# The Money and Politics
# of Criminal Justice Policy

# The Money and Politics of Criminal Justice Policy

O. Hayden Griffin, III
Vanessa H. Woodward
John J. Sloan, III

CAROLINA ACADEMIC PRESS
Durham, North Carolina

Library of Congress Cataloging-in-Publication Data

Names: Griffin, O. Hayden, III, author. | Woodward, Vanessa H., author. | Sloan, John J., author.
Title: The money and politics of criminal justice policy / O. Hayden Griffin, III, Vanessa H. Woodward, and John J. Sloan, III.
Description: Durham, North Carolina : Carolina Academic Press, [2016] | Includes bibliographical references and index.
Identifiers: LCCN 2015044376 | ISBN 9781611635171 (alk. paper)
Subjects: LCSH: Criminal justice, Administration of--United States--History.
| Crime--United States--History. | Crime prevention--United States--History. | Law enforcement--United States--History. | United States--Politics and government.
Classification: LCC HV9950 .G75 2016 | DDC 364.973--dc23
LC record available at http://lccn.loc.gov/2015044376

Carolina Academic Press
700 Kent Street
Durham, NC 27701
Telephone (919) 489-7486
Fax (919) 493-5668
www.cap-press.com

Printed in the United States of America
2018 Printing

*To anyone who has questioned the process.*

# Contents

# List of Tables

# Preface

When people think of criminal justice, a number of ideas come to mind. Typically, none of these ideas are wrong, but they only paint part of the picture. Criminal justice comprises a myriad of philosophies, organizations, and systems, making it challenging to define. Whether speaking of criminal justice in the context of education or government, its meaning is multifaceted. At a very basic level, one may argue that a criminal justice system is designed to increase social control, through both proactive and reactive means. Specifically, a system of criminal justice should protect its citizens from harm (proactively) and enforce control by punishing those who have violated the law (reactively). In the United States, theoretically, the system is assumed to provide the same rights and protections to all; however, some may argue that money has immense influence on the system. For example, some argue the more money and privilege a person has, the more likely they are to receive protection by the criminal justice system, yet escape liability when they are accused of a crime. Moreover, the cost of crime control can be exorbitant, making it challenging for the criminal justice system to operate within its budgetary confines.

## Defining Criminal Justice

Unfortunately, this description only scratches the surface of the complexities of the criminal justice system. The criminal justice system incorporates multiple roles that encompass all stages of social control, from the enforcement of criminal law to the various methods used to punish and/or rehabilitate those who have been convicted of violating these laws. While the system would ideally function independently of political and monetary influence, their influence is evident within each stage of the system. Even more problematic is that at times, money both obstructs and facilitates the goals of the system. There is a symbiotic relationship between those who have money and the system: each relies heavily on the other.

Within this text, our goal is to provide readers with a critical analysis of the relationship among money, politics, and the criminal justice system by examining the influence of money and politics on the agencies and processes that criminal justice comprises. Each of the chapters that follow addresses how money and politics influence an agency (e.g., police departments) or a stage in the criminal justice process. However, before we provide a brief description of each chapter, we would like to provide some background information that we believe is necessary to understand our perspective on these issues.

Regarding the formation of law, many philosophers from the Age of Enlightenment have argued that humans should willingly relinquish part of their sovereignty to the state in exchange for societal protection from harm, an idea known as the social contract. Decisions regarding what behaviors should be prohibited operate through utilitarian ideals that are best administered through a democratic process. If the majority of citizens believe that a behavior is harmful, legislation should be enacted prohibiting the behavior and, on the other hand, those behaviors that are deemed acceptable should continue to be lawful.

Why is there such a divide on the meaning of criminal justice? Theoretically, justice should be representative of objectivity and righteousness. Yet, attempting to implement justice through a formal system muddles its meaning, primarily because of individuals' varying status and power. Contrary to the ideals of Enlightenment thinkers, some Marxist theorists would argue that notions of a social contract are a farce and what behaviors are legal or prohibited is dictated by the ruling elite. In many instances, the ruling elite will purposefully criminalize behaviors in which the working class or poor are likely to engage for purposes of further strengthening the control that the ruling elite exerts upon society.

## Politics and the Constitution

Political power coupled with opposing political views also diminishes the objectivity of the criminal justice system. Acts that seem universally wrong (such as killing or raping an individual) can result in incredibly different punishments. These punishments boil down to the context of the act, the law, and the predominant political beliefs during the time period in which the act occurred. For instance, if a killing was premeditated or particularly brutal, the offender could be sentenced to life imprisonment, or depending on the circumstances, could be put to death. On the other hand, a killing that occurred when a person was in the heat of passion is classified as manslaughter, not murder, and carries a more lenient penalty. Sometimes, killing another human being is not seen as an act of evil. Killing during war not only does not warrant punishment—it can be revered as a heroic act. Additionally, if person A killed person B because person B was threatening them with deadly force, this would be considered self-defense, and not only would the person who committed the killing not be punished, their actions would typically be considered justified under the law.

When we deconstruct the details of varying punishments for varying crimes, it becomes difficult to justify the proposition that notions of crime and punishment are universal or somehow based on what Aristotle called "natural law." If principles of law are not universal or based upon some universal notions of justice, then perhaps we should look to other sources of law. One such example is the supreme document of law within the United States (the Constitution). This document is so sacred that a signed copy of it is on display in the National Archives in Washington, D.C., in a bulletproof case with inert gases inside to preserve it. The document is so well protected that it can even be lowered into a bomb shelter to ensure it will be preserved for future generations (a little more extreme than a sign at a museum that reads "do not touch the paintings"). Yet the Constitution was written exclusively by white men who owned property (often referred to as the "Founding Fathers" or the "Framers"), the elite among the only class of people eligible to vote at the time. The Constitution replaced the former Articles of Confederation, which many people at the time believed had established an ineffective form of government that relied too heavily on the individual states and gave little authority to the federal government. The Constitution established a stronger central government, but still left some power to the individual states. Support for this change in government was not universal. Supporters of the Constitution were known as "federalists," and opponents of the Constitution were intuitively called "anti-federalists."

Within Article Five of the Constitution, the Founding Fathers outlined the process by which the Constitution could be changed, known as "amending" the Constitution. Thus, before it could even be ratified, the Constitution actually had to be amended. Some people who were fearful of a powerful central government had complained that the Constitution had failed to include a list of basic rights for citizens. This argument was quickly addressed by the addition of ten amendments to the Constitution, which are collectively known as the Bill of Rights. The Bill of Rights confers, among others, the seemingly sacred privileges of freedom of speech, the right to remain silent, and the protection against cruel and unusual punishment. Yet there are many exceptions to these amendments. Seemingly, everyone knows that a person cannot claim freedom of speech while yelling "fire" in a crowded theatre. The right to remain silent ("nor shall [a defendant] be compelled in any criminal case to be a witness against himself" is the actual text in the Fifth Amendment) only applies to spoken testimony, and any recordings, writings, fingerprints, and/or DNA evidence can be used against a person at trial. Regarding the protection against cruel and unusual punishment, the United States Supreme Court and other lower courts often interpreted this protection based upon the standard of "evolving standards of decency." Essentially, the Court tries to consider what the views of contemporary society are and if the punishment is essentially cruel and unusual within a modern society.

After the Constitution was ratified, it was amended seventeen more times. Among the changes were the Thirteenth Amendment, which outlawed slavery, the Fourteenth Amendment, which granted equal protection to people regardless of race, the Seventeenth Amendment, which made United States Senators directly elected by the people instead of by state legislatures, and the Nineteenth Amendment, which gave women the right to vote. The Twenty-First amendment actually *repealed* the Eighteenth Amendment, which had prohibited the manufacture or sale of alcohol within the United States. Thus, although the Constitution may well have been enacted "in order to form a more perfect union," it was not universally enacted at the time; many people in the United States were excluded from taking part in creating the document; and the meaning of the words found in the document have often been disputed and required interpretation by the courts. If the document was in fact sacred and based upon universal rights or natural law, perhaps it would be clearer in its meaning and would not have to be interpreted so frequently. Additionally, society's ever-changing values have required changes to the Constitution.

# Law, Social Control, and Criminal Justice

If we cannot ascertain a sense of natural law or what is right/wrong through societal beliefs or government, perhaps the only place left to look is religion. Many people have argued that legal codes reflect religious beliefs and values. Indeed, the Ten Commandments, at least in so-called Judeo-Christian countries like the United States, have often been claimed by religious leaders and some politicians as the foundation of any legal code. In countries such as Saudi

Arabia, legal codes are partly, if not entirely, based on religious doctrine found in the Qur'an and Hadith. The United States, which was founded by people who most often had Judeo-Christian beliefs, can certainly claim some inspiration in various religious texts. Murder, theft, and many other behaviors are described as "crimes" in the Christian Bible. Although some actions, such as adultery, would probably be considered immoral in contemporary society, it is unlikely that a person would be prosecuted for them—unless the defendant was a member of the United States military. Some actions, such as worshipping idols or practicing magic, would be considered immoral by only a small minority of Christians in the United States, a country that encourages religious freedom. Although we still might look to religion to identify what behaviors should be considered a crime, the proper punishment for these crimes is another story. In the Bible, the most often prescribed punishments are death, monetary fines, or corporal punishment. Incarceration, one of the punishments used in modern times, was unknown in biblical times.

Although we often look to concepts of universal rights or natural law, constitutions and legal codes, or religion for inspiration in deciding what is morally right and wrong, as well as criminally right and wrong, the ultimate answer is settled through a political process. Based upon American legal principles, before a person can be punished by the state, there must first be a law that prohibits the behavior and there must be some stated penalty for the violation. This cannot occur unless a legislature passes a bill and a governor or the president signs the bill into law. If a proposed law is vetoed by the executive, then a legislature, through a supermajority vote (usually ⅔), can override the veto and the bill becomes law. In some states, like California, laws can be enacted by ballot initiative. For this to occur, a sponsoring citizen will be required to collect a certain number of signatures in support of the proposed initiative from other citizens who are registered to vote. If enough valid signatures are gathered, the ballot initiative will be put up for a vote at the next election. If a majority of voters approve of the initiative, it becomes law.

Not only must law be created within a political process, but criminal justice issues can also become central in many political elections. In 1992, for example, while running for president of the United States, Bill Clinton often advocated that 100,000 additional police officers should be hired to help control burgeoning levels of crime.[1] In 1995, the state of New York reinstituted the death penalty after an eighteen-year absence. Reinstituting the death penalty had been one of the central pledges on which Governor George Pataki had based his campaign.[2] In 1993, while running for governor of Virginia, George Allen's cornerstone campaign promise was to abolish parole for incarcerated offenders.[3] Aside from these examples, gun control, sex offender registries, drug testing of welfare recipients, restoration of voting rights for people with felony convictions, victim's rights, and many other issues have become important issues in political campaigns. Not only are these issues important to the general social welfare, but some criminal justice personnel—including judges, attorney generals, county sheriffs, and district attorneys—occupy elected positions. For the most part, candidates for these positions will be judged solely based on the positions they take on issues relating to the criminal justice system.

So how do politics affect a person's beliefs about the criminal justice system? Elliott Currie equated political views with criminal justice beliefs by contrasting "due process liberals" with "crime control conservatives."[4] Using Herbert Packer's notion that competing values inform the operation of the criminal justice system, what he labeled as "crime control" and "due process" models of criminal justice,[5] Currie argued people who tended to be more liberal were more likely to value human rights and believe that governments should be less punitive towards people who broke the law. People who were more conservative would believe that the ultimate goal of the criminal justice system is to reduce crime and keep people safe. If that meant diminishing everyone's civil rights, doing so was to achieve the goal of less crime.[6] Yet, in reality, such easy distinctions are rare. Although the Republican Party has traditionally been known as the "law and order" party, that distinction has recently waned, as more Republicans call for repealing mandatory sentences for low-level drug offenders and the end of "three strikes and you're out" laws. Beginning with the election of Bill Clinton, Democratic candidates for major state and national offices have endorsed tactics associated with a crime control model. Further complicating the picture is the fact "libertarians" or "progressives" can be found in both political parties. Libertarians are typically people who advocate for limiting government power in nearly all segments of society—economic, education, etc.—while progressives typically see government as the solution to social ills and advocate for increased government intervention in social problems. In recent times, Libertarians have complained about everything from what they consider harsh drug laws to policies that allow law enforcement to stop and frisk people with little provocation. To Libertarians, these are examples of unnecessary government infringement on people's liberty. Progressives actually agree with libertarians' opinions on these issues, but for entirely different reasons. To them, rather than sending drug offenders to jails and/or prisons, the country should embrace drug prevention measures such as expanded, state-sponsored drug rehabilitation. Regarding stop and frisk policies, while sup-

porting them in theory, progressives worry that such tactics unfairly target
racial or cultural minorities and the poor. Thus, political affiliation affects
people's views of the criminal justice system in ways beyond the simple "crime
control" or "due process" models posited by Packer.

Historical context is also important for understanding how political attitudes shape the passage of laws. Just like anything else, attitudes toward issues
in criminal justice trend and vary over time. For instance, not so long ago, if
a man had sex with a woman against her will, this situation was not really
thought of so much as a crime against the woman, but instead as a crime
against her father or husband (if she was married). Generally, members of society believed that if people knew the woman was no longer a virgin, regardless of whether it was by choice, a father would have a difficult time marrying
off his daughter. If the woman was married, she was considered the property
of her husband and the rape had caused his property to become damaged. Social attitudes about rape eventually began to change where both men and
women perceived rape as a violent crime and the woman as the victim (not
her husband or father), which led to rape being punishable by death until 1972,
when the Supreme Court ruled that the death penalty for rape was unconstitutional. In contemporary America, the punishment for rape (or lesser sexual
assaults) can vary from probation to life imprisonment.[7]

Speaking on drug policy, the historian David Musto argued that American
attitudes towards drugs are akin to a swinging pendulum. Some historical periods have been marked by more tolerant attitudes towards drugs, while other
periods are marked by stricter control of drugs. Musto noted that the late 1960s
and 1970s were the most recent period of relative tolerance for drugs like marijuana. It was during those decades that many states relaxed sentencing policy
and some even decriminalized possession of small amounts of marijuana for
personal use. The 1980s saw a backlash against drug use, partly as a result of
the perceived excesses of the time. Much tougher sentences for drug offenders became the norm and decriminalization all but disappeared.[8]

Similar shifts in attitudes have also occurred regarding what should be the
proper punishment for crime. Although many Americans believe incarceration is both the norm and has existed for a long time, neither is the case. Further, policies resulting in mass incarceration are quite recent as well. Prior to
the 1980s, rehabilitation — rather than deterrence, incapacitation, or retribu-
tion — was the guiding philosophy behind criminal sentencing policy. [9] However, which of these justifications for criminal sanctions you believe is the most
(or least) important is often shaped by your political views.

As stated earlier, money matters; it has an immense influence on criminal justice policymaking. Prisons and jails do not appear out of thin air—they cost money. Money is not only required to build these facilities, but also to maintain and staff them, and ensure the inmates living in them have access to the basic necessities of food, clothing, and medical care. Not only do we provide money to support prisons and jails, but for all other aspects of the criminal justice system as well: probation and parole officers, police officers, judges, prosecutors, clerks of the courts, and countless other people who are paid salaries and benefits (e.g., medical and other benefits like retirement or disability pay) for their work in law enforcement, the courts, and corrections. All of these expenditures account for significant portions of local and state budgets (which can be cut during economic slowdowns or enhanced during periods of economic growth).

Although criminal justice expenditures can be the target of budget cuts and some people may even question the need to spend so much money maintaining the criminal justice system, there is another rationale for preserving the system. The criminal justice system creates jobs—*a lot* of them—not only for the people who work in the system directly, but also for those who support and provide secondary benefits to the system. When facilities need to be built, this will require architects, construction companies, and perhaps most importantly, workers who actually construct the facilities. Uniforms worn by inmates and prisoners alike must be manufactured by textile companies. Food for inmates helps employ farmers. Automobiles for police officers are manufactured by domestic car companies. The list of industries that both support and are aided by the criminal justice system is endless. Cuts to budgets for the agencies that make up the criminal justice system hurt not only the agencies themselves, but also the ancillary industries. Most directly, budget cuts can make criminal justice workers' jobs tougher by limiting resources or, if the cuts are severe enough, cause them to lose their jobs. A well-funded criminal justice system will keep many people employed, many of whom are registered voters. Budgets cuts directly affecting them might result in decisions made at the ballot box to support—or not support—political candidates. Few politicians would ever want to appear to *not* support the men and women who make the criminal justice system work!

Now that we have considered some potential monetary benefits of the criminal justice system, it is time to consider some of its negative monetary costs. What is the most basic need of any criminal justice system? People who break the law and warrant punishment. Without inmates in a correctional facility, all you have is an empty building. Without people breaking laws, a police officer in a car is just a man or woman with nothing to do. The fewer the number of people who break the law, the less need there is for a criminal justice system and, certainly, the fewer the people whom governments will have to pay to prevent and prosecute crimes. Yet, before we start to argue that more people breaking laws and being punished is economically beneficial, there are a number of things we must consider. First, regardless of whether certain acts are legal or illegal, there is still a monetary cost attached to them. Shoplifting, for example, costs companies money that, in turn, causes prices to rise as they attempt to replace that lost revenue. Therefore, regardless of whether shoplifting is legal or illegal, there is still a cost associated with the act. Second, even when a direct monetary cost of crime does not exist, a social cost does. We must remember that people who commit crime are human beings—fathers and mothers, sons and daughters—and may have others who depend on their emotional and financial support. Although society may be safer by incapacitating these people through locking them up in prison or jail, having them languishing in jails and prisons makes them a drain on the economy. Not only does the government have to pay money to house these people, but also they are not adding their labor to the economy (the economic benefits of prison labor is an issue we will discuss in a later chapter). Prisoners are neither spending nor making money outside the prison walls or jail cells; they are certainly not paying taxes. Furthermore, these people are not financially supporting their families. If an incarcerated parent is the sole custodial parent, children may be forced to live with relatives or into the foster care system. Thus, not only have we punished the offender who is incarcerated, we have also punished his or her family as well. This has a negative effect in the short term, but this lack of support and displacement could contribute to the criminogenic behavior of family members down the road.

Now that we have briefly discussed how politics and money affect criminal justice, we must consider one more issue before concluding this chapter. At what point do we find a phenomenon a problem? A similar question should be, after defining a phenomenon as a problem, how do we determine that something in the criminal justice system is not working and requires some change to the system? For instance, relative to other public places, schools have always been safe places, even today. However, if we listen to the media, whose presence and scope of coverage seems to be ever expanding, school shootings almost seem to be frequent, and always increasing in frequency. Although school shootings are certainly tragic, these incidents are *not* common. Similarly, the media also depicts numerous other criminal behaviors as either bizarre or increasing. These constant reports, if believed, can make us feel like we are not safe anywhere. This is not surprising though. If you look hard enough in a country of over 370 million people within a world of over six billion people, you are likely to find most anything.

# Politics and Crime in America

As previously mentioned, our purpose in writing this book is to provide readers a critical analysis of the role played by money and politics in criminal justice policy. By critical, we mean not accepting the status quo, but instead questioning it and trying to uncover its inner workings. We will not, however, advocate any particular political ideology.

Our first goal is to analyze how political issues affect policy. In many instances, we will present criminological/criminal justice research to illustrate how the political framing of an issue is more important than actually considering whether a particular policy choice is sound because it works. In doing so, we endeavored to be as unbiased as possible, although bias is never completely overcome. Regarding money, we first want to show that money matters in the criminal justice system. There are not only costs from the commission of crime, but there are also costs associated with preventing and prosecuting crime. Beyond this, we want people to understand that the criminal justice system is an industry like any other. Crime is a multi-billion-dollar industry. The criminal justice system is one of the nation's largest employers. One common urban legend is that some scientist invented a gasoline combustion engine that would allow a car to drive 90–100 miles on a single gallon of gas. Consumers have not been able to purchase this engine because an oil company promptly bought the patent. If a fuel-efficient engine of this caliber were available, oil companies could potentially lose profits. Now, we are not suggesting that a cure for crime is out there, or if it were, that it is being suppressed. Yet the criminal justice system is an industry and many of the decisions that are made or the process itself can be more about collecting money or keeping people employed than actually promoting justice, even if we could develop a satisfactory definition of what exactly justice is.

We have organized the book in the following manner: In Chapter 1, "Government & Politics within the United States," we discuss the nature of government and politics in the United States. Of specific concern is the American system of federalism, whereby the federal government and state governments share governance. While criminal justice was primarily a state responsibility at the founding of the United States, the federal government has had a con-

tinuing role in, and influence over, criminal justice, which has important implications.

In Chapter 2, "The Political Economy of Crime," we present various criminological theories that examine the role of politics and money in the criminal justice system. The purpose here is to ground readers in different theoretical
explanations that scholars have developed to explain why money and politics
play a large role in creating law and policy, and effects of money and politics
on the day-to-day operation of the criminal justice system.

In Chapter 3, "A Brief History of the United States Criminal Justice System," we provide a condensed history of how criminal justice policy developed
in the United States. This evolution is hardly accidental—money and politics
have played a role since the beginning.

In Chapter 4, "The Cost of Crime," we provide analysis of what the true
cost of crime in the United States is. As we describe in the chapter, figuring
out the true costs of crime can be a difficult exercise since some costs, such as
federal and state budgets for criminal justice, are easy to obtain, but other costs
related to crime are not so easily determined.

In Chapter 5, "The Mythology (and Reality) of Crime and Justice in the
United States," we describe some of the myths that have developed about crime.
What we mean by mythology is the fact that there are many different faulty or
inaccurate reasons disseminated to justify various phenomenon within the
criminal justice system.

In Chapter 6, "The Politicization of Crime and Justice in the United States,"
we describe different types of interest groups in the United States that are both
interested in and help to shape crime policy. While we cannot provide any definitive answers, we can say that these groups certainly have an effect on the
criminal justice process and the formation of policy.

In Chapter 7, "The Political Economy of Policing," we identify the different
public and private agencies that engage in policing. We also examine how police budgets are developed, the costs of policing for society, and who actually
profits from policing. We explore various political issues that affect the practice of policing as well in the chapter.

In Chapter 8, "The Political Economy of Courts," we identify the different
public and private agencies that make up the American criminal court system,
including how budgets are developed for courts, what costs society incurs from
courts, and who actually profits from courts. We also describe various political issues affecting the administration of courts.

In Chapter 9, "The Political Economy of Corrections," we turn our attention to the different public and private agencies involved with corrections in

America. Again, we examine how budgets are developed for corrections, what costs society incurs from corrections, and who actually profits from corrections. Likewise, we also describe the various political issues that affect the practice of corrections.

Chapter 10 concludes the book. In this chapter we summarize what we believe are the most important points we have made in the book, as well as examine what the future may hold for the criminal justice system.

# Notes

1. Marion, Nancy. 1997. "Symbolic Policies in Clinton's Crime Control Agenda." *Buffalo Criminal Law Review*, 1(1): 67–108.

2. Kuziemko, Ilyana. 2006. "Does the Threat of the Death Penalty Affect Plea Bargaining in Murder Cases? Evidence from New York's 1995 Reinstatement of Capital Punishment." *American Law and Economics Review*, 8(1): 116–142.

3. Petersilia, Joan. 1999. "Parole and Prisoner Reentry in the United States." *Crime and Justice*, 26: 479–529.

4. Currie, Elliott. 2013. *Crime and Punishment in America*. London: Macmillan.

5. Packer, Herbert. 1968. *The Limits of the Criminal Sanction*. Stanford, CA: Stanford University Press.

6. Currie, Elliott. 2013. *Crime and Punishment in America*. London: Macmillan.

7. Little, Nicholas J. 2005. "From No Means No to Only Yes Means Yes: The Rational Results of an Affirmative Consent Standard in Rape Law." *Vanderbilt Law Review*, 58: 1321–1364.

8. Musto, David. 1999. *The American Disease: Origins of Narcotic Control*. 3rd Edition. New York: Oxford University Press.

9. Clear, Todd R., Michael D. Reisig, and George F. Cole. 2012. *American Corrections*. 10th Edition. Stamford, CT: Cengage.

# The Money and Politics
# of Criminal Justice Policy

# Chapter 1

# Government and Politics in the United States

## Chapter Outline

- Introduction
- States' Rights and State Autonomy
- Federalism, the States, and Criminal Justice
  - Federalism
  - Interpreting the Constitution
  - The Constitution and Criminal Justice Issues
- Expanding the Power of the Federal Government in Criminal Justice
- Interstate Commerce and Taxing Powers
  - The Mann Act
  - The Harrison Narcotic Act
  - Gun-Free School Zones Act of 1990
  - Contemporary Issues of States' Autonomy
- The Courts & Selective Incorporation of the Bill of Rights
  - Federal Grants to States
  - The Law Enforcement Assistance Administration
- Key Terms
- Key People
- Key Cases
- Discussion Questions

## Learning Objectives

- Evaluate the role of common law in the United States' legal system
- Compare and contrast modes of interpretation of the Constitution
- Outline the changes in states' autonomy over time

- Identify and explain contemporary issues of states' autonomy within criminal justice
- Identify and explain the importance of the Law Enforcement Administration Association

# Introduction

Thomas "Tip" O'Neill (D-MA) served as Speaker of the United States House of Representatives from 1977–1987. While much can be said about Tip, he is perhaps best known for his slogan that "all politics is local."[1] The reason O'Neill's statement is so well known is because it captures the original intent of American politics: a politician must have the support of their local district to continue in office. Moreover, O'Neill was arguing that regardless of how much ordinary citizens seem to hate politicians, that hatred often becomes insignificant when speaking of their own elected officials. If people in a local district perceive their elected officials as "hardworking" and "fighting for their interests," then people will generally support the individual politician. Moreover, if the politician has obtained federal funding for projects earmarked for their district, commonly referred to as "pork," elected representatives will escape the wrath of voters—often leading to their further success in politics.

Not surprisingly, the success of the criminal justice system is contingent on not only generating local support, but also procuring funding for its operations—some of which comes from local sources, some from the state, and some from the federal government. (In Chapter 4, we document how much each state and the federal government spend on preventing, investigating, and sanctioning crime and criminals.) The money has to come from somewhere, and traditionally *local* governments—cities and counties—bear the brunt of those costs. Table 1.1 shows the distribution of justice expenditures across all levels of government (federal, state, and local) for fiscal year 2009 (the most recent year for which justice expenditure data are available). As highlighted by the table, local governments shoulder the largest percentage of direct expenditures for the criminal justice system, including over one-half of the total direct expenditures, about 51 percent of law enforcement direct expenditures, and some 40 percent of judicial/legal direct expenditures. The exception is corrections, where state governments shoulder about 60 percent of direct expenditures.

Federal, state, and local budgets must allocate funds for police, courts, and corrections—the agencies of criminal justice—to operate. Not only has this been the case from the founding of the United States, but from the earliest days of colonial rule as well. British settlers brought with them **common law**,[3]

### Table 1.1. Percentage Distribution of Expenditures for the Justice System in 2009[2]

| Activity | Percent Distribution | | |
|---|---|---|---|
| | Federal Government | State Governments | Local Governments |
| Total justice system expenditures<br>    Direct expenditures | 18.2 | 31.3 | 50.5 |
| Police protection<br>    Direct expenditures | 22.6 | 10 | 67.4 |
| Judicial and legal operations<br>    Direct expenditures | 22 | 38.1 | 39.8 |
| Corrections<br>    Direct expenditures | 8.9 | 58.6 | 32.5 |

a. *Total expenditures* are direct and intergovernmental expenditures of a government. "Expenditure" is all amounts of money paid out, net of recoveries and any correcting transactions, other than for retirement of debt (including interest), investment in securities, extensions of loans, or agency transactions. *Intergovernmental expenditures* comprise payments from one government to another, including grants-in-aid, shared revenues, fiscal assistance, and amounts for services performed by one government for another on a reimbursable or cost-sharing basis (e.g., payments by one government to another for boarding prisoners).
b. *Direct expenditures* are all expenditure except those classified as intergovernmental and is further divided into two categories: Direct current includes salaries, wages, fees, commissions, and the purchase of supplies, materials, and contractual services. Capital outlay includes expenditure for the three object categories of construction, equipment, and purchase of land and existing structures.
Local government data are estimates subject to sampling variability. Federal Government data are for the fiscal period beginning October 1, 2008 and ending September 30, 2009.

a legal system rooted in judicial precedent—rather than legislative dictate—that guided judicial decision making in future, similar cases. Common law relies on "common" holdings by judges based on the principle that it is unfair to treat similar facts (cases) differently on different occasions (when they appear before different judges).[4] The accumulated body of precedent is referred to as "common law" and binds all future decisions. In cases where parties may disagree on what the law says about a particular set of facts, in a common law system, a court reviews past precedent in the case to reach a decision. Assuming a similar dispute has been resolved in the past, the court is then bound to follow the reasoning used in the prior decision, known as the principle of *stare decisis* ("let the decision stand").[5] If, however, the court finds the current dispute is distinct from previous cases—a "**matter of first impression**"—judges have both the authority and duty to make law by creating precedent.[6] Thereafter, the new decision becomes precedent and binds future courts to decide similar cases the same way. Some of the key features of common law systems include:

- There is not always a written constitution or codified laws;
- Judicial decisions are binding—decisions of the highest court can generally only be overturned by that same court or through legislation;
- Extensive freedom of contract—few provisions are implied into the contract by law (although provisions seeking to protect private consumers may be implied);
- Generally, everything is permitted that is not expressly prohibited by law.[7]

A continuing controversial issue in the United States is to what degree the federal government should regulate the actions and laws of the states. A related question, and perhaps the guiding principle of this chapter, is how does the question of state versus federal authority affect the American criminal justice system?

## States' Rights and State Autonomy

Over time, rather than simply relying on legal precedent, the colonies (later, the states) drafted and adopted legal codes that codified the principles found in the common law. In addition to these state codes—both civil and criminal—many cities and towns adopted municipal ordinances. There are many reasons that this arrangement in government works. Different states (and cities and towns) have different needs—different ways of doing things. If you grew up in Northeast Tennessee, for example, and ventured to New Orleans, you might find some of the customs there, such as drive-thru daiquiri shops, bizarre. If you traveled to Detroit, you could find drive-thru beer and wine stores where you can order everything from a single can of beer to multiple kegs. Indeed, the notion of *states' rights* has enjoyed a strong presence in American political culture, an example of which is found in the case of *New State Ice Co. v. Lippmann*, where Supreme Court Justice **Louis Brandeis** referred to the states as "laboratories of democracy."[8] What Justice Brandeis meant was that it is important that individual states are able to maintain at least some self-rule so that local customs could be preserved, their citizens' unique needs planned for, and, in some cases, experiments with various methods of regulating or permitting behavior attempted.

This is not to say that the notion of states' rights is without controversy when states face challenges to their autonomy.[9] For example, it was not until the 1950s that the Supreme Court began dismantling segregation and its vestiges, a bastion of Southern states' rights.[10] More recent controversies have involved state bans on gay marriage and the legalization of the recreational use of marijuana by Alaska, Colorado, Oregon, and Washington. In the former controversy, the Supreme Court has allowed to stand three federal circuit courts' rulings overturning several states' banning of gay marriage.[11] Concerning the latter issue, the federal courts have not yet addressed the constitutionality of the states of Alaska, Colorado, Oregon, and Washington legalizing recreational marijuana.[12] The Supreme Court has, however, ruled in *United States v. Oakland Cannabis Buyers' Cooperative*[13] and *Gonzales v. Raich*[14] that the federal government has the right to regulate and criminalize cannabis, even if the drug is being used for medical reasons. Politicians in other states are closely watching these developments to determine whether they should have their state follow a similar course of action.[15] However, in some instances, states are actually suing in federal court, hoping that the states that have legalized marijuana will be barred from continuing this policy. Both the attorney generals of Nebraska and Oklahoma have argued that marijuana is being diverted into their states and states such as Colorado are ignoring federal law.[16]

Maintaining state sovereignty has fallen short within the criminal justice system. While criminal justice remains primarily the responsibility of the states, there has been a growing federal presence in criminal justice, in regards to both the growing list of federal crimes and federal oversight of state policy. How does this occur? To understand how the presence of the federal government in criminal justice has increased, one need understand the foundations of the American system of government.

## Federalism, the States, and Criminal Justice

The United States is a **republic**, meaning that under its form of government, citizens elect representatives to state and federal legislative bodies who are then supposed to act in the interests of the electorate. The distinction between a republic and a **democracy** has important legal significance and is not trivial. In Article IV, Section 4, of the U.S. Constitution one finds the *guarantee clause* that every state will have a republican form of government—as opposed to a monarchy (where a king or queen is in charge) or dictatorship (where one individual or group runs the government).[17] In effect, the Constitution is dictating that no state may join the union unless it is a republic and accepts the notion of "liberty and justice for all." Prominent also is the guarantee that minority individual rights are a priority and will be protected by the Bill of Rights (generally, the first ten amendments to the Constitution and the Fourteenth Amendment, which made them applicable to the states).[18] In contrast, a democracy is a "dictatorship by the majority," wherein the minority only enjoys those rights or privileges granted by the majority.[19]

The American colonists who revolted from their British colonial masters and set into motion the creation of a new nation were full of catchy slogans such as "No taxation without representation," "Don't tread on me," or Patrick Henry's famous line from a speech to the Virginia House of Burgesses, "Give me liberty or give me death." While catchy, these mantras focused solely on the rebellion—not the after effects of a successful revolution. In particular, little thought apparently went into determining what *type* of government would be formed and how it would avoid becoming similar to the government that they had just fought to expel. The sole issue on which the colonists seemed united was ridding themselves of what they believed was the tyrannical rule of King George III.

At least part of the problem was that there was not much precedent for the Founding Fathers to rely upon in forming a new government. Wars of this type were usually over disputed claims of royal succession or by oligarchic nobles who wanted more say in government (such as the case when a group of English nobles forced King John to sign the Magna Carta). Additionally, there was little to no precedent to follow regarding how to establish a *democratic* form of government. While England had Parliament and France had the Estates General, both countries also had monarchies that would routinely ignore these legislative bodies. This left only one other example for the Founding Fathers: Athens, in Ancient Greece. From 507 B.C. to around 460 B.C., all adult male citizens (around 40,000 in total) had the opportunity to participate in the *ekklesia*, the assembly of Athens.[20] The problem was that instituting a similar form of government in the United States would have been impossible. The *ekklesia* ruled over a single city; the founding fathers had to create the government for a brand-new nation that stretched thousands of miles from Maine to Georgia. Having every white male property owner in the country descend upon a single place for a governing session would have been impossible.

After **General Charles Cornwallis** surrendered to **George Washington** at Yorktown on October 19, 1781, the new nation had to decide how to govern itself. While it was obvious that the American colonists were fighting for freedom, how to go about implementing a government that centered on the premise of "liberty for all" was strange and led to conflict. The only idea the founders seemed to agree upon was that the new nation would *not* have a strong central government. At present, it is easy to take for granted what being an American means without realizing that, at one point, there was no clear definition of what was "an American." Citizens of the time were far more likely to feel kinship with the state in which they resided than in a brand new country. As one can imagine, becoming the United States of America was a long and arduous process.

## Federalism

While the word never appears in the Constitution, **federalism** is the foundation on which the United States government is built and refers to the sharing of power between the national (federal) and state governments. Because the states existed first, their representatives were most concerned about what role a federal government for the new nation would play and how much power it would be given. While the **Articles of Confederation**[21] created a "united" group of states, the confederation also created a weak central government (Congress), having only the power to declare war and negotiate peace treaties but little else, including not having the power to tax citizens to pay for the debts accumulated during the Revolutionary War.[22] In reality, the governing structure of the Articles of Confederation was more akin to the present-day United Nations than it is to the current structure of the United States government. Without a central authority, conflicts quickly emerged between representatives of the various states, leaving them generally dissatisfied with the Articles of Confederation. Opponents argued that a system of government required a federal authority that had ultimate power, especially the ability to conduct foreign policy, maintain and regulate an economic system, and raise and maintain an army, among other activities. The question that remained was one of balance: how to implement a supreme authority without creating a tyrannical system of government?

After the Revolutionary War and realizing the country faced a problem of having a weak central government, members of Congress issued a resolution in February of 1787 calling for a convention to amend the Articles of Confederation. There, delegates considered a new form of government, federalism, under which shared power would occur between the states and a more robust central government. Over the span of four months, the delegates created a new government consisting of three branches—legislative, judicial, and executive—drastically expanded Congressional power, and produced the Constitution, which provided the basis of how the government would work.[23] Unlike the Articles of Confederation, under the new Constitution, there would be two separate legislative bodies: the House of Representatives and the Senate. The delegates of smaller states had wanted a legislative body that maintained equal voting rights under the Constitution. Larger states wanted a legislative body where the number of legislators would be based upon the population of each state. In what is known as the Connecticut Compromise, the delegates agreed to have one legislative body based upon state population size and another legislative body where states had equal voting rights.[24] Furthermore, the delegates agreed that slaveholding states could count three-fifths of their enslaved population for representation and taxation purposes.[25]

The Constitution, then, is clearly the foundation for the republic. The problem is that it was written some 230 years ago and, in places, is vague as to what the Founders intended. For example, a well-debated part of the document is the Second Amendment, which reads "A well-regulated militia, being necessary to the security of a free state, the right of the people to keep and bear arms, shall not be infringed." What does this mean? For example, does an individual citizen have the right to own unlimited numbers of firearms of *any* kind? Is the government restricted from imposing regulations on the ownership, carrying, sale, or trading of firearms? What is a "well-regulated militia?" Is that simply today's National Guard? Or, what about the so-called religious clauses of the First Amendment, which read "Congress shall make no law respecting an establishment of religion, or prohibiting the free exercise thereof ..." What constitutes Congress "establishing" religion? What does "free exercise" mean?

## Interpreting the Constitution

Whenever there is debate over the meaning of the Constitution, the issue is actually over how to best *interpret* the words found in the document. While we may be able to grasp the original intent of the Founding Fathers, it is impossible to know whether their intent would have remained constant to the present day. Who is to say if the Founding Fathers lived today whether they might not think differently than they did at the time the document was created?

*Modes of Interpretation.* While there are numerous ways of interpreting the Constitution,[26] perhaps the most common methods—whose supporters have aligned themselves into opposing camps—involve interpreting the Constitution in light of what its words meant *when they were written* (so-called "**strict constructionists**") and interpreting the Constitution as a *living document* whose words are then interpreted in light of the current environment ("**living Constitutionalists**").[27]

The arguments of strict constructionists and living constitutionalists both have merit.[28] On the one hand, if we ignored the intent of legislation, we could end up arbitrarily deciding which law is "good" and which law is "bad." By considering the intent of those who brought forth the law to begin with, we more fully understand both the expressed purpose of the law as well as the spirit in which it was presented for ratification. On the other hand, the Founding Fathers were only one group of people who lived over two hundred years ago, were not representative of either the United States population in the 1700s or the United States population now, and were comprised solely of white, male, property owners (including slave owners). It is, therefore, an open question over how they would govern in a world complete with the Internet, automobiles, airplanes, cellphones, and countless other unimaginable circumstances. The only thing we can state with certainty is that both sides of this debate are fairly entrenched and this issue will provide further controversy in the years to come.

Additionally, regardless of how the justices on the Supreme Court actually interpret the meaning of the Constitution, noteworthy is the fact the Supreme Court exercises no legal authority beyond having the final say in a case. The Court must ultimately rely on the executive branch of government—either the president or state governors—to enforce their rulings. For example, when the Court ordered desegregation of the public schools "with all deliberate speed" in its famous ruling in *Brown v. Board of Education*[29] (which is discussed later in this chapter) some of the Southern states balked at doing so. As a result, the president had to order the National Guard to enforce the ruling.[30]

## *The Constitution and Criminal Justice Issues*

At first glance, the main body of the Constitution seems to focus very little on issues that affect the criminal justice system. For example, the only crime that is explicitly defined in the Constitution is treason—not exactly a commonly prosecuted offense. Unlike the Articles of Confederation, the Constitution granted the federal government the ability to tax, regulate the borders of the United States, and print money. These new powers led not only to the ability to regulate, but also to the ability to prosecute people who violated legislation enacted by Congress regarding these duties. Enforcement of these laws was not only important to maintain a working economic system, but also to ensure the federal government actually had enough money to operate. Indeed, since Congress did not enact a permanent income tax until 1913, the federal government sought other sources of revenue, most often through taxes on goods. The problem with doing so was that people were not always supportive of these taxes.

One example of this (which you may remember from your American history class) is the **Whiskey Rebellion** in 1791, which became one of the first challenges to the presidency of George Washington. The Whiskey Rebellion involved a group of frontier farmers who believed a tax on whiskey was an abuse of federal authority and wrongly targeted a demographic that relied on crops such as corn, rye, and grain to earn a profit. Because shipping such produce east was risky due to poor storage and dangerous roads, farmers frequently distilled their grains into liquor, which was much easier to preserve and ship. While large-scale farmers easily incurred the financial strain of the additional tax, smaller farmers were less able to do so without falling into dire financial straits.[31] President Washington considered this issue to be so important to the new and fledgling American government that he personally led over 12,000 militiamen to put down the rebellion. The importance of this is twofold: President Washington's actions were crucial to reinforce the authority of the federal government over matters of taxation, and there was the simple fact the new country needed the revenue that was being generated by these taxes. Washington, however, had to be careful how he handled the rebellion. The government of the newly founded country could not possibly establish credibility by crushing its citizens with taxes, considering this was the exact idea that had inspired the American Revolution. Washington also had to show citizens the government was serious about imposing and collecting the taxes necessary to fund its operations. His response was to first issue a public statement indicating the rebels' behavior would not be tolerated and supporters who participated with the rebels or sheltered them would be arrested and prosecuted; he soon thereafter gathered the militia to march on the rebels. His plan worked: by the time the militia reached them, the rebels had completely dispersed.

As we discussed earlier, there was great concern about how the states could maintain their autonomy with the federal government acting as the central authority. Furthermore, some (particularly the anti-federalists) were concerned that the establishment of a federal government would strip individuals of their liberty. Thus, prior to consenting to a new form of government, many delegates to the Constitutional Convention demanded a list of guaranteed rights for the people. The first ten amendments, known by most people as the Bill of Rights, represent the basic rights granted to citizens by the United States government.[32] Furthermore, these amendments address many of the complaints that American colonists had towards the British during colonial rule. Perhaps most telling of this is the Third Amendment, which prohibits the government from quartering troops in people's homes. While it is hard to imagine the need to exercise this right in present times, it was of the utmost importance at that time. Presently, there are certain rights that seem automatic, such as protections of the freedom of speech, the right against unreasonable search and seizures, and from cruel and unusual punishment. In reality, these rights were anything but automatic when the Constitution and Bill of Rights were enacted. Indeed, prior to passage of the Fourteenth Amendment, in many rulings or refusals to hear cases, the Supreme Court routinely ruled the Bill of Rights only applied to the federal government and the individual states were free to violate any of these provisions as they saw fit.

There is a bit of irony here, considering that a revolution was fought in the name of freedom from tyrannical control but accepted such behavior from state governments. As the Tenth Amendment to the Constitution states, "The powers not delegated to the United States by the Constitution, nor prohibited by it to the States, are reserved to the States respectively, or to the people."[33] While some modern politicians have campaigned on power being returned to the states based on the Tenth Amendment, former senator and presidential candidate Robert Dole literally carried a copy of the Tenth Amendment in his pocket and Texas governor Rick Perry has campaigned for president on a seemingly "**Tenth Amendment platform**," arguing that power needs to be returned the states.[34] Such arguments were unnecessary at the time of the ratification of the Constitution. Except for those powers specifically mentioned in the Constitution, all other power resided in the states.

## Expanding the Power of the Federal Government in Criminal Justice

While in its early years the power of the federal government to prosecute criminals was typically limited to prosecuting cases involving taxation, immigration, and counterfeit currency, the power to prosecute crimes such as murder, thefts, assault and batteries, rape, and other similar crimes was reserved for the states. Lawrence Friedman has noted there are places in the United States where state jurisdiction does not exist. For example, the federal government has always been responsible for operating the criminal justice system in the District of Columbia, on federal lands, in all existing territories, and in any new colonies that the United States obtained. Given the growing colonial ambitions of the United States at the time the Constitution was ratified, it was necessary for the federal government to substantially involve itself in the administration of criminal justice beyond just the state level. Furthermore, as the fighting force of the United States transitioned from a standby citizen militia to a permanent standing army, the federal government would ultimately oversee the military justice system that governs the behavior of all members of the armed forces worldwide.[35] However, as Friedman noted, until the 1900s, the number of federal criminal cases was miniscule compared to that of states' criminal cases.[36] Even today, in comparison with the states, there are fewer federal criminal prosecutions.

There are many reasons the federal government expanded its role in criminal justice within the United States. Perhaps most importantly is the fact that over a span of some 200 years, the United States became less a collection of segregated states and more of an integrated country. This was partially attributable to new modes of transportation that developed, including railroads, automobiles, and airplanes, which made traveling from state to state easier, and which increased connectivity among citizens. As a result, people are now far less likely to live their entire lives without venturing beyond the confines of where they were born and raised than was the case 200 years or even 50 years ago. Furthermore, as the country grew in physical size and population, the federal government continually expanded, not just in the number of people in its employ, but also the amount of money that runs through its coffers. One of the reasons for this growth has been the continually expanding federal register of legislation.[37] Yet, despite this growth, the same restrictions upon the legislative reach of the government still remain. So, how exactly has the federal government managed to increase its role in criminal justice despite clear constitutional hurdles? There are three ways that the federal government has been able to assert itself: creative use of interstate commerce and taxing powers, selective incorporation of the Bill of Rights into the individual states, and federal grants to the states.

# Interstate Commerce and Taxing Powers

## The Mann Act

In 1910, Congress enacted the **Mann Act**.[38] According to the language of the legislation, the law made it a felony "to knowingly transport women or girls in interstate or foreign commerce for the purpose of prostitution, debauchery, or any other immoral purpose." In 1986, the statute was amended, and "women or girls" were replaced with "individuals."[39] Michael Conant has argued that while there was not any particular legislative *need* to prevent the trafficking of boys or men, the amendment was still important, as it represented a broader effort to make all federal legislation gender neutral.[40]

The Mann Act is controversial for many reasons. Social scientists have suggested the legislation was the result of a "moral panic."[41] Erich Goode and Bachman Ben-Yehuda, for example, stated the law was primarily passed to combat the problem of "white slavery," a fear associated with the mass immigration of Chinese workers into the western United States. Racist sentiments were commonly focused toward this immigrant population involving a distinct fear of white women being lured into opium dens run by and for Chinese immigrants, where they would be exposed to all manner of debauchery. According to Goode and Ben-Yehuda " 'white slavery' proved to be a 'perfect storm' of a moral panic—a complete figment of the media's imagination."[42]

Instead of representing restraint on human trafficking, the law was frequently used as a mechanism to reinforce majority views of sexuality and race.[43] Perhaps the quintessential example of this was when Jack Johnson, famous for being the first African-American heavyweight-boxing champion of the world, was charged with violating the Mann Act.[44] Johnson was known to frequently flaunt societal norms, especially within the Jim Crow era. A behavior that especially irked the white establishment was that Johnson would frequently involve himself romantically with white women. As a seeming effort to put him back in his place, Johnson was charged in 1912 for violating the Mann Act.[45] The alleged prostitute that Johnson was transporting across state lines was a woman named Lucille Cameron who was, in reality, Johnson's fiancé. While Johnson was originally charged with Cameron's abduction, those charges were dismissed after Cameron refused to cooperate. As a result, Johnson was charged and ultimately convicted of violating the Mann Act.[46] He had to serve a year and a day (the maximum sentence) in prison. This was not the only case where charges were filed for violation of the Mann Act: both the actor Charlie Chaplin and the musician Chuck Berry were charged with violating the Mann Act.[47]

This is not to say that human trafficking is not an enormous issue within the United States and other countries.[48] However, the intent of the Mann Act was not stopping human traffickers. Consider: the federal government has always been able to regulate immigration, and prior to the enactment of the Mann Act, kidnapping was a crime that only existed at the state level. At the time of its passage, the Mann Act seemed more like an excuse for the federal government to intrude upon the states and exert authority that was neither necessary nor desired. The legislation quickly gave rise to an important legal question: was it appropriate for the federal government to have such authority? That question was answered in *Hoke v. United States.*[49] In that case, Effie Hoke was charged in federal court for "unlawfully, feloniously, and knowingly persuad[ing], induc[ing], and entic[ing]" Annette Baden from New Orleans, Louisiana, to Beaumont, Texas, for the purposes of engaging in prostitution. Hoke was convicted of violating the Mann Act and sentenced to prison. She challenged her conviction, arguing that the regulation of prostitution was a state matter and the federal government had exceeded its legislative authority. While the Court ultimately agreed that the regulation of prostitution was a state matter, it also ruled that the Mann Act was properly based on the authority of Congress to regulate interstate commerce. The Court believed the law was not targeting prostitution per se, but regulating illegal behavior that occurred while crossing state lines.[50] Thus, the Supreme Court ruled that so long as a law was sufficiently based upon economic activity or commerce, Congress had the ability to regulate certain types of behavior.

Putting aside for the moment that the passage of the Mann Act was seemingly based on a moral panic and that many prosecutions for violations of the law arose from dubious claims, one element of the law does seem plausible. As we mentioned earlier, by the turn of the 20th century the United States had become more of a unified country and less a collection of states. People were routinely travelling greater distances, and it would be inevitable that legislation would be needed to track crimes and criminals that crossed state lines. Numerous cases and events highlight this point, perhaps the most famous being the kidnapping of the son of the famous 20th-century aviator Charles Lindbergh. That case highlighted the need for the federal government to track kidnapping cases that crossed state lines.[51] Furthermore, the 1920s and 1930s was the era of bank robbers and bandits such as Bonnie and Clyde and John Dillinger.[52] To combat these criminals, it was not only necessary to enact federal legislation, but also to create federal agencies to enforce these new laws.

Into this void stepped **J. Edgar Hoover**, who served as the first director for the Federal Bureau of Investigation (FBI).[53] In addition, the Federal Bureau of Narcotics and Dangerous Drugs (later renamed the Drug Enforcement Administration, or DEA) was founded and directed by **Harry Anslinger**.[54] These two men would preside over their respective agencies for decades—in Hoover's case, some 50 years, and in Anslinger's case, 32 years. It quickly became apparent that the federal government could not only justify its authority to enforce legislation because crimes crossed state lines, but the government could also prosecute crimes against persons who engaged in behavior that had the *possibility* of crossing state lines, *regardless of whether the crossing occurred.*[55] This became abundantly clear in 1914 with the passage of the Harrison Narcotic Act.[56]

## *The Harrison Narcotic Act*

The Harrison Narcotic Act placed regulations on all physicians licensed to prescribe opiates and/or cocaine to their patients. These physicians had to register with the federal government, pay appropriate taxes on the transactions, and dispense medications in "good faith."[57] According to David Musto, the Harrison Narcotic Act was intended as a record-keeping act and was based upon the taxing powers of Congress. There was a general consensus that basing the legislation on any other power of Congress would be viewed as a power grab to establish national policing powers. This was particularly controversial since most people believed this went beyond the authority of Congress.[58] This belief seemed briefly prophetic when two years in later, in *United States v. Jin Fuey Moy*,[59] the Supreme Court ruled that the Harrison Narcotic Act was a revenue-based act and *not* a criminal statute. The Court further ruled that Congress was not permitted to create legislation of this type that included *criminal* penalties for its violation. Unless transactions crossed state borders, Congress could not usurp the authority of states to regulate criminal behavior within their borders. However, only three years later, the Supreme Court changed its mind and in two decisions, *United States v. Doremus*[60] and *Webb et al. v. United States*,[61] ruled that although the Harrison Narcotic Act was primarily a revenue measure, its secondary purpose was to reduce both substance abuse and the sale of drugs to those who were not prescribed to receive opiates and/or cocaine.

While the Supreme Court was seemingly content with what generally could be referred to as an expansionist view of the powers of Congress regarding drug regulation, this view did not immediately apply to other areas of regulation. When **Franklin D. Roosevelt** was elected president in 1932, he promised a "New Deal" of legislation to manage the economic depression that was strangling the United States.[62] As part of the New Deal, President Roosevelt proposed many ambitious projects that he believed would not only create scores of new jobs, but also provide necessary regulation of various industries. The problem, however, was the Supreme Court continually ruling that many of these new laws were unconstitutional, arguing that the regulations went beyond the power Congress enjoyed to regulate interstate commerce. Unhappy with the Supreme Court's hindrance to his plans, President Roosevelt devised a radical solution. Arguing that many of the justices were elderly (over 70) and probably overworked, President Roosevelt proposed adding a new justice to the Supreme Court for every member over the age of 70.[63] If the law had passed, it would have expanded the number of justices on the Supreme Court from 9 to 15. Critics saw this as an attempt of "court packing" and argued the only motive of the president was adding new members to the Court who shared Roosevelt's agenda.[64] Although President Roosevelt's plan never came to fruition, it did seem to have the desired effect. One year later, in *West Coast Hotel Co. v. Parrish*,[65] the Supreme Court acquiesced and, by a narrow 5–4 margin, allowed the state of Washington to enact minimum wage legislation, one of Roosevelt's signature plans under the New Deal.

After the *Parrish* decision, the Supreme Court troubled President Roosevelt no further, and it seemed as if an expansionist reading of Congressional ability to regulate interstate commerce would continue. Perhaps the quintessential example of this view was passage of the **Civil Rights Act of 1964**.[66] The law was an omnibus bill that sought to end discrimination in many areas, including voter registration, school segregation, and employment. Additionally, the bill targeted business owners who refused to serve people based upon race, color, religion, sex, or national origin. Another example was the **Comprehensive Drug Abuse Prevention and Control Act of 1970**.[67] Similarly based upon the federal government's ability to regulate interstate commerce, the drug control legislation was far-reaching and provided a comprehensive system of classifying drugs based upon different criteria, such as medical utility, potential for abuse, and potential harm of the substances. The legislation also allows the Drug Enforcement Administration to set quotas of what quantities of drugs can be made. Furthermore, the legislation provided support for substance abuse treatment and drug research. Over the years, the legislation has been amended several times and each change has provided additional regulations for the federal government to oversee.[68]

## The Gun-Free School Zones Act of 1990

At the time, it seemed as though the federal government had free reign to enact legislation that affected the state regulation of crime. It was not until 1995 that the trend in the federal government's control over state crime was blunted. In 1990, Congress passed and President Clinton signed into law the **Gun-Free School Zones Act of 1990** as part of the omnibus Crime Control Act of 1990.[69] The Gun-Free School Zones Act of 1990 prohibits any unauthorized person from knowingly possessing a firearm at any place the person can reasonably believe is a school zone. In *United States v. Lopez*,[70] the Supreme Court ruled that Congress had gone too far and passed legislation that went beyond the scope of interstate commerce. The government had argued that possession of a firearm within an educational setting would most likely lead to a violent crime. As a result, this would eventually affect the economy, as it would lead to a higher cost for insurance, which in turn would affect people's spending and limit their travel, which would, once again, affect the economy. In a 5-4 decision, the majority argued that upholding the act would set a dangerous precedent and that if allowed to stand, Congress could essentially argue that *any* behavior could be shown to somehow affect the economy.

## Contemporary Issues of States' Autonomy

The Supreme Court came to a similar conclusion in *United States v. Morrison*,[71] when the Court invalidated a section of the **Violence Against Women Act of 1994**.[72] Here, the Court ruled that Congress lacked the authority to enact a statute such as the Violence Against Women Act under the Commerce Clause or the Fourteenth Amendment, as the statute did not regulate an activity that *substantially affected* interstate commerce, nor did it redress harm that had been caused by the state's actions or inaction.[73]

Some observers point to these cases as indicative of the originalist perspective they claimed characterized the Court at the time, which under Chief Justice William Rehnquist was more conservative and gave greater respect to states' rights.[74] Yet that is not the whole story. Five years after the *Morrison* decision the Supreme Court turned aside a challenge to the Controlled Substances Act of 1970[75] in *Gonzales v. Raich*.[76] In 1996, California passed Proposition 215 the **Compassionate Use Act of 1996**, which allowed patients to use marijuana for medicinal purposes when prescribed by a physician. Although California may have recognized that marijuana had medicinal value, the Controlled Substances Act [77] (part of the Comprehensive Drug Abuse Prevention and Control Act of 1970) did not. According to the Controlled Substances Act, marijuana is a Schedule I drug, which means it has no medical utility and is not approved for any medical use. Perhaps sensing earlier decisions of the Rehnquist-led Supreme Court, Raich argued that since the residents of California were growing marijuana in California for the purposes of medicinal use, this did not constitute interstate commerce, as no marijuana was being transported across state lines. Instead, it was intrastate commerce that was beyond the authority of Congress to regulate. Unfortunately for Raich, the Court rejected this argument and ruled that the Controlled Substances Act was a *general law* that regulated drugs which are continually trafficked in interstate commerce, both legally and illegally. Furthermore, the Court argued that it was only a matter of time until California-grown marijuana would be transported across state lines and thus would inevitably become interstate commerce.[78]

While there is the need for some people to debate the ability of Congress to regulate interstate commerce, in actuality, there have only been two recent cases of significance where the Supreme Court ruled that Congress had exceeded its regulatory authority. As long as Congress does not go beyond the latitude it has to regulate interstate commerce, legislation it passes involving such activities will usually pass constitutional muster. Frankly, this is not a surprise. Not only is Congress continually passing new laws that make additional behaviors potential crimes, but also in these instances, federal law enforcement (e.g., FBI, Secret Service, or the DEA) has greater resources than does local law enforcement. Although we might see local detectives grumble when the "Feds show up" on television shows such as *Law & Order*, any time a criminal investigation crosses state lines or involves complex financial matters, federal law enforcement is likely to take over an investigation or case. Critics view this as federal authority encroaching into state matters, but even with the greater federal reach into traditionally state criminal justice, there is seemingly more than enough crime to keep both parties busy.

# The Courts and Selective Incorporation of the Bill of Rights

As we previously discussed, one of the guiding principles of common law is the Latin phrase *stare decisis*, which generally means "Let the decision stand."[79] This guiding principle is the foundation on which is built the common law's system of precedent—similar cases should reach similar outcomes. Precedent is primarily practical; once a ruling has been made in one case, it is then applied to future decisions. Such a system offers some sense of predictability, an important feature to a legal system. However, a system built on *stare decisis* and precedent does not always encourage innovation. The Supreme Court will sometimes *distinguish* new cases from previous cases as a reason to bypass or ignore precedent, but it is loath to simply abandon established legal rules. Perhaps the quintessential example of this was the Court's decision in *Brown v. Board of Education*,[80] which (as mentioned earlier) ended racial segregation of public schools. Some sixty years prior, the Court in *Plessy v. Ferguson*[81] upheld a state law that allowed racial segregation under the principle of "separate but equal." People often argue that *Brown* overturned the decision in *Plessy*, but that is a simplistic interpretation of the Court's ruling. In *Brown*, the Court stated that maintaining segregated educational systems would always be discriminatory because it was inevitable one of them—most likely the one serving African Americans—would always be inferior. Thus, the "separate but equal" principle was not explicitly overruled, but rather, the Court focused on equality in educational opportunity for minorities. This notion was further elaborated upon in the Court's decision in *United States v. Virginia*,[82] where the Court ruled that gender-segregated educational institutions (in this case, Virginia Military Institute (VMI) for men, and Virginia Women's Institute for Leadership at Mary Baldwin College) did not provide equal educational experiences.

Why are these rulings important? As we have demonstrated, the Supreme Court, as an institution, can be quite stubborn. Instead of just saying that "separate but equal" was a bad idea and should not have been established as legal precedent, the Court had to find other avenues to essentially reach the same conclusion. Just like most people or organizations, the Court hates to admit it was wrong, and will oftentimes avoid doing so unless absolutely necessary. The issue of "separate but equal" exemplifies the Court's reluctance to change precedent; however, they were eventually able to overturn precedent without having to explicitly state that the particular precedent was a bad idea. The Court was unable to use such tactics when it came to the applicability of the Bill of Rights to the states. In fact, the Supreme Court found itself backed into a corner with no visible exit.

In *Hurtado v. California*,[83] **Joseph Hurtado** was charged with capital murder. There was nothing really unique regarding the facts of his case; however, what was of interest to the Supreme Court were procedural issues arising after Hurtado's arrest. Hurtado was charged by information, or in layman's terms, a direct criminal complaint was filed against Hurtado, and the case did not go before a grand jury before he was officially indicted. At the time, many states followed this practice. Although most people would readily associate the Fifth Amendment with the right to remain silent, it also provides additional protections. One of those provisions is that whenever a person is charged with a capital or "infamous" crime, the defendant must be indicted by a grand jury before going to trial. Clearly, this stipulation was in conflict with the process that California had undertaken in Hurtado's case. Yet, in 1884, the protections of the Bill of Rights *did not apply to the states*. This situation created a quandary for the Supreme Court. While it wanted to maintain precedent, the Court simultaneously held due process of law in high regard. Hurtado's attorney seized upon this idea and argued that due process required something more; that procedural protections found in the common law brought from Great Britain required greater protections from the power of the state for citizens. Unfortunately for Hurtado, his argument largely fell upon deaf ears, and seven justices (just like so many times before) ruled that the Bill of Rights only placed restrictions *on the federal government* and did not apply to the individual states.

Although it was likely no comfort to Joseph Hurtado, his case sparked an idea for **Justice Harlan**, which he addressed with his lone dissenting opinion. Sixteen years before Hurtado's case had reached the Supreme Court, the Fourteenth Amendment was added to the United States Constitution. One of three amendments passed after the conclusion of the Civil War, the Fourteenth Amendment guaranteed due process and equal rights to *all citizens*. Although most people at the time probably assumed that the purpose of the Fourteenth Amendment was to give rights to everyone who had been freed by the Thirteenth Amendment, which had abolished slavery, Justice Harlan believed the

Fourteenth Amendment provided greater protections to citizens. According to the language of the amendment, it "imposed upon the states the same restrictions, in respect of proceedings involving life, liberty, and property, which had been imposed upon general government." Justice Harlan believed this meant that the Fourteenth Amendment essentially *guaranteed* that the protections of the Bill of Rights should be applicable to the states. This new position has been called the *incorporation doctrine*. Written in a dissent, it would take many years before the incorporation doctrine would first appear in concurring and later majority opinions. Today, almost of all of the Bill of Rights has been incorporated unto the states.

Many people view these added protections from state governments as long overdue, while others believe that once again, the federal government has inserted its metaphorical nose where it does not belong, by going beyond the scope of its power and unfairly usurping the power of the states. As of now, the only way that the states can deviate from these rulings is if they provide greater protections from the government than is required, such as states provide attorneys to suspects regardless of whether they request representation. Thus, the states can give *more* rights than what the federal government requires, but not *less*. This is not to say that people's rights are no longer violated and that the states always follow the standards set by the Supreme Court. Indeed, people's rights are violated every day. However, until a court has recognized this violation of rights, people do not have any recourse until a court intervenes. Were the actions of the Supreme Court regarding the selective incorporation of the Bill of Rights unto the states long overdue or heinous act of judicial activism? Once again, that all depends upon your perspective.

## *Federal Grants to States*

The last example of federal authority affecting state policy is something that affects many individuals in college. Ever wonder why the drinking age in every single state is 21? For that degree of uniformity to exist, it would seem Congress would have to pass a law. From our discussion of the powers of Congress under interstate commerce, it would certainly seem like the Supreme Court would be fine if Congress had enacted such legislation. However, that is not the case. Like many other laws, establishing the legal drinking age for citizens is primarily a state issue. Until the 1960s, many states had legislation establishing the minimum drinking age at 21. However, during the late 1960s and early 1970s, many states lowered their drinking age to 18. States did not do this for safety reasons; they did it for political reasons. At that time, the United

States was embroiled in the Vietnam War, which, as you may remember from American history, was not popular with large segments of the American population. One of the most prevalent arguments about placing age limits on legal alcohol consumption was how a young man could be sent overseas to fight for his country, but that country would not allow him to drink a beer. After American forces left Vietnam, the pressure to maintain 18 as the minimum legal drinking age subsided.

During the next few years, many states changed their drinking ages back to 21, citing many studies that found that raising the drinking age resulted in fewer highway fatalities. However, some states maintained a minimum drinking age under 21. As Alexander Wagenaar noted, many lobbying groups supported raising the legal drinking age to 21. Among these groups were the National Transportation Safety Board, the National Council on Alcoholism, the Presidential Commission on Drunk Driving, and the American Medical Association. However, the *real* motivation to change the drinking age came from the federal government. Instead of establishing a national standard, the federal government (beginning in July of 1984) began *withholding* portions of federal highway grants to states that did not have a minimum legal drinking age of 21.[84] This approach is quite clever. The federal government is not, in the strictest sense, *requiring* the individual states to do anything. Instead, they are merely denying a benefit if the individual states do not comply with a stated policy goal. While this may seem like two distinct procedures, practically speaking, there is no functional difference. Highway grants are not small and often account for millions, if not billions, of dollars for each state. There would need to be a lot of people from the ages of 18–20 buying a lot of alcohol to make up for this loss of income through taxes paid on purchased alcohol. Certainly, you could come up with other ways that having a drinking age under 21 could have economic benefits—such as encouraging spring breakers or other youngsters who desire a place they could legally drink. However, given the added safety benefits and the guaranteed income from the federal government, it is little wonder that every state now has a minimum drinking age of 21. Withholding highway funds dramatically affected a single issue area (the drinking age), but perhaps the most dramatic impact the federal government has had on state and local criminal justice policy was the omnibus **Safe Streets Act**, which was enacted in 1968.[85] The act was responsible for the creation of the Law Enforcement Assistance Administration (LEAA), an agency within the Department of Justice that not only had a profound effect on crime policy, but also accelerated the establishment of criminal justice programs at many state universities.[86]

## The Law Enforcement Assistance Administration

According to Malcolm Feeley and Austin Sarat, the Safe Streets Act was enacted during a time when it was popular to metaphorically declare "war" on different social problems.[87] The act was passed in the wake of President Lyndon Johnson's declaration of a "war on poverty" and just before President Richard Nixon's "war on drugs." Feeley and Sarat argued that the legislation was in line with many government solutions to problems, one of merely "throwing money" at them. Beyond creating new funding to fight crime, the act created an entirely new federal agency, **the Law Enforcement Assistance Administration** (LEAA), responsible for overseeing the disbursement of these funds. The LEAA also set an example for creating similar agencies at the state level — such as state planning agencies (SPAs), offices (SPOs), and commissions (SPCs), and "regional planning units" (RPUs) — that would establish innovative strategies to curb or eliminate crime. The LEAA became a mechanism through which the states received up to billions of dollars to fight crime. Evaluations of the efficacy of these allocations to the individual states were difficult because of high turnover among personnel at state agencies responsible for administering the funds, frequent reorganization of these agencies, shifting emphases and mission goals within them, and variability in their scope and size. However, as Feeley and Sarat, among other criminologists, have noted, evaluating the effect of new crime policies can be difficult.[88] How effective any crime prevention program can be at reducing or preventing crime is difficult to establish, although much progress has been made on that front since Feeley and Sarat wrote about the LEAA.[89]

Feeley and Sarat provided an explanation for the creation of LEAA-funded crime prevention programs they described as "splashy, highly publicized, expensive [and] a regular and well-known part of the landscape of American politics."[90] Such politicized processes can create policy dilemmas when government agencies are supposed to produce results while interest groups lobby for the creation of more government programs. Feeley and Sarat argued this belief is rooted in President Franklin Roosevelt's "New Deal," which created many federal projects for the simple purpose of providing people employment during the Great Depression. These programs were later expanded during the 1960s, when there was growing optimism that government programs and spending could solve most social problems. However, despite noble intentions, the creation of bureaucracies is often self-perpetuating, and keeping them funded and staffed can become more important than the agencies' ultimate goal. Feeley and Sarat argued that governments are good at spending money on targeted issues, such as the interstate system. However, when issues are complicated, government intervention is just as likely to further complicate issues as it is to solve them. Furthermore, many politicians who favor allocating the monies are not overly concerned with producing tangible results; delivery of resources to their constituents is the key to getting elected and re-elected, rather than measurably beneficial policy outcomes.[91]

Ultimately, the LEAA was abolished in 1982. In no way, however, was this an end to the federal government providing money to its states to fund crime expenditures. In fact, it was merely the beginning. Currently, the modern day version of the LEAA is the Bureau of Justice Assistance (BJA), which, like its predecessor, still provides billions of dollars to the states for criminal justice expenditures. These expenditures are vital to many state governments. The question of whether this is representative of a good system is still controversial.

Although evaluations of these programs often produce mixed results, it is typically hard to declare that certain programs are failures. In a politicized environment where everyone is competing for federal grants, programs are often short-lived and, in many cases, do not have enough to time to implement programs as they were intended. Voters and politicians are not exactly known for their patience, and the pressure to keep the federal gravy train of dollars rolling and produce results often leads to the creation of new programs rather than sticking with old ones and trying to determine what exactly went wrong.

# Key Terms

- Common law
- *Stare decisis*
- Matter of first impression
- Republic
- Democracy
- Federalism
- Articles of Confederation
- Strict constructionists
- Living constitutionalists
- Whiskey Rebellion
- Tenth Amendment platform
- The Mann Act
- The Harrison Narcotic Act
- Civil Rights Act of 1964
- Comprehensive Drug Abuse Prevention and Control Act of 1970

- The Gun-Free School Zones Act of 1990
- Violence against Women Act of 1994
- Compassionate Use Act of 1996
- Safe Streets Act
- The Law Enforcement Assistance Administration

# Key People

- Thomas "Tip" O'Neill
- Louis Brandeis
- General Charles Cornwallis
- George Washington
- J. Edgar Hoover
- Harry Anslinger
- Franklin D. Roosevelt
- Joseph Hurtado
- Justice Harlan

# Key Cases

- *New State Ice Co. v. Lipmannb*
- *United States v. Oakland Cannabis Buyers' Cooperative*
- *Gonzales v. Raich*
- *Brown v. Board of Education*
- *United States v. Jin Fuey Moy*
- *United States v. Doremus*
- *Webb et al. v. United States*
- *West Coast Hotel Co. v. Parrish*
- *United States v. Lopez*
- *United States v. Morris*
- *Plessy v. Ferguson*
- *United States v. Virginia*
- *Hurtado v. California*

# Discussion Questions

1. Name and define some of the key features of a common law system. How is the current United States legal system different from a common law system? How is it similar?
2. Why did cities and towns begin to develop municipal ordinances?
3. Is the United States a republic, a democracy, or both? What is the distinction between a republic and a democracy? Make sure to explain your answer.
4. Explain the differences between how originalists and living constitutionalists interpret the Constitution. Then select a contemporary issue in the courts and describe how originalists might interpret the issue and how living constitutionalists might interpret the issue.
5. Describe the occurrences of the Whiskey Rebellion. What was the significance of this event?
6. What is the "Tenth Amendment platform"? What is its relevance today, and would the same relevance have existed in colonial times?
7. What is the Mann Act? Describe some of the controversies surrounding the act.
8. Identify and describe two current issues regarding states' autonomy.
9. Describe the political influence on the creation and maintenance of the LEAA.

# Notes

1. O'Neil, Thomas. 1995. *All Politics is Local and Other Rules of the Game*. Boston: Adams Media.

2. Kyckelhahn, Tracey. 2014. *Justice Expenditure and Employment Extracts, 2009—Final*. Retrieved on November 2, 2014 at: http://www.bjs.gov/index.cfm?ty=pbdetail &iid=5048.

3. Holmes, Oliver W. 1881. Retrieved on November 2, 2014 at: http://biotech.aw. lsu.edu/Books/Holmes/claw06.htm.

4. Arnold-Baker, Charles. 2008. *The Companion to British History*. London: Loncross Denholm Press.

5. Legal Information Institute. n.d. "*Stare Decisis.*" Retrieved on November 3, 2014 at: http://www.law.cornell.edu/wex/staredecisis.

6. See, for example, *Marbury v. Madison*, 5 U.S. 137 (1803).

7. Public Private Partnership in Infrastructure Resource Center. n.d. "Key Features of Common and Civil Law Systems." Retrieved on November 3, 2014 at: http://www.world bank.org/public-private-partnership/legislation-regulation/framework-assessment/legal-systems/common-vs-civil-law#Common_Law_System.

8. New State Ice Co. v. Liebmann. 285 U.S. 262. 1932.

9. See, for example, Sullivan, Kathleen. 2006. "From States' Rights Blues to Blue States' Rights: Federalism after the Rehnquist Court." *Fordham Law Review* 75(2): 799–814.

10.  See, for example, Katagiri, Yakashira. 2001. *The Mississippi State Sovereignty Commission: Civil Rights and States' Rights*. Oxford, MS: University Press of Mississippi.

11.  Barnes, Robert. 2014. "Supreme Court Takes No Action on Same Sex Marriage Cases, for Now." *The Washington Post*, October 2, 2014, Retrieved on November 4, 2015 at: http://www.washingtonpost.com/politics/supreme-court-bypasses-same-sex-marriage-cases-for-now/2014/10/02/1d2747b0-4a39-11e4-891d-713f052086a0_story.html.

12.  Caldwell, Suzanna, and Laurel Andrews. 2014. "Everything You Wanted to Know About Legalizing Marijuana (But Weren't Sure You Could Ask)." *Alaska Dispatch News*, October 25, 2014. Retrieved on November 3, 2014 at: http://www.adn.com/article/20141025/everything-you-wanted-know-about-legalizing-marijuana-werent-sure-you-could-ask.

13.  United States v. Oakland Cannabis Buyers' Cooperative. 532 U.S. 483. 2001.

14.  Gonzales v. Raich. 545 U.S. 1. 2005.

15.  Milligan, Susan. 2014. "Pro-Pot Push: The Next Gay Marriage." *U.S. News & World Report*, August 13, 2014. Retrieved on November 3, 2014 at: http://www.usnews.com/news/articles/2014/08/13/push-to-legalize-marijuana-echoes-same-sex-marriage-efforts.

16.  Glass, Kevin. 2014. "Neighboring States Sue Colorado over Marijuana Legalization." *Townhall.com*. Retrieved on April 19, 2015 at: http://townhall.com/tipsheet/kevinglass/2014/12/19/neighboring-states-sue-colorado-over-marijuana-legalization-n1934069.

17.  Annenberg Classroom. n.d. Article IV Section 4. Retrieved on November 3, 2014 at: http://www.annenbergclassroom.org/page/article-iv-section-4.

18.  Brennan, William J. 1961. "The Bill of Rights and the States." *New York University Law Review*, 36:761–805.

19.  Nitty Gritty Law Library. nd. "Republic vs. Democracy." Retrieved on November 3, 2014 at: https://www.1215.org/lawnotes/lawnotes/repvsdem.htm.

20.  Hansen, Mogens H. 2010. "The Concepts of *Demos, Ekklesia*, and *Dikasterion* in Classical Athens." *Greek, Roman, and Byzantine Studies*, 50:499–536.

21.  Monk, Linda. nd. "Federalism." Retrieved on November 3, 2014 at: http://www.pbs.org/tpt/ constitution-usa-peter-sagal/federalism/#.VFepFGznbIU.

22.  *Ibid*.

23.  *Ibid*.

24.  Jillson, Calvin and Thornton Anderson. 1978. "Voting Bloc Analysis in the Constitutional Convention: Implications for an Interpretation of the Connecticut Compromise." *The Western Political Quarterly*, 31(4): 535–547.

25.  Ohline, Howard. 1971. "Republicanism and Slavery: Origins of the Three-Fifths Clause in the United States Constitution." *The William and Mary Quarterly*, 28(4): 563–584.

26.  Linder, Douglas. 2014. "Exploring Constitutional Law." Retrieved on November 3, 2014 at: http://law2.umkc.edu/faculty/projects/ftrials/conlaw/home.html.

27.  For an example of the former type of Constitutional interpretation see *Marsh v. Chambers* 463 U.S. 783 (1983), where the Court upheld the Nebraska legislature's practice of beginning each legislative session with a prayer. An example of the latter is found in *Griswold v. Connecticut*, 381 U.S. 479 (1965) where the Supreme Court ruled that a husband and wife have a "right to privacy" from state law that made it a crime to use contraception. Nowhere in the Constitution is the "right to privacy" explicitly mentioned, let alone mentioned as a right.

28.  Linder, Douglas. 2014. "Exploring Constitutional Law." Retrieved on November 3, 2014 at: http://law2.umkc.edu/faculty/projects/ftrials/conlaw/home.html.

29.  Brown v. Board of Education, (1955). 349 U.S. 294.

30.  Bill of Rights Institute. 2010. *Brown v. Board of Education*. Retrieved November 8,

2014 from http://billofrightsinstitute.org/resources/educator-resources/lessons-plans/landmark-cases-and-the-constitution/brown-v-board-of-education-1954/.

31. Digital Encyclopedia of George Washington. 2014. "Whiskey Rebellion." Retrieved on November 8, 2014 at: http://www.mountvernon.org/research-collections/digital-encyclopedia/article/whiskey-rebellion/.

32. With the states' ratification of the 14th Amendment in 1868, the Bill of Rights became applicable to them.

33. United States Constitution, Amendment X.

34. Gerson, Michael. (2011, July 25). "Rick Perry's Passion for States' Rights." *The Washington Post*. Retrieved on May 13, 2014 at: http://www.washingtonpost.com/rick-perrys-passion-for-states-rights/2011/07/25/gIQAWa2WZI_story.html.

35. 10 U.S.C. 47.

36. Friedman, Lawrence M. 1993. *Crime and Punishment in American History*. New York: Basic Books.

37. *Ibid*.

38. In total, the statute reads: "Whoever knowingly transports any individual in interstate or foreign commerce, or in any Territory or Possession of the United States, with intent that such individual engage in prostitution, or in any sexual activity for which any person can be charged with a criminal offense, or attempts to do so, shall be fined under this title or imprisoned not more than 10 years, or both." 18 U.S.C. 2421.

39. Legal Information Institute. 2014. 18 U.S.C. § 2421—Transportation—Generally. Retrieved on November 10, 2014 at: http://www.law.cornell.edu/uscode/text/18/2421.

40. Conant, Michael. 1996. "Federalism, the *Mann Act*, and the Imperative to Decriminalize Prostitution." *Cornell Journal of Law and Public Policy*, 2(1):99–118.

41. Rohloff, Amanda and Sarah Wright. 2010. "Moral Panic and Social Theory: Beyond the Heuristic." *Current Sociology*, 58(3), 403–419. For a classic example of this line of research, see Stanley Cohen. 2002 [1972]. *Folk Devils and Moral Panics*. New York: Routledge.

42. Goode, Erich and Nachman Ben-Yehuda. 2002. *Moral Panics: The Social Construction of Deviance*. Malden, MA: John Wiley & Sons, Ltd., p. 6.

43. Langum, David J. 1994. *Crossing Over the Line: Legislating Morality and the Mann Act*. Chicago, IL: University of Chicago Press.

44. Weiner, Eric. 2008. "The Long Colorful History of the *Mann Act*." Retrieved on November 8, 2014 at: http://www.npr.org/templates/story/story.php?storyId=88104308.

45. Burns, Ken. 2005. *Unforgiveable Blackness: The Rise and Fall of Jack Johnson*. Washington, DC: WETA. Retrieved on November 8, 2014 at: http:///www.pbs.org/unforgivableblackness/index.html.

46. Gilmore, Al-Tony. 1973. Jack Johnson and White Women: The National Impact. *The Journal of Negro History*, 58(1):18–38.

47. Weiner, Eric. (March, 11, 2008). "The Long, Colorful History of the Mann Act." NPR.org. Retrieved on May 21, 2014 at: http://www.npr.org/templates/story/story.php?storyId=88104308.

48. United States Department of State. 2014. *Trafficking in Persons Report*. Washington, DC: U.S. Department of State.

49. Hoke v. United States, (1913). 227 U.S. 308.

50. *Ibid*.

51. Federal Bureau of Investigation. 2014. *The Lindbergh Kidnapping*. Retrieved on November 10, 2014 at: http://www.fbi.gov/about-us/history/famous-cases/the-lindbergh-

kidnapping.

52. Legends of America. 2014. "20th Century America: Prohibition and Depression Era Gangsters." Retrieved on November 10, 2014 at: http://www.legendsofamerica.com/20th-gangsters.html.

53. Federal Bureau of Investigation. 2014. "History: John Edgar Hoover." Retrieved on November 10, 2014 at: http://www.fbi.gov/about-us/history/directors/hoover.

54. See, for example, the collected papers of Henry J. Anslinger available at the Pennsylvania State University library archives. See: http://www.libraries.psu.edu/findingaids/1875.htm.

55. McCoy, Kelli Ann. 2010. *Claiming Victims: The Mann Act, Gender, and Class in the American West, 1910–1930s.* Unpublished doctoral dissertation, Department of History, University of California San Diego.

56. 38 Stat 785 Ch. 1. Retrieved November 11, 2014 from http://www.law.cornell.edu/topn/ harrison_act_of_1914.

57. *Ibid.*

58. Musto, David F. 1999. *The American Disease: Origins of Narcotic Control.* 3rd Edition. New York: Oxford University Press.

59. United States v. Jin Fuey Moy, (1916). 241 U.S. 394.

60. United States v. Doremus, (1919). 249 U.S. 86.

61. Webb et al. v. United States, (1919). 249 U.S. 96.

62. Roosevelt Institute. nd. "The New Deal." Retrieved on November 12, 2014 at: http://rooseveltinstitute.org/policy-and-ideasroosevelt-historyfdr/new-deal.

63. Holloman III, John H. 1970. "The Judicial Reform Act: History, Analysis and Comment." *Law and Contemporary Problems,* 35(1): 128–150.

64. Thompson, Dorothy 1937. "Roosevelt Goes Too Far in Packing the Court." *Washington Star,* February 10, 1937, p. 1.

65. West Coast Hotel Co. v. Parrish, (1937). 300 U.S. 379.

66. 42 U.S.C. §2000d *et seq.*

67. 21 U.S.C. §801 *et seq.*

68. Ratliff, John. nd. "History of Drug Laws and Restrictions in the U.S." Retrieved on November 12, 2014 at: http://facultypages.morris.umn.edu/~ratliffj/psy1081/drug_laws.htm.

69. Public Law No. 101–647.

70. United States v. Lopez, (1995). 514 U.S. 549.

71. United States v. Morrison, (2000). 529 U.S. 598.

72. 42 U.S.C. §13701 *et seq.*

73. *Ibid.*

74. Biskupic, Joan. 2005. "Rehnquist Often Sided with States Over Federal Power." *USA Today,* September 4, 2005.

75. 21 U.S.C. §812.

76. 545 U.S. 1 (2005).

77. 21 U.S.C. §812.

78. Gonzales v. Raich, (2005). 545 U.S. 1.

79. We are not Latin scholars, so we will not definitively state the authoritative literal translation (many different variations are offered), but the phrase essentially means "let the decision stand."

80. Brown v. Board of Education, (1954). 347 U.S. 483.

81. Plessy v. Ferguson, (1896), 163 U.S. 537.

82. United States v. Virginia, (1996). 518 U.S. 515.

83. Hurtado v. California, (1884). 110 U.S. 516.

84. Wagenaar, Alexander C. 1986. Preventing Highway Crashes by Raising the Legal Minimum Age for Drinking: The Michigan Experience 6 Years Later. Journal of Safety Research, 17:101–109.

85. 42 U.S.C. § 3711.

86. Barker, Thomas. 2010. "Law Enforcement Assistance Administration (LEAA)." In Bonnie S. Fisher and Steven Lap (Eds.), *Encyclopedia of Victimology and Crime Prevention*. Thousand Oaks, CA: Sage Publications.

87. Feeley, Malcolm M. and Austin D. Sarat. 1980. *The Policy Dilemma: Federal Crime Policy and the Law Enforcement Assistance Administration*. Minneapolis, MN: University of Minnesota Press.

88. *Ibid.*

89. Sherman, Lawrence W., David P. Farrington, Brandon C. Welsh, and Doris L. MacKenzie (Eds.). 2002. *Evidence Based Crime Prevention*. New York: Routledge.

90. Feeley, Malcolm and Austin D. Sarat. 1980. *The Policy Dilemma: Federal Crime Policy and the Law Enforcement Assistance Administration*. Minneapolis, MN: University of Minnesota Press.

91. *Ibid.*

# Chapter 2

# The Political Economy of Crime

## Chapter Outline

- Introduction
- Punishment and Politics
  - Cesare Beccaria
  - The Social Contract
  - Law and Social Solidarity
  - Conflict and Lawmaking
  - Conflict and Politics
  - Conflict and Marxism
  - The Influence of Marxism in Criminological Theory
- Power and Control in the United States
  - Black Codes and Jim Crow Laws
  - Discrimination and Legislation
  - Socioeconomic Status and the Law
  - Labeling Theories of Crime
  - Strain Theories of Crime
- Conclusion
- Key Terms
- Key People
- Key Cases
- Discussion Questions

## Learning Objectives

- Identify the role of deterrence in politics, crime, and punishment
- Identify and explain the relationship between criminological theory, money, and politics

- Evaluate the relevance of the social contract in contemporary issues of crime and politics
- Compare and contrast conflict and consensus theories of law and crime
- Examine the relationship between social norms and law

# Introduction

The primary role of **criminological theory** is to explain why people commit crime. Theorists approach the study of crime from different perspectives, some at the macro or ecological level, where explaining crime *rates* is the focus, others at the micro level, where explaining why specific *individuals* engage in illegal behavior is the guiding orientation. The former group of theories is perhaps best illustrated by those focusing on concentrated disadvantage to explain crime, and emphasizing such factors as racial heterogeneity, family disruption, and inequality, while the latter group is perhaps best illustrated by so-called "control theories" which focus on factors like bonds with larger social institutions such as schools, families, or church. While few of these theories focus *exclusively* on money and politics as causal agents for crime or criminality, many theories at least mention their possible role in explaining crime or criminality.

# Punishment and Politics

## *Cesare Beccaria*

A long tradition in both sociological and criminological theory emphasizes the fact that conflicts between groups of people are ultimately settled through a politicized process, and as many of these theories indicate, the winners typically are those from the most powerful or wealthy classes of society.[1] Since this book focuses on money and politics, this chapter describes how money and politics have played a role in criminological theory. Please keep in mind, we are not writing a book about theory, we are merely pointing out how theory can inform our discussion of money and politics and how these two entities affect criminal justice policy.

Although not developed on the grounds of politics or money per se, Cesare Beccaria (1739–1794), considered by many to be the "father of modern criminology," shared his theory of crime in *On Crimes and Punishments*, originally published in 1764.[2] Beccaria lived in Italy at a time when great reforms in the law were being advocated throughout Europe. At the time, formal legal codes were almost nonexistent, people could be arrested for merely offending the crown, and judges were practically limitless in their discretionary power. A person could be found guilty of an act that was subjectively and spontaneously labeled a crime, and a judge could punish the guilty person however he saw fit. In his early twenties, Beccaria became close friends with Pietro and Alessandro Verri and formed an intellectual circle called "the academy of fists," which focused on reforming the criminal justice system. Through this group, Beccaria became acquainted with French and British political philosophers such as Hobbes, Hume, Diderot, Helvetius, and Montesquieu.[3] The group discussed literature and philosophy, and somewhat contrary to the groups that you and your friends might belong to today, Beccaria's friends assigned him homework, which was to write an essay on penology. The result of this essay was *On Crimes and Punishment.*

To learn more about the state of penology at the time, Beccaria visited prisons in Italy with the Verri brothers. As a result of his visits, Beccaria came to the conclusion that the brutal and arbitrary punishments he observed were actually counterproductive to reducing crime. Rather, he argued that the unfairness he witnessed seemed more like the desperate acts of a punitive state than a rational response to illegal behavior, and would inevitably lead to resentment of the government by the people. Beccaria's position on crime and punishment is based in two key philosophical theories of the day: **social contract** and utility. Concerning the social contract, Beccaria argued that punishment is justified only to defend the social contract and to ensure that everyone will be motivated to abide by it. Concerning utility (perhaps influenced by Helvetius), Beccaria argued that the method of punishment selected should be that which serves the greatest public good.[4]

Beccaria stated that for criminal sanctions (punishment) to be effective, they should be dictated by three elements that worked in concert: certainty, severity, and celerity.[5] For Beccaria, the certainty of punishment referred to the probability the sanction would in fact be imposed on lawbreakers, while the severity of punishment referred to the amount of punishment received. Finally, the celerity of punishment referred to the speed with which the punishment was administered. These ideas ultimately became the basis for what we now know as **deterrence theory**. Deterrence assumes humans are rational actors who pursue behavior that maximizes their pleasure (utility) and minimizes their pain. When faced with an opportunity to break the law, deterrence assumes people will weigh the costs and benefits of doing so—what would be gained (e.g., money from selling drugs) versus what would be lost (e.g., their liberty from being incarcerated)—and choose the action that maximizes the benefits and minimizes the pain. If the benefits of the behavior are perceived to outweigh the costs, the individual will choose the behavior. Thus, for punishment to be effective, the costs of crime—the punishment—had to outweigh the benefits.[6]

Beccaria argued that if the government appropriately implemented these three elements of punishment, a particular offender would be deterred from committing the same crime again. Beccaria referred to this as *specific deterrence*. Even more, he argued that other people would become aware of the crime and the punishment received by an offender and these people would also be deterred from committing that crime, which Beccaria referred to as *general deterrence.*[7]

As mentioned previously, Beccaria was especially concerned with what he viewed as the draconian punishments of his day. Essentially, Beccaria believed that the "punishment should fit the crime," meaning that if the punishment was lenient but the offense serious, neither the individual being punished nor those aware of the light punishment would be dissuaded from committing that same crime in the future. However, punishment that was *too* severe would be equally ineffectual. Beccaria believed punishments that were unfair or too harsh would lead to people believing that the government is unjust and illegitimate. Therefore, brutal punishments would actually *encourage* more law breaking than they would prevent. To alleviate these concerns, punishment had to be "just right," where serious crimes like armed robbery would be punished more severely than lesser crimes like petty theft. Beccaria also believed that if punishment was uncertain or unnecessarily delayed, it would seem less real to a person, as the punishment would no longer be associated with the crime. Thus, if punishment is either unlikely to occur or far off in the future, people would not be deterred in the present.[8] Alex Piquero came to this conclusion when he found that many youthful serious offenders, who believed that they would die at an early age, perceived there was no reason to follow the law since no punishment would be forthcoming because they would most likely be dead.[9]

Beccaria was only 26 years old when he published *On Crimes and Punishment*. At the time he wrote it, neither sociology nor criminology existed, yet many of his ideas (which were influenced by other intellectuals of his day) still heavily impact our ideas of law and punishment. Furthermore, his ideas have been somewhat modernized into other theories of crime, such as the calculations explicitly found in rational choice, situational crime prevention, and routine activities theories. Although the terminology used in these theories may be different from that found in Beccaria's writings, the terminology is still based upon the same principle that humans are rational actors seeking to maximize their pleasure and minimize their pain. Although it is difficult to calculate exactly which pleasures and pains individuals most people desire or wish to most avoid, a society's laws, and the punishment of those who violate those laws, will likely affect how the members of that society behave.

The degree to which deterrence is effective is dependent on the time we take to make a decision. For instance, if we are coming home from a long run and think about stopping to get some ice cream, we may be discouraged if we rationally review all the consequences. We will likely come to the conclusion that getting ice cream is not a healthy choice and that our workout will have been useless. On the other hand, we could argue that the ice cream is our reward for running. Both of these could plausibly be rational arguments. However, if we are really craving ice cream, some of that rationality may go out the window. In fact, we may not even think to weigh the various consequences of that action—we may just eat the ice cream, and only later think of the consequences. This may seem like a silly comparison; however, those who believe in deterrence would argue that we make decisions that are based on weighing the degree of happiness to the degree of pain. However, when emotions (like that craving for ice cream) take over, this is when we often make rash decisions that we later regret.

Notions of deterrence are incorporated within many aspects of our lives. For instance, every time you hear a politician say that we need tougher laws to prevent crime, they are referencing deterrence. Every time you go into a convenience store and see a sign that states that there is under $100 in the register and no safe is present in the facility, the store is posing a question to every would-be robber: is that small amount of money worth the potential penalties associated with robbing this store? Even when you were a child, your parents guaranteed that if you did something bad, you would be punished accordingly. If you look around, you will realize that methods of deterrence are everywhere.

## *The Social Contract*

When a theory of crime is focused on the process of lawmaking, it is inevitable that the role of money and/or politics will be integrated in the theory's explanations. One of the first examples of this originated during the Enlightenment period with the development of the **social contract**. The social contract is generally based upon the idea that there must be an exchange of a person's freedoms for protection from the state. The social contract has been applied to numerous topics, including the natural rights of human beings, the nature of political authority, the limits of a sovereign's authority, and many other ideas.[10] Although we would be hesitant to rank the importance of each idea, the work of **Thomas Hobbes** (1588–1679) is likely the most significant to the field of criminology. Hobbes lived a long life in Europe during some very turbulent times. Despite his longevity, Hobbes would write in his well-known *Leviathan* that human life was effectively "solitary, poor, nasty, brutish, and short."[11] Writing during one of many English civil wars that occurred in his lifetime, Hobbes argued it was necessary to have a strong state government to bring order to the chaos of life. Hobbes's idea of the social contract involved people giving up some of their liberty to the state so that they would in turn be protected by the state.[12] Thus, people should be willing to submit to a state authority so that they could be safeguarded against possible threats—giving up some freedom is necessary for the trade-off in security.

Hobbes's statements seem prophetic, as they are just as relevant today as they were over 350 years ago. The extent to which individuals should relinquish their liberties has been an ongoing debate within American history. The terrorist attacks of September 11, 2001, or the mass shootings at Sandy Hook Elementary school are just two events that have renewed interest in how much liberty people should be willing to give up so that society can be protected.

## *Law and Social Solidarity*

Over 200 years after Hobbes's Leviathan, **Emile Durkheim** (1858–1917), who is considered by many to be the "father of modern sociology," published *The Division of Labor in Society*.[13] In the book, Durkheim explored "totality of beliefs and sentiments common to the average citizen of the same society."[14] Durkheim argued that law mattered in both examples of social solidarity. In mechanical solidarity, legal sanctions tended to be **repressive**—to purposely inflict suffering or loss on the offender—because criminal offenses/offenders shocked the collective conscience. In a society characterized by mechanical solidarity, there tends to be a defined normative social order, and not only do social pressures among people enforce this order, but the presence of law does as well. In societies characterized by organic solidarity, legal sanctions are more **restitutive**, seeking to return things to the way they were before the infraction.[15] In both cases, Durkheim argued that law generally reflects the larger moral order. Furthermore, law is important not only because it reinforces the normative order and sense of morality, but also when someone violates the law, society reaffirms their behavior as unacceptable by punishing the offenders, which helps create in those who abide by the law a sense of moral superiority. If laws are not enforced, people might begin to question the necessity of the laws or why they should conform to them. Such a situation could lead to a complete breakdown in social order.[16]

So why bring up the work of Hobbes and Durkheim? They make two important points. The first is that people should be willing to cede some of their freedom (how much is certainly debatable) so that they can live in a secure state. The second is that law reinforces social order. These two ideas serve as a basis for what are known as **consensus theories of law**.[17] Proponents of consensus theories argue that society is organized around agreement—that people implicitly agree that certain behaviors are so wrong as to warrant formal intervention by the state. There is also agreement about the structure of larger social institutions—political, religious, familial, etc. From the consensus perspective, in a democracy or a republic, legislation is developed and passed *that satisfies the most people*, usually through some form of voting process.[18] Perhaps a more simple way to state this principle would be to say that the majority rules, but there is consensus that such should be the state of affairs. The problem here is that only in rare circumstances can everyone be satisfied, and there will thus be some disappointed people whenever a law is passed. Being a part of the minority within a decision is inevitable, but remembering that each individual was included in the process should yield at least some satisfaction.

As you might expect, not all social scientists—particularly sociologists and criminologists—agree with such an interpretation of social organization or how law functions. A competing perspective is known as **conflict theory**, and its proponents posit a much different view of how society is organized. Generally, conflict theorists argue that society is organized around competing interests, specifically, groups competing for power and privilege. As these groups come into or fall out of power, change occurs in larger social organization, including the major institutions—political, religious, familial, economical, etc. Concerning law, conflict theorists argue that the law at any given time reflects the interests of those in power at the time. For example, during the 1960s, as a result of tremendous pressure mounted by civil rights proponents, Congress passed legislation that outlawed segregation and gave minorities a set of basic rights concerning participation in the political process (e.g., the 1964 Voting Rights Act). More recently, well-funded interest groups associated with the conservative wing of the Republican Party have pressed for legislation at the state and federal levels that would reduce taxes on the wealthy and spending on the "social safety net," create "voucher programs" or publicly funded "charter schools" to allow parents to send children to private schools or charter schools instead of failing public schools, abolish or severely restrict regulations on business and the financial sector of the economy, restrict abortion and immigration, and create new requirements for voting, such as requiring a picture ID to vote.[19] Concurrently, various interest groups representing the more liberal wing of the Democratic Party counter with a set of competing legislative agendas that emphasize raising taxes on the wealthiest among us, reducing military spending, expanding the social safety net, enhancing regulations on business and the financial sector of the economy, expanding the availability of abortion and family planning services for women, increasing spending on public schools, etc.[20] During the 2014 midterm elections, the United States Senate was "up for grabs," along with governorships in multiple states. As a result, both sides pumped billions of dollars into the campaign in an effort to influence the public. According to conflict theorists, those groups—whether Republican or Democrat—wielding the most power will "rule" the country. Furthermore, once acceding to power, the groups will change or alter the political process so that they not only ensure their future dominance in society, but also minimize the role of those less powerful in producing change.[21]

## Conflict and Lawmaking

So, to what degree or scope do conflict theories predict that conflict will mar the political process? That depends upon the theorist. For instance, in 1938, **Thorsten Sellin** (1896–1994) argued that all societies possess conduct norms. If a society was relatively homogenous in terms of values and beliefs, then these conduct norms might not present much of a problem because people would likely have similar ideas of what the normative structure of society should be. However, as a society became more heterogeneous, conflicting values and disagreements about how society should be structured would occur.[22] Similar to the ideas of Durkheim, Sellin stated that conduct norms would often be codified into legislation. This could result in the arrest and punishment of people who violated the conduct norms of society. Sellin believed that when nations colonized other nations or lands, the possibility for oppression was greatest because the dominant society would not only subjugate the colonized nation through some form of military force, but would follow that up by requiring the newly colonized people to conform to conduct norms that were most likely completely foreign to them.[23]

In the original edition of his text *Theoretical Criminology* (published in 1958), **George Vold** (1896–1967) proposed *group conflict theory*, in which he argued that societies are often composed of different interest groups that will continually struggle for supremacy. This struggle is continuous and issues never seem to actually be settled. Instead, societies are often marked by periods of uneasy peace where the losing interest groups bide their time until they are again able to compete for power. Vold believed that consensus was never achieved, just periods of "uneasy adjustment." He argued that conflict is natural in a society because humans form groups based upon common interests, whether economic, political, or religious. These groups form not only because of common interests, but because these interests could be furthered by legislation through collective action. When new interests or issues emerge, either new groups form or existing groups take positions on these issues that are typically consistent with their existing beliefs.[24]

## Conflict and Politics

Even the most casual observer of politics would recognize the presence of competing groups within their society. In the United States, the two most powerful political parties are the Democrats and Republicans. Who wields power in different branches of government, although clearly affected by geography, often shifts between these two parties over time. Similar results occur in other countries, such as the battles between the Conservative Party and Labour Party in the United Kingdom, and the Christian Democratic Union/Christian Social Union, the Social Democratic Party, the Left Party, the Alliance '90/ Green, and the Free Democratic Party in Germany. Countries like Germany can be particularly instructive on the dynamics of interest groups because competing parties there may form alliances to form a majority in government. Unlike the United States (which has a government structure that seems to encourage the formation of only two political parties), countries with more than two political parties illustrate the complex dynamics of how different interest groups can join together and fall apart.

So, why is this talk of political parties and group conflict important to crime? Vold argued that the nature of the legislative process is finding compromises between opposing interests. Ultimately, the interests groups with the most power will be able to reflect their values within the law. Some of the interests groups that end up losing will simply abide by the winning groups' regulations, biding their time until they once again wield power; however, others within the losing interest groups will simply disregard the regulations, perceiving the ratification of law as being based on power, not justice. In 1968, Edward Suchman provided an example of such behavior in an article he wrote about marijuana use among college students. He argued that marijuana use was more common among college students, whose behaviors went against the traditional normative values of society.[25] He referred to such behavior as a "hang-loose" ethic.[26] Since that time we have seen the growth of an entire marijuana culture, sometimes referenced around the concept of "420" (pronounced four-twenty, not four-hundred-and-twenty), which allegedly originated at San Rafael High School in 1971 among a group of about a dozen pot-smoking students who called themselves the "**Waldos**" and invented the term as shorthand for the time of day (4:20 p.m.) the group would meet to smoke pot.[27] Yet, in the case of marijuana, we may eventually see one of those cases where the minority interest eventually became the majority. On October 22, 2013, the Gallup Poll announced that, for the first time, a majority of Americans favored legalization of marijuana.[28] Furthermore, in 2013, voters in both Colorado and Washington approved recreational use of marijuana in their states. Voters in the states of Alaska and Oregon and voters in Washington, DC, would follow suit in 2014. Although these laws currently conflict with federal regulations of marijuana and the possibility of nationwide legalization of marijuana is far from certain, this case illustrates how minority interests groups might show both their defiance to criminal laws enacted by other interest groups and how eventually minority interest groups may overtake the majority opinion.

Although ideological conflict can be between political parties or philosophies, conflict can also be based upon single issues or sets of interrelated issues, which is discussed in Chapter 6. In some instances, groups (such as Campaign to End the Death Penalty) are merely lobbying against the federal government and the individual states that still use the death penalty as a form of punishment. In other cases, you will have interest groups that compete with each other for issue supremacy. For instance, the National Rifle Association and Brady Campaign are continually at odds over the regulation of firearms in the United States.[29] Both groups accuse the other of promoting policies that put people at risk. Although lobbying groups may find politicians who are sympathetic to their cause, this does not stop these politicians from stating that they have the best interests of the United States at heart.

In the Netflix drama *House of Cards*, the American political system is portrayed as hopelessly corrupt. Politicians and lobbyists are often shown engaging in shady deals that most Americans would find unseemly. Although some of the events in the television show might seem a little over the top or unrealistic, the wheeling and dealing that occurs is likely spot on. In 1999, an article appeared in the *Los Angeles Times* recounting that President Bill Clinton was requesting $6 billion for proposed military operations in Kosovo. The appropriations Bill Clinton received from Congress was $12.9 billion, twice the amount of Clinton's request. While one may presume that Congress believed Clinton was in need of more funds to achieve these military goals, in actuality Congress had added other spending projects to the bill during the legislative amendment process. Thus, if Clinton wanted his money for his proposed military options, he would also have to sign off on these other projects.[30] Amendments or "riders" are commonplace in the legislative process. Seemingly every representative has their hand out and wants something for agreeing to the process. Although many decry these political machinations as the main culprit of the United States' excessive spending, referring to them as **"pork-barrel politics"** (perhaps most famously Senator John McCain [R-AZ]), in reality many also benefit from this brand of politics—as long as they are the winners of this process. Those representatives who have their pet projects funded can later go home to their constituents and tell them of their hard-working efforts to fight to ensure their interests were met. Few politicians would ever admit they liked being in Washington or that they condoned the legislative process as long as they were able to bring the money home to their constituents.

Vold described some criminal behaviors as the actions of "minority power groups" and believed the criminal law could be an effective weapon against competing interest groups. By enacting legislation criminalizing behavior important to minority groups, the political process can be an effective tool in efforts to keep certain groups in the minority.[31] In 1969, during the turbulence of the civil rights movement and the Vietnam conflict, Austin Turk argued that "political power determined legality."[32] He argued it was rare for one group of people to wield enough power to rule in complete disregard of all others. When coalitions form, they sometimes are able to affect law, the final form of which reflects the compromises of those involved. Regarding the losers in the process, Turk argued, "For those groupings who have lost out, or never really competed, in the struggle to control legal mechanisms will be edicts. For them, to live in a legal order is to be dominated."[33] He went on to say that the primary condition that would predict conflict was the organization and sophistication of the parties. Turk believed that authorities had organization because they were able to occupy the positions they did. The ability of subjects to organize predicts the likelihood of them protesting the actions of the authorities. Strength often comes in numbers, and Turk believed that better organization was likely to bolster the position of subjects and result in them being more likely to stand up to the authorities.[34]

## Conflict and Marxism

The ideas of Vold and Turk are just two perspectives on conflict within the traditions of sociology and criminology. Yet, no discussion of conflict is complete without discussing the ideas of **Karl Marx** (1818–1883). Marx is a polarizing figure in almost any discussion of government and his name has incorrectly become synonymous with communism. While he, along with **Friedrich Engels** (1820–1895), wrote *The Communist Manifesto*, neither should be held responsible for the occurrences in the Soviet Union, China, or any other self-identified communist countries. Marx studied both history and society using the scientific method, identified patterns and trends using that methodology, and attributed the results he discovered as the result of social conflict. At the core of Marx's theory is the argument that in all societies, a dominant class (the bourgeoisie) exercises domain over a subordinate class (the proletariat). However, that domination is not uncontested, does not last long, and results in large-scale social change: "The history of all hitherto existing society is the history of class struggles."[35] For Marx, class struggle is the driving force of social change and social conflict is at the heart of all historical processes. Marx goes on to identify ownership of, or control over, the means of production as the source of power for the dominant class in society. Marx argued that what is produced, how it is produced, and how it is exchanged profoundly affected society and its organization. Finally, and perhaps most importantly, above all else, Marx's analyses were a critique of capitalism—its dilatory effects on owners, workers, and entire social systems. Marx believed that eventually capitalism would be destroyed as the dominant economic system when the proletariat would rise up and overthrow the bourgeoisie and a new economic system would be created: socialism.

So why have we taken this detour into political philosophy? Taken at face value, Marxist theory seems unrelated to crime, as Marx was certainly not a criminologist (indeed, Marx considered thieves, swindlers, robbers, etc., as members of the *lumpenproletariat*, or miscreants).[36] Indeed, the term "criminologist" did not even exist in Marx's time. However, criminologists *have* applied Marxist thought both to explaining the existence of crime and to understanding the law and its operations.

In terms of Marxist criminology, according to Mark Lanier and Stuart Henry, the perspective makes the following points:

- *All* social institutions in a capitalist society—political, economic, familial, educational—are shaped by capitalism, as are individual social identities, and social action.
- Capitalism, *by its very nature*, creates class conflict (owners of the means of production versus workers).
- Crime/criminality are *responses to capitalism* and its contradictions (e.g., generating and maintaining a surplus labor force of the unemployed and underemployed; oppressive conditions created by capitalism that help to inspire violence).
- Law in a capitalist society both *facilitates and conceals* the crimes of the dominant class.
- In capitalist societies, *crime is "functional"* in the sense it provides opportunities to members of the surplus labor force to earn money and for

those involved with controlling crime to have jobs. Crime is also functional because it helps justify and maintain a legal system that maintains
exploitation of the non-capitalist classes.
- The response by capitalist societies to crime is *shaped by law*.[37]

Further, proponents of the orientation have further "split" Marxist thought
into two streams, *instrumental* and *structural*, designed to describe the role
of the state in generating crime and influencing the behavior of law.[38] **Instrumentalists** argue "[t]here is a direct and crude relationship between the ruling
economic classes and the government"[39] where political elites have explicit ties
to the capital class and work on their behalf to pass laws and create enforcement mechanisms that support them. Structural Marxists, or **structuralists**, by
contrast, argue that the relationship between the state and the capitalist class
is more autonomous, with political elites working to ensure the survival of the
capitalist *system* rather than working on behalf of any one member of the capitalist class. Thus, political elites might pass laws that could damage members
of the capitalist class but which, in the long run, would help ensure the survival of the capitalist economic system. For structuralists, the contradictions
of capitalism create disturbances that must be contained or controlled; failing
to do so would create conditions ripe for revolution and the potential overthrow of the capitalist system. To address this, political elites—to maintain
*ideological* dominance rather than *coercive* dominance over the working
classes—enact laws that benefit the less powerful while also ensuring no one
capitalist comes to dominate the system ("one person cannot get too powerful at the expense of the economic system" as a whole).[40] Interestingly, both
structuralists and instrumentalists would likely agree that because law is imposed by the ruling classes upon the working classes, perpetrating a crime
could be viewed as a "revolutionary act" against an illegitimate social order.[41]

## The Influence of Marxism in Criminological Theory

**Marxism** has never been particularly popular in the United States, and that
lack of popularity is reflected in criminological thought.[42] However, there are
three points that Marxist criminologists have developed that are important to
the subject of money, politics, and crime. The first relevant point was developed by **Willem Bonger** (1876–1940). In his 1916 book *Criminality and Economic Conditions*, Bonger argued that a capitalistic economic system typically
encourages greed and selfish behavior, which likely gives more affluent people
unfair advantages that they will use to further enrich themselves at the expense
of the lower classes.[43] The ideas of Edwin Sutherland (whom we have never

seen identified as a Marxist) essentially echo those of Bonger. Sutherland suggested that not only were more affluent people able to commit crimes that are typically more damaging to society, but also, many people will not think of these actions as "criminal" in a capitalistic society.[44] Such an ethic can be commonplace. John Conklin's text *"Illegal but Not Criminal:" Business Crime in America* got its title from a businessman who was trying to rationalize his own criminal behavior.[45]

The second relevant point regarding Marx is that he engaged in what is now known as *structural* analysis (see previous discussion). Essentially, Marx examined the different structures of a society and discussed how these structures played a part in dictating the rules of society. Thus, when a person engages in a Marxian critique, they are not necessarily promoting a communist agenda (although they certainly could), they are merely pointing out how the organization and structures of a society either promote or inhibit certain types of behavior. One such structural approach is to use *political economy* as a framework. As Michael Lynch has noted, this approach has been underutilized in criminology and criminal justice, but political economy has been applied in many different academic disciplines. For Lynch, political economy is "the use of an explanation that establishes a connection between the economic system and the social sphere, and highlights the influence of economic relations on social relations and institutions."[46] Lynch argued that since the mid-1850s, political economy has been frequently associated with Marxian, radical, and heterodox economic explanations.[47] He utilized a political economic framework in combination with Marxian principles to explain the drop in crime that has taken place in the United States since the early 1990s.[48] In a later work, Lynch and several co-authors used the same paradigm of political economy and Marxism to provide a theoretical rationale to consider "**green criminology**" and how we might better analyze global ecological harms within the discipline of criminology.[49]

Another structural approach to examine the influence of politics and money in criminology is the state-corporate crime paradigm, similar to the instrumental Marxist orientation. The paradigm has many inspirations, including Karl Marx and the work of Edwin Sutherland.[50] Additionally, the work of **Richard Quinney** and **William Chambliss** argued the United States and many other capitalist societies have a "**corporatist nature**" which seems to blindly protect the interests of corporations. Some may wonder who is really running the state: the government or corporate bigwigs.[51] In a series of articles, book chapters, and one book, Ronald Kramer, Raymond Michalowski and David Kauzlarich described their framework for a state-corporate crime paradigm. They argued that great power and great crimes are inseparable. Furthermore, when economic and political powers unite for a cause, the harms produced by this con-fluence of events are often exacerbated.[52] This paradigm, of a state either col-lusive with corporations or indifferent to maintaining safety regulations that will curb the behavior of corporations, has been used to explain several events. These include the events that led to explosion of the space shuttle Challenger,[53] a fire at an Imperial Food Products chicken-processing plant in Hamlet, North Carolina,[54] and many other incidents where scholars believe the government had varying roles of responsibility in allowing and/or causing corporations to harm people.

The third major point we can take from Marxist criminology involves group conflict. Many of the previous works we have mentioned noted that compet-ing values exist between competing groups of people. The group that prevails is usually able, to some degree, to impose its version of what should be con-sidered the **"normative order"** in society. Marx himself predicted that the lower classes might be essentially forced into crime because they did not believe in the larger norms and values of society, and/or they did not have the means to compete in a capitalistic society. Additionally, controlling these groups of peo-ple diverts resources away from capitalistic production. Steven Spitzer further developed this idea with his concepts of **social junk** and **social dynamite**. He noted that there are many unemployed people who are not a threat to the state. In some instances, they may be unemployed because they are elderly, devel-opmentally disabled, dependent upon others, or they simply do not wish to par-ticipate within the economy. Spitzer referred to this class as social junk. While members of this group may represent a drain on the economy, they do not pose a direct threat to the normative capitalistic order. However, those who do *not* participate in the economy but instead question the legitimacy of the social order are referred to as social dynamite and represent a "real" threat to society. Spitzer noted that while the criminal justice system is used to control social dynamite, because social junk is a more benign problem, social welfare agencies are called upon to manage it.[55]

# Power and Control in the United States

## Black Codes and Jim Crow Laws

The United States has a long history of controlling certain groups of peo-ple, particularly minority groups, with slavery undoubtedly being the most notorious example. This form of social control was enforced by law and there was nothing subtle about it. After enactment of the Thirteenth Amendment to the United States Constitution and the abolition of slavery, the desire by powerful whites to institutionally control African Americans did not dissipate. After the Civil War, states and localities in the South enacted what are now known as **black codes** and **Jim Crow laws** that purposely reinforced African Americans as "second-class citizens" despite the end of slavery. For example, some common elements of black codes in the South included:

- Race was defined by blood; the presence of any amount of black blood made one black.
- Employment was required of all freedmen; violators faced vagrancy charges.
- Freedmen could not assemble without the presence of a white person.
- Freedmen were assumed to be agricultural workers and their duties and hours were tightly regulated.
- Freedmen were not to be taught to read or write.
- Public facilities were segregated.
- Violators of these laws were subject to being whipped or branded.[56]

Jim Crow laws also explicitly created legal rules for African Americans, including:

- Prohibiting marriages between whites and Negroes, Indians, or persons of Negro or Indian descent to the third generation.
- White and black children could only be taught in separate public schools.
- Seats on all buses would be segregated by race.[57]

This system of institutionalized racism[58] persisted until the civil rights movement of the 1950s and 1960s systematically began challenging in court legally supported segregation of the races, and the United States Supreme Court began striking down these laws because they violated the Fourteenth Amendment and its guarantee of equal protection under the law.[59]

## Discrimination and Legislation

Although the Supreme Court effectively ended the practice of enacting legislation that had the strict purpose of enacting a system of discrimination, to this day, the Supreme Court has been reluctant to overturn legislation that seems to *produce* a discriminatory effect without a clear discriminatory *intent*. One area of criminal justice that has seen its share of litigation relating to potential discriminatory treatment without discriminatory intent is the United States' prison system. For much of the twentieth century, the courts generally relied upon a **hands-off doctrine**[60] when it came to intervening in the operation of prisons, whether at the state or federal level, and justified this orientation by looking to the **separation of powers** implied by several articles of the Constitution: the judiciary should not interfere with the running of prison systems by the executive branch of government.[61] Beginning approximately in the 1960s with the onset of the **prisoners' rights movement**,[62] appeals courts at the federal level effectively ended the practice of the courts minimizing their intervention into prison administration and management with the case of *Holt v. Sarver*, where the U.S. Court of Appeals for the 8th Circuit ruled the entire prison system in the state of Arkansas was operating in a way that violated the Eighth Amendment, and the United States Supreme Court upheld that ruling several years later.[63] During the 1970s, the United States also saw the beginnings of what would become a nearly fifty-year-long experiment in **mass incarceration**,[64] where incarceration rates nationally skyrocketed over 400% between 1972 and today.[65] While there are many possible reasons for the increase, including tougher sentencing practices, increased arrests, increased prison construction, and others,[66] one of the most cited culprits is the **war on drugs**, which began under President Richard M. Nixon and came into full force during the administration of President Ronald Reagan.[67]

## Socioeconomic Status and the Law

Generally, the poor have always been disproportionately affected by both prison and punishment.[68] The expansion of the use of incarceration as a primary tool to deal with drugs has only exacerbated this problem. All you have to do is read some of the titles of scholarly books and articles on prison and punishment to reach this conclusion, such as John Irwin's *The Warehouse Prison: Disposal of the New Dangerous Class*[69] and Jeffrey Reiman and Paul Leighton's *The Rich Get Richer and the Poor Get Prison*.[70] Even if you were to dismiss these titles as biased, some of the figures would be harder to ignore. For instance, Todd Clear and colleagues discussed that in 1980, there were three times more African American men in college than in prison. Today, African American men are more likely to go to prison than college or serve in the military. Despite being approximately 12% of the total population of the United States, African Americans account for almost 40% of arrests for violent crime and roughly 25% of arrests for property crimes. Furthermore, some reports estimate that there are five times more white drug users than African American drug users, yet African Americans are 13.4 times more likely to be sent to prison for drug charges.[71]

Some explanations for these statistics are simply extensions of the influence of wealth in the United States.[72] Since minorities are more likely to come from impoverished backgrounds, they are less likely to have the resources to insulate them from arrest or hire adequate representation for a criminal trial.[73] The argument about class and the legal system only begins to uncover the complexities of the relationship between race and crime. As mentioned previously, African Americans were first controlled in the United States by the institution of slavery and later through black codes and Jim Crow legislation. Scholars such as Michelle Alexander, Justin Smith, and Loic Wacquant[74] have argued that mass incarceration, which has disproportionately affected African Americans, is merely the new means through which marginalization and control of this population occurs. Not only does prison have the effect of warehousing African Americans away from society, but the aftereffects of prison are just as controlling. For instance, when one completes a job application, he or she will usually have to check a box if they are a convicted felon. Most often, this diminishes their chances of being called in for an interview, let alone being offered a job, and severely damages a candidate's future employment options. Furthermore, not only do most states not allow prisoners to vote, but many states also forbid convicted felons to vote. Thus, not only have tens of thousands of people in American been incarcerated and have trouble finding a job as a result of their incarceration, but they also no longer have a say in the political process that helped create the circumstances in the first place by creating draconian laws relating to the control of drugs.

## Labeling Theories of Crime

Labeling theory began with the work of **Frank Tannenbaum** and **Edwin Lemert**[75] and had its origins in **symbolic interactionism**, a group of sociological theories that focus on how individuals understand themselves, their roles, and their identities.[76] A core tenet of symbolic interaction is Cooley's notion of the "Looking-Glass Self,"[77] whereby one comes to understand and regard him- or herself through the eyes of others. However, symbolic interactionism became more recognized among sociologists and psychologists with the publishing of Mead's *Mind, Self, and Society*[78] and Dewey's *Human Nature and Conduct*.[79] Tannenbaum and Lemert both argued that if punishment included stigmatization, then one may internalize not only that their actions were bad, but that they might be a bad person as well. Tannenbaum referred to this process as "tagging," and Lemert was actually the first person to use the word "label" in such a context.[80] Regardless of the specifics, labeling theory can best be described as a **social process theory**, which emphasizes that the key to understanding social behavior is to understand how individuals subjectively perceive their social reality and how they interact with others to create, sustain, and change.[81]

While **Howard Becker** contributed to our understanding of labeling theory as a social process theory, there is also a different type of labeling theory found within his text *Outsiders* operating as a **legal process theory**. Becker argued that there was nothing necessarily wrong with smoking marijuana and nothing particularly deviant about the people who engaged in this behavior. Yet, Becker argued that certain people, whom he called *moral entrepreneurs*, had other motives for attaching a deviant label to this behavior. To illustrate, Harry Anslinger wanted to promote his agency, the Federal Bureau of Narcotics and Dangerous Drugs. Other people who held negative feelings towards minorities would attach a deviant label to marijuana and then associate smoking the plant with particular minorities through a seemingly double stigmatization process. By criminalizing a behavior, moral entrepreneurs were able to essentially tie a newly deviant behavior to a group of people toward which they already held negative attitudes.[82] While most criminologists would not consider labeling theory a conflict theory, labeling processes involving power differentials—the power of those doing the labeling to be successful, and the lack of power by the labeled to stop them—fit nicely into arguments made by conflict theorists about the role of power in society. Both **Austin Turk** and Richard Quinney made just such arguments when they observed that lawmaking is a set of choices that inevitably benefit some people at the expense of others.[83] Legislation provides some moral repudiation of the act simply by stating that a behavior is prohibited; however, if people do not believe the act is deviant they are less likely to either abide by or respect the law. The labeling process can be used by anyone who seeks to demonize a behavior.

## Strain Theories of Crime

In Chapter 5, we discuss crime myths. While not a crime myth per se but a myth nonetheless, the **American Dream** is considered by some theorists to have harmful effects on those who believe in it.[84] According to Steven Messner and Richard Rosenfeld, the American Dream is a "broad cultural ethos that entails a commitment to the goal of material success, to be pursued by everyone ... under conditions of open, individual competition."[85] There are many variations of this dream. Some simply state that if you work hard and live right, you will get everything you need in America, while others hear that everyone can become wealthy in America. Interestingly, these stories are not unique to the United States. In the 1400s and 1500s European explorers went in search of places such as the Seven Cities of Gold, Eldorado, the Fountain of Youth and countless other fictional places believing them to contain vast wealth. Modern variations of these stories recount how a homeless high school student managed to be awarded a full scholarship to Harvard or how Bill Gates and Mark Zuckerberg dropped out of the same university and became billionaires.

While we cannot say with absolute certainty that places like Eldorado exist, we do know the stories of the homeless student, Bill Gates, and Mark Zuckerberg are true. Yet one inconvenient detail is often omitted from these stories of these people's successes: all three were geniuses! Keep in mind that "off the chart" intelligence is not something that is equally distributed among the masses!

So what can be the harm with telling tales to get young people to study hard and behave? Well, maybe none. Yet other people have argued that these abundant tales of wealth in America are actually damaging. Perhaps the first to do so was **Robert Merton** (1910–2003), one of the greatest sociologists of the twentieth century. In developing a new theory about deviance and crime, Merton borrowed a term coined by Durkheim called "anomie." To Durkheim, anomie was a state of normlessness that occurred during times of rapid social change, which could then lead to rapid changes in human desires. This state of anomie could then cause maladaptive forms of coping, and, in extreme cases, people might commit suicide because they cannot properly regulate their desires.[86] Merton argued that the primary goal of those residing in the United States was to obtain wealth. Furthermore, another related goal was the notion of *winning* (said long before Charlie Sheen uttered the phrase). However, we all know that generally, in most competitions, there is a winner and a loser. Even when we attempt to avoid the labels in little league sports by not officially keeping score, there is still a team who scored more runs, points, or goals. According to Merton, since not everyone can win, to keep a fair field of play, rules must be created and emphasized. Therefore, even if you lose, you should be proud you played fairly. This is perhaps why we tell kids after a sporting event that they need to shake hands with the opponents and say "good game." Despite these notions of fair play and rituals that even try to reinforce these rules, Merton believed that the ultimate goal of winning was often the only thing that people internalized. In a land where stories of wealth are abundant, there are bound to be people who are unhappy that they were left behind in the race to the top. Similar to Marx's ideas, Merton argued that success is desirable, and in the United States, wealth is synonymous with success. Thus, when conventional avenues to achieve wealth are ineffective, one may cheat or commit crime in an attempt to reach their goal of success. Merton noted that many people who obtained wealth illegitimately were still afforded some amount of respect, while the people who simply played by the rules received nothing but empty words of encouragement. The pressure to obtain wealth is felt by many, yet this pressure, according to Merton, disproportionately affected the lower class because structural disadvantages in life often blocked them from obtaining wealth. One common adage is that it takes money to make money and if you need money, then banks do not want to give it to you.[87]

Merton did not argue that those who were unable to obtain wealth conventionally would inevitably engage in criminal behavior. Merton argued that there were many people who would continue to play by the rules, even if wealth was never achieved. He classified these people as "**conformists**" and "**ritualists**." Conformists were those who work hard, play by the rules, and doggedly attempt to obtain the American Dream. Regardless of the outcome, conformists will continue their ongoing struggle to obtain the dream. Unlike conformists, ritualists will reject the American Dream and do not believe they will ever obtain any great wealth, yet they will still follow the rules because they see no alternatives. According to Merton, there are three forms of deviant coping for people who could not legitimately obtain the American Dream. Innovators not only believe in the American Dream, they want to achieve it. Yet, they do not have the legitimate means to obtain it. Therefore, they will often turn to crime to obtain wealth. **Retreatists** are people who realize that they will never obtain the dream and essentially drop out of society. According to Merton, many of these people will become alcoholics or drug abusers. Lastly, some people will not only reject the American Dream, but they will also reject the rules and the entire system and engage in rebellious acts. So how did Merton predict which people would choose which path? He believed that the inability of people to obtain the American Dream and particularly the gap between their aspirations and expectations was likely to produce strain. The more strain they felt, the more likely they were to engage in a deviant form of coping. Merton believed that the lower classes often suffered from the most strain because they had the fewest opportunities to obtain the American Dream.[88]

In their text *Crime and the American Dream*, **Steven Messner** and **Richard Rosenfeld** provided a slightly different account of how the American Dream can be damaging to society. Messner and Rosenfeld departed from Merton's class-based argument that the lower class is predominantly affected by the strain of obtaining wealth. Instead, they provided a critique on American values and priorities. Similar to Merton, Messner and Rosenfeld believed that the goal of obtaining wealth is overemphasized and can be destructive. However, Messner and Rosenfeld argued that perhaps what is just as damaging is the promotion of individualism in American society. They believed that instead of glamorizing a culture where people continually compete to obtain more, often at the expense of others, American society should instead emphasize institutions that can bring people together. Messner and Rosenfeld argued that a greater emphasis on families and communities would not only make American society more harmonious, but would also provide a sense that a crime committed is not an action against some other individual who is competing with you, but instead a member of your family or community. According to Messner and

Rosenfeld, a change in priorities in values and promoting a sense of togetherness will lessen current priorities that drive us apart and encourage crime.[89]

# Conclusion

This chapter is not intended as a survey of all theory that attempts to explain crime. Indeed, there are many excellent textbooks that already do this. Instead, we wanted to present theories and ideas that we believe in some way make accommodations for the effect of money and politics on this process. Although we discussed a wide range of ideas, there are many other works assessing the quality of these theoretical propositions that due to space constraints we were unable to include. Additionally, there are several other theories that you might argue have money or politics at their core, or are affected by these phenomena. We do not write this chapter as a definitive account. Instead, we just want to get the ball rolling and potentially introduce some ideas that might inspire others to imagine theory in the same way.

# Key Terms

- Criminological theory
- Deterrence theory
- Social contract
- Restitutive legal sanctions
- Repressive legal sanctions
- Conflict theory
- Consensus theory
- Waldos
- Pork-barrel politics
- Marxism
- Structuralists
- Instrumentalists
- Green criminology
- Corporatist nature
- Normative order
- Social junk
- Social dynamite
- Black codes
- Jim Crow laws

- Hands-off doctrine
- Separation of powers
- Prisoners' rights movement
- Mass incarceration
- War on drugs
- Labeling theory
- Symbolic interactionism
- Social process theory
- Legal process theory
- The American Dream
- Conformists
- Ritualists
- Retreatists

# Key People

- Cesare Beccaria
- Thomas Hobbes
- Emile Durkheim
- Thorston Sellin
- George Vold
- Karl Marx
- Friedrich Engels
- Willem Bonger
- Richard Quinney
- William Chambliss
- Frank Tannenbaum and Edwin Lemert
- Howard Becker
- Austin Turk
- Robert Merton
- Steven Messner and Richard Rosenfeld

# Key Cases

- *Holt v. Sarver*

# Discussion Questions

1.  What is the role of deterrence in crime and politics?
2.  Explain the differences and similarities between consensus and conflict theories.
3.  Is the social contract still relevant today? Explain and provide examples.
4.  To what extent do conflict theories predict that conflict will mar the political process? How does the differ among conflict theorists?
5.  Describe the relationship between social norms and law. Make sure to cite specific examples from the text.
6.  Why did President Bill Clinton receive over twice what he requested for proposed military operations in Kosovo? What is the significance of this?
7.  Imagine the United States government decided to adopt Marxist practices. What effect do you think this would have on the frequency of crime? How do you think this would affect the punishment of crime?

# Notes

1. Stanley, Timothy (2012). Are Politicians Too Rich to Understand Us? Anonymous (n.d.). *CNN News*. Retrieved on October 21, 2014 at: http://www.cnn.com/2012/06/12/opinion/stanley-money-in-politics/index.html.

2. Beccaria, Cesare. 1963. *On Crimes and Punishment*. Translated with an Introduction by Henry Paolucci. New York: Macmillan. Original work published in 1764.

3. Anonymous (n.d.). Cesare Beccaria. Internet Journal of Philosophy. Retrieved on October 21, 2014 from http://www.iep.utm.edu/beccaria/.

4. *Ibid.*

5. Beccaria, Cesare. 1963. *On Crimes and Punishment*. Translated with an Introduction by Henry Paolucci. New York: Macmillan. Original work published in 1764.

6. Akers, Ronald L. and Christine S. Sellers. Criminological Theories: Introduction, Evaluation, and Application. 6th Edition. New York: Oxford University Press; Bernard, Thomas J., Jeffrey B. Snipes and Alexander L. Gerould. 2010. Vold's Theoretical Criminology. 6th Edition. New York: Oxford University Press.

7. Beccaria, Cesare. 1963. *On Crimes and Punishment*. Translated with an Introduction by Henry Paolucci. New York: Macmillan. Original work published in 1764.

8. Beccaria, Cesare. 1963. *On Crimes and Punishment*. Translated with an Introduction by Henry Paolucci. New York: Macmillan. Original work published in 1764.

9. Piquero, Alex. In Press. Take My License n' All that Jive, I Can't See ... 35: Little Hope for the Future Encourages Offending Over Time. *Justice Quarterly*. Available Online First.

10. Bernard, Thomas J., Jeffrey B. Snipes and Alexander L. Gerould. 2010. *Vold's Theoretical Criminology*. 6th Edition. New York: Oxford University Press.

11. Hobbes, Thomas. 1982. *Leviathan*. London: Penguin. Original Work Published in 1651.

12. *Ibid.*

13. Durkheim, Emile. 2014. *The Division of Labor in Society*. Edited by Steven Lukes, Translated by W.D. Halls. New York: Simon and Shuster. Original work published in 1893.

14. *Ibid*, p. 176.

15. Anonymous. 2014. Division of Labor in Society by Emile Durkheim—summary and analysis. The Cultural Studies Reader. Retrieved on October 21, 2014 at: http://culturalstudiesnow.blogspot.com/2014/04/division-of-labor-in-society-by-emile.html.

16. Durkheim, Emile. 2014. *The Division of Labor in Society*. Edited by Steven Lukes, Translated by W.D. Halls. New York: Simon and Shuster. Original work published in 1893.

17. Bernard, Thomas. 1983. *The Consensus-Conflict Debate: Form and Content in Social Theories*. New York: Columbia University Press.

18. Akers, Ronald L. and Christine S. Sellers. *Criminological Theories: Introduction, Evaluation, and Application*. 6th Edition. New York: Oxford University Press; Bernard, Thomas J., Jeffrey B. Snipes and Alexander L. Gerould. 2010. *Vold's Theoretical Criminology*. 6th Edition. New York: Oxford University Press.

19. Tea Party Movement Platform (n.d.). Ten core beliefs of the modern-day Tea Party movement. Retrieved on October 23, 2014 at: http://www.teaparty-platform.com.

20. Democratic National Platform (2013). Moving America forward. Retrieved on October 23, 2014 at: http:/www.democrats.org/democratic-national-platform.

21. Akers, Ronald L. and Christine S. Sellers. *Criminological Theories: Introduction, Evaluation, and Application*. 6th Edition. New York: Oxford University Press.

22. Goff, Collin 2010. "Culture, Conflict and Crime." In Francis T. Cullen and Pamela Wilcox (Eds.), *Encyclopedia of Criminological Theory*, vol. I. Thousand Oaks, CA: Sage, pp. 823–826.

23. Sellin, Thorsten. 1938. *Conflict and Crime*. New York: Social Science Research Council.

24. Bernard, Thomas J., Jeffrey B. Snipes and Alexander L. Gerould. 2010. *Vold's Theoretical Criminology*. 6th Edition. New York: Oxford University Press.

25. *Ibid.*

26. Suchman, Edward. 1968. "The "Hang-Loose" Ethic and the Spirit of Drug Use." *Journal of Health and Social Behavior*, 9(2): 146–155.

27. Halnon, Karen B. 2010. "The Power of 420." In James A. Inciardi and Karen McElrath (Eds.). *The American Drug Scene: An Anthology*. New York: Oxford University Press.

28. Swift, Art. October 22, 2013. "For First Time, Americans Favor Legalizing Marijuana." *Gallup*. Retrieved on March 13, 2014 at: http://www.gallup.com/poll/165539/first-time-americans-favor-legalizing-marijuana.aspx.

29. See: The Brady Campaign to End Firearm Violence, http://www.bradycampaign.org/ and the Institute for Legislative Action (ILA), the lobbying arm of the National Rifle Association (NRA), http://home.nra.org/nraila.

30. Hook, Janet. 1999. "Clinton Would Pay a Price for Getting Kosovo Funding." *Los Angeles Times*. Retrieved on April 13, 2014 at: http://articles.latimes.com/1999/may/06/news/mn-34516.

31. Bernard, Thomas J., Jeffrey B. Snipes and Alexander L. Gerould. 2010. *Vold's Theoretical Criminology*. 6th Edition. New York: Oxford University Press.

32. Turk, Austin. 1969. *Criminality and Legal Order*. Chicago: Rand McNally & Company, p. 32.

33. *Ibid.*

34. *Ibid.*

35. Marx, Karl and Frederich Engels. 1998. *The Communist Manifesto.* Trans. Samuel Moore. London: Merlin Press Ltd., p. 34. Original work published in 1848.

36. *Ibid.*

37. Lanier, Mark and Stuart Henry. 2010. *Essential Criminology.* Philadelphia: Westview Press, pp. 314–315.

38. *Ibid*, pp. 316–317.

39. *Ibid*, p. 316.

40. *Ibid*, p. 317.

41. Bernard, Thomas J., Jeffrey B. Snipes and Alexander L. Gerould. 2010. *Vold's Theoretical Criminology.* 6th Edition. New York: Oxford University Press.

42. See, for example, Klockars, Carl. 1979. "The Contemporary Crises of Marxist Criminology." *Criminology*, 16: 477–515.

43. Bonger, Willem. 1916. *Criminality and Economic Conditions.* Boston: Little, Brown.

44. Sutherland, Edwin. 1940. "White-collar Criminality". *American Sociological Review*, 5: 1–12.

45. Conklin, John E. 1977. *"Illegal but Not Criminal": Business Crime in America.* Englewood Cliffs, NJ: Prentice-Hall.

46. Lynch, Michael J. 2013. "Political Economy and Crime: An Overview." *Journal of Crime and Justice*, 36; 137–147, p. 138.

47. *Ibid.*

48. Lynch, Michael J. 2013. "Reexamining Political Economy and Crime and Explaining the Crime Drop." *Journal of Crime and Justice*, 36: 248–262.

49. Lynch, Michael J., Michael A. Long, Kimberly L. Barrett and Paul B. Stretesky. 2013. "Is it a Crime to Produce Ecological Disorganization? Why Green Criminology and Political Economy Matter in the Analysis of Global Ecological Harms." *British Journal of Criminology*, 53: 997–1016.

50. Michalowski, Raymond J. and Ronald C. Kramer. 2006. *State-Corporate Crime: Wrongdoing at the Intersection of Business and Government.* New Brunswick, NJ: Rutgers University Press.

51. Quinney, Richard. 1974. *Critique of the Legal Order: Crime Control in a Capitalist Society.* Boston: Little Brown; Quinney, Richard. 1977. *Class, State and Crime: On the Theory and Practice of Criminal Justice.* New York: Longman.

52. Kramer, Ronald C. 1985. Defining the Concept of Crime: A Humanistic Perspective. *Journal of Sociology and Social Welfare*, 12, 469–487; Michalowski, Raymond J. and Ronald C. Kramer. 2006. *State-Corporate Crime: Wrongdoing at the Intersection of Business and Government.* New Brunswick, NJ: Rutgers University Press; Kramer, Ronald C., Raymond J. Michalowski, and David Kauzlarich. 2002. "The Origins and Development of the Concept and Theory of State-Corporate Crime." *Crime & Delinquency*, 48: 263–282.

53. Kramer, Ronald C. 2006. "The Space Shuttle Challenger Explosion." In Raymond J. Michalowski and Ronald C. Kramer. 2006. *State-Corporate Crime: Wrongdoing at the Intersection of Business and Government.* New Brunswick, NJ: Rutgers University Press, pp. 27–44.

54. Aulette, Judy R. and Raymond Michalowski. 1993. "Fire in Hamlet: A Case Study of State-Corporate Crime." In Kenneth D. Tunnell (Editor), *Political Crime in Contemporary America: A Critical Approach.* New York: Garland Publishing, pp. 171–206.

55. Spitzer, Steven. 1975. Toward a Marxian Theory of Deviance. *Social Problems*, 22(5), 641–651.

56. Anonymous (n.d.). Black Codes and Jim Crow Laws. Retrieved on October 25, 2014 at: https://sites.google.com/a/email.cpcc.edu/black-codes-and-jim-crow/black-code-and-jim-crow-law-examples.

57. *Ibid.*

58. Hughes, Robin. 2014. "Ten Signs of Institutional Racism." Retrieved on October 25, 2014 at: http://diverseeducation.com/article/64583/.

59. See, for example, *Brown v. Board of Education of Topeka*, 347 U.S. 483 (1954).

60. See, for example, Sigler, Robert and Chadwick Shook. 1995. "The Federal Judiciary and Corrections: Breaking the Hands-Off Doctrine." *Criminal Justice Policy Review*, 7: 245–254.

61. Articles I, II, and III of the Constitution specifically outline the powers vested to the Legislative, Judicial, and Executive branches of government. It is from these articles the notion of "separation of powers" arises. See, for example, Persson, Torsten Gerard Roland and Guido Tabellini. 1997. "Separation of Powers and Political Accountability." *Quarterly Journal of Economics*, 112: 1163–1201.

62. Jacobs, Bruce. 1980. "The Prisoners' Rights Movement and Its Impact: 1960–1980." *Crime and Justice*, 2: 429–470.

63. Holt v. Sarver, (1971). 442 F.2d 304; Hutto v. Finney, (1978). 437 U.S. 678.

64. Clear, Todd, Bruce Western, and Steve Redburn (Eds.). 2014. *The Growth of Incarceration in the United States: Exploring Causes and Consequences*. Washington, DC: The National Academies Press.

65. Clear, Todd R., George F. Cole, and Michael D. Reisig. 2013. *American Corrections*. 10th Edition. Belmont, CA: Cengage.

66. *Ibid.*

67. Drug Policy Alliance. n.d. A Brief History of the Drug War. Retrieved October 25, 2014 from http://www.drugpolicy.org/new-solutions-drug-policy/brief-history-drug-war.

68. Western, Bruce. 2010. "Decriminalizing Poverty." Retrieved on October 25, 2014 at: http://www.thenation.com/article/157007/decriminalizing-poverty.

69. Irwin, John. 2005. *The Warehouse Prison: Disposal of the New Dangerous Class*. Los Angeles: Roxbury.

70. Reiman, Jeffrey and Paul Leighton. 2010. *The Rich Get Richer and the Poor Get Prison: Ideology, Class, and Criminal Justice*. 9th Edition. New York: Pearson.

71. Clear, Todd R. George F. Cole, and Michael D. Reisig. 2013. *American Corrections*. 10th Edition. Belmont, CA: Cengage.

72. Western, Bruce. 2010. "Decriminalizing Poverty." Retrieved on October 25, 2014 at: http://www.thenation.com/article/157007/decriminalizing-poverty.

73. Breger, Marshall J. 1982. "Legal Aid for the Poor: A Conceptual Analysis." *North Carolina Law Review*, 60: 281–363.

74. Alexander, Michelle. 2012. *The New Jim Crow: Mass Incarceration in the Age of Colorblindness*. New York: The New Press; Smith, Justin. 2012. "Maintaining Racial Inequality through Crime Control: Mass Incarceration and Residential Segregation." *Contemporary Justice Review*, 15: 469–484; Wacquant, Loic. 2001. "Deadly Symbiosis: When Ghetto and Prison Meet and Mesh." *Punishment & Society*, 3: 95–134.

75. Tannenbaum, Frank. 1938. *Crime and Community*. Boston: Ginn; Lemert, Edwin. 1951. *Social Pathology*. New York: McGraw-Hill.

76. Stryker, Sheldon. 2008. "From Mead to Structural Symbolic Interaction." *Annual Review of Sociology*, 34: 15–31; Turner, Jonathan. 2001. *Handbook of Sociological Theory*. New York: Kluwer Academic/Plenum Publishers.

77. Cooley, Charles Horton. 1902. *Human Nature and the Social Order*. New York: Charles Scribner's Sons.

78. Mead, George Herbert. 1934. *Mind, Self, and Society*. Chicago: University of Chicago Press.

79. Dewey, John. 1922. *Human Nature and Conduct: An Introduction to Social Psychology*. New York: Carlton House.

80. Tannenbaum, Frank. 1938. *Crime and Community*. Boston: Ginn; Lemert, Edwin. 1951. *Social Pathology*. New York: McGraw-Hill.

81. Huck, Jennifer and Camie Morris. 2014. "Social Process Theories." In Jay Albanese (Ed.), *Encyclopedia of Criminology and Criminal Justice*. New York: Wiley-Blackwell.

82. Becker, Howard. 1963. *Outsiders: Studies in the Sociology of Deviance*. New York: Free Press.

83. Quinney, Richard. 1970. *The Social Reality of Crime*. Boston: Little Brown; Turk, Austin. (1969). *Criminality and Legal Order*. Chicago: Rand McNally & Company.

84. Messner, Steven and Richard Rosenfeld. 2013. *Crime and the American Dream* (5ed). Belmont, CA: Cengage.

85. Ibid, p. 6.

86. Durkheim, Emile. 1951. *Suicide*. Translated by John A. Spaulding and George Simpson. New York: Free Press. Original work published in 1897.

87. Merton, Robert K. 1957. *Social Theory and Social Structure*. Glencoe, IL: Free Press.

88. *Ibid*.

89. Messner, Steven F. and Richard Rosenfeld. 1994. *Crime and the American Dream*. Belmont, CA: Wadsworth.

# Chapter 3

# A Brief History of the United States Criminal Justice System

## Chapter Outline

- Introduction
- Colonial America
  - Law during Colonial Times
  - Law Enforcement in the 20th Century
- Courts
  - Courts in Colonial Times
  - Growth and Expansion of the Courts
- Police
  - Police in Colonial Times
  - Growth and Expansion of Police
- Corrections
  - Corrections in Colonial Times
  - Growth and Expansion of Corrections
- Conclusion
- Key Terms
- Key People
- Key Cases
- Discussion Questions

## Learning Objectives

- Describe the development of the criminal justice system in Colonial America
- Examine the role of the courts throughout the development of the United States

- Examine the role of law enforcement throughout the development of the United States
- Examine the role of corrections throughout the development of the United States
- Compare and contrast the frequency and types of punishments in the United States, historically and currently
- Assess the importance of Vollmer's methods of professionalizing police
- Compare and contrast the Auburn System and Pennsylvania System

# Introduction

In this textbook, we argue that money and politics are the driving force behind criminal justice policy. Thus, we believe it important to illustrate how money and politics have been at the heart of the American criminal justice system over time, despite changes occurring to the system itself. As this chapter's title indicates, rather than presenting a complete history of the American system of criminal justice, this chapter presents a "brief" history of the system that highlights and presents analyses of key periods where fundamental change occurred.[1] In this chapter the most important point we make is that while the philosophies guiding the American criminal justice system have changed dramatically over time, the influence of money and politics has not.

# Colonial America

For purposes of discussing the American criminal justice system, we start with English settlers' colonization of Jamestown in 1607. As you may remember from American history classes, the greatest struggle for these settlers was merely surviving in a new and strange land, which, as **Lawrence Friedman** described it, caused the colonists to consistently live in a state of desperation.[2] Furthermore, as Kathryn Preyer pointed out, **Colonial America** was not highly populated. By 1760, for example, only seven cities in America (if you could actually call them that) had a population of more than 3,000 people, which is smaller than many present-day high schools. Preyer further noted that by the dawn of the American Revolution, the highest-populated city in the American colonies was New York, with just more than 23,000 people, while London had 900,000 inhabitants at that time. The majority of people in Colonial America lived in small towns or villages of less than 1,000 people.[3]

Given the precarious position in which American colonists found themselves—living in small communities with no central authority nearby—colonial punishments for deviants and law-breakers were both swift and brutal. Recall that the American colonialists had brought **common law** with them from Britain, but the harsh conditions of the new land, including constant fear of starvation, mutiny, and hostile relations with indigenous people, created in colonialists the belief that crime in any form could not be tolerated because it could jeopardize the group's survival.[4] Yet at the same time, because colonial communities were often small and tightly knit, informal social control administered by members of the group both discouraged crime and made apprehending and punishing offenders relatively simple. According to Mark Jones and Peter Johnstone, this cultural practice essentially made every colonialist a "police officer."[5] There was also the fact that colonists were living in a strange, hostile land, and trying to flee prosecution for a crime one had committed was not really an option—to where could one flee?[6]

## Law during Colonial Times

While the Americanized version of English common law would eventually take hold in the colonies, more pressing concerns shaped the implementation and enforcement of law. The first English colonists to North America had hoped to find gold and other forms of wealth that had been so plentiful in South America, which had been colonized by the Spanish and Portuguese. Instead, the English colonists found a hostile land, with threats arising from the native population and a host of new conditions, including diseases the colonists had never before encountered. Since there was no easy wealth to be found, the colonists needed to become farmers to survive. However, as many of the colonists were not the type of men who had sought a life of farming in the New World, many of them protested having to work in the fields. To keep the men working and in line, **Captain John Smith**, Admiral of New England and leader of the Virginia Colony, enforced a type of military law among the colonists. Punishment for various offenses ranged from withholding food to **corporal punishments** (such as flogging), to death for certain crimes, including sodomy, rape, sacrilege, trading with or attacking indigenous Americans, larceny, and murder.[7] Kathryn Prayer also documented that the crimes of treason, murder, arson, rape, burglary, robbery, larceny, theft of horses, witchcraft, assault, and battery were all prosecutable offenses as well.[8]

As the stability of the American colonies increased and new settlers (including women and children) began to arrive, the need for military justice waned.[9] The American colonies began to adapt English common law for their own purposes, but the justice system was not without its problems. For instance, in the Virginia Colony, only minor crimes could be tried in county courts. All criminal cases that included the punishment of "life or member" had to be tried in a general court. Yet the only general court that existed in the Virginia Colony was in the capital of the colony, which originally was Jamestown but was later relocated to Williamsburg and finally to Richmond. Given that transportation was largely by horseback, it was no small feat to have to escort a prisoner to court. The only exception to this policy was in regards to the treatment of slaves and criminal complaints. Prior to 1692, criminal allegations against slaves had to be prosecuted in the colonial capital. However, at the time, many slaveholders believed this a burdensome process and consistently argued that the resulting loss of labor by the slave was a problem. As a result, special courts were created in the individual counties, called **the Courts of Oyer and Terminer**. This matter of convenience came at a cost to enslaved persons—in these courts, slaves were not entitled to a jury trial.[10]

Perhaps the best way to summarize criminal justice in Colonial America is how Lawrence Friedman described it: a "system of amateurs."[11] Unlike in contemporary America, where many (if not most) people who work in the criminal justice system need either specialized training or any number of university, graduate, or professional degrees to gain employment, in the colonies those working in the criminal justice system had very little training and few had degrees of any type—even prosecutors or judges. Further, while jury trials existed, these proceedings were rare and trials were usually presided over by magistrates.

In colonial times, perhaps the only true "professionals" were sheriffs, who were appointed by the governor of a colony to enforce the law and essentially serve as what Friedman referred to as "the chief agent of government."[12] Sheriffs were in charge of jury selection, as well as maintaining the jail in their country (there were no prisons in the colonies). However, many of these sheriffs did not act professionally. In Pennsylvania, for example, there was a problem with some sheriffs who were extorting money from inmates or selling them alcoholic beverages. Both of these practices were prohibited by a 1730 state law.

Beyond sheriffs, law enforcement officials consisted of constables and night watchmen.[13] As David Johnson described it, almost as soon as the various colonies had been established, local ordinances were passed that allowed constables to be appointed by colony officials. Townspeople also formed a "watch" consisting of six watchmen, one constable, and several volunteers who patrolled the colony at night. Initially run by a combination of obligatory and voluntary participation, the 17th-century watch typically reported fires, maintained order in the streets, raised the "hue and cry" (pursuing suspected criminals with loud cries to raise alarm), and captured and arrested lawbreakers. Constables had similar tasks, which included maintaining health and sanitation and bringing suspects and witnesses to court—frequently for such conduct as working on the Sabbath, cursing in public places, and failing to pen animals properly.[14]

Hiring competent constables was problematic in many parts of the colonies and some places resorted to drafting them, much like a nation-state drafts its soldiers. Needless to say, many of the draftees were not happy about being selected. Some constables neglected their duties or would hire someone else to perform them. Watchmen were also employed to patrol the streets of larger towns and cities at night. Constables and night watchmen often had little real authority and were oftentimes victimized by hardened criminals of the time, who would not think twice before resisting arrest or committing battery.[15] Throughout the 1700s and into the 1800s, law enforcement was reactionary rather than proactive—the watch usually responded to criminal behavior only when requested by victims or witnesses. Without monetary incentive in certain areas, apprehending criminals was not always a priority.[16] According to David Johnson, the 1700s saw more people settling in towns and building more shops and businesses, which meant more work for the watch. Seaports, bustling with sailors and overseas trading ships, boosted the merchant class economy but also caused unprecedented social problems that affected law enforcement. Taverns were built to entertain sailors in port cities, and public drunkenness, brawls, and prostitution became more common. As police work became increasingly time-consuming and difficult, fewer men volunteered for the watch and many evaded their mandatory duties. Issuing fines to those who did not show up only punished the poor—those who were most unable to pay. To curb this, some towns and cities instituted a paid watch.[17]

The solution to these problems was to create a new and improved law enforcement system that was first implemented in London in 1829: a stronger, more centralized, *preventive* police force, designed to deter crime from happening rather than to react once it had occurred. In 1833, Philadelphia organized an independent, 24-hour police force. In 1838, the Boston Police force was established, with a day police and night watch working independently. New York City followed suit in 1844, becoming the New York City Police Department in 1845. Police departments were now headed by police chiefs appointed by political leaders—typically city mayors. While it still had its flaws, this "new" method of policing more closely resembled a modern day police department.[18]

Philadelphia, in 1749, became one of the first cities to pass a law that restructured the watch to solve many of the aforementioned problems. Officials, now called wardens, had the authority to hire watchmen as needed, their powers were increased, and a special tax was collected that was paid to the watch. Male citizens were no longer obligated to work when summoned and only men interested in a paid job applied. Philadelphia's reform was not the ultimate solution, but it fueled progress and inspired others to make similar improvements. Even with positive developments like these, colonial law enforcement still required drastic change. During the Industrial Revolution of the early 19th century, the number of factories, buildings, and people surged substantially. New York, for example, jumped from a population of 33,000 in 1790 to 150,000 in 1830. The overall boom in industrial growth and overcrowding brought more crime, riots, public health issues, race and socio-economic divisions, and general disorder.[19]

## Law Enforcement in the 20th Century

The 20th century witnessed three major movements that resulted in major shifts in American policing: **the political era, the reform era**, and the **community era**.[20] As Michael Hooper has described them, the political era was so named because of the close ties between police and local politicians, and dated from the 1840s through the early 1900s. The reform era (also referred to as the professional era) developed in reaction to the shortcomings of the political era and focused on moving policing into the ranks of a formal profession. The reform era took hold during the 1930s but began to erode during the late 1970s, as its emphasis on reactive law enforcement, clearing as many crimes via arrest as possible, and little interaction with the neighborhoods being policed, as well as the legacy of racism caused turmoil in police-community relations. The 1970s saw the advent of the community era, so named because of its emphasis on police-community partnerships in solving crime problems. By the end of the 20th century, "**community policing**" had become ingrained as both a strategy and a philosophy, and continues to this day to be the umbrella descriptor in the literature, even for the array of information-based practices characteristic of evolved contemporary police agencies.[21]

# Courts

While this section of the chapter is called "courts," there are really three components covered: courts, the law, and the legal profession. Each greatly affects the others such that change in one is likely to cause change in the others.

In Chapter 1, we discussed how the Constitution established the basic rights of American citizens and procedures that must be followed. However, we did little to discuss the law itself, except that American law is based upon the common law developed in Great Britain. While there are certainly vestiges of common law remaining, it has been largely replaced by statutory law. As Lawrence Friedman noted, this was purposeful. Many people may debate whether the American Revolution was a revolution at all or merely one group of aristocrats getting rid of another group of aristocrats. Yet, there was one clear distinction that made it revolutionary—within the new nation there was a complete absence of any mention of royal authority. Some colonists wanted to rid themselves of royal authority because they believed God and the law should be the only authorities in the newly created United States. Some of the Founding Fathers found fault with royal authority because it was wavering and the whims of a monarch could put any person in prison without reason. This included judges who, acting on behalf of a monarch, could develop new common law crimes to punish what they arbitrarily considered bad behavior.[22]

## *Courts in Colonial Times*

One of the ways that the new nation liberated itself of the last vestiges of monarchy was to codify the common law into statutory law. From that point forward, for someone to be found guilty of a crime, a law had to exist at the time the behavior occurred, meaning a common law rule could not simply be created by a judge to legitimize an illegal conviction. While this idea may have seemed novel, it was not. Most of the founding fathers were well read and familiar with the contemporary philosophy and theory of the day. For example, many of those responsible for creating the new government were influenced by the writings of **Cesare Beccaria**, the Italian jurist and philosopher who was a proponent for the codification of law, as well as doing away with arbitrary penalties for violating laws. In 1812, the Supreme Court ruled in *United States v. Hudson and Godwin* that there was no such thing as federal common law crimes, and thus, for any defendant to be found guilty of a federal crime, a federal law had to exist that specifically prohibited the behavior in question. Many of the states were a bit slower to follow suit, and many failed to declare that no state common law crimes existed. This was evident in an 1881 case in Pennsylvania where a citizen was convicted of a common law crime of "stuffing ballot boxes." Yet Friedman argued that this was one of only a few isolated cases; as he noted, both Ohio and Indiana explicitly banned the practice of prosecuting people for common laws crime in 1842 and 1852, respectively.[23]

Along with the creation of a constitutional form of government, the founders designed a federal court system relatively quickly, and that system has remained largely unchanged to the present day. Shortly after the passage of the Constitution and before the Constitutional Convention voted on the Bill of Rights, **the Judiciary Act of 1789** was enacted. Article III of the Constitution established a Supreme Court, but left to Congress the authority to create lower federal courts as needed. Principally authored by Senator Oliver Ellsworth of Connecticut, the Judiciary Act of 1789 established the structure and jurisdiction of the federal court system and created the position of attorney general. Although amended throughout the years by Congress, the basic outline of the federal court system established by the First Congress remains largely intact today.[24]

The legislation created three different types of courts that fit within a hierarchal order. In the federal court system, at the lowest level are the federal district courts. These are considered trial courts of general jurisdiction and hear both civil and criminal cases. There is also a United States bankruptcy court associated with each United States district court. Each federal judicial district has at least one courthouse, and many districts have more than one.[25] The Judiciary Act of 1789 created 13 district courts; in 2009, there were 94 district courts employing a total of 678 judges. There would probably be more judges today except for the fact that in 1968, Congress passed the Federal Magistrates Act of 1968 to replace the position of commissioner, a position that had served the federal judiciary since the 1790s, with that of federal magistrates.[26]

In the mid-1960s members of the congressional judiciary committees and judges on the Judicial Conference of the United States recognized the need for revisions to the commissioner system. Commissioners were still paid by a fee system, the appointment process varied from court to court, and there were no uniform criteria for selection. Members of Congress and federal judges also wanted to relieve the congestion of the federal court dockets by expanding the judicial responsibilities of the commissioners. The Federal Magistrates Act of 1968 created the new title and expanded magistrates' authority to conduct misdemeanor trials with the consent of defendants, serve as special masters in civil actions, and assist district judges in pre-trial and discovery proceedings as well as appeals for post-trial relief. The act also authorized a majority of district judges on any court to assign to magistrates "additional duties as are not inconsistent with the Constitution and laws of the United States." In 2009, there were 523 full-time magistrates.[27]

Occupying the next highest second judicial position in the hierarchy are circuit courts (these are essentially appeals courts). Originally, there were only three circuits, and each circuit comprised two federal district judges and a

Supreme Court Justice. Ultimately, this system was inefficient and exhausting for the judges so Congress changed how the circuit courts were organized. Today, the 94 federal judicial districts are organized into 12 regional circuits, each of which has a court of appeals, plus the DC Circuit. Each circuit has between six and 28 judges, one of which is the chief judge for the circuit, who has administrative duties in addition to hearing cases and is selected by his or her peers based on seniority within that circuit. In 2009, there were 179 circuit court judges.[28]

The circuit courts of appeals' primary task is to determine whether the law was correctly applied by a trial court, whether a federal district court or a state court. A court of appeals hears challenges to district court decisions from courts located within its circuit, as well as appeals from decisions of federal administrative agencies. In addition, the Court of Appeals for the Federal Circuit has nationwide jurisdiction to hear appeals in specialized cases, such as those involving patent laws and cases decided by the United States Court of International Trade and the United States Court of Federal Claims. Most appeals heard by the appeals courts are heard by a panel of three judges randomly selected from the entire panel of judges in the circuit. However, under some circumstances, the entire roster of judges in the circuit will hear an appeal, known as an *en banc* hearing.[29]

At the pinnacle of the hierarchy of federal courts is the Supreme Court of the United States. While Article III of the Constitution created the Supreme Court, no details about the court's structure or operation were provided. The original Judiciary Act helped remedy this oversight by calling for the appointment of one chief justice and four associate justices. Today, there is one chief justice and eight associate justices.[30] As we recounted in Chapter 1 in some detail, the Supreme Court is the highest court in the United States and the court of absolute last resort.

While it is relatively easy to document the establishment of federal courts (since there is a federal law serving as a definitive record of the event), studying the evolution of state courts is more difficult. As we noted earlier, in Colonial America criminal courts met infrequently and in many instances people had to travel some distance to reach them. Outside the historical records of these judicial centers, accounts of how courts operated in the early history of the United States are often incomplete. As Joseph Spillane and David Wolcott have observed, criminal justice researchers have often neglected to examine the development of state courts in the United States.[31]

Under the common law system, courts consisted of a judge, the parties who had some dispute with one another, and ultimately a jury that would decide the case. One of the reasons courts met so infrequently during the 1800s was because there was often no police force to investigate crimes and no prosecutor to bring charges. If a person believed they had been the victim of a crime, then they had to press charges on their own behalf.[32] Considering how sparsely populated the early United States was and the lack of professionals to advocate for people who had been accused of crimes, it is little wonder **vigilante justice** occurred.[33] As Lawrence Friedman noted, the lack of governmental regulation and professionals seeking justice for victims inevitably led to people taking the law into their own hands. This was especially rampant on the American frontier, which, by definition, was often beyond the scope of civilization and the law.[34]

Throughout the 1800s, for example, different localities and cities tried many different tactics to increase the efficiency of courts. Philadelphia experimented with appointing an **alderman** to oversee low-level cases and many localities gave similar duties to their justices of the peace. Ultimately, by the early 1900s, most places in America had standardized their courts.[35] Today, although there is still considerable variation among state courts, most have four tiers, starting with low-level magistrate or limited jurisdiction courts, followed by trial courts of general jurisdiction, appellate courts, and some form of supreme court.[36]

## Growth and Expansion of the Courts

While the explosion of the American population during the 18th, 19th, and 20th centuries alone might explain the vast expansion of the United States court system, two other factors likely played a role as well: the passing of ever more laws by state and federal legislative bodies and the growth of the legal profession in the United States. Without question, one reason for the growth and expansion of state and federal courts over the past 300 years—not only in terms of the number of courts and judges but in the number of cases coming into the courts—was due to increases in the United States population. Consider that in 1700, the *entire population* of the United States was about the same as that of the city of Birmingham, Alabama, in 2015—about 222,000 people. By 2010, according to census data, the population of the United States had grown to nearly 309 million people, or about a 1,400% increase. With more people one would expect would come more business for the courts, both civil and criminal, and that is exactly what happened. However, at least two other forces were at work as well, both of which are tied to what John Walker and Harold Vatter have described as the social and ideological streams of American culture.[37]

The first of these forces involved Congress and the states passing ever more laws and regulations necessary to govern an increasingly complex society and those laws resulting in more business for the courts. As America evolved from the Colonial period, governed by a combination of informal norms and common law, to the present, where vast bureaucracies oversee most aspects of our lives, changes occurred both in the number of laws passed and in the content of these laws. As we discussed in Chapter 2 and as predicted by the French sociologist Emile Durkheim,[38] as American society moved from an agrarian-based economy to one based in industry and finally to one based in information, it became increasingly complex in not only its institutional arrangements (economical, political, educational, familial) but in the everyday interactions among its members. As a result, more law was needed to oversee these complexities and those complexities resulted in more cases coming to the courts.

**Roscoe Pound**, who was Dean of Harvard Law School for twenty years, as well as one of America's top legal scholars, wrote in 1912 that more than half of the people arrested the previous year were charged with crimes that had only been prohibited by law in the previous twenty-five years.[39] **Justin Miller** documented in 1927 that the creation of white-collar crimes, laws governing the use of automobiles and other vehicles, laws regulating building construction, and various laws that seek to protect the public health all greatly added to legal codes.[40] During the 20th century, the United States prohibited alcohol for thirteen years (1920–1933) and began "wars" on poverty, crime, and drugs. All of these efforts were made possible by passing laws; some of them, like the war on crime and the war on drugs, greatly increased the frequency of people breaking laws.[41] More recently, a plethora of legislation has been passed to regulate various computer crimes.[42] Perhaps the key lesson here is that governments will greatly expand criminal codes to address perceived problems, but in very few cases do governments dispose of laws that criminalize past behavior. Thus, the number of prohibited acts generally increases over time.

In conjunction with burgeoning legal codes was also the growth of the legal profession.[43] As David Friedrichs has noted, none of the earliest settlers to the American colonies were lawyers.[44] Given the harsh brutality of early colonial life, practicing law was not a typical career choice and many of the earliest settlers to the United States were also hostile to attorneys. As is true in contemporary America, lawyers were often members of the upper class, and in Colonial times, one who was a member of the upper class was also considered a royalist, responsible for the widespread discrimination and oppression in Great Britain that caused many of the colonists to leave in the first place. This hostility was so widespread that some of the colonies actually forbade people from collecting fees for engaging in legal services. As commerce and trade grew in the colonies, so did the importance of having people who understood the law. Some people began to practice law on a part-time basis and eventually, by the time of the American Revolution, several of the Founding Fathers were attorneys. Alexis de Tocqueville noted that attorneys seemed to represent the closest thing to aristocracy in the United States. Contemporary America is not much different—a disproportionate number of politicians at all levels of government are attorneys.[45]

Perhaps the greatest surprise in the growth of the legal profession in the United States is the sheer number of attorneys that have been produced, especially during the post-WWII period. To illustrate, in 1850, the ratio of lawyers to the American population was about 1:969. By 1950, the ratio was about 1:709.[46] By 1980, that ratio had shrunk to about 1:300, and today the ratio is about 1:257.[47] According to Matt Leichter, between 1970 and 2014 law schools conferred just over 1.6 million degrees and state bars issued nearly two million legal licenses (excluding reciprocity but including many duplicates).[48] At least part of this explosive growth in the legal profession was due to attractive salaries earned by lawyers,[49] the so-called "litigation explosion" that occurred in this country,[50] the growth in demand for legal services fueled at least in part by the removal of barriers on lawyers advertising their services,[51] and an increase in the number of accredited law schools.[52] All of these helped fuel even more business for the courts.

Additionally, one type of attorney—the prosecutor—represents a uniquely American invention. As we mentioned previously, in Colonial America any time a person wanted to press criminal charges against another, they were responsible for filing those charges themselves with a court. This was the procedure within common law, both in the American colonies and Britain. As Jack Kress has noted, it was not until 1879 that Great Britain would establish the Office of Director of Public Prosecutions.[53] Yet, as Patrick Devlin has stated, the director handles only a small number of prosecutions and most of these are done in capital or other serious cases. Most prosecutions involve cases that are filed by police. However, common law traditions are still preserved, and the Director of Public Prosecutions and police officers are not acting according to the duties of their office, but as private citizens who have an interest in maintaining the law and order of society.[54] Thus, as Kress argued, the presence of American district attorneys who seemingly simultaneously act as police, prosecutors, magistrates, grand juries, petit juries, and judges is somewhat of an anomaly given the common law roots of the United States. What is really interesting, though, is no one is quite sure how this position came about. As Kress stated, how the position of prosecutor was created in the United States is something of a "historical mystery." Both France and the Netherlands, countries that practice Roman—or what some call civil law (not to be confused with the American civil law system that governs lawsuits), have a public prosecutor. Yet Connecticut and Virginia both created public prosecutors in 1704 and 1711, respectively. How or whether these actions were influenced by continental European society is unknown.[55]

By the late 1900s, political scientists began referring to the "courtroom workgroup" to describe the relationships among judge, prosecutor, and defense attorney.[56] Some people believe members of the workgroup, rather than operating as independent agents with different roles (prosecutor as advocate for the people, defense attorney as advocate for his or her client, and judge as neutral arbiter), work together to quickly and efficiently process as many criminal cases as possible without trial. In effect, the courtroom workgroup's allegiances are to clearing the court's docket of cases and not to ensuring that justice is administered in a fair and effective manner. The workgroup concept helps account for the disjuncture that exists between a formally advocated adversarial system and patterns of individual behavior that researchers have identified occurring in criminal trial courts. Characterizing the activities of trial courts in terms of a workgroup also helps explain uniformities researchers report with work outputs such as classification of criminals, the categorization of crimes, and the sentencing behavior of judges.[57]

While it is nice that we have prosecutors looking out for our safety and defense attorneys to protect our rights, as John Langbein pointed out, the growth of these two professions dramatically affected the workload of each court.[58] In a system where citizens had to file charges with the courts—which were often far away and thus reduced the likelihood of charges being filed—and where a judge had to only to work with a jury, many cases could be disposed of in a short time. This is one of the reasons that courts did not have to meet as frequently. Once prosecutors and defense attorneys were introduced into the proceedings, the process dragged on and the amount of time it took to dispose of a case greatly increased. Furthermore, with the enhanced professionalization of the legal practice, rules of evidence, procedures, and other aspects of the legal process became more complex.[59]

Additionally, as we previously documented, the vast expansion of law gave the growing number of prosecutors more cases to process. Furthermore, in addition to the expansion of law, as we documented in Chapter 1, decisions by the United States Supreme Court mandated that any defendant who is charged with a crime and who faces the loss of his or her liberty—even for one day—has a right to an attorney whether the defendant can afford one or not. This also greatly increased the amount of work available for defense attorneys.

One method that has since been implemented to speed up this process or make court dockets clear quicker is the **plea bargain**.[60] Indeed, **Herbert Packer** described the plea bargaining process as essentially a streamlining of the entire criminal justice system.[61] Yet the plea bargain is seemingly just a part of the growing complexity of law and punishment and the expansion of the legal profession. As Albert Alschuler argued, when a defendant was not represented by counsel and the only penalties available as punishment ranged from death, to corporal punishment, to monetary fines, judges would typically not allow a defendant to plead guilty. The trial process was seen as a necessary part of due process.[62] Yet, today, jury trials seem more like rarities and, depending on the jurisdiction, more than ninety-five percent of all guilty verdicts are achieved through plea bargaining.[63]

# Police

According to **Samuel Walker,** three factors have affected the historical development of the police in the United States. While some modern day citizens may dispute this, the first factor is that the Anglo-American tradition of law holds dear the principle of protecting individual liberties. Under the principle, strict procedures are developed to protect citizens from police abuses. For example, the Constitution's Bill of Rights places limits on what the government (i.e., the police) can do when a citizen is suspected of a crime. The second factor is the strict system of federalism under which the states and localities are responsible for operation of their own police forces. This is very different from many other countries, which have national police forces. The third factor that has affected the development of police is that local control of police has led to the creation of some 18,000 separate law enforcement agencies in contemporary America.[64]

## Police in Colonial Times

As we mentioned earlier in the chapter, the primary law enforcement positions that existed in Colonial America were sheriffs, constables, and watchmen. Sheriffs, which still exist in the present day, evolved from being appointed by a royal governor to being elected officials in all but two states after the American Revolution. In Rhode Island, sheriffs are still appointed by the governor while in Hawaii, sheriffs are appointed by the chief justice of the state supreme court. While sheriffs have a variety of duties, their primary functions include operating the county jail, providing protection to county courts, and providing law enforcement services to unincorporated areas of the country.[65] In many rural areas of the United States, a sheriff can be the most powerful locally elected official. Unlike sheriffs, the position of constable is mostly a relic of colonial times. Even in localities that still have a constable, most of their traditional duties have been ceded to police departments.[66]

Many criminal justice historians have written about early America often being both lawless and violent. American mistrust of authority routinely prevented the creation of more standardized police forces.[67] While those within the role of watchmen performed many of the rudimentary duties that modern police perform, according to Samuel Walker, the first modern law enforcement agency was actually the slave patrol.[68] As David and Melissa Barlow argued, this showed that the creation of the police in the United States was not actually due to social progress, but instead, was instituted to protect the social order of that time. During the 1740s, the city of Charleston, South Carolina, created a mounted daytime patrol. By 1837, this agency employed one-hundred officers, whose primary duty was slave patrol. To accomplish this, officers monitored the travel of slaves and free blacks. The slave patrol was responsible for checking documents, enforcing the local slave codes, protecting white society against slave revolts, and, just as important, tracking and catching runaway slaves. Americans at this time would not accept what was viewed as tyranny of the free population, but to maintain the social order of the time and maintain the institution of slavery, it was viewed as necessary.[69]

## *Growth and Expansion of Police*

The move towards a permanent police force was also in part to control unruly populations. Throughout the 1800s, the United States began to rapidly industrialize. This change was not only from a migration of domestic populations to American societies, but also from massive increases of immigration from other countries, especially among Irish, German and other European populations. As cities began to grow and periods of instability related to downturns in the labor market began to periodically occur, acts of violence began to increase within cities. These periods of violence frequently included actions of mob violence and riots. It was clear that the old system of using a few constables and watchmen was outdated, and many cities began to experiment with combining these two positions into what more resembled modern police. Yet, this transition was hardly a smooth one. While modern police began to take shape in London in 1829 at the direction of **Sir Robert Peel**, the federalist system of the United States effectively prevented the establishment of any modernized police force. It was not until well into the 1900s that police officers would wear uniforms and carry an air of authority. During the 1800s, the primary responsibility of police seemed only to minimize violence.[70] As Joseph Spillane and David Wolcott noted, many police forces in the 1800s did not curb violence by making arrests. Instead, police officers responded to violence with violence. Perhaps the most notorious example of this type of behavior was by an officer named **Alexander "Clubber" Williams**, who openly boasted that violence was the best way to prevent violence and crime, and against whom more than 350 complaints for using excessive force were filed.[71]

Violence was not the only problem associated with police officers in the 1800s. A similar problem was that officers were routinely corrupt. In some ways, this was merely a sign of the times. Many cities were controlled by political machines and bosses who viewed their respective cities as their fiefdoms. Police officers were often a tool of these political machines and bosses. Furthermore, a problem that continues to this day is that police officers are underpaid and susceptible to corruption beyond the corrupting influence of whatever political machine or boss dominated their respected city.[72] In addition to these problems, as David and Melissa Barlow have argued, police officers had an additional loyalty that they had to maintain, perpetuating the industrialization of the United States and protecting big business. As they noted, one of the reasons that such high rates of violence existed was mob-action — especially riots, which were commonly perpetrated by people who could not find work. Furthermore, riotous behavior also frequently occurred due to the efforts by many people to form labor unions. Police officers were often called to quell these actions and maintain the dominant ideological political order of the day — capitalism.[73] While the existing police forces may have been viewed as tools of the corporate order, many corporations viewed them as so incompetent that they developed their own police agencies or hired corporate detective agencies to protect themselves from crime.[74]

The reform of police forces from unprofessional, reactionary squads to something resembling modern police did not take place overnight. As Samuel Walker noted, one of the struggles to reform policing was battling corruption and attempting to separate the police from being a tool of political machines and bosses to maintain control of turbulent cities.[75] Furthermore, efforts to reform police efforts occurred as a broader part of progressivism that was popular during the late 1800s and early 1900s. Many people argued that American society needed to protect its citizens from the evils of big business and other forms of endemic corruption.[76] Among the earliest voices who advocated the need for police reform were **August Vollmer** and **Richard Sylvester**. Sylvester was Chief of Police of Washington, DC, from 1898 to 1915. Not only did he advocate reform, but he served as President of the International Association of Chiefs of Police (IACP). Vollmer was Chief of Police in Berkeley, California, from 1905 to 1932. Vollmer's name has become synonymous with modern police administration.[77]

August Vollmer noted that police work was complex and policing in a modern world had many different and sometimes contradictory responsibilities.

For instance, he noted that the suppression of vice in the United States was hopelessly corrupting and specialized agencies were needed to try to combat these problems. Along similar lines, many politicians allowed organized criminals to operate and police departments needed to be removed from the corrupting influence of politics. Vollmer argued that policing was difficult work and many people were unsuited for it. He argued that this problem was aggravated by the seemingly omnipresent way of recruiting police officers at the time—political appointees who seemed to have no knowledge of what it took to be a police officer. Vollmer believed that the only thing that would overcome these inadequacies was if police officers received considerably more training. In addition to better training, Vollmer also believed that police needed to take advantage of the most modern technology available. He argued that criminals always seemed to be a step ahead of the police and it was a wonder that ill-equipped police officers were able to apprehend as many criminals as they did.[78] Perhaps one of the biggest innovations initiated by Vollmer was hiring officers who had either attended or graduated from college.[79]

Echoing the words of August Vollmer, Samuel Walker posited that three factors have influenced the modernization of police: **professionalization**, the introduction of modern **communications technology**, and calls for equal justice that arose from the civil rights movement. Regarding professionalization, it was important for police officers to begin wearing uniforms. Police officers in the 1800s gained authority through violence; the presence of a uniform helps lend credibility to officers and in many instances allows officers not to resort to such a baser instinct. Additionally, although many people point to military structure as an inspiration for the command hierarchy of modern police forces, Walker argued that police organizations often operate as businesses as well. Furthermore, while police agencies can never completely separate themselves from the politics of the places where they serve, distancing themselves from being mere tools of a political machine is vital to maintaining credibility among an often skeptical citizenry.[80]

One of the biggest changes to police forces was the implementation of modern technology. Perhaps foremost among these changes was the addition of the automobile to police work. Beginning in the 1920s, police officers on foot found they could do little to curb criminals who fled in automobiles.[81] As August Vollmer noted, the proliferation of automobiles in the United States seemed to increase crime. Criminals were suddenly able to not only flee in automobiles from the scenes of crimes, but they were also able to drive to new locations that had not been previously accessible to commit additional criminal activity.[82] By the 1960s, only a few cities still used police foot patrols as their primary police presence. While the automobile might have been viewed as a technological necessity, the omnipresent police car patrolling the streets often depersonalized police work. Many people in policing bemoan the limited communication between police officers and citizens within the community. Furthermore, as Samuel Walker noted, many racial minorities in the United States viewed the increase in police cars and the ability of multiple cars and officers able to show up at a scene in a short period of time as a further sign that police officers in ethnic minority neighborhoods were nothing more than an occupying army. Such a climate has led many people to call for an increase in foot patrols by police officers, and efforts to improve relations between police and communities are staples of one of variant of modern policing—community policing.[83]

While the automobile was certainly important to the evolution of modern police work, another invention might have been more valuable—the two-way police radio. Before the invention, if a person needed police assistance, they either had to hope that a police officer would happen to walk by or go find one. After the invention of the telephone, citizens were able to call a police station, and then a police dispatcher was able to contact a police officer via the two-way radio. As Samuel Walker noted, the ability of citizens to be able to "call the cops" raised citizens' expectations of police officers. This resulted in a marked increase in workload and, as a result, police departments not only needed to become more efficient, but they had to hire more officers and more equipment for those officers to effectively perform their jobs. While in some ways, the telephone made up for the lack of personal relationships that citizens had with police due to a decrease in foot patrols, citizens were now able to contact police and request immediate assistance. As a result, police officers had to deal with new issues, such as family problems and more crimes in progress. While this allowed police officers to intervene and protect citizens from many dangerous situations, it also more often placed police officers in situations that could lead to them being put in danger.[84]

One of the biggest steps towards the modernization of a police force is overcoming their violent past, a step that is still a work in progress. In 1929, President Herbert Hoover appointed **the Wickersham Commission**, which was the first national commission on crime. Two years later, the Wickersham Commission released its report.[85] While the report covered many areas of the criminal justice system, one of the themes within the report was that there was an unacceptable amount of violence still perpetrated by police officers.[86] Not only was the violence perpetrated as a means of street-justice, but police officers frequently beat or tortured people suspected of crimes. Particularly susceptible to this type of treatment were members of minority communities.[87] Many of these police tactics led to what many people have referred to as "the **due**

**process revolution**" by the United States Supreme Court, when it mandated in a series of rulings that most of the Bill of Rights was applicable to the states. The Court and the many supporters of these decisions hoped it would curb police brutality and help protect the rights of citizens.

Obviously, the advancements of police organizations did not end in the 1930s. Even newer technology than the automobile, telephone, and radio, such as fingerprinting, DNA, and a host of other technologies, would revolutionize the work of police investigation. Different strategies such as "hot spots" and CompStat would change the ways in which police administrations would deploy officers and change the goals of police work. Additionally, just as August Vollmer discussed, occurrences like the "war on drugs" would dramatically change police practices. These innovations and many more will be discussed in more depth in Chapter 7.

# Corrections

Finally, at the back end of the criminal justice system is corrections—the punishment meted out to offenders once they have been arrested, tried (or pled guilty), and convicted of violating the law. In some ways, the United States actually began as an experiment in corrections, as some of the early colonists had been banished to America by the English courts as punishment for their crimes. **Banishment**, or as some people refer to it, exile, has ancient origins. Indeed, some people might cite the biblical account of the expulsion of Adam and Eve from the Garden of Eden as the first instance of banishment. Many ancient societies, such as Babylon, Greece, and Rome, would prescribe the punishment of banishment for a variety of crimes. The length of banishment would either be a prescribed number of years, or in some cases, the offender would simply be banished permanently.

The punishment of banishment was usually practiced in two forms. In some instances, people who were banished were simply told to leave a certain area or jurisdiction, and, as long as they did not return, they would receive no further punishment. In more extreme cases, an offender would not only be banished, but would also be forced into some sort of servitude or slavery. By the time English settlers had founded Jamestown, prisons in Great Britain and other European countries were severely overcrowded. The collapse of feudalism had thrown the region into social chaos, and along with a deterioration of economic conditions, there was an overflow of criminals arriving in the courts.[88] Additionally, religious persecution was frequent in Europe, and there were many people seeking a place where they could worship in a manner that they saw fit.[89]

## Corrections in Colonial Times

While some settlers came to the American colonies seeking fame and fortune (such as the aforementioned Captain John Smith) and others were fleeing persecution, some of the colonists had been loaded on ships and "transported" to a variety of penal colonies, one of which was the United States. This practice began in 1619 with the transportation of one hundred English convicts from England to the colony of Virginia. The entire colony of what later became the State of Georgia was founded in 1733 for the specific purposing of housing English debtors and criminals.[90] The transportation of English convicts to the American colonies continued until American independence.[91]

While some people might view banishment as an antiquated practice (indeed, many state constitutions explicitly ban the punishment), some types of banishment still occur in the United States today. For example, although the punishment of banishment is officially prohibited by the state constitution of Georgia, some criminals are given the punishment of being banned from 158 out of the 159 counties in Georgia. While some offenders may choose to live in that one county in which they are allowed to reside, many of them end up leaving the state. Indeed, it seems like that may be the actual purpose of the punishment.[92]

While not necessarily banishing people, many states will still place restrictions on places that people can live after they have been convicted of a crime. As Richard Tewksbury noted, restrictions of these types are most often used against sex offenders. Essentially, these laws are designed to prohibit registered sex offenders from living, working, and/or loitering near certain places. The most common restrictions prohibit sex offenders from being near schools; however, the list of places that children populate can quickly grow to include child-care facilities, parks, playgrounds, recreational facilities, swimming pools, school bus stops, and any other place that children frequent. Thus, adhering to the law can become increasingly burdensome. In a Georgia statute enacted in 2006, the penalty for violating these restrictions is a felony, which can result in from ten to thirty years in prison as punishment. The problem quickly becomes, where can sex offenders (or other people who have targeted restrictions on where they can live) live or work that is not too close to one of these protected places? As a result of these policies, sex offenders typically are forced to live in extremely rural or isolated areas.[93]

Beyond banishment as punishment, **capital punishment** has existed in America since its origins. In 1608, merely a year after Jamestown was founded, the first state-sanctioned execution took place. Since that time, more than 20,000 people, more than 97% of whom have been men, have received the death penalty under some form of colonial, local, state, federal, or territorial authority in the United States.[94] While capital punishment arrived in (what would become) the United States soon after English settlers arrived, controversy regarding the practice of capital punishment continues to the present. As we stated earlier, many of the people who sought refuge in the United States were fleeing religious and other forms of persecution. One of the major fears of new settlers to the United States had been the high rate of capital punishment in Great Britain for much of its history. During the 1700s and 1800s, critics viewed the death penalty as a symbol of state tyranny and some religious groups, such as the Quakers, advocated for an end to the death penalty in the American colonies and later in the United States.[95]

In Great Britain, the punishment of death was associated with as many as 150 crimes; however, in the American colonies and later in the United States, far fewer offenses were **capital crimes**. In what Robert Bohm has described as the extreme of capital punishment statutes, the Puritans of the Massachusetts Bay Colony designated twelve offenses as capital crimes: idolatry, witchcraft, blasphemy, murder, manslaughter, poisoning, bestiality, sodomy, adultery, man-stealing, false witness in capital cases, conspiracy, and rebellion. In 1682, Pennsylvania outlawed the imposition of capital punishment for all crimes except treason and murder. Beginning in the 1830s, many states moved the execution of criminals from public forums to behind the privacy of prison walls; public executions ended in the United States in the 1930s.

Rates of execution in the United States have waxed and waned, peaking in the 1930s. Beginning in the 1950s, imposition of death sentences began to drop.[96] In 1972, the Supreme Court ruled in *Furman v. Georgia* that the death penalty was not necessarily unconstitutional per se, but the procedures for implementing the death penalty in the United States were unconstitutional. The effect of the decision was to declare thirty-nine states' laws that allowed capital punishment unconstitutional. Four years later, in *Gregg v. Georgia*, the Supreme Court ruled that capital punishment could proceed after those states enacted statutes with greater clarity and protections. Today, the death penalty is only allowed for the federal crime of treason (which is rarely prosecuted) and for first-degree murders that involve various aggravating circumstances.[97] Additionally, the intellectually disabled and juveniles are exempt from capital punishment as a result of Supreme Court rulings in 2002 and 2005, respectively.[98]

Since 1976 and the *Gregg* decision that allowed executions to begin anew, the United States seems to be on a trajectory to abolish capital punishment through a process of inertia. In 1999, a peak in post-*Gregg* executions occurred when 98 people were put to death. Since then, a steady decline in executions has occurred, where in 2014 only 35 people were executed.[99] Additionally, multiple states have either placed moratoria on executions or have abolished capital punishment altogether.[100] Finally, recent trends in public opinion polling show that support for capital punishment by Americans is waning and is currently at levels not seen since the 1970s.[101]

While no longer practiced by the federal or state governments, **corporal punishment** was an integral part of the criminal justice system until the 1800s. As Preyer has documented, corporal punishment in Colonial America often targeted servants and slaves—generally, those who could not afford to pay fines.[102] Preyer found that people who were neither slaves nor servants were three times more likely to be ordered to pay a fine than face corporal punishment once convicted of a crime like "immorality," which called for forty lashes as punishment. Actions by servants or slaves that were considered "insubordinate" could result in the offender receiving up to one hundred lashes on the offender's bared back. In addition to whippings, Preyer described other corporal punishments available for offenders that included brandings, placing a person in wooden stocks or a pillory, public cages, forcing people to wear symbols on their clothing, or cutting off a part of a person's body, such as an ear.[103] While corporal punishment was an integral part of punishment within Colonial America, the practice fell into disfavor beginning in the 1800s. Friedman has noted that since slaves or domestic servants were often the targets of corporal punishment, critics considered it a form of barbarism or tyranny against regular citizens. In response to these critics, many states began to outlaw corporal punishment, beginning with Massachusetts in 1805. Eventually, the practice was strictly confined to prisons and schools, and parents for disciplining their children.[104] Ultimately, corporal punishment was abolished in the federal criminal code in 1839 and most of the states followed suit. The final documented state-sponsored corporal punishment was a whipping, which took place on June 16, 1952, in Delaware, which did not officially abolish corporal punishment until 1986.[105]

Lawrence Friedman has argued that one of the greatest reasons the United States renounced the use of corporal punishment for criminal offenders was the growing reliance on incarceration as the primary means to punish those convicted of serious crimes.[106] Robert Bohm has even suggested that if penitentiaries had been available for use earlier in American history, the abolition of capital punishment might have gained greater public support.[107]

The original intent of incarceration was to hold people only until their trials were held. Beginning in the 1500s, European countries began to employ the idea that incarceration for differing periods of time was actually *de facto* punishment. As a result, facilities known as **houses of detention** or **prisons** were constructed.[108] Indeed, the great 18th century philosopher and lawyer Cesare Beccaria argued that the death penalty should be replaced with life imprisonment.[109] Jeremy Bentham, also an 18th century jurist and social reformer, offered his idea of the perfect prison, the **Panopticon**, which employed deterrence and prevention to reform prisoners who were housed within its walls. Envisioned as an "Inspection House," Bentham described the Panopticon as a circular building with the prisoners' cells arranged around the outer wall and the central point of the building dominated by an inspection tower. From this tower, the prison's "inspector" could look into the cells at any time—and even be able to speak to the prisoners in their cells via an elaborate network of "conversation tubes"—though the inmates themselves would never be able to see the inspector himself.[110] While two prisons in the United States were influenced by the Panopticon (Eastern State Penitentiary in Pittsburgh, Pennsylvania, and four cell houses at prison facilities in Statesville, Illinois), no prison has ever truly modeled Bentham's design.

In the United States, the first prison began as a wing of the Walnut Street Jail, located in Philadelphia, Pennsylvania, around 1788. This wing of the facility was given a new name—the **penitentiary**. Prisoners housed in the penitentiary were held in solitary confinement to keep them separate from the bad influence of the other prisoners and to give them ample to reflect upon their bad deeds, pray, and repent before God. Each inmate was provided a Bible to aid in this lofty goal. The very name penitentiary was developed as the facility was intended to be filled with penitent prisoners. After the Walnut Street Jail became overcrowded, Eastern State Penitentiary was constructed outside Philadelphia in 1829 for the sole purpose of keeping inmates in solitary confinement. Due to this model of incarceration originating in Pennsylvania, it was aptly named the **Pennsylvania System**.[111]

Penologist and former prison warden Thomas Murton has referred to the Pennsylvania system as a **theocratic system** of prison management.[112] Among supporters, the belief was that crime resulted from a sinful lifestyle; rehabilitation occurred when the inmate rejected sin and embraced the ideals of Christianity. While perhaps well intentioned, a fatal flaw soon became apparent: the negative effects of solitary confinement on prisoners' mental health.[113] Many prisoners, some of whom may have suffered from various forms of mental illness before they were incarcerated, began to deteriorate under the extreme form of isolation. Inmates began showing such symptoms as appetite and sleep disturbances, anxiety, panic, rage, loss of control, paranoia, hallucinations, and self-mutilation. Instead of making prisoners better, this type of incarceration tended to make them worse. Therefore, the Pennsylvania system was mostly abandoned within a few years.[114]

## *Growth and Expansion of Corrections*

One of the reasons that it was so easy for many states to abandon the Pennsylvania System was that a different system was already available. In 1821, the state of New York opened a new prison in Auburn. The state had experimented with the Pennsylvania System of incarceration, but abandoned the practice in 1824 after multiple incidents where inmates went insane and committed suicide. Elam Lynds was appointed warden at the newly constructed penal facility in Auburn, New York, the year the facility opened, and rather than implementing a system of solitary confinement, Lynds developed a **congregate system** of inmate management, which is now known as either the New York or **Auburn System** of inmate management. While inmates were still held in solitary confinement at night, inmates comingled during the day while completing numerous public works projects. Inmates were officially prohibited from speaking to each other, but were at least able to have some human contact.[115]

While the Pennsylvania System was largely a faith-based system of corrections, Thomas Murton argued that the Auburn System was a **work-ethic system** of incarceration. Rather than sin and sinful lifestyles being the root of crime, instead, crime was the result of sloth. Thus, instead of teaching inmates reverence (which was not completely abandoned), to improve themselves inmates needed to be taught a work ethic. Some of the tasks that inmates performed were monotonous and unproductive. For instance, a group of inmates might be forced to simply dig holes in the ground and then fill them back up or move rock piles from place to place.[116] However, not all inmate projects were meaningless exercises to teach self-discipline. By the 1840s, the inmates at Auburn Prison were producing a number of goods that could be given to the state, and prisoners from Auburn even built the newer prison at Ossining, New York, which is more commonly referred to as Sing Sing. In the southern and western United States, states would actually engage in what is known as the **lease system** and directly lease their prisoners to private individuals or companies. This system was in many ways akin to slavery, and inmates were forced to work long hours doing various forms of farming or plantation work. However, since the owners of these companies had no ownership stake in the prisoners and knew there were plenty more available, work conditions were generally horrible and many inmates suffered injuries or died.[117]

The Auburn System is well known for forcing inmates to dress in striped uniforms while walking in lock step, which readers have likely seen depicted in movies or television shows. The Auburn System is also famous, or perhaps infamous, for another reason. Unlike in today's prisons, where inmates receive paltry sums of money (e.g., 30 cents per hour) for working, inmates in the

Auburn System worked for free under the guise they were "repaying" their "debt" to society. Under such a system, the fruits of inmates' labor helped make the institution self-sustaining and, in some cases, allowed it to turn a small profit.

Another innovation relating to inmate work was the **convict-lease system**, popular in the South and West in the late 19th and early 20th centuries. Douglas Blackmon's research on this system uncovered the fact that after the Civil War, many Southern states leased their convicts to local farmers and industrialists for minimal sums of money as a "solution" to the problem of how to house inmates after most of the prisons in the South had been destroyed during the war. As part of the lease agreements, inmates would be housed and fed—thereby eliminating costs and increasing revenues. Soon, large-scale markets for convict laborers developed, and entrepreneurs created businesses whose function was to buy and sell labor leases for a profit. Unlike during slavery, convict leaseholders made minimal investments in the laborers and had little incentive to treat them well. As a result, convict laborers were subjected to horrible working conditions and many were injured, often fatally. Because the supply of convict laborers was large and the system addressed a pressing need, the convict-lease system was highly profitable for both the states and employers.[118] It was not until the 1920s that public sympathy toward the plight of convict laborers grew to the point where the South ended the practice and chose instead to devote convict labor to public works projects via the use of chain gangs. Recently, at least some states have begun experimenting with modern versions of the convict-lease system[119] and chain gangs.[120]

Thomas Murton also observed that, beginning in the 1870s, the **reformatory model of incarceration** began in the United States. The Pennsylvania and Auburn systems operated on the beliefs that correcting sinfulness and sloth in inmates, respectively, were ways of changing inmate behavior and reducing reoffending. Under the reformatory model, crime was a product of a lack of education and/or vocational training in offenders. Teaching inmates to fear and respect God and work hard was not enough to keep them out of trouble; instead, to keep inmates from recidivating, they needed a career or at least the tools to help them obtain a career.[121] In 1876, Zebulon Brockway was appointed superintendent of the Elmira Reformatory in New York, and he designed a regiment for first-time offenders between the ages of sixteen and thirty. At the time, inmates were sentenced to serve between one year and some maximum number of years based on the crime for which they had been convicted—what is known as an **indeterminate sentence**. If an inmate progressed through a series of educational programs before their sentence was officially over, the inmate could receive an early release, known as **parole**. Parole is granted by a

**parole board,** which is given the authority to do so by the state. Inmates petition a parole board for a hearing at which evidence is introduced relating to why (or why not) the offender should receive early release. A parole board hears from witnesses representing both the interests of the state and an offender's interests. The board then renders its decision. If a board denies a petition, an offender is then eligible to reapply according to an established timetable. If a board grants a petition, an offender is soon released from prison.

While on parole, an offender is required to periodically communicate with his or her **parole officer,** obtain stable housing, and abide by certain restrictions on liberty, such as not consuming alcohol or illegal drugs; not possessing firearms; and not fraternizing with known offenders. There may also be special conditions for parole, such as requiring a parolee to participate in drug or alcohol treatment, obtain gainful employment and stay employed, and pursue a GED. Should a parolee violate any of these conditions or be rearrested for a new offense, they have violated their parole agreement and can be returned to prison by a court to serve the remainder of their sentence. Questions remain to this day about the utility of parole.[122]

Brockway's reforms seemed to be effective, but structural problems, such as continual facility overcrowding, frustrated many of the reforms Brockway championed.[123] Furthermore, even Brockway himself questioned whether inmates in his program actually reformed, or if they were merely going through the motions in hope of gaining early release, a concern that remains today with critics of parole.[124]

Parole has multiple origins, including with **Captain Alexander Maconochie,** who oversaw operations of various prisons throughout the British Empire, and **Sir Walter Crofton,** who oversaw prison facilities in Ireland. In the United States, one of the first places in which parole originated was with the **houses of refuge** for juvenile delinquents, which originated in 1825 in New York City and were funded by wealthy philanthropists and progressives and intended to serve as the institutional embodiment of the larger "child saver" movement.[125] Originally, these facilities were designed to provide a place to live for dependent and neglected children, but soon enough, the facilities also accepted boys who had been convicted of crimes in criminal courts. Houses of refuge were designed to both educate and discipline the juveniles housed in these facilities, and many juveniles would stay in them until they turned twenty-one, the age of majority at the time. However, many of the juveniles were also released early through a process called **binding out.** What this meant was that prior to their 21st birthday or the end of their sentence, juveniles were released either to various tradesmen as apprentices or to wealthy families as domestic servants. In effect, they received an early release from their term of confinement.[126]

By the end of the nineteenth century, more than half of the states allowed for the parole of inmates.[127] By 1910, every federal prison had a parole board, and in 1930, the federal government established a United States Board of Parole, which replaced all of the individual parole boards housed at federal correctional facilities. By 1925, forty-six states had parole statutes. Parole would remain a controversial practice in the United States; by 2002, sixteen states and the federal government had abolished discretionary release by parole boards.[128]

Another form of conditional release is probation, the antecedents of which date back hundreds of years in the form of benefit of clergy, judicial reprieve, and recognizance. Probation occurs as an alternative to incarceration (be it jail or prison), whereby an offender is released back into the community under a strict set of conditions, some of which all probationers receive (called general conditions) and some of which are special conditions unique to a specific offender. General conditions include such stipulations that the probationer will not engage in a new offense or possess a firearm, and will communicate with his or her probation officer on a set schedule. Special conditions tend to be tailored to each offender's needs and may include stipulations such as a curfew, stable employment, or drug treatment. Failure to abide by the stipulations of the probation agreement may mean revocation of an offender's probation and being resentenced to jail or prison for the entire term established by law for the conviction offense.

In the United States, one man is responsible for developing probation: **John Augustus**. A shoemaker by trade, Augustus was also a social advocate, reformer, and supporter of the temperance movement. In August of 1841, Augustus was in court when he observed a disheveled looking defendant being escorted into the courtroom. Augustus conversed with the defendant and found that he had problems with alcohol. Augustus decided to pay for the man's bail, with the permission of the court. Under Augustus's guidance, the man sobered up, and when he appeared for sentencing three weeks later, the court found a tremendous change for the better in the defendant. As a result, he only received a small fine from the court. During the course of what would soon be his life's work, Augustus supervised nearly 2,000 people, most of whom were in court as a result of struggles with alcohol. While Augustus seemed to have somewhat of a soft spot in his heart, he did not take on supervising people in a haphazard manner. Augustus conducted thorough background checks for anyone he thought of supervising. Essentially, he engaged in every activity that modern probation officers now undertake. The only difference was that Augustus did this on his own and never received any support from the state. He died in 1859, and in that same year, the state of Massachusetts, where Augustus had lived and worked, established the first probation law in the United States. Today, every state and the federal government have probation as a punishment, and it is the most common punishment dispensed in criminal courts.[129] Like parole, probation remains controversial.

The work of Zebulon Brockway and other correctional reformers would carry into the twentieth century. People like **Howard Gill** (who was appointed superintendent of the Norfolk State Prison Colony in 1927) and **Sanford Bates** (who was appointed the first director of the Federal Bureau of Prisons in 1929) would push rehabilitation into what some scholars now refer to as the **medical model** of corrections. This push was an outgrowth of the emerging behavioral and social sciences. As psychology and sociology grew in prominence, many researchers and practitioners began to believe that various social, psychological, and biological characteristics might be the cause of a person's criminality, or at least a contributing factor. Several states actually built special correctional facilities so that inmates could undergo more comprehensive studies to determine the source of their criminality.[130]

During his 2004 Presidential Address to the American Society of Criminology, **Francis Cullen** stated that when he attended graduate school during the 1960s, "the rehabilitative ideal was near hegemonic in corrections."[131] Yet, the dominance of rehabilitation was soon to change. Crime increased dramatically during the 1960s and 1970s as the baby boom generation entered its late teenage and early adult years. American cities were beginning to decay at the same time that high-paying, relatively low-skilled manufacturing jobs disappeared. The 1960s and early 1970s were also a time of unrest as young people protested the war in Vietnam, marijuana and other drugs made inroads into the middle class, and the civil rights movement reached its pinnacle. America also began a costly "war" on poverty under President Johnson's Great Society initiative. Furthermore, Americans began experiencing high levels of fear that they would suffer criminal victimization. White flight from major urban areas resulted in tremendous shifts in the demographics of American cities, declining tax bases, and the rise of "bedroom community" suburbs. Meanwhile, minorities, who often remained in the cities, suffered with substandard housing, declining prospects for good jobs, segregation, and poor relations with the police. All of these forces helped ignite major riots in many metropolitan areas, including Detroit, Chicago, Los Angeles, New York and Philadelphia. The Republican Party officially endorsed "get tough" crime control policies that involved greater use of incarceration and longer sentences for felons. Given that government seemed relatively powerless to bring law and order to American cities, Democrats had little evidence or support to counteract the coming wave of increasingly punitive policies to address crime. Furthermore, many politicians and scholars alike began to question the notion that criminals could be rehabilitated based on a major report from **Robert Martinson** and his colleagues, which seemed to conclude that "nothing works."[132] The so-called Martinson Report became fuel for critics who called for abandoning rehabilitation as the basis for correctional policy, unleashing the police to fight a "war" on crime, reducing or eliminating the discretion of judges at sentencing (to be replaced with mandatory sentences and sentencing guidelines), and abolishing parole.

Beginning in the 1970s and into the 1980s a new age of corrections developed, one that Malcolm Feeley and Jonathan Simon called "**The New Penology**," which they described as a correctional philosophy emphasizing the minimization of risk to the detriment of individuals within the correctional system. While the most important goal was keeping offenders from recidivating, this goal was not being met by employing treatment strategies. Instead, the correctional system would rely more on incarceration and keeping high-risk offenders from mingling with general society. Despite the beginnings of a drop in violent crime during the early 1990s, the United States seemed increasingly committed to locking up more and more of its citizens for longer periods of time, often through variations of **mandatory sentencing laws**, which required that inmates serve either their complete prison sentence or a substantial portion of it.[133] Such policies led the country to incarcerate more of its citizens than any other Western, democratic, post-industrial society. As the title of his book indicates, Travis Pratt described America as *Addicted to Incarceration*. By 2008, the United States incarcerated a full one percent of its population (more than two million people in prisons and jails). Such an occurrence seems especially troubling when considering the rate of imprisonment, since the United States does not have the world's largest population, prides itself on the concept of freedom, and does not prohibit its citizens from engaging in political activity that is unpopular with the current political regime that is in control.[134] In addition to so many incarcerated citizens, in 2008, more than four million Americans were on probation and slightly more than 800,000 were on parole.[135]

As Travis Pratt has noted, one of the primary reasons the United States ended up controlling such a large percentage of its population through the correctional system is due to politics. In 1964, when **Barry Goldwater** ran for the United States presidency against incumbent President Lyndon B. Johnson, Goldwater trumpeted new policies to get tough on crime. While Goldwater ultimately lost the election, this mantra would be later picked up by **Richard M. Nixon**, who would win two terms as president. Not only would the Republican Party fully embrace such law-and-order rhetoric, but so too would the Democratic Party. According to Pratt, embracing crime control policies was essentially political capital. As a result, various politicians enacted a plethora of get-tough-on-crime policies, such as mandatory minimums, an expansion of the war on drugs, and various habitual offender legislation, like "three-strikes laws."[136]

While the past thirty to forty years have seen an unprecedented expansion of the number of people under correctional control in the United States, it seems that change might be underway. Beginning in 2010, for the first time in more than thirty years, correctional populations began to decrease.[137] Two factors seem to have influenced this trend. The first, which has been documented by criminologists for some time, is that increasingly punitive policies do not seem to decrease crime.[138] The second factor, as we will illustrate in Chapter 4, is that despite many people benefitting from them, crime controls are expensive and absorb significant proportions of both state and federal budgets. Reducing these costs are one of the easiest ways to reduce expenditures. As Todd Clear, George Cole, and Michael Reisig noted, several states have reduced corrections budgets and even closed prison facilities. This has happened in states that are controlled by Democrats as well as Republicans.[139] Perhaps the most unlikely of advocates for sentencing reforms is former Republican Speaker of the House Newt Gingrich, who once championed the Conservative Revolution in 1992. He now has become one of the most vocal people campaigning for reduced sentences and less expenditures to fund the American correctional system.[140] How long this trend lasts is anyone's guess, but for at least the immediate future, it seems that the trend in corrections is to try to reduce population as well as costs.

# Conclusion

Criminal justice began in the United States with a brief term of militarized order to protect the few Europeans who inhabited these British colonies. As more people settled in the country, this strict form of law and order waned. American colonists and later American citizens rejected many forms of law and order as tyrannical and indicative of the mother country from which they had revolted. However, as this new nation embraced freedom for some, the genesis of social controls began with efforts to control its minority populations. Over the course of time, as many citizens were freed from at least official policies of bondage and people began to move to cities, new problems arose that required criminal justice to become formalized. Since then, the rationales behind law, order, and punishment have changed to justify one of the highest correctional populations in the world and an increasingly wide range of behaviors that are prohibited or controlled. Although the need to supervise so many citizens may be waning, it is difficult to tell if this is merely a fad or a modern trend.

# Key Terms

- Colonial America
- Common law
- Corporal punishments
- The Courts of Oyer and Terminer
- Political era
- Reform era
- Community era
- Community policing
- The Judiciary Act of 1789
- Vigilante justice
- Alderman
- Plea bargain
- Professionalization (of police)
- Communications technology
- Wickersham Commission
- The Due Process Revolution
- Banishment
- Capital punishment and capital crimes
- Houses of detention
- Prisons
- Panopticon
- Penitentiary
- Congregate system
- Auburn system
- Work-ethic system
- Lease system
- Convict-lease system
- Reformatory model of incarceration
- Indeterminate sentence
- Rehabilitation
- Probation
- Parole
- Parole board

- Parole officer
- Houses of refuge
- Binding out
- Medical model
- "The New Penology"
- Mandatory sentencing laws

# Key People

- Lawrence Friedman
- Captain John Smith
- Cesare Beccaria
- Samuel Walker
- Herbert Packer
- Roscoe Pound
- Justin Miller
- Sir Robert Peel
- Alexander "Clubber" Williams
- August Vollmer
- Richard Sylvester
- Captain Alexander Maconochie
- Sir Walter Crofton
- John Augustus
- Howard Gill
- Sanford Bates
- Francis Cullen
- Robert Martinson
- Barry Goldwater
- Richard Nixon

# Key Cases

- *United States v. Hudson and Godwin*
- *Gregg v. Georgia*
- *Furman v. Georgia*
- *Trop v. Dulles*
- *Atkins v. Virginia*
- *Roper v. Simmons*

# Discussion Questions

1.  American colonists were fearful of starvation and mutiny, which left them intolerable to any type of crime. Even though there was no centralized support to enforce the law, each colonist could act as a police officer. This was an effective approach, considering that there were small communities, which increased informal social control. In present times, how is informal social control still effective? How is it ineffective? Does this vary among communities? Explain and provide examples.

2.  Lawrence Friedman described the criminal justice system in Colonial America as a "system of amateurs." Do you agree or disagree with this description? Use examples from the reading to defend your opinion.

3.  During colonial times, why were there so many instances of vigilante justice? What could have prevented acts of vigilante justice?

4.  Describe the development of the legal profession in the United States.

5.  August Vollmer is predominantly responsible for the professionalization of police in the United States. Identify and explain his contributions. Now, imagine that his contributions had never existed. Identify how policing would currently be less (or more) efficient.

6.  Both banishment and corporal punishment were popular forms of punishment in colonial times. What would be different in the U.S. currently if these were still popular forms of punishment?

# Notes

1. For a more comprehensive analysis of the history of the American criminal justice system, see: Friedman, Lawrence M. 1993. *Crime and Punishment in American History*. New York: Basic Books; Jones, Mark and Peter Johnstone. 2012. *History of Criminal Justice*. New York: Anderson Publishing; Spillane, Joseph F. and David B. Wolcott. 2013. *A History of Modern American Criminal Justice*. Thousand Oaks, CA: SAGE.

2. Friedman, Lawrence M. 1993. *Crime and Punishment in American History*. New York: Basic Books.

3. Preyer, Kathryn. 1982. "Penal Measures in the American Colonies: An Overview". *The American Journal of Legal History*, 26(4): 326–353.

4. Friedman, Lawrence M. 1993. *Crime and Punishment in American History*. New York: Basic Books; Preyer, Kathryn. 1982. "Penal Measures in the American Colonies: An Overview". *The American Journal of Legal History*, 26(4): 326–353.

5. Jones, Mark and Peter Johnstone. 2012. *History of Criminal Justice*. New York: Anderson Publishing.

6. *Ibid.*

7. *Ibid.*

8. Preyer, Kathryn. 1982. "Penal Measures in the American Colonies: An Overview". *The American Journal of Legal History*, 26(4): 326–353.

9. Jones, Mark and Peter Johnstone. 2012. *History of Criminal Justice*. New York: Anderson Publishing.

10. Preyer, Kathryn. 1982. "Penal Measures in the American Colonies: An Overview". *The American Journal of Legal History*, 26(4): 326–353.

11. Friedman, Lawrence M. 1993. *Crime and Punishment in American History*. New York: Basic Books

12. *Ibid.*

13. Monkkonen, Eric H. 1992. "History of the Urban Police." Pp. 547–580 in Michael Tonry and Norval Morrids (Eds.), *Modern Policing*. Chicago: University of Chicago Press.

14. Johnson, David R. 1981. *American Law Enforcement: A History*. Wheeling, IL: Forum Press.

15. Friedman, Lawrence M. 1993. *Crime and Punishment in American History*. New York: Basic Books.

16. Johnson, David R. 1981. *American Law Enforcement: A History*. Wheeling, IL: Forum Press

17. *Ibid.*

18. *Ibid.*

19. *Ibid.*

20. Walker, Samuel. 1977. *A Critical History of Police Reform: The Emergence of Professionalism*. Lexington, MA: Lexington Books.

21. Hooper, Michael K. 2014. "Acknowledging Existence of a Fourth Era of Policing: The Information Era." *Journal of Forensic Research and Crime Studies*, 1(1):1–4.

22. Friedman, Lawrence M. 1993. *Crime and Punishment in American History*. New York: Basic Books.

23. *Ibid.*

24. Henderson, Dwight F. 1971. *Courts for a New Nation*. Washington, D.C.: Public Affairs Press.

25. About Federal Courts. Retrieved May 11, 2015 from http://www.uscourts.gov/about-federal-courts/court-role-and-structure.

26. Federal Magistrates Act of 1968. 82 Stat. 1107.

27. Federal Judicial Center. nd. "History of the Federal Judiciary." Retrieved on May 11, 2015 at: http://www.fjc.gov/history/home.nsf/page/judges_magistrate.html.

28. Champion, Dean John, Richard D. Hartley and Gary A. Rabe. 2012. *Criminal Courts: Structure, Process, and Issues*. 3rd Edition. New York: Pearson.

29. *Ibid.*

30. *Ibid.*

31. Spillane, Joseph F. and David B. Wolcott. 2013. *A History of Modern American Criminal Justice*. Thousand Oaks, CA: SAGE.

32. *Ibid.*

33. Brown, Richard M. 1975. *Strain of Violence: Historical Studies of American Violence and Vigilantism* New York: Oxford University Press.

34. Friedman, Lawrence M. 1993. *Crime and Punishment in American History*. New York: Basic Books.

35. Spillane, Joseph F. and David B. Wolcott. 2013. *A History of Modern American Crim-*

*inal Justice.* Thousand Oaks, CA: SAGE.

36. The U.S. may be characterized as having a "dual system" of courts reflecting the two hierarchies of courts in America: the federal system and the states. For discussion, see Dean J. Champion Richard D. Hartley, and Gary A. Rabe. 2012. *Criminal Courts: Structure, Process, and Issues.* 3rd Edition. New York: Pearson.

37. Walker, John F. and Harold G. Vatter. 1997. *The Rise of Big Government in the United States.* New York: Routledge.

38. Durkheim, Emile. 2014. *The Division of Labor in Society.* Edited by Steven Lukes, Translated by W.D. Halls. New York: Simon and Shuster. Original work published in 1893.

39. Pound, Roscoe. 1930. *Criminal Justice in America.* New York: Henry Holt.

40. Miller, Justin. 1927. "The Compromise of Criminal Cases." *Southern California Law Review,* 1:1.

41. Goode. Erich. 2011. *Drugs in American Society,* 8th ed. Boston: McGraw-Hill.

42. Hollinger, Richard C. and Lonn Lanza-Kaduce. 1988. "The Process of Criminalization: The Case of Computer Crime Laws." *Criminology,* 26(1): 101–126.

43. According to the American Bar Association (ABA), in 2014 there were 1,281,432 *licensed* (practicing) attorneys in the United States. This figure does not include the thousands more not actively practicing law. American Bar Association (nd). Lawyer Demographics. Retrieved May 19, 2015 from http://www.americanbar.org/content/dam/ aba/administrative/ market_research/ lawyer-demographics-tables-2014.authcheckdam.pdf.

44. Friedrichs, David O. 2006. *Law in our Lives: An Introduction.* 2nd Edition. Los Angeles: Roxbury Publishing Company.

45. *Ibid.*

46. Segal, Robert M. and John Fei. 1953. "The Economics of the Legal Profession: An Analysis by States." *American Bar Association Journal,* 39(2): 110–116.

47. Jacoby, Jeff. 2014. "US Legal Bubble Can't Pop Soon Enough." Retrieved on May 19, 2015 at: http://www.bostonglobe.com/opinion/2014/05/09/the-lawyer-bubble-pops-not-moment-too-soon/qAYzQ823qpfi4GQl2OiPZM/story.html.

48. Leichert, Matt. nd. "Lawyer Overproduction." Retrieved on May 19, 2015 at: https:// lawschooltuitionbubble.wordpress.com/original-research-updated/lawyer-overproduction/.

49. Zahorsky, Rachel M. 2011. "What America's Lawyers Earn." Retrieved on May 19, 2015 at: http://www.abajournal.com/magazine/article/what_americas_lawyers_earn.

50. Galanter, Marc. 1986. "The Day After the Litigation Explosion." *Maryland Law Review,* 46(1):3–39.

51. Hallgarn, Helena and Ann Björk. 2013. "Future of Legal Services and the Development of Legal Knowledge Management." *Voxpopulii,* August 23, 2013. Retrieved on May 19, 2015 at: https://blog.law.cornell.edu/voxpop/2013/08/30/future-of-legal-services-and-the-development-of-legal-knowledge-management/.

52. Hanson, Mark. 2015. "As Law School Enrollment Drops, Experts Disagree on Whether the Bottom is in Sight." *ABA Journal.* Retrieved on May 19, 2015 at: http://www.aba-journal.com/ magazine/article/as_law_school_enrollment_drops_experts_disagree_on_ whether_the_bottom.

53. Kress, Jack M. 1976. "Progress and Prosecution". *Annals of the American Academy of Political and Social Science,* 423: 99–116.

54. Devlin, Patrick. 1960. *The Criminal Prosecution in England.* London: Oxford University Press.

55. Kress, Jack M. 1976. "Progress and Prosecution". *Annals of the American Academy*

*of Political and Social Science*, 423: 99–116.

56. Eisenstein, James and Herbert Jacob. 1977. *Felony Justice: An Organizational Analysis of Criminal Courts*. Boston, MA: Little, Brown and Company. See also: Sloan, John J. and JoAnn L. Miller. 1990. "Repeat Player Police Officers and Prosecutorial Charge Reduction Decisions: A Case Study." *American Journal of Police* 9(1): 163–168. Sloan and Miller argue that police officers—particularly narcotics officers—are also members of the courtroom workgroup.

57. Clynch, Edward J. and David W. Neubauer. 2008. "Trial Courts as Organizations: Critique and Synthesis." *Law and Policy*, 3(1): 69–94.

58. Langbein, John H. 1978. "The Criminal Trial Before the Lawyers." *The University of Chicago Law Review*, 45, 263–316.

59. *Ibid.*

60. Langbein, John H. 1979. "Understanding the Short History of Plea Bargaining." *Law & Society Review*, 1979:261–272.

61. Packer, Herbert L. 1968. *The Limits of the Criminal Sanction*. Stanford, CA: Stanford University Press.

62. Alschuler, Albert W. 1979. "Plea Bargaining and its History." *Law & Society Review*, 13:211–245.

63. Champion, Dean John, Richard D. Hartley and Gary A. Rabe. 2012. *Criminal Courts: Structure, Process, and Issues*. 3rd Edition. New York: Pearson.

64. Walker, Samuel. 1999. *The Police in America*. 3rd Edition. New York: McGraw-Hill.

65. Strope, Walter and Sam Swindell. 2014. "Sheriffs and County Law Enforcement." Pp. 1–5 in Jay Albanese (Ed.), *The Encyclopedia of Criminology and Criminal Justice*. New York: Wiley Online Library.

66. Walker, Samuel. 1999. *The Police in America*. 3rd Edition. New York: McGraw-Hill.

67. Friedman, Lawrence M. 1993. *Crime and Punishment in American History*. New York: Basic Books; Spillane, Joseph F. and David B. Wolcott. 2013. *A History of Modern American Criminal Justice*. Thousand Oaks, CA: SAGE; Walker, Samuel. 1999. *The Police in America*. 3rd Edition. New York: McGraw-Hill.

68. Walker, Samuel. 1999. *The Police in America*. 3rd Edition. New York: McGraw-Hill.

69. Barlow, David and Melissa Hickman Barlow. 1999. "A Political Economy of Community Policing." *Policing: An International Journal of Police Strategies and Management*, 22: 646–674.

70. Friedman, Lawrence M. 1993. *Crime and Punishment in American History*. New York: Basic Books; Spillane, Joseph F. and David B. Wolcott. 2013. *A History of Modern American Criminal Justice*. Thousand Oaks, CA: SAGE; Walker, Samuel. 1999. *The Police in America*. 3rd Edition. New York: McGraw-Hill.

71. Spillane, Joseph F. and David B. Wolcott. 2013. *A History of Modern American Criminal Justice*. Thousand Oaks, CA: SAGE.

72. Friedman, Lawrence M. 1993. *Crime and Punishment in American History*. New York: Basic Books; Spillane, Joseph F. and David B. Wolcott. 2013. *A History of Modern American Criminal Justice*. Thousand Oaks, CA: SAGE; Walker, Samuel. 1999. *The Police in America*. 3rd Edition. New York: McGraw-Hill.

73. Barlow, David and Melissa Hickman Barlow. 1999. "A Political Economy of Community Policing." *Policing: An International Journal of Police Strategies and Management*, 22: 646–674.

74. Spillane, Joseph F. and David B. Wolcott. 2013. *A History of Modern American Crim-*

*inal Justice*. Thousand Oaks, CA: SAGE.

75. Walker, Samuel. 1999. *The Police in America*. 3rd Edition. New York: McGraw-Hill.

76. Friedman, Lawrence M. 1993. *Crime and Punishment in American History*. New York: Basic Books; Spillane, Joseph F. and David B. Wolcott. 2013. *A History of Modern American Criminal Justice*. Thousand Oaks, CA: SAGE; Walker, Samuel. 1999. *The Police in America*. 3rd Edition. New York: McGraw-Hill.

77. Walker, Samuel. 1999. *The Police in America*. 3rd Edition. New York: McGraw-Hill.

78. Vollmer, August. 1971. *The Police and Modern Society*. Montclair, NJ: Patterson Smith. Original work published in 1936.

79. Spillane, Joseph F. and David B. Wolcott. 2013. *A History of Modern American Criminal Justice*. Thousand Oaks, CA: SAGE; Walker, Samuel. 1999. *The Police in America*. 3rd Edition. New York: McGraw-Hill.

80. Walker, Samuel. 1999. *The Police in America*. 3rd Edition. New York: McGraw-Hill.

81. *Ibid*.

82. Vollmer, August. 1971. [1936]. *The Police and Modern Society*. Montclair, NJ: Patterson Smith.

83. Walker, Samuel. 1999. *The Police in America*. 3rd Edition. New York: McGraw-Hill.

84. *Ibid*.

85. Spillane, Joseph F. and David B. Wolcott. 2013. *A History of Modern American Criminal Justice*. Thousand Oaks, CA: SAGE.

86. Friedman, Lawrence M. 1993. *Crime and Punishment in American History*. New York: Basic Books; Walker, Samuel. 1999. *The Police in America*. 3rd Edition. New York: McGraw-Hill.

87. Walker, Samuel. 1999. *The Police in America*. 3rd Edition. New York: McGraw-Hill.

88. Clear, Todd R., George F. Cole and Michael D. Reisig. 2013. *American Corrections*. 10th Edition. Belmont, CA: Cengage.

89. Friedman, Lawrence M. 1993. *Crime and Punishment in American History*. New York: Basic Books.

90. Clear, Todd R., George F. Cole and Michael D. Reisig. 2013. *American Corrections*. 10th Edition. Belmont, CA: Cengage.

91. Friedman, Lawrence M. 1993. *Crime and Punishment in American History*. New York: Basic Books.

92. Alloy, Jason S. 2002. "158-County Banishment in Georgia: Constitutional Implications under the State Constitution and the Federal Right to Travel." *Georgia Law Review*, 36: 1083–1108.

93. Tewksbury, Richard. 2007. "Exile at Home: The Unintended Collateral Consequences of Sex Offender Residency Restrictions." *Harvard Civil Rights—Civil Liberties Law Review*, 42: 531–540.

94. Bohm, Robert M. 2003. *Deathquest II: An Introduction to the Theory and Practice of Capital Punishment in the United States*. Cincinnati, OH: Anderson Publishing.

95. Friedman, Lawrence M. 1993. *Crime and Punishment in American History*. New York: Basic Books.

96. Bohm, Robert M. 2003. *Deathquest II: An Introduction to the Theory and Practice of Capital Punishment in the United States*. Cincinnati, OH: Anderson Publishing.

97. Clear, Todd R., George F. Cole and Michael D. Reisig. 2013. *American Corrections*. 10th Edition. Belmont, CA: Cengage.

98. *Atkins v. Virginia*, (2002). 536 U.S. 304; *Roper v. Simmons*, (2005). 543 U.S. 551.

99. Death Penalty Information Center. "Executions by Year Since 1976." Retrieved on May 19, 2015 at: http://www.deathpenaltyinfo.org/executions-year.

100. Death Penalty Information Center. 2015. "Capital Punishment in Flux." Retrieved on May 19, 2015 at: http://www.deathpenaltyinfo.org/death-penalty-flux.

101. Gallup. 2014. "The Death Penalty." Retrieved on May 19, 2015 at: http://www.gallup.com/poll/1606/death-penalty.aspx.

102. Preyer, Kathryn. 1982. "Penal Measures in the American Colonies: An Overview." *The American Journal of Legal History*, 26(4): 326–353.

103. *Ibid.*

104. Friedman, Lawrence M. 1993. *Crime and Punishment in American History*. New York: Basic Books.

105. Hall, Daniel E. 1995. "When Caning Meets the Eighth Amendment: Whipping Offenders in the United States." *Widener Journal of Public Law*, 4: 403–459.

106. Friedman, Lawrence M. 1993. *Crime and Punishment in American History*. New York: Basic Books.

107. Bohm, Robert M. 2003. *Deathquest II: An Introduction to the Theory and Practice of Capital Punishment in the United States*. Cincinnati, OH: Anderson Publishing.

108. Clear, Todd R., George F. Cole and Michael D. Reisig. 2013. *American Corrections*. 10th Edition. Belmont, CA: Cengage.

109. Bernard, Thomas J., Jeffrey B. Snipes and Alexander L. Gerould. 2010. *Vold's Theoretical Criminology*. 6th Edition. New York: Oxford University Press.

110. The Bentham Project. nd. "The Panopticon." Retrieved on May 19, 2015 at: https://www.ucl.ac.uk/Bentham-Project/who/panopticon.

111. Clear, Todd R., George F. Cole and Michael D. Reisig. 2013. *American Corrections*. 10th Edition. Belmont, CA: Cengage.

112. Murton, Thomas. O. 1979. "Prison Management: The Past, the Present, and the Possible Future". Pp. 5–53 in *Prisons: Present and Possible*, edited by M.E. Wolfgang. Lexington, MA: Lexington Books.

113. Haney, Craig. 2003. "Mental Health Issues in Long-Term Solitary and 'Supermax' Confinement." *Crime and Delinquency*, 49(1):124–156.

114. Murton, Thomas. O. 1979. "Prison Management: The Past, the Present, and the Possible Future". Pp. 5–53 in *Prisons: Present and Possible*, edited by M.E. Wolfgang. Lexington, MA: Lexington Books.

115. Clear, Todd R., George F. Cole and Michael D. Reisig. 2013. *American Corrections*. 10th Edition. Belmont, CA: Cengage.

116. Murton, Thomas. O. 1979. "Prison Management: The Past, the Present, and the Possible Future". Pp. 5–53 in *Prisons: Present and Possible*, edited by M.E. Wolfgang. Lexington, MA: Lexington Books.

117. Clear, Todd R., George F. Cole and Michael D. Reisig. 2013. *American Corrections*. 10th Edition. Belmont, CA: Cengage.

118. Blackmon, Douglas A. 2008. *Slavery by Another Name*. New York: Random House.

119. Atkins, Joe. 2011. "Crime Pays for the Private Prison Industry and Modern-Day Convict Leasers." Retrieved on May 20, 2015 at: http://www.southernstudies.org/2011/08/voices-crime-pays-for-the-private-prison-industry-and-modern-day-convict-leasers.html.

120. Fraser, Steven and Joshua B. Freeman. 2012. "21st Century Chain Gangs." Retrieved on May 20, 2015 at: http://www.salon.com/2012/04/19/21st_century_chain_gangs/.

121. Murton, Thomas. O. 1979. "Prison Management: The Past, the Present, and the Possible Future". Pp. 5–53 in *Prisons: Present and Possible*, edited by M.E. Wolfgang. Lexington, MA: Lexington Books.

122. Solomon, Amy L., Vera Kachnowski, and Avi Bhati. 2005. *Does Parole Work?* Washington, DC: The Urban Institute. Retrieved on May 20, 2015 at: http://www.urban.org/research/ publication/does-parole-work.

123. Clear, Todd R., George F. Cole and Michael D. Reisig. 2013. *American Corrections*. 10th Edition. Belmont, CA: Cengage.

124. *Ibid.*

125. Platt, Anthony. 2009 [1969]. *The Child Savers: The Invention of Delinquency*. Camden, NJ: Rutgers University Press.

126. Lundman, Richard J. 2001. *Prevention and Control of Juvenile Delinquency*. 3rd Edition. New York: Oxford University Press.

127. Friedman, Lawrence M. 1993. *Crime and Punishment in American History*. New York: Basic Books.

128. Clear, Todd R., George F. Cole and Michael D. Reisig. 2013. *American Corrections*. 10th Edition. Belmont, CA: Cengage.

129. Lundman, Richard J. 2001. *Prevention and Control of Juvenile Delinquency*. 3rd Edition. New York: Oxford University Press.

130. Clear, Todd R., George F. Cole and Michael D. Reisig. 2013. *American Corrections*. 10th Edition. Belmont, CA: Cengage.

131. Cullen, Frank T. 2005. "The Twelve People Who Saved Rehabilitation: How the Science of Criminology Made a Difference". *Criminology*, 43(1): 1–42. Quote on Page 3.

132. Martinson, Robert. 1974. "What Works?—Questions and Answers About Prison Reform," *The Public Interest*, 35: 22–54.

133. Feeley, Malcolm M. and Jonathan Simon. 1992. "The New Penology: Notes on the Emerging Strategy of Corrections and its Implications". *Criminology*, 30(4): 449–474.

134. Pratt, Travis C. 2009. *Addicted to Incarceration: Corrections Policy and the Politics of Misinformation in the United States*. Thousand Oaks, CA: SAGE.

135. Clear, Todd R., George F. Cole and Michael D. Reisig. 2013. *American Corrections*. 10th Edition. Belmont, CA: Cengage.

136. Pratt, Travis C. 2009. *Addicted to Incarceration: Corrections Policy and the Politics of Misinformation in the United States*. Thousand Oaks, CA: SAGE.

137. Clear, Todd R., George F. Cole and Michael D. Reisig. 2013. *American Corrections*. 10th Edition. Belmont, CA: Cengage.

138. Beckett, Katherine and Theodore Sasson. 2004. *The Politics of Injustice: Crime and Punishment in America*. Thousand Oaks, CA: SAGE; Clear, Todd R., George F. Cole and Michael D. Reisig. 2013. *American Corrections*. 10th Edition. Belmont, CA: Cengage; Pratt, Travis C. 2009. *Addicted to Incarceration: Corrections Policy and the Politics of Misinformation in the United States*. Thousand Oaks, CA: SAGE.

139. Clear, Todd R., George F. Cole and Michael D. Reisig. 2013. *American Corrections*. 10th Edition. Belmont, CA: Cengage.

140. Cohn, Gary. 2014. "Newt Gingrich and Jay–Z Find Common Cause in a Prison Reform Proposition". *The Huffington Post*. Retrieved on March 21, 2015 at: http://www.huffingtonpost.com/2014/10/23/proposition-47_n_6038310.html.

# Chapter 4

# The Cost of Crime

## Chapter Outline

- Introduction
- The True Cost of Crime
  - Federal and State Expenditures for Criminal Justice
  - Interpreting the Cost of Crime
  - Jobs in the Criminal Justice System
- Crime and Crime Victims
  - Cost of Violent Crime
  - Cost of Property and White-Collar Crime
  - Fear of Crime
  - The Benefits of Crime
- Conclusion
- Key Terms
- Key People
- Discussion Questions

## Learning Objectives

- Identify the financial gains from various crimes
- Compare and contrast the direct and indirect costs of crimes
- Identify and evaluate the criminal justice system from an economic approach
- Identify and explain methods of interpreting the cost of crime

## Introduction

What exactly is the cost of crime? Similar to many questions regarding crime, there is no easy answer. Consider the following scenario: Smith is driving his new BMW convertible home from work one evening, and while stopped at a traffic light, is approached by Jones, who produces a large-caliber handgun and demands that Smith surrender the car or be shot. Smith complies and surrenders the car. Jones drives off at a high rate of speed. How much did this event cost? When considering the cost of this or any crime Kathryn McCollister and colleagues[1] have argued we must consider the **direct or fixed costs** to the victim—economic losses that include payments for medical services, lost time from work, and property damage or loss. Some of the direct costs involve criminal justice system costs—government funds directed at the criminal justice system including support for the police, the courts, and corrections. However, there are also **speculative costs** that accrue from crime. These include indirect losses suffered by victims, such as pain and suffering, mental health problems, or declines in quality of life. In theory, if one tallied the losses associated with direct and speculative costs, one could then have an overall estimate of the economic costs of crime in the United States. As we will see, however, even when doing so, at best we will be able to develop a general estimate of the costs of crime.

# The True Cost of Crime

In reviewing estimates of the annual cost of crime, one finds conflicting figures. In 2012, for example, David Anderson estimated that the cost of crime in the United States was $1.7 trillion annually. In compiling this estimate, he noted that over $200 billion was spent on government expenditures for police protection, correctional facilities, and the legal and judicial costs in prosecuting crimes. Other costs Anderson mentioned were $164 billion that Americans spent paying employees simply to lock and unlock doors. Computer viruses and other computer security issues cost businesses approximately $78 billion each year.[2] Conversely, Kathryn McCollister and colleagues noted that 23 million criminal offenses were committed in 2007 and economic losses in that same year were $15 billion.[3] Which of these estimates is closer to the truth? Although it would seem that determining the cost of crime is a relatively straightforward effort, the reality is that identifying the cost of crime can actually be a highly subjective undertaking. Indeed, to properly calculate the economic costs of crime we would need to make decisions about many subjective factors that could spawn disagreement, such as what is the value of a human life? What is the cost associated with a victim suffering post-traumatic stress disorder (PTSD) as a result of being raped? We will argue that certain considerations need to be taken into account when trying to answer the question of how much crime costs each year. In doing so, we suggest factors that, while not all scholars would agree are 100% appropriate, most would accept at least some of as reasonable indicators that should be used when trying to estimate how much crime costs each year. We believe that in using our factors, one can develop one's own estimate while also understanding that certain biases and subjectivity are part of the equation as well.

The first major dimension we consider is determining the **fixed costs of crime**. Fixed costs, according to economists, are "costs that do not depend upon the number of times a criminal act is committed."[4] For example, the fixed costs of a thief stealing a $100 vase from an antiques shop are $100—the value of the item taken. That individual value does not change whether the thief steals one vase from the shop, or one hundred of them. Assuming the price is equal to its value, the particular item is worth $100. In other words, fixed costs are the direct financial losses suffered by victims. Returning to our BMW example, the fixed cost of the robbery in the scenario is the actual value of the car—say, $55,500. To estimate the fixed costs of *all* armed robberies, we would thus add up the value of *all* property taken during robberies and arrive at a particular figure.

Fixed costs also include the costs associated with criminal justice agencies that respond to crime: the police, the courts, and correctional agencies. Returning again to our BMW example, the police officer who responded to the call from Smith is paid a salary and provided a benefits package, which is hypothetically $50,000 annually. Let us say the officer works 40 hours per week, 52 weeks a year, or about 2080 hours. At $50,000 per year, the officer's fixed costs to her department are approximately $48 per hour. Let us then assume the officer spent 10 hours on the case from beginning to end, so the fixed costs of *that particular robbery* for the police in Smith's case would be $480. We would then repeat this exercise for all the other crimes that happened in a given year to identify the fixed costs for the police of the crimes to which they responded. We would then repeat this exercise to determine the fixed costs of prosecuting the case, which includes the time spent on the case by one or more prosecutors. There will also be court costs (assuming the case goes to trial) as well as costs for a public defender assigned the case. Assuming the defendant is convicted and sentenced to prison, there are also fixed correctional costs associated with incarcerating offenders. You can well imagine how quickly these fixed costs add to a very large number!

Conversely, *speculative costs* of crime are the indirect costs that accrue to crime victims and include factors such as lost wages, pain and suffering, etc. Although the courts have attempted to estimate these costs by considering factors such as lost wages and/or pain and suffering, the figures settled upon are typically determined on a case-by-case basis and are, therefore, variable. In some instances, states may even cap the damages one can receive as the result of being a crime victim. Nonetheless, if one decides to file a lawsuit against the person(s) who victimized them, the courts assess an appropriate monetary award that reflects the degree of damage which the plaintiff/victim has endured.

Finally, other costs of crime are not so easy to estimate; these expenditures go beyond any direct calculation of cost. These can be considered **unknown costs**. For instance, as a result of experiencing victimization some people will become fearful of being victimized again. Friends, relatives, and acquaintances of the victims may also become fearful of becoming victims. Such a belief can dramatically affect the quality of a person's life. The person might become agoraphobic and never leave their house. Although a person might not go to this extreme, someone who greatly fears becoming a victim might severely alter his or her daily routine from "normal" people, who are merely acting pragmatically.

## Federal and State Expenditures for Criminal Justice

In 2003, the **Bureau of Justice Statistics** (BJS) released a report *Justice Expenditure and Employment in the United States, 2003*.[5] This information can be seen in Table 4.1. As its title clearly indicates, BJS recounted how much was spent on the criminal justice system within the United States. According to the report, the federal government, the individual states, and localities spent $185 billion for police protection, corrections, and judicial and legal activities. In 2003, $83 billion was spent on police protection, $41.5 million was spent on the court system, and $60.8 billion was spent on corrections. The report noted the total of $185 billion represented a five-fold increase in criminal justice system costs compared to those of $36 billion in 1982. The *Sourcebook of Criminal Justice Statistics*, which is maintained by the Hindelang Criminal Justice Research Center at the University at Albany, found that by 2006, criminal justice expenditures had risen to $214.5 billion.[6] Finding recent expenditures of federal criminal justice spending is not difficult. In 2012, the United States Department of Justice was allocated a budget of $26.8 billion.[7] Yet law enforcement at the federal level is not monopolized by the Department of Justice. In large response to the terrorist acts of September 11, 2001, the Department of Homeland Security was created. In 2013, the agency had a budget of $60.68 billion.[8] Additionally, the federal judiciary received $6.9 billion in 2013.[9] The most recent reliable figures that we can produce which reflect state and local measures of criminal justice spending is the 2010–2011 United States Census. The report noted that the states and localities spent roughly $214.3 billion to maintain their criminal justice and court systems.[10] Thus, if we added these figures together, we could estimate that the United States annually spends roughly $248 billion on criminal justice. If we consider the Department of Homeland Security as a criminal justice agency, this amount increases to $308.6 billion.

Many people mistakenly think of the United States Census as merely a tedious exercise that results in nothing more than population record keeping. What many people do not know is that the Census Bureau collects much more data than on simply who lives where. It provides information at tract, city, county, and state-level regarding households, businesses, and government. From the most recent Census (as can be seen in Table 4.2), we were able to access recent figures on how much each state allocates various forms of funding, including expenditures for criminal justice. As you can see, criminal justice is not the greatest expense that states have, but it is certainly substantial. In the next table, we break down criminal justice expenditures by the three common areas of the discipline: judicial, police, and corrections.

## Interpreting the Cost of Crime

The picture that emerges from the numbers we have shared is rather simple: the United States spends a great deal of money on criminal justice. Yet, numbers are generally meaningless until we put them into context. The BJS report of 2003 noted that local and state governments devoted approximately 7.2% of all budgetary expenditures to criminal justice that year. To put this amount in perspective, the BJS noted that localities and states spent almost four times this amount on education, twice as much on public welfare, and about the same amount on hospitals and health care.[11] According to the 2010-2011 Census, 5.45% of state and local budget expenditures were dedicated to criminal justice spending and another 1.36% of these budget expenditures were dedicated to maintaining court systems. Thus, there appears to be a slight decrease in the percentage of state-level criminal justice spending from 2003 to 2011. Indeed, the states' governments spent four times more on education (30.8%), public welfare and hospitals (38.9%), and even slightly more on transportation (8.5%) than they did on the criminal justice system.

Another way to look at the cost of crime is to compare states' expenditures to that of companies' expenditures in the private industry. As you can see in Table 4.2 (*Market Values of the Most Profitable Companies Internationally*), annual criminal justice expenditures in the United States are greater than the market value of the most profitable companies across the world! Such a finding seems staggering.

Table 4.1. Expenditures by State (by 10,000)

| State | Population | Total Expenditures | Education | Social Services | Transportation | Judicial | Police | Corrections |
|---|---|---|---|---|---|---|---|---|
| Alabama | 4,779,758 | 4,216,102.8 | 1,477,975.1 | 1,769,805.2 | 364,713.0 | 41,241.1 | 114,053.7 | 75,657.1 |
| Alaska | 710,231 | 1,468,704.0 | 378,563.4 | 442,374.6 | 279,726.9 | 22,660.5 | 32,732.4 | 29,017.9 |
| Arizona | 6,392,015 | 5,253,381.9 | 1,491,898.4 | 2,151,906.9 | 459,500.9 | 92,857.6 | 209,938.3 | 151,451.0 |
| Arkansas | 2,915,916 | 2,376,876.0 | 937,267.2 | 1,048,299.2 | 222,655.7 | 20,601.0 | 54,336.2 | 57,775.6 |
| California | 37,253,959 | 45,471,058.4 | 11,386,258.6 | 17,072,259.2 | 2,578,000.3 | 888,674.2 | 1,508,460.9 | 1,436,524.6 |
| Colorado | 5,029,196 | 5,157,392.5 | 1,501,212.1 | 1,377,099.5 | 424,919.1 | 67,584.7 | 165,017.4 | 123,731.9 |
| Connecticut | 3,574,097 | 4,067,569.0 | 1,282,058.4 | 1,469,807.5 | 235,161.9 | 68,845.6 | 107,303.4 | 69,453.7 |
| Delaware | 897,936 | 989,673.6 | 350,059.4 | 398,299.1 | 93,621.9 | 15,478.4 | 29,047.0 | 26,774.1 |
| Florida | 18,802,690 | 16,406,221.2 | 4,268,378.5 | 6,105,838.0 | 1,625,888.4 | 219,904.1 | 735,001.0 | 439,227.3 |
| Georgia | 9,687,663 | 7,809,354.9 | 2,736,922.6 | 2,789,372.5 | 579,507.4 | 101,525.1 | 227,386.2 | 244,616.8 |
| Hawaii | 1,360,301 | 1,438,890.7 | 379,620.9 | 564,757.8 | 115,691.8 | 23,830.7 | 38,614.0 | 19,148.9 |
| Idaho | 1,567,652 | 1,206,599.3 | 337,812.9 | 555,377.1 | 166,596.3 | 18,953.0 | 38,118.5 | 30,073.8 |
| Illinois | 12,830,632 | 13,077,709.6 | 3,803,223.9 | 4,285,086.7 | 1,251,421.0 | 146,080.1 | 462,334.7 | 223,700.7 |
| Indiana | 6,483,797 | 5,265,197.3 | 1,820,907.5 | 2,147,761.6 | 478,399.3 | 48,220.7 | 129,559.2 | 102,592.9 |
| Iowa | 3,046,857 | 3,032,489.7 | 1,104,360.9 | 1,317,007.6 | 335,943.4 | 33,982.9 | 64,412.0 | 54,146.8 |
| Kansas | 2,853,116 | 2,652,937.4 | 962,203.7 | 1,002,726.3 | 277,253.3 | 30,194.6 | 73,337.3 | 51,717.5 |
| Kentucky | 4,339,357 | 3,906,243.0 | 1,272,234.8 | 1,744,609.9 | 375,831.4 | 50,673.4 | 70,088.4 | 75,297.5 |
| Louisiana | 4,533,372 | 4,875,659.3 | 1,338,104.0 | 1,856,935.9 | 562,683.5 | 72,824.6 | 150,561.8 | 136,986.7 |
| Maine | 1,328,361 | 1,261,044.2 | 372,378.5 | 649,344.3 | 145,273.6 | 9,640.3 | 26,419.7 | 19,731.9 |
| Maryland | 5,773,623 | 5,761,227.7 | 2,022,417.4 | 2,118,574.9 | 494,215.1 | 79,449.9 | 216,284.7 | 175,705.1 |
| Massachusetts | 6,547,629 | 7,551,917.1 | 2,079,871.4 | 3,254,403.4 | 458,588.3 | 95,833.7 | 211,642.0 | 107,307.6 |
| Michigan | 9,883,701 | 8,980,018.1 | 3,182,085.6 | 3,423,643.0 | 529,983.1 | 111,131.7 | 237,665.0 | 228,951.5 |
| Minnesota | 5,303,925 | 5,568,358.1 | 1,699,169.7 | 2,701,742.6 | 602,652.8 | 70,043.8 | 165,206.8 | 88,849.0 |
| Mississippi | 2,967,299 | 2,730,771.7 | 788,283.3 | 1,437,752.1 | 280,372.6 | 22,714.4 | 66,077.0 | 62,311.1 |
| Missouri | 5,988,923 | 4,979,004.8 | 1,518,245.5 | 2,030,956.5 | 535,687.8 | 46,793.2 | 166,972.6 | 87,227.0 |

Table 4.1. Expenditures by State (by 10,000) *continued*

| State | Population | Total Expenditures | Education | Social Services | Transportation | Judicial | Police | Corrections |
|---|---|---|---|---|---|---|---|---|
| Montana | 989,417 | 929,356.0 | 278,551.7 | 327,186.7 | 153,467.0 | 15,400.4 | 25,758.7 | 25,894.9 |
| Nebraska | 1,826,341 | 1,947,998.7 | 630,229.4 | 580,216.3 | 190,817.0 | 17,839.0 | 41,155.4 | 38,472.1 |
| Nevada | 2,700,552 | 2,326,734.3 | 609,344.2 | 613,778.0 | 319,880.6 | 44,982.4 | 114,608.0 | 70,718.3 |
| New Hampshire | 1,316,469 | 1,163,743.5 | 407,584.7 | 439,589.4 | 112,066.3 | 11,528.7 | 35,215.3 | 18,910.6 |
| New Jersey | 8,791,909 | 10,123,655.3 | 3,290,110.2 | 3,303,403.8 | 727,582.9 | 147,677.9 | 334,354.5 | 210,059.0 |
| New Mexico | 2,059,183 | 2,241,545.2 | 774,318.6 | 1,057,493.5 | 201,641.1 | 31,814.6 | 63,659.1 | 63,906.4 |
| New York | 19,378,105 | 29,960,235.8 | 8,014,878.2 | 12,358,476.6 | 1,989,427.2 | 422,240.5 | 901,747.1 | 620,589.2 |
| North Carolina | 9,535,471 | 8,084,949.5 | 2,605,139.2 | 3,361,228.5 | 650,536.6 | 75,121.6 | 245,591.6 | 217,113.3 |
| North Dakota | 672,591 | 713,712.1 | 243,616.1 | 213,520.3 | 155,456.0 | 7,622.5 | 15,263.2 | 13,863.3 |
| Ohio | 11,536,503 | 11,623,147.9 | 3,742,593.2 | 4,916,746.5 | 813,425.2 | 175,354.7 | 319,813.9 | 197,607.1 |
| Oklahoma | 3,751,357 | 3,065,910.0 | 1,050,413.4 | 1,301,196.1 | 416,128.1 | 33,108.7 | 89,716.2 | 66,623.3 |
| Oregon | 3,831,073 | 3,993,220.3 | 1,188,504.7 | 1,464,599.2 | 336,392.2 | 43,889.9 | 107,754.2 | 106,154.3 |
| Pennsylvania | 12,702,379 | 13,274,770.0 | 3,870,723.8 | 5,926,190.9 | 1,538,956.8 | 166,955.2 | 313,308.8 | 329,382.0 |
| Rhode Island | 1,052,567 | 1,144,482.2 | 317,059.9 | 492,848.4 | 71,933.5 | 12,234.3 | 35,640.9 | 19,948.7 |
| South Carolina | 4,625,360 | 4,278,413.0 | 1,352,700.1 | 2,004,080.6 | 267,190.5 | 35,049.2 | 105,863.2 | 67,590.7 |
| South Dakota | 814,180 | 701,364.4 | 242,292.9 | 226,619.7 | 149,943.1 | 7,837.1 | 16,246.7 | 16,559.4 |
| Tennessee | 6,346,113 | 5,514,719.7 | 2,745,104.7 | 2,469,476.0 | 424,823.0 | 60,835.5 | 171,261.3 | 102,937.8 |
| Texas | 25,145,561 | 22,102,998.4 | 8,432,678.9 | 8,017,553.5 | 1,928,327.9 | 270,619.8 | 658,167.3 | 608,346.6 |
| Utah | 2,763,885 | 2,492,789.0 | 879,154.5 | 730,314.0 | 334,046.6 | 34,375.3 | 65,859.3 | 49,967.8 |
| Vermont | 625,745 | 692,219.1 | 250,683.1 | 314,526.8 | 94,826.7 | 7,039.8 | 17,285.3 | 12,719.4 |
| Virginia | 8,001,031 | 6,922,514.3 | 2,500,491.5 | 2,586,612.8 | 715,960.8 | 82,739.7 | 204,071.2 | 230,054.0 |
| Washington | 6,724,543 | 7,489,962.0 | 2,139,090.4 | 2,520,980.4 | 780,844.1 | 83,367.6 | 157,089.1 | 162,562.6 |
| West Virginia | 1,852,999 | 1,640,037.0 | 606,955.0 | 722,338.3 | 218,609.2 | 21,612.6 | 35,689.3 | 32,870.0 |
| Wisconsin | 5,686,983 | 5,669,601.5 | 1,894,056.7 | 2,323,202.0 | 622,345.3 | 59,365.7 | 177,029.5 | 159,357.8 |
| Wyoming | 563,626 | 866,624.7 | 284,869.7 | 280,824.8 | 116,028.7 | 11,563.9 | 21,377.6 | 20,656.7 |

**Table 4.2. Market Values of the Most Profitable Companies Internationally**

| Company | Country | Market Value |
| --- | --- | --- |
| ICBC, China | China | $237,300,000,000 |
| China Construction Bank | China | $202,000,000,000 |
| JPMorgan Chase | United States | $191,400,000,000 |
| General Electric | United States | $243,700,000,000 |
| Exxon Mobil | United States | $243,700,000,000 |
| HSBC Holdings | United Kingdom | $213,100,000,000 |
| Royal Dutch Shell | Netherlands | $213,100,000,000 |
| Agricultural Bank of China | China | $150,800,000,000 |
| Berkshire Hathaway | United States | $252,800,000,000 |
| PetroChina | China | $261,200,000,000 |
| Total | | $2,209,100,000,000 |

(Many factors were considered in ranking these companies; market value was only one measure.)[12]

## Jobs in the Criminal Justice System

Not only does the United States heavily fund criminal justice, but also this funding results in the creation of jobs—a lot of them. In 2003, the BJS found that in total, the criminal justice system employed 2,361,193 people. Among the total were 253,367 federal employees, 733,570 state employees, and 1,374,256 local employees.[13] Over 1.5 million of these jobs were for security and law enforcement agencies, and their distribution is shown in Table 4.3, *Law Enforcement Employees within the United States*. In 2008, BJS found that 12,501 local police departments were operating in the United States. These departments had approximately 593,000 full-time employees, of which 461,000 were sworn police officers.[14] In 2007, over 3,000 county sheriffs' offices in the U.S. employed approximately 369,000 people, of which 49% were sworn officers.[15] In 2008, American Indian tribes operated 178 law enforcement agencies that employed 4,500 full-time personnel, of which 66% were sworn officers.[16] During the 2004–2005 school year, four-year universities and colleges with 2,500 or more students employed 25,000 for campus law enforcement personnel, of which 52% were sworn personnel.[17] In 2009, publicly funded crime labs employed 13,100 full-time personnel.[18] In 2006, a total of 648 state and local law enforcement academies provided training to law enforcement officers. These academies employed 10,000 full-time and 28,000 part-time instructors.[19]

In 2012, the United States Department of Justice was allocated a budget of $26.8 billion and employed 113,543 people. The agency, which is presided over by the United States attorney general, includes many different divisions, such as the Federal Bureau of Investigation, the Drug Enforcement Administration, the United States Attorneys, the United States Marshall Service, the Bureau of Alcohol, Tobacco, Firearms, & Explosives, and the Bureau of Prisons. Thus, the agency oversees the three major areas of the criminal justice system of the federal government: police, courts, and corrections. Yet, law enforcement at the federal level is not monopolized by the Department of Justice. The Department of Homeland Security had a budget in 2013 of $60.6 billion. Among the agency's twenty-two subunits are the United States Customs & Border Protection, Transportation Security Administration, United States Coast Guard, the United States Immigration & Customs Enforcement, the United States Secret Service, and the Federal Emergency Management Agency. In 2013, the agency employed nearly 240,000 people. Yet, although these agencies are primarily responsible for the federal government's commitment to the criminal justice system, many other agencies have law enforcement responsibilities as well.

According to the Bureau of Labor Statistics,[32] in 2012 there were about 3,500,000 positions within the field of criminal justice (See Table 4.4, *Job Position Availability in Criminal Justice by Sector Bureau of Labor Statistics*). Putting that in context, the Census reports show that the United States population in 2012 was approximately 313 million, and of that, 154.4 million were in the labor force (meaning, 16 and older). Thus, over two percent of all persons employed in the U.S. (public and private) have a job attributable to criminal justice. How does this compare to other companies? Table 4.5 (*U.S. Job Positions Availability in Largest Companies*) shows the top ten United States employers with the number of job positions each company provides. Not surprisingly, **Wal-Mart** employs more United States residents than any company within the U.S. Internationally, Wal-Mart employs 2.2 million people, and more than half of those employees are residing in the United States. On average, there are 100 Wal-Mart or Sam's Club stores in each state! Even in Wyoming, the least populated state, with less than 600,000 residents, there are ten Wal-Mart Super Centers and two Sam's Clubs.[33] Yet, when we put that number in comparison to criminal justice, the government employs approxi-

Table 4.3. Law Enforcement Employees within the United States

| Employees | f | % |
|---|---|---|
| Federal Law Enforcement[20] | 120,000 | 6.99 |
| Department of Justice[21] | 113,543 | 6.62 |
| Homeland Security[22] | 240,000 | 13.98 |
| State Agencies[23] | 94,095 | 5.48 |
| Local Police[24] | 593,000 | 34.55 |
| Sheriff's Offices[25] | 369,000 | 21.50 |
| Special Jurisdiction[26] | 104,943 | 6.11 |
| Constable/Marshal[27] | 1,169 | 0.07 |
| American Indian Law Enforcement Agencies[28] | 4,500 | 0.2 |
| Campus Law Enforcement[29] | 25,000 | 1.46 |
| Publicly Funded Crime Labs[30] | 13,100 | 0.76 |
| State and Local Law Enforcement Academies[31] | 38,000 | 2.21 |
| Total | 1,716,350 | —— |

mately three times more individuals than Wal-Mart companies. Keeping in mind that these numbers are reported estimates, if we summed the number of employees from all the top ten companies *except* Wal-Mart, the total (3,477,000) is actually slightly less than that of criminal justice employees (3,518,750).

Thus, as we have shown, crime creates jobs—a lot of them—and there are millions of people involved in trying to reduce, prevent, and prosecute it.

# Crime and Crime Victims

Perhaps the greatest harm that a person can do to another person is to take their life. Attempts to calculate the cost of a human life are hopelessly controversial. For instance, during a lawsuit against the **Ford Motor Company** involving the safety of a car the company used to produce called the Pinto, plaintiffs suing the company tried to offer evidence that the Ford Motor Company valued a human life at $200,000, and used this as a measuring stick against

Table 4.4. U.S. Job Position Availability in Criminal Justice by Sector

| Sector | f |
|---|---|
| Probation Officers and Correctional Treatment Specialists | 86,780 |
| Lawyers* | 581,920 |
| Judges | 27,200 |
| Paralegals and Legal Assistants | 267,030 |
| Judicial Law Clerks | 11,200 |
| Court Reporters | 18,590 |
| Criminal Justice and Law Enforcement Teachers, Postsecondary | 14,020 |
| Law Teachers, Postsecondary | 15,260 |
| First-Line Supervisors of Correctional Officers | 44,830 |
| First-Line Supervisors of Police and Detectives | 99,860 |
| Bailiffs | 16,240 |
| Correctional Officers and Jailers | 434,870 |
| Detectives and Criminal Investigators | 109,230 |
| Fish and Game Wardens | 6,320 |
| Parking Enforcement Workers | 9,210 |
| Police and Sheriff's Patrol Officers | 632,000 |
| Transit and Railroad Police | 4,140 |
| Animal Control Workers | 13,890 |
| Private Detectives and Investigators | 23,390 |
| Gaming Surveillance Officers and Gaming Investigators | 9,150 |
| Security Guards | 1,046,420 |
| Transportation Security Screeners | 47,200 |
| Total | 3,518,750 |

*Not all lawyers practice criminal law.

Table 4.5. U.S. Job Positions Availability in Largest Companies[34]

| Company | $f$ |
|---|---|
| Wal-Mart | 1,300,000 |
| Yum! Brands | 523,000 |
| McDonald's | 440,000 |
| IBM | 434,000 |
| United Parcel Service | 399,000 |
| Target | 361,000 |
| Kroger | 343,000 |
| Home Depot | 340,000 |
| Hewlett-Packard | 332,000 |
| General Electric | 305,000 |
| Total | 4,777,000 |

the potential money the company might be liable for when settling a lawsuit. The plaintiffs believed this was a sign of callousness on the part of the company, both putting a value on human life, as well as making it what they considered a relatively low figure. The plaintiffs argued that the value of a human life was worth considerably more. In actuality, the source of the $200,000 value for a human life was developed by the National Highway Traffic Safety Administration.[35] Instead of considering the alleged callousness of a corporation, Kathryn McCollister and colleagues argued that there is other value in trying to estimate what the monetary cost is to victims of homicide and other crimes generally. They argued that considering crimes in terms of dollars and cents is valuable when considering the cost effectiveness of crime prevention programs, substance abuse treatment versus incarceration, community policing, and any other programs that seek to lower crime rates.[36]

## Cost of Violent Crime

If we want to consider what the monetary cost to society is of different crimes, we must first determine how many crimes have occurred. A convenient source of this information is the **Uniform Crime Report** (UCR) compiled annually by the FBI, which presents figures on the total number of crimes known to the police and breaks down that total into different categories and specific offenses. According to the UCR, in 2012, there were 14,827 homicides.[37] Using the $200,000 figure as the value of a human life, the direct costs of homicide in 2012 was $2,965,500,000. McCollister and colleagues, writing in 2010, developed modern considerations of the cost of being a victim of different crimes. Using different metrics, they argued that being the victim of murder presents a cost of anywhere from $1,278,424 to $8,982,907 per victim.[38] Using the higher figure, we could estimate the fiscal loss from murder in 2012 alone at $128,338,792,309.

The indirect costs of homicide are a bit harder to gage, considering that the greatest cost has occurred—the victim's life. As we stated earlier, an objective calculation for determining the cost of a human life is challenging and often varies from person to person. However, determining the personal cost to the homicide victim who lost his or her life is nearly impossible—there is no way to account for that individual's indirect costs. There are, however, indirect costs to the other victims of homicide—the victim's family and friends. They are likely to suffer emotionally and psychologically. Furthermore, if the victim provided monetary support to his/her family, there may be financial struggles. Additionally, the death of a loved one costs time—time to grieve, to contact friends and family, to plan a funeral, to settle the estate of the deceased, and to settle life insurance claims.

There are many crimes besides homicide where a victim suffers indirect costs. Although determining the degree of heinousness of a crime can be entirely subjective, we believe many people agree that the most violent and harmful crimes after murder would be rape and sexual assault. The indirect costs to a victim of sexual assault are significant. Not only is this a brutal crime of violence, but victims are often left with severe psychological trauma, which could lead to years of therapy. Many victims of this crime might never fully recover. Additionally, a victim of rape may be accused of lying or those closest to him/her may at least doubt their claim of being victimized. Furthermore, most often, the victim and offender knew one another prior to the incident, which can create a number of issues with family or friends. Lastly, as somewhat of a final indignity, to ensure prosecution of the offense, a woman will have to testify in open court to an incident that many victims will consider shameful and embarrassing. While rape shield laws may protect victims to an extent, they do not protect against embarrassment, which many victims have equated to "being raped all over again."[39]

In order to examine the social cost of rape, we must first examine how frequently rape and sexual assault occur within the United States. According to the UCR, in 2012, 84,376 forcible rapes were reported to law enforcement.[40] To put this in perspective, the FBI reports that a forcible rape occurred every 6.2 minutes, and that 26.9 people out of 100,000 were forcibly raped in 2012.

McCollister and colleagues estimated the cost of rape and sexual assault is between $41,247 and $240,776 per incident.[41] If we take these estimates at face value, that could mean that rapes and sexual assaults reported in 2012 have or will cost the United States somewhere between $3.5 and $20.3 billion. With that being said, actually attempting to estimate the fiscal cost of rape and sexual assault is probably futile. The most troubling issue is that the reported sum of 84,376 forcible rapes is only a fraction of the crimes that actually occur. The Bureau of Justice Statistics reported that from 2006–2010, two out of three rapes/sexual assaults were not reported to the police by victims, revealing that the dark figure of sexual assault vastly overshadows the figure of sexual assaults known to the police.[42] This is not a revelation; indeed, according to government reports as far back as the 1970s, for every rape reported somewhere, between three and ten rapes went unreported. Mary Koss and colleagues argued that even this government estimate is inadequate. Based upon victimization surveys they have conducted, they found that 53.7% of the women they surveyed suffered some form of sexual victimization. While all of these incidents do not necessarily reach the level of forcible rape or other standards of sexual assault, nonetheless, we have a large number of women reporting that they have been the victim of a crime.[43]

## Cost of Property Crime and White-Collar Crime

Although still considered a violent crime, we are presenting robbery as a property crime, considering that the major motivation for the commission of robbery is obtaining money or property. According to the UCR, in 2012, there were an estimated 354,520 robberies. The FBI estimated the losses from these robberies at $414 million.[44] In 2012, there were an estimated 2,103,787 burglaries, which accounted for an estimated $4.7 billion loss in property.[45] An estimated 6,150,598 larceny-thefts were committed in the same year, with an estimated loss of $987/incident, which totals to an estimated $6,070,640,226.[46] In 2012, an estimated 721,053 motor vehicle thefts occurred, with an estimated $4.3 billion in losses.[47] Together, these losses account for approximately $15.5 billion in 2012 alone. Obviously, this is a lot of money, even to someone like Bill Gates or Mark Zuckerberg. Yet this is probably small potatoes compared to financial crimes that occur worldwide.

In 1939, a joint conference was held between the American Sociological Society (now known as the American Sociological Association) and the American Economic Association (AEA). After the president of the AEA, Jacob Viner, delivered his presidential address, **Edwin Sutherland**, the president of the American Sociological Society, took his turn at the podium. Besides being president of the organization, Sutherland was also well known in sociological circles. He was the author of a widely used textbook called *Criminology* and frequently advocated in journal articles for more rigorous use of the scientific method in sociological research. Within his presidential address, Sutherland stated that he hoped to find a way to integrate research within business and sociology.[48]

Sutherland argued that at the time, most criminological theories merely focused on crimes committed by poor people, because the study of crime predominantly focused upon official statistics and conviction rates. Sutherland believed that society seemed to concentrate too much on what he called "street crimes" and gave little attention to "crimes in the suites." He coined the term "white-collar crime" to depict financial crimes and scams that were most often committed by people within the upper class of society. Although these offenses were not crimes of violence, from a financial standpoint, Sutherland believed that these crimes were far more damaging to the American economy than were street crimes like robbery or burglary. For instance, Sutherland noted that in one year, a single officer within a grocery store chain embezzled $600,000, or more than six times the money taken in five hundred robberies and burglaries that had been committed against that same grocery store. Furthermore, Sutherland noted that "public enemies" one through six (the old term for what became the FBI's Ten Most Wanted) obtained $130,000 through various robberies and burglaries. Yet **Ivan Krueger**, a white-collar criminal who died in 1932, swindled individuals and businesses out of approximately $250 million through elaborate financial schemes and fictitious companies he established.[49] This would be equal to over $4.2 billion today!

Edwin Sutherland's arguments from the 1940s remain valid today. Over several years, hedge fund manager **Bernie Madoff** duped friends, relatives, and investors out of $65 billion.[50] Thus, one man independently and over time accounted for direct financial losses comparable to those associated with all property crimes that the UCR reported in five years. Although the sheer amount of money Bernie Madoff swindled might stand out, other recent financial scandals have occurred that have cost the United States billions as well. Some examples of these scandals include the financial collapse of the company Enron, risky stock trading practices at J.P. Morgan, money-laundering allegations against HSBC, and ex-Tyco CEO Dennis Kozlowski embezzling $150 million from his company. Although none of the victims of these financial crimes had a gun pointed at their head or suffered direct physical harm, many people lost their life savings, had the stocks they owned devalued, and financial markets as a whole were negatively affected by these events. Indeed, two years to the day after his father Bernie Madoff was arrested, **Mark Madoff** hanged himself in his apartment. Mark had worked for many years in his father's company, had been recently named in a civil lawsuit, and some suspected he would eventually face criminal charges. He left behind a wife, a four-year-old daughter, and a twenty-two-month-old son, who was found sleeping in a bedroom adjoining the one in which his father had just committed suicide.[51]

If we had more space in this chapter (or this textbook for that matter), we could discuss at length other ways white-collar crimes can harm people. Unsafe working conditions can lead to the illness or death of employees. This can lead to medical bills and lost or reduced time a person can work. Obviously, if an employee is killed on the job, that person is no longer providing for their family. Some companies have manufactured dangerous products that can harm or kill consumers. Furthermore, many companies needlessly pollute the environment. We do not want to overlook the positive contributions that many corporations make to our lives, but many of the companies cause a lot of harm, which costs us all.

## *Fear of Crime*

In his first Inaugural Address in 1933, Franklin D. Roosevelt stated that "[t]he only thing we have to fear is fear itself—nameless, unreasoning, unjustified terror which paralyzes needed efforts to convert retreat into advance." While FDR's statement has become a commonly used quote, its meaning is too easily forgotten. Fear is a powerful motivator that guides our behaviors and beliefs. This is evident within the criminal justice system; the fear of crime changes our daily lives and activities. Most of us would likely not go for a nighttime stroll alone in downtown Detroit without at least some apprehension! Moreover, fear also influences whether we will support certain criminal justice policies.

Fear, anxiety, and anger are all natural responses to conflict,[52] including criminal victimization. Fear of victimization arises from both direct and indirect experiences with crime. The media strongly influences our fear, as well as societal trends of fear (we will talk about this more in Chapter 5). Studies have shown that gender influences fear, with women tending to be more fearful of victimization regardless of the substantive crime involved. As a result, fear tends to affect their behavior more than it does the behavior of men.[53] Changes within the community can have a substantial effect on fear of crime, which can then result in increased social isolation and mistrust of neighbors.[54] Conversely, increased social ties can also *increase* fear of crime, due to improved communication of criminal events.[55] Moreover, fear of crime can instigate mo-bilization, which can then affect the population composition of an area.

There is no real way to measure the cost of fear—it is simply too abstract, and is most often indirect. Yet one can easily argue its indirect costs are immense. Fear drives society to support and implement reactive and more punitive methods of crime control, which costs money. While other emotions may influence punishments, fear is definitely a front-runner for driving costly policies such as "three-strikes" laws, zero tolerance in schools, and mandatory sentencing. We would like to claim that formal rationality that is based on research and statistics drive our decisions. In this case, however, fear most likely prevails.

## The Benefits of Crime

Although it can be somewhat of a controversial topic, when considering the costs of crime, we must also consider that crime may actually have **benefits**. It is hard to imagine how benefits can accrue from human misery, besides to those who commit crime. Yet the reality is that many people in society actually benefit from the presence of crime. For example, crime leads to jobs in police departments, prosecutors' offices, the courts, and in corrections. Further, the private security industry exists because people either actually need or perceive they need protection from criminals. Gun manufacturers often advertise their products as needed for self-defense, while crime is a staple of mass media—both electronic and print. Without crime, mass media would have to fill the empty space or time with other newsworthy events that attract viewers or readers. Lastly, criminals who make large sums of money will spend at least some of the money through legitimate transactions. A vendor may unwittingly be profiting from the ill-gotten gains of criminals.

In our analysis of the fixed costs of crime, we noted the vast expansion of criminal justice spending over the last twenty years. For every police or correctional officer who needs to be hired, the result is a person with a job. The uniforms they wear are manufactured by various companies. The firearms, Tasers, handcuffs, and other tools of the trade are likewise manufactured by different companies. Most of the vehicles that police officers drive are manufactured and produced by American automobile manufacturing companies, such as General Motors, Ford, and Chrysler. Prisons and jails do not appear out of thin air. Every facility had to be built and this meant construction jobs were created for thousands of workers. While most people would like to see drops in crime levels, if these drops are drastic, it could mean a reduced need for jail and prison space and fewer people employed by criminal justice agencies. Todd Clear and colleagues noted that many unions who represent police officers and correctional workers will often lobby state legislatures to pass legislation that criminalizes more behaviors or for tougher sentencing policies. More people who break the law and need to be supervised by the criminal justice system can mean stable employment for many workers.[56]

Erich Goode made a similar point about drug dealers. Although television commercials have presented drugs as a drain on the economy and as a source of the sponsorship of terrorism (which the drug trade is), as Goode noted, most drug dealers spend a lot of the money they make. This results in benefits such as sales of clothing, jewelry, motor vehicles, property, and many other items.[57] The recent movie *The Wolf of Wall Street* chronicled the life of convicted stockbroker Jordan Belfort. The movie has become somewhat controversial because of the decadent and often wasteful spending habits of the people depicted in the movie, made the worse by the fact the money was fraudulently obtained.

Squandering money that is not one's own is undoubtedly harmful. However, this could be approached differently. All of Belfort's lavish parties were catered by some company or restaurant, the drinks that were provided were bought with this fraudulently obtained money, yet some company profited. If done right, decadent entertainment required a division of labor. Thus, some companies and their employees legally profited off Belfort's fraudulence. The Eagles guitarist and hard-partier, Joe Walsh, in his song "Life's Been Good," made reference to his recklessness with few consequences. When he destroyed or damaged hotel property, it was easy for him to pay for the destruction. In fact, he employed people specifically for that purpose. Although the hotel room was damaged, someone later had to make repairs. The hotel might have been short a room for one night, as Walsh indicated; however, he probably paid for the room until it was in service again and for whoever the contractor was that was hired to complete necessary repairs.

# Conclusion

Obviously, we are not arguing that crime is "good" for society in either economic or moral terms. Yet many people *do* benefit from crime. More crime can lead to more jobs, considering that someone will need to arrest these new suspects. People who are arrested are entitled to a defense attorney, and there is also a prosecutor, judge, and bailiffs who get paid as well. If a person is convicted, they might either end up on probation, where they will be supervised by a probation officer, or incarcerated and supervised by corrections officers in a secure facility that someone had to build. Although financial crimes harm people and the economy, money, unless it was fictitious or literally set on fire, does not simply disappear. White-collar criminals will often "reinvest" the money someplace else, and while we may feel sorry for the people who had the money taken from them, someone else down the line that we often would not label a criminal might later profit. Crime can be a business, and sometimes, it helps if we consider it that way.

# Key Terms

- Direct or fixed costs of crime
- Speculative (or indirect) costs of crime
- Bureau of Justice Statistics
- Wal-Mart
- Ford Motor Company
- Uniform Crime Report
- Fear of crime
- Benefits of crime

# Key People

- Edwin Sutherland
- Bernie Madoff
- Ivan Krueger
- Mark Madoff

# Discussion Questions

1) In this chapter, we used both homicide and sexual assault to show some of the indirect costs of crime. Identify two other crimes and explain their indirect costs, and how they differ from their direct costs.
2) You discover that both violent and property crime rates have doubled in your hometown. Identify and explain how this would affect the costs and benefits of crime. Who will this crime surge harm? Who will this surge benefit? Make sure to explain your answers.
3) Imagine that you are a hotel owner and discover that during his stay, Kanye West managed to cause about $60,000 in damage. The room will need all

new furniture and the plumbing will need to be repaired. Who will this benefit? As the hotel owner, how do you benefit?

4) Compare the costs and profits of the criminal justice system to the costs and benefits of a major business, such as Wal-Mart. How are these costs similar?

5) How is the criminal justice system like a major business? How does it differ? Explain the role of fear of crime in determining the indirect costs of crime.

# Notes

1. McCollister, Kathryn E., Michael T. French, and Hai Fang. 2010. "The Cost of Crime to Society: New Crime-Specific Estimates for Policy and Program Evaluation." *Drug and Alcohol Dependence*, 108(1–2): 98–109.

2. Anderson, David A. 2012. "The Cost of Crime." *Foundations and Trends in Microeconomics*, 7(3): 209–265.

3. McCollister, Kathryn E., Michael T. French, and Hai Fang. (2010). "The Cost of Crime to Society: New Crime-Specific Estimates for Policy and Program Evaluation." *Drug and Alcohol Dependence*, 108(1–2): 98–109.

4. Stanley, Timothy J. 1995. "Radar Detectors, Fixed and Variable Costs of Crime." Retrieved on May 23, 2015 at: http://papers.ssrn.com/sol3/papers.cfm?abstract_id=219.

5. Hughes, Kristen A. 2006. *Justice Expenditure and Employment in the United States, 2003*. Washington, DC: U.S. Department of Justice.

6. Sourcebook of Criminal Justice Statistics: University at Albany. Retrieved on May 23, 2015 at: http://www.albany.edu/sourcebook/.

7. U.S. Department of Justice Overview. Retrieved on May 23, 2015 at: http://www.justice.gov/jmd/2014summary/pdf/fy14-bud-sum.pdf#bs.

8. U.S. Department of Homeland Security: Budget-in-Brief, Fiscal Year 2014. Retrieved on May 23, 2015 at: http://www.dhs.gov/sites/default/files/publications/MGMT/FY%202014%20BIB%20-%20FINAL%20-508%20Formatted%20%284%29.pdf.

9. United States Courts: Fiscal Year Funding and Cost Containment Initiatives. Retrieved on May 23, 2015 at: http://www.uscourts.gov/FederalCourts/UnderstandingtheFederalCourts/AdministrativeOffice/DirectorAnnualReport/annual-report-2012/fiscal-year-funding-cost-containment-initiatives.aspx#funding.

10. United States Census Bureau: State Government Finances. Retrieved on May 23, 2015 at: http://www.census.gov/govs/state/.

11. Hughes, Kristen A. 2006. *Justice Expenditure and Employment in the United States, 2003*. Washington, DC: U.S. Department of Justice.

12. The World's Biggest Companies. 2015. *Forbes*. Retrieved on May 23, 2015 at: http://www.forbes.com/global2000/list/.

13. Hughes, Kristen A. 2006. *Justice Expenditure and Employment in the United States, 2003*. Washington, DC: U.S. Department of Justice.

14. Reaves, Brian A. 2012. *Hiring and Retention of State and Local Law Enforcement Officers, 2008*. Washington, DC: U.S. Department of Justice.

15. Burch, Andrea M. 2012. *Sheriffs' Offices, 2007—Statistical Tables*. Washington, DC: U.S. Department of Justice.

16. Perry, Steven W. 2013. *Tribal Crime Data Collection Activities.* Washington, DC: U.S. Department of Justice.

17. Reaves, Brian A. 2008. *Campus Law Enforcement, 2004–05.* Washington, DC: U.S.

18. Durose, Matthew R., Kelly A. Walsh and Andrea M. Burch. 2012. *Census of Publicly Funded Forensic Crime Laboratories.* Washington, DC: U.S. Department of Justice.

19. Reaves, Brian A. 2009. *State and Local Law Enforcement Training Academies, 2006.* Washington, DC: U.S. Department of Justice.

20. Federal Law Enforcement Officers, 2008, NCJ 238250, June 2012.

21. U.S. Department of Justice Overview. Retrieved on May 23, 2015 at: http://www.justice.gov/jmd/2014summary/pdf/fy14-bud-sum.pdf#bs.

22. U.S. Department of Homeland Security: Budged-in-Brief, Fiscal Year 2014: Retrieved on May 23, 2015 at: http://www.dhs.gov/sites/default/files/publications/MGMT/FY%202014%20BIB%20-%20FINAL%20-508%20Formatted%20%284%29.pdf.

23. Reaves, Brian A. 2011. *Census of State and Local Law Enforcement, 2008.* Washington, DC: U.S. Department of Justice.

24. Reaves, Brian A. 2012. *Hiring and Retention of State and Local Law Enforcement Officers, 2008.* Washington, DC: U.S. Department of Justice.

25. Burch, Andrea M. 2012. *Sheriffs' Offices, 2007—Statistical Tables.* Washington, DC: U.S. Department of Justice.

26. Reaves, Brian A. 2008. *Census of State and Local Law Enforcement.* Washington, DC: U.S. Department of Justice.

27. *Ibid.*

28. Perry, Steven W. 2013. *Tribal Crime Data Collection Activities.* Washington, DC: U.S. Department of Justice.

29. Reaves, Brian A. 2008. *Campus Law Enforcement, 2004–05.* Washington, DC: U.S.

30. Durose, Matthew R., Kelly A. Walsh and Andrea M. Burch. 2012. *Census of Publicly Funded Forensic Crime Laboratories.* Washington, DC: U.S. Department of Justice.

31. Reaves, Brian A. 2009. *State and Local Law Enforcement Training Academies, 2006.* Washington, DC: U.S. Department of Justice.

32. Bureau of Labor Statistics: Occupational Employment Statistics. Retrieved on May 23, 2015 at: http://www.bls.gov/oes/current/oes_stru.htm#21-0000.

33. http://corporate.Wal-Mart.com/our-story/locations/united-states#/united-states/wyoming.

34. Hess, Alexander E.M. 2013. "The 10 Largest Employers in America." *USA Today.* Retrieved on May 23, 2015 at: http://www.usatoday.com/story/money/business/2013/08/22/ten-largest-employers/2680249/.

35. Schwartz, Gary T. 1991. "The Myth of the Ford Pinto Case." *Rutgers Law Review,* 43: 1013–1068.

36. McCollister, Kathryn E., Michael T. French, and Hai Fang. 2010. "The Cost of Crime to Society: New Crime-Specific Estimates for Policy and Program Evaluation." *Drug and Alcohol Dependence,* 108(1–2): 98–109.

37. Uniform Crime Reports: Murder. Retrieved on May 23, 2015 at: http://www.fbi.gov/about-us/cjis/ucr/crime-in-the-u.s/2012/crime-in-the-u.s.-2012/violent-crime/murder.

38. McCollister, Kathryn E., Michael T. French, and Hai Fang. 2010. "The Cost of Crime to Society: New Crime-Specific Estimates for Policy and Program Evaluation." *Drug and Alcohol Dependence,* 108(1–2): 98–109.

39. Olson, Kristin. 2001. "Comprehensive Justice for Victims of Pornography-Driven Sex

Crimes: Holding Pornographers Liable While Avoiding Constitutional Violation." *Oregon Law Review* 80: 1067–1105.

40. Uniform Crime Reports: Forcible Rape. Retrieved on May 23, 2015 at: http://www.fbi.gov/about-us/cjis/ucr/crime-in-the-u.s/2012/crime-in-the-u.s.-2012/violent-crime/rape.

41. McCollister, Kathryn E., Michael T. French, and Hai Fang. 2010. "The Cost of Crime to Society: New Crime-Specific Estimates for Policy and Program Evaluation." *Drug and Alcohol Dependence*, 108(1–2): 98–109.

42. Langton, Lynn, Marcus Berzofsky, Christopher Krebs and Hope Smiley-McDonald. 2012. *Victimizations Not Reported to the Police, 2006–2010*. Washington, DC: U.S. Department of Justice.

43. Koss, Mary P., Christine A. Gidycz, and Nadine Wisniewski. 1987. "The Scope of Rape: Incidence and Prevalence of Sexual Aggression and Victimization in a National Sample of Higher Education Studies." *Journal of Consulting and Clinical Psychology*, 55(2): 162–170.

44. Uniform Crime Reports: Robbery. Retrieved on May 23, 2015 at: http://www.fbi.gov/about-us/cjis/ucr/crime-in-the-u.s/2012/crime-in-the-u.s.-2012/violent-crime/robbery.

45. Uniform Crime Reports: Burglary. Retrieved on May 23, 2015 at: http://www.fbi.gov/about-us/cjis/ucr/crime-in-the-u.s/2012/crime-in-the-u.s.-2012/property-crime/burglary.

46. Uniform Crime Reports: Property Crime. Retrieved on May 23, 2015 at: http://www.fbi.gov/about-us/cjis/ucr/crime-in-the-u.s/2012/crime-in-the-u.s.-2012/property-crime/larceny-theft.

47. Uniform Crime Reports: Motor Vehicle Theft. Retrieved on May 23, 2015 at: http://www.fbi.gov/about-us/cjis/ucr/crime-in-the-u.s/2012/crime-in-the-u.s.-2012/property-crime/motor-vehicle-theft.

48. Geis, Gilbert and Colin Goff. 1983. "Introduction," pp. x–xxxiii. In Edwin H. Sutherland, *White Collar Crime: The Uncut Version*. New Haven, CT: Yale University Press.

49. Sutherland, Edwin H. 1940. "White-collar Criminality." *American Sociological Review*, 5: 1–12.

50. Henriques, Diana B. 2011. *The Wizard of Lies: Bernie Madoff and the Death of Trust*. London: Macmillian.

51. Sherwell, Philip and Richard Blackden. December 12, 2010. "Bernard Madoff's Massive Financial Swindle Claims its Latest Victim as his Son Mark Commits Suicide." *The Telegraph*. Retrieved on March 8, 2014 at: http://www.telegraph.co.uk/finance/financetopics/bernard-madoff/8196670/Bernard-Madoffs-massive-financial-swindle-claims-its-latest-victim-as-his-son-Mark-commits-suicide.html.

52. Freiburg, Arie. 2001. "Affective versus effective justice: Instrumentalism and emotionalism in criminal justice." *Punishment & Society*, 3: 265–277.

53. Valentine, Gill. 1989. "The Geography of Women's Fear." *Area, 21*(4): 385–390.

54. Ross, Catherine E. and Sung Joon Jang. 2000. "Neighborhood Disorder, Fear, and Mistrust: The Buffering Role of social ties with neighbors." *American Journal of Community Psychology, 28*(4): 401–420; Skogan, Wesley. (1986). "Fear of Crime and Neighborhood Change." In Albert Reiss and Michael Tonry. (Eds.) *Communities and Crime* (pp. 203–229). Chicago, IL: University of Chicago Press.

55. Ross, Catherine E. and Sung Joon Jang. 2000. "Neighborhood Disorder, Fear, and Mistrust: The Buffering Role of Social Ties with Neighbors. *American Journal of Community Psychology, 28*(4): 401–420.

56. Clear, Todd R., Michael D. Reisig, and George F. Cole. 2012. *American Corrections*. 10th Edition. Stamford, CT: Cengage.

57. Goode, Erich. 2012. *Drugs in American Society*. 8th Edition. New York: McGraw Hill.

# Chapter 5

# The Mythology (and Reality) of Crime and Justice in the United States

## Chapter Outline

## Learning Objectives

- Describe the role of mythmaking in American society
- Evaluate the power of the media in mythmaking
- Examine the effect that crime myths have on criminal justice policies
- Identify the role of moral panics in crime myths
- Assess the motivations behind mythmaking for various stakeholders

# Introduction

When someone mentions myths, one of the first things that might come to mind is the mythology of Ancient Greece. Tales of the gods, such as Zeus and his brothers and sisters overthrowing their parents (the Titans), have not only been depicted in popular culture (such as in the movie *Clash of the Titans*), but mythology is also frequently taught as literature in many high school and college classrooms.

Although seemingly just anachronisms today, mythology was important to ancient peoples because it provided them ways to understand the complexities of their world. For example, nearly every culture has its own creation myth that answers the basic question "how did we get here?" Importantly, myths such as the creation myth serve various functions. Not only do they help people answer questions about from where humans originated, but they influence people's frames of reference, impacting how they think about the world, their place in it, and the relationship they have with their surroundings.[1]

Today, people continue to seek answers to questions about the state of affairs in the world and their place in it. Human beings have the seemingly irrepressible need to understand and internalize what happens in the world around them. Stories, and the myths they contain, are thus used to help people "make sense" of an increasingly complex and interconnected world. As David Naugle has suggested, "[W]hat human beings think, say, and do emerge out of the basic stories that inform their lives. Overarching stories are necessary to make sense of the world as well as one's own life and social context."[2]

In the modern world, one way stories and the myths they contain find their way into social life is through urban legends. According to Annette Lesak:

> "[U]rban Legends are derived from the age-old tradition of folklore, or, the passing on of stories from groups and individuals ... "Urban" just means modern or current. These tales are often described as apocryphal, of questionable authority, or [as] fictitious. Many Urban Legends change over time as the teller ... inject[s] their own details, sometimes without even realizing it. Urban Legends are usually spread through word of mouth; however ... e-mail has vastly propelled the dissemination of some Urban Legends."[3]

Lesak suggested urban legends are "ridiculous, outrageous, and frightening," "can take another shape throughout the years and across many tellings," but possess at least a modicum of truth. With urban legends, the teller, rather than having experienced the event him- or herself has instead heard the story from someone else—a friend, or a friend of a friend. Urban legends usually possess a great many "friends of a friend," as the teller provides particulars about the events at the heart of the story. Ultimately, urban legends, as is true of other stories and legends, impart a lesson in morality (not necessarily of the deep "meaning of life" variety), are interpreted differently depending on the individual teller and listener, and are typically related to some issue in society: crime, sexuality, drugs, etc.[4] These legends can involve a serial killer who nearly kills a young couple who were "parking" or a psychopath who puts some form of poison on the top of a soda can. Parents may tell their children different tales of boogeymen who will abduct or kill them if the child goes to some hazardous place or tell stories of all the horrible things that happened to a person because they failed to study in school or experimented with alcohol, tobacco, or drugs.

## *Mythmaking*

Not only do humans tell stories to explain the current state of the world, we engage in mythology to justify our actions relating to various issues — some of which become the substance of urban legends. Americans like to think they are critical thinkers who can rise above myths, including those about crime and criminal justice. In actuality, Americans are fallible in not only believing myths, but also perpetuating them. For example, have you ever been in an informal argument or debate with someone and started exaggerating the facts to make your point? Perhaps you are discussing gun control and you support gun laws. You know that somewhere, at some time, you read an article stating that having a gun in the home puts the residents of that home at a greater risk of being killed with that same gun.[5] You do not remember the details of the study, where it was published, or to what extent guns in the home increases the risk. Making an argument for gun control using such ambiguous evidence would not be very impressive. So perhaps you replace the unknowns with "facts" to make your point. Some increase in risk becomes "two times more likely"; a study conducted at some time becomes a study conducted "within the last two years." Although it may seem harmless, you have played a role in disseminating information that may have *some* truth to it, but also some exaggeration. Just like a game of telephone, as this story is passed from person to person, the distinction between the truth and fiction becomes increasingly less discernible.

**Mythmaking** is also an important function of government. According to Murray Edelman, governments are inevitably entrusted with easing the anxiety of the citizens they serve.[6] While some governments are certainly better than others at protecting the safety and rights of their people, no government can promise complete security. Therefore, a government will engage in mythmaking to help calm the fears of its citizenry. *How* these myths are used, however, is entirely dependent upon those in power. For instance, one government may use myths to justify providing its citizens with greater rights than are enjoyed by citizens elsewhere, while a different government may use the same myths to justify repressing the rights of its citizens. Furthermore, mythmaking can be used to show preferential treatment to certain classes of people. As Edelman noted, many countries scapegoat their poor and state that the reason these people are poor is because they are "lazy." Such a myth not only provides a justification for why some people are poor, but overlooks the role of a country's elites as well as the role of government in contributing to the poverty of poor citizens.[7]

Criminal justice is routinely surrounded by mythology that takes many forms, in particular, "catch phrases." In some instances, myths become the foundation on which not only criminal justice policy but larger social policy is built. "Exceptionalism," "all people are created equal," and the "land of opportunity" are often used to describe the United States; yet these catch phrases mean different things to different people. Importantly, in some cases, these types of myths can be beneficial in some regards and harmful in others. Some people will view these myths as goals to strive for, and if they happen to fail and not meet a goal, they just need to try harder. On the other hand, some people see these myths as a complete farce and as cruel slogans designed to perpetuate a chronically unfair system. In a similar vein, mythology is not just used to perpetuate a system, but also is often used to justify certain policies. Laws such as "three-strikes laws" not only sound catchy, but there is the convenient baseball metaphor—if a law is based upon a slogan from America's pastime, it must be beneficial. Yet many three-strikes laws were passed in the 1990s, a time in the United States when crime was already declining.[8] Furthermore, these laws were based upon the premise that locking up "chronic" criminal offenders for longer periods of time would ultimately lead to a decrease in crime—an assertion that is subject to heavy debate among criminologists.[9] Additionally, many of the worst and most violent offenders in the United States were already serving long prison sentences because many states had already passed mandatory sentences for many types of crime during the 1980s and 1990s.[10] Thus, before we could even see the results on crime rates of three-strikes laws, the need for them quite possibly did not exist.

In Chapter 2, we discussed the work of **Emile Durkheim** and how he argued that societal norms are often reflected in the law. Durkheim also argued that crime was necessary ("functional") so that law-abiding citizens could see what would happen to them if they violated the law. Punishing criminal offenders reinforces the norms of a society and establishes firm boundaries between deviance and conformity.[11] According to **Robert Bohm**, Durkheim's argument was essentially that law served as the "**social glue**" that held society together. Thus, many people will argue if the law is not enforced, society may very well fall apart.[12] Yet, as discussed in Chapter 2, Bohm and others have argued that law is established by those in power to reflect their interests; they pick and choose what types of behavior should be prohibited. Therefore, if laws are arbitrarily enacted to further the interests of one group over another, myths will inevitably be created to legitimize those laws and crime control strategies associated with them.

Bohm believed that two unfortunate consequences often arise from the creation of **crime myths**. The first is they inspire short-term "quick fixes" to problems. For governments and politicians alike, it seems more important to *appear* they are solving a problem than *actually* formulating a well-crafted long-term solution. Knee-jerk reactions, however, can be problematic as they can have unintended consequences and actually cause more harm than good.[13] The second negative consequence of myth creation is that society may actually come to *believe* the myth that supported a policy.[14]

So, how does a crime myth come into existence? **Victor Kappeler** and **Gary Potter** described this process by examining the role of each contributing party: the public, the media, and politicians.[15] Robert Bohm broke these parties down further to include criminologists, criminal justice officials, and social elites. Each of us is familiar with a particularly horrific crime that has sparked public reaction. These events are typically rare, which is why the public is fascinated with them and therefore demands more information. The media plays its role by supplying enhanced coverage of the event, which in turn produces a public outcry for action. An abstract "call and response" occurs among the public, the media, and politicians. For instance, when a mass shooting occurs, the public is fearful, yet captivated. To satisfy this fascination, the media provides extensive coverage of the event, and integrates into its coverage the personal stories of victims as well as investigative angles in an effort to "get at the truth."[16]

Myths about crime and criminal justice are ubiquitous. Their abundance is attributable to a number of factors, all of which play a pertinent role. First, there are groups who facilitate the creation of crime myths and groups who perpetuate them, including politicians, media, individuals, and interest groups.[17]

What gives power and life to myths about crime and criminal justice are the emotions they generate, which become integrated within every aspect of mythmaking and myth-perpetuating. In particular, crime brings up emotions of fear, fascination, and anger, which creates the perfect breeding ground for mythmaking. The irony of crime myths is that their endurance within American society is partially due to a set of assumptions about crime and criminals. First, there is a general belief among people that crime is not normal, and that any crime, but particularly street crime, disrupts everyday life. Second is the notion that there are clear distinctions between "good" (victims) and "bad" (criminals) people. Lastly, there is an assumption that criminals victimize individuals who are pure and powerless.[18]

# Themes of Crime Myths

As Victor Kappeler and Gary Potter have documented, crime myths often include three common themes.[19] The first theme is one of *difference*. Crime myths are routinely developed around unpopular groups in society be they the poor, immigrants, or members of racial or ethnic minorities. For example, a commonly held myth about immigrants is that they "bring crime to our towns and cities."[20] In some instances, the myths involve straightforward racist or prejudicial beliefs about members of different groups. In other cases, myths develop around different subcultural groups—people who simply engage in patterns of behavior that those in the mainstream of life can neither relate to nor understand (e.g., "MS-13 gang members are participating in a 'gang initiation rite' wherein they rear-end a car from behind and then shoot the driver when he or she exits the vehicle to check for damage").

The second theme of crime myths often includes helpless or innocent victims who require additional protection, such as children or the elderly. Here, the presumption is that *all* crime victims are blameless, preyed upon by "bad" people (criminals). For example, one of the strongest myths in American culture is that children are innocent, in a moral sense. While many victims have never been involved in any criminal activity, there is a substantial overlap between victims and offenders. This gives rise to presumptions that children who are the victims of sexual predation, violence, theft, etc., did nothing to warrant the harm they suffered. While this is often true, a number of crime victims have engaged in criminal behavior themselves.

The third theme of crime myths, according to Kappeler and Potter, involves threatened societal values.[21] Such a theme is reminiscent of the ideas of Durkheim we discussed earlier and Bohm's concept of laws as the social "glue" of society.[22] Kappeler and Potter essentially argued that crime myths are centered on the concept of "society as we 'know' it" and the idea that there are predictable patterns in social life, that people know the difference between "right" and "wrong," and that most of the time, our lives are safe. Crime, however, threatens social order and could possibly destroy the world as we know it.[23]

## Crime Myths and the Media

While crime myths arise from many sources, one of the most common creators and perpetuators of crime myths are the media. The power that media enjoy is a frequent topic of criminological research.[24] Moreover, within the field of criminal justice, one cannot simply discount the impact (both negative and positive) the media has on outcomes including arrests, convictions, and sentences received by offenders. The criminal justice system and mass media share a symbiotic yet sometimes conflicting relationship. The media continually want information from those within the criminal justice system (the police, prosecutors, parole board members); however, they are often reluctant to give information back to the system. Yet, occasionally, the give and take relationship can work beautifully—the police use the media as a tool to gain information from the public, and the media is able to provide information the public desires. The media needs the criminal justice system, and the criminal justice system needs the media. While this is consistent, the timing of that need from both parties varies, giving one organization more power at any given time.

One frequent topic regarding the media is determining exactly what motivates media coverage of various events, including crimes. For instance, **Edward Herman** and **Noam Chomsky** have provided one of the more radical views of the media.[25] They argued the American media is essentially the mouthpiece of both the government and elites in the United States. Herman and Chomsky argued that the American media is essentially the propaganda machine of the government and frequently either disseminates messages from the government or fails to properly investigate when government claims could easily be debunked.[26] Other commentators, such as Leonard Downie and Robert Kaiser, have argued the media has a corrupting influence on American culture in the name of profit. Rather than serving as a guardian against government infringement upon citizens' rights, the American media are entirely dependent upon advertisers, which in turn are influenced by the number of viewers or readers a particular media outlet draws. The media has learned that "sensationalized" news is likely to attract viewers, who then attract advertisers, which then results in profits for the conglomerates that control most forms of media in the U.S.[27] The mass media has also learned that it must not offend advertisers for fear they will take their dollars elsewhere.[28]

**Erich Goode** provided a different take on mass media's role in generating crime news. Goode noted that different forms of media have different audiences. Everything from *The New York Times*, to *The Washington Post*, to ESPN, to *People* magazine, to local news programming has a different audience that media outlets are trying to reach. It is not necessarily that media outlets are ignoring certain topics and pushing a particular agenda; instead, they are simply trying to give their audience the type of news or programming they believe the audience wants.[29]

While criticizing the media is frequently a fun topic, the field of journalism strives to achieve high levels of professionalism. Journalists are supposed to be independent and neutral from the news they cover and are supposed to ensure that they comply with professional standards and ethics of the field. Yet questions have arisen about the neutrality of journalists as media have increasingly been moving from print form to the Internet, and as ever increasing numbers of "citizen journalists" create blogs, "report" and provide commentary on the news, blurring the lines between professional journalist and amateur.[30]

Regardless of the various motives of media, as Katherine Beckett and Theodore Sasson have stated, Americans seem to "have a love-hate relationship with crime." They argued Americans seem to be fascinated with crime and not only are crime stories among the most read, but Americans love stories about crime in popular media, such as television and movies. This interest in crime stories has made it the most common topic within American news media stories. Yet, according to Beckett and Sasson, this is not simply a case of the media just giving the American public what it wants. They documented that various government agencies, such as the National Institute on Drug Abuse and the Drug Enforcement Administration, frequently issue press releases about the danger of drugs hoping that the releases will receive ample attention from media. Additionally, not only does the media put too much focus on crime, but, according to Beckett and Sasson, the media most frequently report on what are statistically speaking the rarest crimes, including murder and rape. Furthermore, the media commonly contributes to the false perception that not only is crime on the rise, but criminals are engaging in ever-increasing numbers of bizarre and brazen crimes.[31]

As Victor Kappeler and Gary Potter argued, crime myths are created, persist over time, and have the power to influence attitudes, partly because of how American media covers crime stories. First, crime stories are ubiquitous, regardless of whether the source is electronic or print. This is particularly true for local news outlets, again whether print or electronic. Generally speaking, local media provide a steady stream of crime stories, particularly those involving violent crime—especially murder (the *least* commonly occurring serious crime) to meet the need for what Franklin Gilliam and Shanto Iyengar dubbed "action news."[32] Because crime news contributes disproportionately to news content, other newsworthy stories and issues are not given the same level of coverage. This results in media giving crime stories greater attention than they deserve. Additionally, crime stories typically include social contexts (e.g., the ghetto) or depictions (e.g., offenders as disproportionately young, African American males) that reinforce what Peter Berger and Thomas Luckmann termed the "**social construction of reality**."[33] Berger and Luckmann theorized that both objective knowledge (e.g., what *criminologists* know about crime) and subjective knowledge (e.g., what a particular *individual* knows about crime) are products of the society in which one lives, which includes the institutions that embody it and the individuals who embrace it.[34] Similarly, in helping to socially construct the reality of crime, media inadvertently reinforce depictions of social and economic conditions. In its rush to document the *crime du jour*, the media will often depict a certain type of crime as either "new" or increasing, but seldom is that the case. More often, media *reports* the behavior as new or increasing simply because the media had not previously given the issue any attention. Media stories often recount incidences of bizarre crimes and just as quickly move on to a new issue. Only in rare cases is there follow-up which includes a more mundane explanation of what was initially deemed "bizarre" behavior. Lastly, media exaggeration often generates fear among certain segments of the population. This not only reinforces the supposed "truth" of the coverage, but often ensures consumers will return for additional coverage of the event.[35]

## Moral Panics

It may seem as though sensationalized news stories are a modern phenomenon, but that is not the case. Although sensationalized crime stories have existed for some time, perhaps the first person to sociologically analyze media accounts was **Stanley Cohen** in 1972. In the first edition of his book *Folk Devils and Moral Panics*, Cohen discussed the fact that media attention paid to different groups was often both exaggerated and distorted. "**Folk devils**," according to Cohen, were created by media and the public, usually as scapegoats for a variety of perceived social ills. In turn, Cohen argued, a **moral panic** will occur when a problem or event is blown out of proportion. Cohen initially developed the concept to describe BBC depictions of riots occurring in the 1950s and 1960s between rival gangs of young males in London, the "Mods" and the "Rockers."[36] Cohen argued that UK media coverage of the fights turned the "mod" subculture into a negative symbol of delinquency and deviance. "Moral panics" have also been used to describe overreactions to and distortions of a plethora of issues including crime in general, child molestation, pedophile priests, undocumented immigrants, terrorism, flag desecration, and countless other issues.[37] Philip Jenkins even used a variation of the phrase when he coined the term "synthetic panics" to describe what he called "overzealous media accounts of designer drugs."[38]

## *The Myth of Crime Itself*

According to many scholars, one of the biggest myths perpetuated about the American criminal justice system is our notion of crime itself.[39] Beginning with Edwin Sutherland, who argued that there was often a distinction made in American society between "crime in the streets" and "crime in the suites," a long list of scholars have provided evidence that the criminogenic behavior of elites in the United States is traditionally dealt with through the civil courts—or dismissed altogether—while the behavior of street criminals is aggressively pursued in the criminal courts.[40] In later research, Sutherland documented how many of America's most well-respected corporations frequently engaged in illegal behavior.[41] As Robert Bohm has argued, the distinction between "**white-collar crime**" and "**street crime**" is a frequently repeated myth within the American criminal justice system.[42] Sutherland's original purpose was to illustrate that white-collar crime was far more costly to society in monetary terms than was street crime.[43] Future scholars, such as Marshall Clinard and Peter Yeager, would point out that not only did white-collar crime cost American society more from a monetary standpoint, but it resulted in more deaths and injuries as well.[44] Homicides that occur with a gun, knife, bomb, arson, vehicular manslaughter, etc., are fairly easy to document. Deaths resulting from the deliberate indifference of corporate owners or from regulatory failures are much harder to establish.[45] As Bohm noted, the first category of deaths are aggressively prosecuted in American criminal courts, while latter are often described as "accidents" and represent the myth that white-collar crime is nonviolent.[46]

## *The Myth of Criminal Groups*

Somewhat related to the notion that Americans arbitrarily pick and choose which behaviors should be considered criminal, Harold Pepinsky and Paul Jesilow have argued that crime myths often state that certain groups of people are more likely to be criminals and certain groups of people are more likely to be law-abiding citizens.[47] Along similar lines, Victor Kappeler and Gary Potter have argued that crime myths catalog various social actors into artificial distinctions between law-abiding citizens, criminals, crime fighters, and victims.[48] Perhaps the most well-known account of such a phenomenon comes from **Howard Becker** in his book *Outsiders*, where he discusses how **Harry Anslinger**, then Director of the Federal Bureau of Narcotics and Dangerous

Drugs (FBN), engaged in a public relations campaign during the 1930s that sought to expose the "dangers" of a relatively unknown plant at the time: marijuana. Anslinger spun fantastic tales describing how people who used marijuana became violent or went insane. He was particularly fond of telling one story of how a young man in his teens axe-murdered his entire family after smoking marijuana, leaving out the fact that the young man had a history of mental illness and violent outbursts. Additionally, Anslinger also recounted that users of marijuana were frequently from minority populations, especially blacks and recent immigrants from Mexico, while also identifying jazz musicians as among the main culprits of marijuana use. To illustrate, he told another fantastic story of a jazz piano player who could, while under the influence of marijuana, play faster than any human should. Becker argued these were nothing more than sensationalized stories, and there was nothing especially dangerous about marijuana or the people who smoked it. Instead, Becker argued that this was simply an instance of people in power having the ability to label certain behaviors—in this case, marijuana use—as "deviant." From Becker's perspective, there is nothing inherently deviant about *any* behavior. Rather, behavior only becomes *labeled* as deviant due to those in power having the ability to apply the label and those labeled as deviant not having the power to deflect it.[49]

Becker also used Anslinger as an example for a new term that Becker coined: **moral entrepreneur.** According to Becker, a moral entrepreneur is one who undertakes an initiative to create a rule about some social evil (e.g., drug use). The entrepreneur's motives may be to elevate the evil to the level of social problem that must be addressed; if successful, the crusade may then lead to the entrepreneur becoming a "professional" rule maker (e.g., being elected to public office or moving to a higher office).[50] Moral entrepreneurs help to create an "us versus them" narrative that clearly defines who should be considered deviant and who should be considered conformist. By creating this new form of deviance—"drug fiend" (or at least drawing attention to it)—Anslinger gave the public a boogeyman who needed to be fought. Who would fight this new boogeyman? Anslinger's fledgling agency, the FBN. In later years, the organization would be renamed something with which you are familiar: the Drug Enforcement Administration (DEA). However, as Richard Bonnie and Charles Whitebread noted, Anslinger did his job a little *too* well. As a result of media hysteria surrounding violent criminals using marijuana, a federal law was passed called the Marihuana Tax Act that essentially prohibited marijuana nationally (most states already had laws their own laws that prohibited the use of marijuana). Anslinger received the law he wanted, but several inventive defense attorneys started to use the defense of "marijuana insanity," which resulted in their clients either being found not competent to stand trial or not guilty by reason of insanity. Ultimately, Anslinger was horrified by this turn of events and immediately tried to get the media and government officials to downplay the harms of marijuana. It is not without irony that Anslinger needed to downplay the public hysteria he helped create.[51]

In addition to Blacks, jazz musicians, and Mexican immigrants being scapegoated for marijuana use, in the early 1900s Chinese immigrants were linked to smoking opium, and Blacks in the South were scapegoated for cocaine use (much as inner-city Blacks were scapegoated for crack cocaine use in the 1980s). During alcohol prohibition, Irish and German immigrants were often associated with heaving drinking. During the 1960s, young people involved in the counterculture movement would be associated with the use of hallucinogens such as LSD. Thus, it always seems there is some demographic group that needs blaming for their drug use. What is rarely discussed by social commentators, the media, or policymakers is that people who are poor and marginalized are easier targets for the *enforcement* of drug laws. If Becker is correct about power being crucial in the development of labels and in their enforcement, elites can use their power, status, and resources to access better lawyers and deflect efforts to label them as "criminals" because of their drug use. Further, elites have more and better access to sophisticated—and costly—drug treatment programs, which can also help minimize exposure to criminal labels, and thereby decrease the likelihood of them entering the criminal justice system.

## The Myth of the Crack Epidemic

While some moral panics can be used to target a specific segment of the public or for the benefit of a particular government agency, other moral panics spawn from the desire of the government and the media to ignore existing social conditions. During the 1980s, for example, the media, politicians, and social commentators warned of a "**crack epidemic**" that was destroying inner-city America. Crack cocaine, the crystal form of cocaine (which normally comes in powder form), is available in solid blocks or "crystals" that vary in color from yellow to pale rose or white. The blocks are then heated and smoked. "Crack" is so named because the crystalized cocaine makes a "crackling" or "popping" sound when heated.[52]

As media accounts revealed, not only did crack cocaine cause near instant addiction for users, the drug was responsible for a rash of homicides in the inner cities. Multiple "experts" feared the plague would soon spread to Middle America. As Craig Reinarman and Harry Levine argued, this fear was unfounded. Crack cocaine was no more abused than were many other drugs available at the time, and most of the violence associated with crack cocaine was in the form of street gangs fighting over turf where they could peddle the drug. The reason crack cocaine became such a problem was because inner cities had been decaying for a long time. These forgotten areas of America contained huge groups of marginalized citizens for whom legitimate job opportunities were lacking. According to Reinarman and Levine, crack cocaine was a catalyst, and the inner cities of America were in a poor state well before the drug arrived. The problem was that no one had bothered to notice. The fact that middle- and upper-class America rarely became involved with crack cocaine serves as a reminder that people wanted any excuse other than neglect for the plight of inner cities.[53]

## The Myth of Crack Babies

Along with the stories of how crack cocaine was destroying America's inner cities and eventually the rest of America were stories of what crack cocaine was going to do to America's next generation of inner-city children. Beginning in 1985, the media warned of a new danger that was associated with crack cocaine use: **crack babies**. According to the stories, children of pregnant crack cocaine users were being born with a range of health problems including premature birth, low birth weight, central nervous system problems, brain damage, and higher risk for Sudden Infant Death Syndrome (SIDS). According to Craig Reinarman and Harry Levine, the "crack baby" stories began with the publication in the *New England Journal of Medicine* of the results of a pilot study of a mere 28 women who had used cocaine during their pregnancy. Ira Chasnoff, the researcher who conducted the study, had given interviews to the media and provided warnings of "cocaine-damaged babies." He would later write, after a more comprehensive study, that he had never *seen* a so-called crack baby and believed he never would. However, media attention for the original story exploded, with some media outlets eventually claiming that "thousands of children" would be born with a wide-range of health defects, have low IQs, and need constant supervision and care. Some media stories claimed as many as 375,000 crack babies were born every year. One newspaper columnist predicted there would be a "biological underclass."[54] Lost in these stories was the fact many women who used crack cocaine came from impoverished backgrounds and lacked many basic necessities like access to competent neonatal care or drug treatment programs. They also abused other substances and were themselves the victims of domestic violence. Therefore, not only were media accounts of crack babies misleading in that they vastly overestimated the number of defective children that would be born to crack-using women in the United States, but the stories scapegoated one drug, crack cocaine, instead of a variety of social conditions, most of which stemmed from poverty and inequality.[55]

## The Myth of Stranger Danger

While some myths within the criminal justice system surround the *type of people* who are likely to engage in criminal behavior, many myths also exist about certain *types of criminals.* One of the best examples of myths that have arisen about criminal offenders involves sex offenders.

**Stranger danger** sums up the danger for children associated with adults whom they do not know. In particular, stranger danger is designed to warn children of pedophiles. Typical of such warnings is the suggestion by the National Crime Prevention Council that "parents can protect their children from dangerous strangers by teaching them about strangers and suspicious behavior, and by taking a few precautions of their own."[56] The problem is that there is scientific consensus that strangers are the least likely to sexually abuse children. Such abuse is far more likely to come from a member of the family or other trusted adult.

In recent years, the dangers associated with sex offenders and how to address their behavior has become an ongoing public policy and criminal justice issue. Like many other areas of criminal justice policy, sex offender legislation itself has a long, often contradictory, and inglorious history in the United States. In an interesting review of the history of sex offender legislation, Derek Logue described changes during the past 200 years in public policy relating to sex offenders.[57] He identified the current era of punitiveness, what he terms the "containment era" (c. 1980–present), as having begun in the late 1970s and early 1980s with a series of high-profile cases including, among others, the disappearance of Etan Patz in New York City in 1979; the John Wayne Gacy serial murders (which occurred between 1972 and 1978 in Illinois) and his trial and conviction in 1980; and the 1981 murder of Adam Walsh in Florida. Logue argued these cases formed a simple but effective narrative: "treat the victim, punish the offender." Single issue victim advocates like John Walsh, along with feminist groups, were loud participants in an increasingly public debate over sex offender policy in the United States, and were part of a larger "war on child molesters" that used mass media to voice their concerns and pressure both state legislatures and Congress to punish, not provide treatment to, sex offenders. Advocates like John Walsh, who founded the National Center for Missing and Exploited Children in 1984, propagated inflated, unverified, and largely unchallenged—but nonetheless influential—statistics that ultimately became the basis for public policy. Logue pointed out there was no room for debate—dissent from the predominant "feminist/victim advocate" view was responded to as being "pro-offender." Experts—even members of other victims' groups—who took a different tact were derided as "apologists for sex offenders" or accused of "devaluing" victims, which helped end the debate.

Logue suggested the 1980s and 1990s marked a return of the "sexual psychopath" view of offenders that held sway in the 1950s. No longer was differentiation made among different *types* of offenders; there was no such thing as a "petty" sex offense. *All* sexually deviant acts—no matter who the victim—were *equally traumatic* to victims, and definitions of abuse were broadened to include anything that made a person feel "uncomfortable," such as hearing sex talk. As a group, men were stereotypically cast as "potential predators," while the "patriarchal family" was a source of exploitation. "Molester" referred to *any* person, whether they had engaged in a single, isolated act of sexual abuse or multiple acts over an extended period. Even a brief sexual act with a willing participant (e.g., an underage partner) was deemed to result in irreparable, lifelong harm. Unlike previous eras, the image of the "monster" was unanimous and even included family members who sexually abused child relatives. These people were no longer dismissed as a "nuisance" or given treatment, but instead faced maximum punishment to "do right by victims." Treatment resources would now be directed to victims, not offenders.

Coinciding with this shift in societal beliefs was the trend of media sensationalism. Tabloid talk shows, sensational coverage of news stories at both the national and local level, "made-for-TV" movies with child abuse themes, and "true-crime" documentaries all played roles in establishing the new "sex offender as monster" paradigm. An explosion of awareness campaigns like the practice of posting missing children on milk cartons helped keep awareness of sexual abuse in the public spotlight.

Legislation regarding sex offender registries and community notification[58] illustrates the emphasis placed on emotion and fear. Many of the laws are named after a child victim of sexual abuse (Megan's Law, the Jacob Wetterling Act, and Dru's Law), and each law has a story behind it that includes a gruesome sexually violent crime committed against a child. Jill Levenson and Leo Cotter have argued that these laws are usually passed based on emotional responses to highly publicized, high profile cases and, therefore, lack adequate rationality.[59] Ironically, irrationality can be harmful to the enforcement of these laws and to the protection of sexually-abused children. Despite the fact that strangers are responsible for only about 3% of reported cases of sexual abuse of children, legislators have repeatedly characterized the pedophile as a stranger who incapacitated or kidnapped a child they did not know. Thus, the methods of preventing sexual assault of children are based on preventing rapes by strangers and not by grandfathers, fathers, or friends of the family, who are much more likely to be sexually abusing children.[60]

While there is certainly myth surrounding the stranger-danger element of sex offender laws, perhaps the widest-known myth involves the generally held belief that recidivism rates of sex offenders are extraordinarily high. One of the biggest challenges to validating this assertion is that partitioning sexual recidivism from general recidivism rates is difficult. Furthermore, there is no consistent operational definition of recidivism (new crimes, new arrests, new convictions, or new sentences). Studies that have examined recidivism rates of sex offenders demonstrate that rates of sexual offenders *sexually* reoffending are generally low.[61] This is problematic. The whole reason that society justifies further restrictions on sex offenders is that they are prone to commit further sex crimes. Although society probably does not want these people committing further crimes like petty theft, society does not subject *all* criminals to these types of restrictions. Richard Tewksbury and Wesley Jennings found that only a small number of sexual offenders who are released from prison are likely to recidivate by committing further sexual crimes. Thus, what is needed is better screening of which offenders are likely to commit further sexual crimes.[62] Furthermore, Richard Tewksbury and Matthew Lee found that studies have consistently demonstrated that the use of sex offender registries and community notification laws have had little to no effect on decreasing sex offender recidivism.[63]

# Conclusion

One of the most important concerns of criminology and criminal justice is challenging various myths that are spread by politicians, the media, and moral entrepreneurs. As we have demonstrated, crime myths are developed for a variety of reasons and serve various functions. Regardless of the rationale that supports a myth, it is important to deconstruct mythology in an effort to find the truth. Deconstructing *crime* mythology is important to not only defuse prejudice and other forms of injustice; at an even more basic level, mythology serves as justification for policies that do not work and often results in confusion over how people conceive crime. This confusion is crucial because whenever we consider reforms, we should try to ascertain why various policies did not work before moving on to another policy, which may very well be supported by knee-jerk reactions from people pushing various agendas.

# Key Terms

- Mythmaking
- Social glue
- Crime myths
- Social construction of reality
- *Crime du jour*
- Folk devils
- Moral panic
- White-collar crime
- Street crime
- Moral entrepreneur
- Crack epidemic
- Crack babies
- Stranger danger

# Key People

- Emile Durkheim
- Robert Bohm
- Victor Kappeler and Gary Potter
- Erich Goode
- Edward Herman and Noam Chomsky
- Stanley Cohen
- Howard Becker
- Harry Anslinger

# Discussion Questions

1. Provide three arguments that support sex offender registration and community notification laws. Then, provide three arguments against these policies.
2. There are numerous crime myths that were not mentioned in this chapter. Identify what you believe to be a crime myth and explain why. Be sure to describe the foundation and perpetuation of the myth.
3. Was there any crime myth in this chapter that surprised you? If so, identify what it was and what about it was surprising. If nothing surprised

you, try to guess what crime myth would be the most surprising and least surprising to American society. Explain why.
4.   What are moral panics? How do moral entrepreneurs further perpetuate myths? How does this affect criminal justice policymaking?
5.   What role does the media have in mythmaking? How do the media affect societal perceptions of crime?

# Notes

    1. Murtagh, Lindsey. n.d. "Common Elements in Creation Myths." Retrieved on March 24, 2015 at: http://dept.cs.williams.edu/~lindsey/myths/myths.html.
    2. Naugle, David. 1999. "Narrative and Life: The Central Role of Stories in Human Experience." Retrieved on March 26, 2015 at http://www3.dbu.edu/naugle/pdf/narrative_and_life.pdf.
    3. Lesak, Annette. 2005. "About Urban Legends." Retrieved on March 26, 2015 at: http://ccb.lis.illinois.edu/Projects/storytelling/alesak/aboutUL.htm.
    4. Whipps, Heather. 2006. "Urban Legends: How They Start and Why They Persist." *Live Science*. Retrieved on March 26, 2015 at: http://www.livescience.com/7107-urban-legends-start-persist.html.
    5. See, for example, Miller, Matthew and David Hemenway. 2008. "Guns and Suicide in the United States." *New England Journal of Medicine*, 359: 672–673.
    6. Edelman, Murray. 1998. "Language, Myths and Rhetoric." *Society*, January/February: 131–139.
    7. *Ibid.*
    8. Walsh, Jennifer. 2007. *Three Strikes Laws*. Westport, CT: Greenwood Press.
    9. Auerhan, Kathleen. 1999. "Selective Incapacitation and the Problem of Prediction." *Criminology*, 37(4):703–734.
    10. Tonry, Michael. 1999. "Why are U.S. Incarceration Rates so High?" *Crime & Delinquency* 45(4): 419–437.
    11. Durkheim, Emile. 1964. *The Division of Labor in Society*. New York: Free Press of Glencoe. Original work published in 1893.
    12. Bohm, Robert M. 1986. "Crime, Criminal and Crime Control Policy Myths." *Justice Quarterly*, 3(2): 193–214.
    13. Tonry, Michael. 2009. "The Mostly Unintended Effects of Mandatory Penalties: Two Centuries of Consistent Findings." *Crime and Justice*, 38(1): 65–114.
    14. Bohm, Robert M. 1986. "Crime, Criminal and Crime Control Policy Myths." *Justice Quarterly*, 3(2): 193–214.
    15. Kappeler, Victor E. and Gary W. Potter. 2005. *Mythology of Crime and Criminal Justice*. Long Grove, IL: Waveland Press.
    16. Bohm, Robert M. 1986. "Crime, Criminal and Crime Control Policy Myths." *Justice Quarterly*, 3(2): 193–214.
    17. Kappeler, Victor E. and Gary W. Potter. 2005. *Mythology of Crime and Criminal Justice*. Long Grove, IL: Waveland Press.
    18. Ibid.

19. *Ibid.*

20. American Civil Liberties Union. 2008. "Immigration Myths and Facts." Retrieved on March 27, 2015 at: https://www.aclu.org/immigrants-rights/immigration-myths-and-facts.

21. Kappeler, Victor E. and Gary W. Potter. 2005. *Mythology of Crime and Criminal Justice.* Long Grove, IL: Waveland Press.

22. Bohm, Robert M. 1986. "Crime, Criminal and Crime Control Policy Myths." *Justice Quarterly,* 3(2): 193–214.

23. Kappeler, Victor E. and Gary W. Potter. 2005. *Mythology of Crime and Criminal Justice.* Long Grove, IL: Waveland Press.

24. See, for example, Surette, Ray. 2014. *Media, Crime and Criminal Justice* (5th ed.). Independence, KY: Cengage Learning.

25. Herman, Edward S. and Noam Chomsky. 2008. *Manufacturing Consent: The Political Economy of the Mass Media.* New York: Random House.

26. Herman, Edward S. and Noam Chomsky. 2008. *Manufacturing Consent: The Political Economy of the Mass Media.* New York: Random House.

27. See, for example, Noam, Eli. 2009. *Media Ownership and Concentration in America.* New York: Oxford University Press.

28. Downie, Jr., Leonard and Robert G. Kaiser. 2002. *The News about the News: American Journalism in Peril.* New York: Alfred Knopf.

29. Goode, Erich. 2012. *Drugs in American Society.* 8th Edition. New York: McGraw Hill.

30. Vos, Tim P., Stephanie Craft, and Seth Ashley. 2012. "New Media, Old Criticism: Bloggers Press Criticism and the Journalistic Field." *Journalism,* 13(7): 850–868.

31. Beckett, Katherine and Theodore Sasson. 2004. *The Politics of Injustice: Crime and Punishment in America.* 2nd Edition. Thousand Oaks, CA: SAGE.

32. Gilliam, Franklin and Shanto Iyengar. 2000. "Prime Suspects: The Influence of Local Television News on the Viewing Public." *American Journal of Political Science,* 44(3):560–573.

33. Berger, Peter and Thomas Luckmann. 1966. *The Social Construction of Reality: A Treatise in the Sociology of Knowledge.* New York: Penguin Putnam, Inc.

34. *Ibid.*

35. Kappeler, Victor E. and Gary W. Potter. 2005. *Mythology of Crime and Criminal Justice.* Long Grove, IL: Waveland Press.

36. Cohen, Stanley. 2002. *Folk Devils and Moral Panics.* 3rd Edition. New York: Routledge.

37. Goode, Erich and Nachman Ben-Yehuda. 2009. *Moral Panics: The Social Construction of Deviance.* 2nd Edition. Malden, MA: Wiley-Blackwell.

38. Jenkins, Philip. 1999. *Synthetic Panics: The Symbolic Politics of Designer Drugs.* New York: NYU Press.

39. Bohm, Robert M. 1986. "Crime, Criminal and Crime Control Policy Myths." *Justice Quarterly,* 3(2): 193–214.

40. Sutherland, Edwin. 1940. "White-Collar Criminality." *American Sociological Review,* 5(1): 1–12.

41. Sutherland, Edwin. 1983. *White Collar Crime: The Uncut Version.* New Haven, CT: Yale University Press.

42. Bohm, Robert M. 1986. "Crime, Criminal and Crime Control Policy Myths." *Justice Quarterly,* 3(2): 193–214.

43. Sutherland, Edwin. 1940. "White-Collar Criminality." *American Sociological Review,* 5(1): 1–12.

44. Clinard, Marshall B. and Peter C. Yeager. 2009. *Corporate Crime*. New Brunswick, NJ: Transaction Publishers.

45. *Ibid.*

46. Bohm, Robert M. 1986. "Crime, Criminal and Crime Control Policy Myths." *Justice Quarterly*, 3(2): 193–214.

47. Pepinsky, Harold E. and Paul Jesilow. 1984. *Myths that Cause Crime*. Cabin John, MD: Seven Locks Press.

48. Kappeler, Victor E. and Gary W. Potter. 2005. *Mythology of Crime and Criminal Justice*. Long Grove, IL: Waveland Press.

49. Becker, Howard S. 1963. *Outsiders: Studies in the Sociology of Deviance*. New York: The Free Press.

50. Becker, Howard S. 1963. *Outsiders: Studies in the Sociology of Deviance*. New York: The Free Press.

51. Bonnie, Richard and Charles H. Whitebread, II. 1999. *The Marijuana Conviction: A History of Marijuana Prohibition in the United States*. 2nd Edition. New York: The Lindesmith Center.

52. "What is Crack Cocaine?" Retrieved March 28, 2015 from http://www.drugfreeworld.org/drugfacts/crackcocaine.html.

53. Reinarman, Craig and Harry G. Levine. 1997. "The Crack Attack: Politics and Media in the Crack Scare." Pp. 18–51 in Craig Reinarman and Harry G. Levine (eds.), *Crack in America: Demon Drugs and Social Justice*. Los Angeles: University of California Press.

54. The quote is generally attributed to *Washington Post* columnist Charles Krauthammer. See, for example, Vargas, Theresa. 2010. "Once Written Off, Crack Babies Have Grown Into Success Stories." *The Washington Post*. Retrieved March 28, 2015 from http://www.washingtonpost.com/wp-dyn/content/article/2010/04/15/AR2010041502434.html.

55. Reinarman, Craig and Harry G. Levine. 2004. "Crack in the Rearview Mirror: Deconstructing Drug War Mythology." *Social Justice*, 31: 182–199.

56. Retrieved March 28, 2015 from http://www.ncpc.org/topics/violent-crime-and-personal-safety/strangers.

57. Logue, Derek. 2012. "Monsters Inc.: A Concise History of Sex Offender Laws." Retrieved March 28, 2015 from http://www.oncefallen.com/history.html. Logue relied on multiple sources, particularly Philip Jenkins' (1998) *Moral Panic: Changing Perceptions of the Child Molester in America* and Chrysanthi Leon's (2011) *Sex Fiends, Perverts, and Pedophiles: Understanding Sex Crime Policy in America*.

58. Bedarf, Abril (1995). "Examining Sex Offender Community Notification Laws." *California Law Review, 83*: 885–939.

59. Levenson, Jill and Leo Cotter. 2005. "The Effects of Megan's Law on Sex Offender Reintegration." *Journal of Contemporary Criminal Justice*, 21(1): 49–66.

60. Garfinkle, Elizabeth. 1993. "Coming of Age in America: The Misapplication of Sex-Offender Registration." *California Law Review*, 91: 163–208.

61. Adkins, Geneva, David Huff, P. Stageberg, L. Prell and S. Musel. 2000. *The Iowa Sex Offender Registry and Recidivism*. Des Moines, IA: Iowa Department of Human Rights; Garfinkle, Elizabeth. 1993. "Coming of Age in America: The Misapplication of Sex-Offender Registration." *California Law Review,* 91: 163–208 Tewksbury, Richard and Wesley G. Jennings. 2010. "Assessing the Impact of Sex Offender Registration and Community Notification on Sex-Offending Trajectories." *Criminal Justice and Behavior*, 37(5): 570–582.

62. Tewksbury, Richard and Wesley G. Jennings. 2010. "Assessing the Impact of Sex Offender Registration and Community Notification on Sex-Offending Trajectories." *Criminal Justice and Behavior*, 37(5): 570–582.

63. Tewksbury, Richard and Matthew B. Lees. 2007. "Perceptions of Punishment How Registered Sex Offenders View Registries." *Crime & Delinquency*, 53(3): 380–407.

Chapter 6

# The Politicization of Crime and Justice in the United States

## Chapter Outline

- Introduction
  - Criminal Justice Interest Groups
  - Research on Criminal Justice Interest Groups
  - Policymaking and Interest Groups
- Single-Issue Interest Groups
  - Mothers against Drunk Driving (MADD)
  - Amethyst Initiative
  - Clery Center for Security on Campus
  - Firearm Advocacy Groups
  - National Rifle Association
  - Handgun Control, Inc.
- General Interest Groups
  - American Civil Liberties Union (ACLU)
  - Southern Poverty Law Center (SPLC)
  - Amnesty International
  - RAND Corporation
  - The Heritage Foundation
- Conclusion
- Key Terms
- Key People
- Discussion Questions

## Learning Objectives

- Describe research conducted on the relationship between criminal justice policymaking and interest groups
- Define single-issue, general-issue, and employee-union interest groups

- Identify major single- and general-issue interest groups
- Classify various interest groups as single or general issue
- Evaluate the role of interest groups within criminal justice policymaking
- Assess the advantages and disadvantages of interest groups within the criminal justice system

# Introduction

Criminal justice policy is not established in a vacuum. In fact, legislation that establishes criminal justice policy is not typically passed without some degree of fanfare. Many laws are enacted with a public signing by a chief executive, whether the president of the United States or a state governor. In some instances, a chief executive who signed a law may do so alone. Many times, however, others who played a role in getting the legislation enacted will appear at the signing ceremony and possibly even be acknowledged. Sometimes these guests will be legislators who either co-sponsored the bill that became law or played some active role in getting the bill through the legislature. In addition to legislators, various "concerned citizens" might appear as special guests at these events or as spectators in the gallery. These people range from crime victims to advocates for crime victims to representatives from lobbying groups interested in having the legislation passed. These concerned citizens and lobbying groups are often effective at bringing attention to an issue and in some cases may dramatically affect the creation or evolution of criminal justice policy.

## *Criminal Justice Interest Groups*

As we noted in Chapter 2, many criminological theories account for the presence of **interest groups**. Indeed, interest groups seem to be at the very heart of conflict theory, which argues that society is littered with interest groups that are continually competing for power. Yet criminological theory tends to speak of interest groups in ambiguous terms, such as power elites, impoverished minority groups, and similar groups that seem to revolve around some measure of socioeconomic status. Many of these concepts are interesting, but it is hard to point to the effectiveness of these vaguely defined interests without first trying to develop a more concrete definition of the types of group of people who attempt to affect criminal justice policy.

## Research on Criminal Justice Interest Groups

Seeking to describe criminal justice interest groups in more concrete terms, **Erika Fairchild** conducted a review of the existing literature in 1981. The results of Fairchild's review demonstrated that very few studies in criminology and criminal justice analyzed the impact of interest groups on criminal justice policy. She found this odd, considering studies of the effect of interest groups on policy are quite common in political science. Fairchild noted that within the few studies that actually did analyze the impact of interest groups and criminal justice policy, the analysis was most often tangential to the main purpose of the research. However, Fairchild noted that interest groups tended to fall into two opposing positions, a law-enforcement lobbying group and a civil liberties group. The law enforcement lobbying group comprises prosecutors and law enforcement officers, while the civil liberties lobbying group is typically composed of the American Civil Liberties Union and other various lobbying groups that support the rights of people who have been convicted of violating the law. Although Fairchild was unable to make any general conclusions due to the limited number of studies, she did make note of three observations regarding interest groups and criminal justice policy. The first was that interest groups that are professionally concerned with criminal justice policy (bar associations, prosecutors and criminal defense attorneys, law enforcement groups, corrections officials, and judges) seemed to have the most effect on policy. The second observation was that the presence (or absence) of interest groups and the agenda these groups supported was largely representative of the political climate within localities and states. For instance, if a state had a more punitive policy towards criminal justice, it was likely there would be more lobbying groups that reflected this perspective. Fairchild's last observation was that new criminal legislation was typically developed by small groups of people, legislation tended to reflect the values of the community, and legislation did not seem to produce much controversy. However, Fairchild qualified her third observation, noting that many of the studies had not comprehensively considered the effect of public opinion on the creation of legislation.[1]

In 2002, **Barbara Ann Stolz**, reached a similar conclusion to the one Fairchild had reached twenty years before. Stolz argued that a comprehensive study of the role of specific interest groups in society was typically reserved for political science and was still quite rare in criminological and criminal justice research. In her research, Stolz identified a multitude of ways in which interest groups participate in the policymaking process: "(1) testify at legislative hearings; (2) provide information or draft legislation to political officials; (3) communicate with public officials through letter writing campaigns by their membership; (4) meet and advise public officials and/or their staff; (5) participate in organized demonstrations; or (6) (hopefully, less frequently) offer bribes."[2] In subsequent research, Stolz documented how various groups, which she referred to as "nonprofessional criminal justice interest groups," educated the public and legislature until the eventual passage of the federal Victims of Trafficking and Violence Protection Act of 2000. Stolz argued that these groups, who were not traditionally interested in criminal justice policy, played a significant role in educating criminal justice policymakers, both about the scope of the problem caused by human trafficking and about the legislative and policy actions that would be needed to help combat the problem.[3]

More recently, Randall Sheldon described the role of interest groups in influencing criminal justice policy in California. Sheldon identified the American Legislative Exchange Council (ALEC) as one of the foremost interest groups influencing criminal justice policy not only in California but nationally. According to Sheldon, ALEC "demonstrates the classic connections between politics, economics and the criminal justice system. The membership consists of private corporation executives, criminal justice officials, and more than one-third of state lawmakers in the country, most of whom are Republicans or conservative Democrats. Several major corporations and corporate foundations contribute money to ALEC."[4]

Sheldon indicated that until recently, ALEC included a "Criminal Justice Task Force" that drafted "model bills" on criminal justice policy (e.g., such issues as three-strikes laws, truth in sentencing, "stand your ground," and mandatory sentencing). Apparently, that group was abolished and replaced with a new group designated the "Public Safety and Elections" task force. This new task force is charged with developing model policies to reduce crime and violence while ensuring integrity and efficiency in the electoral process. Sheldon identifies key members of the new group as including Laurie Shanblum, who is senior director of business development for the Corrections Corporation of America (CCA), the world's largest private prison corporation (CCA is also a member of ALEC). The American Bail Coalition—dedicated to the long-term growth and longevity of the bail bond industry—also has a seat on the Public Safety and Elections task force and is an active member of ALEC. According to data collected by Sheldon from the Lobby Watch project by the Center for Public Integrity, between 1998 and 2004, 1,243 different companies engaged in lobbying efforts in California related to crime, law enforcement, and criminal justice. CCA had the most filings (n=64) and spent some $6.5 million in support of those filings with state legislators. The Arizona Justice Project (AJP)—a public interest "innocence project" that provides counsel for inmates convicted of capital crimes in Arizona—had 38 filings and spent over $2 million in support of them between 1998 and 2004. Other significant activities included filings by the **National Rifle Association** (**NRA**) and **Taxpayers Against Fraud**, which, combined, spent nearly $15 million in support of their filings.[5]

## Policymaking and Interest Groups

Although Stolz described the ways in which lobbying groups influence policy, we would like to develop her criteria in more detail. The most basic way interest groups affect the policymaking process is simply through lobbying of individual legislators. This can be accomplished through a variety of methods, such as writing letters/sending emails or using social media to advance their cause to members of government. Additional tactics include various forms of protest against current policy and direct face-to-face meetings with government officials. Furthermore, interest groups may donate money directly to candidates' political campaigns or to political action committees (known as PACs) that support one or more candidates running for public office. They may also actively campaign for candidates sympathetic to their agendas. Sometimes interest groups will develop model legislation for issues that are salient to them (as illustrated above with ALEC) and may actually have some part of this model legislation incorporated into proposed bills or final legislation. Whenever legislation is being considered, whether at the state level or in Congress, public hearings are often conducted that will identify an issue and possible solutions to it. These hearings are often more spectacle than substance and are used by legislators to directly appeal to the public and show them that legislative bodies are actually working toward solving problems. At many of these hearings, members of interest groups testify and offer various rationales or evidence as to why legislation is needed. Such an action can serve a dual function: not only are interest group members contributing an opinion toward pending legislation, they are able to directly lobby to the public through these hearings, as in many cases the events are televised.[6]

Although there are probably several ways one could organize criminal justice interest groups, we believe these groups can be characterized as *single-issue groups*, *general interest groups*, and *employee unions*. As the name implies, single-issue groups typically focus on one issue (e.g., capital punishment) or a very narrow set of issues (e.g., providing counsel for indigents). Conversely, general interest groups typically have a universal philosophy that spans multiple issues affecting criminal justice. Lastly, employee union interest groups represent various issues within criminal justice policy that are salient to people who work in the criminal justice system. Criminal justice employee union interest groups will be discussed in chapters 7–9.

# Single-Issue Interest Groups

## Mothers Against Drunk Driving (MADD)

Perhaps the best known of all criminal justice single-issue interest groups is **Mothers Against Drunk Driving**, or **MADD**, as most people refer to the group. Founded in 1980, the organization has been credited with transforming American attitudes concerning the dangers of drunk driving.[7] In her analysis, Stolz made specific reference to MADD as transforming Americans' attitudes towards drunk driving from behavior that was a public nuisance to behavior that became a crime.[8] As James Fell and Robert Voas noted, MADD's agenda was not novel. Awareness that drinking and driving was dangerous began in the early 20th century, and the first studies that found a link between increased blood alcohol concentration (BAC) and diminished driving ability were published in the 1930s. Furthermore, the first practical alcohol breath-testing device was invented by **Robert Borkenstein** in 1954. Yet, in American society, most people believed that automobile crashes were infrequent occurrences and largely attributable to human error, and most states that allocated law enforcement resources to drunk driving focused mostly on severely impaired drivers.[9]

In the United States, policy shifts in criminal justice policy often follow tragedy, and this was certainly the case for the creation of MADD. In 1980, **Candy Lightner**, a Sacramento realtor and mother of three, lost her thirteen-year-old daughter Cari to a drunk driver. Cari had been walking with a friend in a bike lane when she was struck from behind by an automobile driven by Clarence Busch. The police determined that Busch was intoxicated when he struck Cari; Busch also had four previous arrests for driving under the influence of alcohol, including an arrest two days before the fatal accident. After a police officer informed Candy Lightner that Busch would most likely face lenient punishment, Ms. Lightner decided to try to do something to prevent other parents from going through what she had experienced and believed a grassroots organization representing the victims of drunk drivers could make a difference. Thus, MADD was born.[10] While often considered the originator of the "get tough" campaign on drunk drivers, MADD was not the first advocacy group to advocate harsher punishments in an effort to curb drunk driving. In 1978, Doris Aiken founded Remove Intoxicated Drivers (RID) in New York.[11]

In an analysis of Candy Lightner's efforts and the development of MADD, **Frank Weed** argued that Ms. Lightner successfully brought to the policy table what others to that point had failed to do.[12] First, she had suffered a horrible loss—her daughter had been killed by a drunk driver. Second, Candy Lightner represented what Frank Weed referred to as "charismatic leadership." Weed argued that Lightner's credibility as a victim and the charismatic leadership she brought to MADD made her highly effective and many people were eager to follow her. After Cari's death, Lightner quit her job and founded the first chapter of MADD in August of 1980. Within a year, Lightner established other chapters throughout California. By May of 1981, MADD had become a national advocacy group and was recognized by the Internal Revenue Service as a tax-exempt organization. According to Weed, Lightner established herself as a crime victim and demanded action. Furthermore, she called on others who had lost family members to crashes involving drunk drivers and granted these people free membership in the organization.[13]

Candy Lightner has described her efforts as being driven by emotion—a mix of anger and grief—and a belief she could make a difference in policy. She also blamed what she perceived as a lax judicial system for failing to adequately punish people who drove while intoxicated. Using those motivations, she became a convincing lobbyist and not only learned how politics worked, but also became a constant presence on television whenever the issue of drunk driving was discussed. Her effectiveness became evident in 1982 when President Reagan established a National Commission Against Drunk Driving and appointed Lightner to the commission's board of directors. Her life even became the subject of a NBC "made-for-TV" movie that aired in March of 1983. She became a nationally known figure, and because of her leadership and the work of people in MADD, drunk driving laws were created in states that lacked such legislation and that legislation gradually got stricter. By the time Lightner ultimately left the organization in 1985, there were 360 local chapters of MADD, which included 600,000 members and donors.[14]

Frank Weed argued that MADD's success seemed strongly correlated with its association with people identified as victims of drunk driving. In a study Weed conducted in 1991, he found that failing to recruit drunk-driving victims in local MADD chapters was a significant cause of chapter failure. Additionally, to remain active, local chapters seemed to require a constant and visible activist agenda. Otherwise, local chapters had difficulties in fundraising.[15] Fundraising was a repetitive issue with MADD, and the organization was cited for running afoul of National Charities Information Bureau guidelines by spending more than 70% of its income for additional fundraising. Additionally, Candy Lightner's place on the board of directors as a victim-advocate eventually created conflict within the organization. Lightner believed that MADD was essentially an extension of herself, and members of MADD were routinely conflicted by Lightner's autocratic leadership style and the belief that the organization was indebted to Lightner for its rapid growth. Ultimately, Lightner's personality became too divisive. Additionally, her practice of taking money from the organization and paying it back later, along with increasing salary demands, led to her ultimately not having her contract with the organization renewed.[16]

Obviously, MADD did not end with the departure of Lightner. While there are certainly other parties who played a role, according to James Fell and Robert Voas, MADD can take credit not only for raising awareness of the problems of drunk driving, but also for the near universal consensus among states that a BAC of .08 is evidence of drunk driving, for the national minimum drinking age of 21, and for the existence of zero tolerance laws (where a BAC of .01 or .02 is enough to convict underage drinkers who drink and drive).[17] Thus, it seems as if the organization accomplished the goals it set. Public awareness of drunk driving has significantly increased, as have the penalties for people who are caught driving under the influence, especially those found to be intoxicated after causing deaths or injuries to others. These occurrences are no longer viewed as just accidents, but willful violations of criminal laws that can result in significant prison time for those convicted. Yet, as Martin Wooster argued, not all of the credit should be given to MADD for changes in the laws. With the general aging of the United States population, there is a lower percentage of younger people on the roads—the most likely demographic to drink heavier and engage in riskier behaviors. Additionally, although highway fatalities have *decreased* significantly since the early 1980s, automobile safety has *increased* significantly, as have the number of drivers and passengers who wear seat belts.[18]

Lonn Lanza-Kaduce and Donna Bishop noted, "We are not arguing either that drunk driving is unproblematic or that drunk driving is a moral act. We too would like to prevent the death, injury and property damage incurred in alcohol-related accidents. However, we are directly challenging the empirical and logical basis, and therefore, the justice, of much of our criminal law on drunk driving."[19] Among the problems that Lanza-Kaduce and Bishop noted is the perceived risk of drunk driving. As they noted, the chances of being involved in an accident while driving intoxicated are 4.5 for every 10,000 drunk driving trips, and the risk of being involved in a fatality are 1 in 330,000 miles of impaired driving. Drunk driving has been marketed as a high-risk endeavor, yet statistics do not seem to back that claim. Additionally, if a person is in an accident while driving under the influence of alcohol, it is presumed that they are responsible for the accident—without any showing of proof that the intoxicated driver *actually caused the accident.* Along similar lines, Lanza-Kaduce and Bishop argued that the .10 BAC that was the standard line of demarcation for drunk driving is only a measure of impairment and does not definitively state with accuracy if a person who registers that BAC is *actually* intoxicated. Relying on such a number as de facto proof essentially flies in the face of the traditional standard burden of proof within American criminal courts that guilt must be proven "beyond a reasonable doubt." Lastly, drunk driving is a crime itself because of the possibility that a person *could* cause harm to others. Yet the law imputes this seemingly dangerous action as a crime in and of itself, even though a person has not caused any harm and most likely does not intend to commit any.[20]

In some ways, MADD might be a victim of its own success. As Martin Wooster noted, in 1987, MADD was invited to be a coalition member of groups that opposed proposed increases on interstate highways of speed limits above 55 miles per hour. At that time, Norma Phillips, who was the president of MADD, declined to participate. She believed that the full resources of MADD needed to be devoted to the mission of the group, that of combating drunk driving. Additionally, Wooster argued in 2000 that the then-current agenda of MADD seemed to reflect an attitude calling for further minimization of the use of alcohol in American society. MADD even sought to obtain funds from the Office of National Drug Control Policy (ONDCP) by arguing that the problems associated with alcohol in American society rivaled those associated with illegal drugs. Barry McCaffrey, then the administrator of ONDCP, argued that the agency did not have the authority to provide MADD with the funds it had requested because reducing alcohol use and abuse was not part of ONDCP's mission. Afterwards, an effort by Congress to include alcohol within the ONDCP's mission was defeated. MADD has lobbied for increases in taxes on alcohol as well as campaigned for taxes on beer to be commensurate with taxes on hard liquor. MADD lobbied the hospitality industry to end all practices that encourage excessive alcohol consumption and in 1999, MADD joined the National Beer Wholesalers Association in support of a bill in Congress that would have allowed prosecution of companies shipping alcohol to states that prohibited the ordering of alcohol through the mail or via the Internet. MADD originally supported the legislation because the organization believed the law would curb underage drinking; however, MADD ultimately withdrew support after deciding that this was a fight between the Wine Institute and the National Beer Wholesalers Association.[21]

While few people have questioned the agenda of MADD regarding drunk driving, some people have questioned the efficacy of maintain a minimum drinking age of 21. In 1989, shortly after the state of Florida raised the state drinking age from 19 to 21, Lonn Lanza-Kaduce and Pamela Richards argued that a law that may have been passed with the best of intentions may not have produced the results legislators were hoping to find. They argued that drinking alcohol is a common and powerful symbol of adulthood and just because the law prohibits drinking does not mean young adults who are not of drinking age are not going to drink. This often leads underage drinkers to engage in fraud by obtaining false identification or associate with people who are willing to break the law and buy alcohol for them. Additionally, since young adults cannot drink in public settings such as bars or restaurants, they must be more secretive about their drinking and potentially engage in riskier behaviors than they would have if they had been able to drink more openly. Furthermore, since underage drinkers (without false identification) cannot purchase alcohol on their own, they are likely to purchase larger quantities and drink until the alcohol is gone since they have may problems storing alcohol they are not supposed to have.[22]

The research of Lanza-Kaduce and Richards provides two lessons. First, many people disregard laws, especially if they believe them unjust (one of the main arguments of conflict theorists). The second lesson is that many people when breaking a law will engage in even riskier behaviors to cover their actions. A certain segment of the population will argue that these people deserve what happens to them and that more punitive laws are needed to prevent this type of behavior. Others, however, take a different approach. For example, some social scientists have argued that policies relating to alcohol use and driving are needed that create *harm reduction*. An illustration of harm reduction relating to alcohol use and driving would be to provide more public transportation (e.g., buses; commuter trains) and more taxi cabs so that people will have a safe and alternative way to travel in lieu of driving. The problem with underage drinking laws and similar regulations is that people will be less likely to utilize harm reduction policies for fear that they might get in trouble for breaking the law. Thus, in many instances, a law does not prevent harm—it actually encourages harm.

## Amethyst Initiative

Due to growing awareness of the unintended consequences of laws that prohibit adults under the age of 21 from legally consuming alcohol, a group formed in 2008 called the **Amethyst Initiative**, which has the singular goal of encouraging the federal government and state legislatures to reconsider the current drinking age. While the formation of the group would probably not be considered Earth-shattering, some readers might be surprised that the group is composed exclusively of American college and university chancellors and presidents. To date, 136 presidents and/or chancellors have joined the initiative, including from Dartmouth College, Duke University, Johns Hopkins University, Ohio State University, Syracuse University, Tufts University, University of Maryland—College 'Park, University of Massachusetts, and Virginia Tech. According to the Amethyst Initiative, a culture of dangerous and clandestine binge drinking has developed among college students. Since this behavior frequently occurs off-campus, colleges and universities have trouble regulating the behavior. The initiative further argues that colleges and universities are often forced to provide "abstinence only" drinking policies that are ineffective. Furthermore, the initiative points out that adults under 21 are allowed to vote, sign contracts, serve on juries, and enlist in the military, but are not allowed to consume alcohol.[23]

## The Clery Center for Security on Campus

Beginning in the late 1980s and continuing today, the **Clery Center for Security on Campus** (henceforth, Clery Center) is another example of a single-issue group which not only affected criminal justice policy in America, it helped create a new social problem: campus crime.[24] The Clery Center was originally founded in 1987 by Connie and Howard Clery as Security On Campus Incorporated using funds received in a civil settlement with Lehigh University after the Clerys' 19-year-old daughter, Jeanne, was brutally raped and murdered by a fellow student in her dormitory room in 1986.[25] During the ensuing 30 years, the Clery Center has dedicated itself to "preventing violence, substance abuse and other crimes on college and university campuses across the United States, and ... compassionately assist[ing] the victims of these crimes" while also working to develop and implement policies intended to make college and university campuses safer.[26]

In their book *The Dark Side of the Ivory Tower: Campus Crime as a Social Problem*,[27] John Sloan and Bonnie Fisher discussed at some length how the Clery Center helped construct campus crime as a new social problem that warranted intervention by first the states and then Congress. Through its lobbying and other advocacy efforts, in 1989 the Clery Center was responsible for Pennsylvania becoming the first state to pass legislation designed to address campus crime.[28] The Clery Center then focused its attention on Congress, and its efforts have been well rewarded: beginning in 1990 and continuing over the next two decades, the Clery Center has been instrumental in getting Congress to pass no less than *six* major pieces of federal legislation, which have fundamentally changed how postsecondary institutions address crime and security on college campuses across the United States.[29]

Without question, the most important piece of legislation the Clery Center was instrumental in having passed is what is now known as the *Jeanne Clery Disclosure of Campus Security Policy and Campus Crime Statistics Act* (hereafter, the Clery Act).[30] Considered "landmark" federal legislation by many observers,[31] the Clery Act fundamentally changed how postsecondary institutions address crime and security on campus by imposing on them several key requirements, including:

- Schools publicly disclose an annual security report that includes crimes reported to campus police, security personnel, counselors, and others for the three most recent calendar years, as well as security policies for the institution including policies for handling of sexual assault complaints and warnings/notifications sent to students and employees (this report is also sent to the U.S. Department of Education, which is charged with enforcing the Clery Act);
- Schools disclose "timely information" through publicly accessible crime logs and warnings issued to the campus community via email, voice mail, text message, or other mechanism relating to ongoing threats to campus health and/or safety;
- Schools protect certain basic rights for accused and victim in cases of alleged on-campus sexual victimization that are taken before campus disciplinary committees.

Failure to comply with these requirements may result in sanctions from the U.S. Department of Education ranging from public warnings to fines of up to $35,000 per violation, to withholding the institutions' federal financial aid in extreme cases.[32]

Given the importance of the Clery Center in influencing campus crime policy, one may wonder whether the Clery Act has had a substantial impact on crime and related issues on college campuses. Recent work by Dennis Gregory and Steven Janosik, among others, suggests it has not.[33] According to Gregory and Janosik, the Clery Act, while an important piece of legislation, is confusing and ill focused. Further, the Clery Act does not appear to have had the positive impact its supports had hoped; there is no evidence parents and students use the information available to them as a result of the Clery Act to make decisions about which college or university to attend. Additionally, the accuracy of crime statistics available as a result of the Clery Act is questionable, largely because so many incidents on campus, especially those involving sexual violence, go unreported to campus authorities. Finally, there is no evidence that constituents—students, faculty members, or staff—perceive college campuses as any more or less safe than they do the communities surrounding them.[34] Finally, some critics have argued that *most* legislation directed at campus crime and security—including the Clery Act—is little more than symbolic public policy intended to make people *feel* safer while doing little to actually address the reality of campus crime.[35]

## Firearm Advocacy Groups

One of the most fascinating examples of single-issue groups are those advocating some position on the presence and regulation of firearms in the United States. Attempting to describe these different groups in purely objective terms can be problematic because so much of the terminology used by these groups is value-laden. For instance, groups supporting fewer restrictions on the ownership and use of firearms in the United States will typically describe themselves as "supporters of gun rights and of the Second Amendment to the United States Constitution." Advocacy groups that support increased restrictions on the ownership and use of firearms are typically referred to as gun control groups, although the two most well-known groups describe themselves as advocates "against gun violence" and "supporters of the Second Amendment to the United States Constitution." How can both sides be supporters of the Second Amendment? Well, this issue boils down to politics, grammar, and use of the comma.

The exact language of the Second Amendment is this: "A well-regulated Militia, being necessary to the security of a free State, the right of the people to keep and bear Arms, shall not be infringed." In 2008, a 5–4 majority of the Supreme Court in the case *District of Columbia v. Heller* overturned a Washington, DC, ban on the ownership of handguns inside city limits. A majority of the Court essentially ruled that the DC legislation limited the ownership of firearms by private citizens, which they believed violated the Second Amendment and the public's right to "keep or bear arms." The four dissenting justices argued strenuously that the Second Amendment did *not* apply to the *private* ownership of weapons but instead was intended to make provisions for the creation and maintenance of a *militia* that would serve in the defense of the newly created United States of America. Since the country now has a more than capable and professional military, the Second Amendment, according to the dissenting justices, is a relic of a time long past and should not be used to allow citizens unfettered ownership of firearms or their use at present.[36]

Essentially, the majority in the case argued there are two clauses in the Second Amendment, one that gives private citizens a right to bear arms and one that provides for a militia and the defense of the United States. The minority of the Court argued that the two clauses of the Amendment are linked and private ownership of firearms is only necessary to maintain the militia. As if that was not problematic enough, some Constitutional scholars have argued that in the versions of the Constitution ratified by many states, the Second Amendment had two or four commas, not three as found in the copy of the Constitution on display in the National Archives.[37] Thus, the number and placement of the commas could significantly affect the meaning of the Second Amendment and ultimately its interpretation by the courts hundreds of years later.

As we mentioned previously, it is common for Supreme Court justices to ponder the original intent of the Founding Fathers, but regarding the Second Amendment, the deconstruction of original intent has gone somewhat extreme. For instance, one analysis of the case suggested that when the Constitution was ratified, people used commas much more frequently than we do today. As a result, perhaps we should not consider the commas *at all* when interpreting the amendment.[38] Regardless, one must wonder if interpretation of the Second Amendment really comes down to commas and basic rules of grammar or merely the political philosophy of an individual justice and what he or she believes is the best way to interpret the words of the amendment.

## *National Rifle Association*

Perhaps the most well-known firearms advocacy group in the United States is the National Rifle Association (NRA). The NRA was founded in 1871 by two Union Army veterans of the Civil War: **Colonel William C. Church** and **General George Wingate**. The two officers formed the group because they were "dismayed by the lack of marksmanship shown by their troops" and hoped to "promote and encourage rifle shooting on a scientific basis." The State of New York chartered the group on November 17, 1871, and the group's first president was Civil War General Ambrose Burnside (whose unusual facial hair was the inspiration behind what we now refer to today as "sideburns"). In 1872, the NRA established a shooting range on Creed Farm on Long Island, New York, and thus began the group's promotion of shooting sports, the primary focus of the organization for its first sixty years of operation. However, in 1934, the NRA created its Legislative Affairs Division, which mailed "legislative facts and analyses" to members. Forty years later, in 1975, the organization formed the Institute for Legislative Action (ILA) and formally began the lobbying for which the group is so well known today.[39] Although the NRA has supported or opposed a plethora of federal, state, and local legislation, the organization notes the purpose of its governmental lobbying activities is "preserving the right of all law-abiding individuals ... to purchase, possess and use firearms for legitimate purposes as guaranteed by the Second Amendment to the U.S. Constitution."[40]

## Handgun Control, Inc.

In 1974, Dr. Mark Borinsky, himself a victim of gun violence, founded the National Council to Control Handguns. On March 30, 1981, John Hinckley, Jr., shot President Reagan, his press secretary, James Brady, and two police officers.[41] During the shooting, Brady suffered a serious head wound that left him partially paralyzed. Although President Reagan allowed Brady to keep the title of "press secretary," he never again worked for the administration. Along with his wife, Sarah, **Jim Brady** became a gun control advocate.[42] Then, in 1991, Sarah Brady became chair of the Center to Prevent Handgun Violence (a sister organization of Handgun Control, Inc. that had been founded in 1983). Handgun Control, Inc. would eventually become the **Brady Campaign to Prevent Handgun Violence** and the Center to Prevent Handgun violence was renamed the Brady Center to Prevent Gun Violence. While the Brady Campaign and Center have supported a number of legislative initiatives, the most well-known was their advocacy of the *Brady Handgun Violence Prevention Act* (commonly referred to as the "Brady Law"), which was signed into law by President Bill Clinton on November 30, 1993. The key component of the legislation was the requirement of a five-day waiting period for purchasing handguns and background checks on those seeking to purchase guns.[43]

In addition to the Brady Campaign and Brady Center, similar groups have formed that advocate for increased regulation of firearms, with perhaps the best known of them being **Everytown for Gun Safety**. Similar to the formation of the Brady Campaign, Everytown for Gun Safety formed from the merger of two existing groups: Moms Demand Action for Gun Sense in America and Mayors Against Illegal Guns.[44] Everytown was formed with a donation of $50 million from former Mayor of New York Michael Bloomberg. During his political career, Bloomberg was consistently a supporter of stricter firearms regulation, but he specifically created Everytown to counteract the influence of the lobbying power of the NRA. In the short time since it was created, Everytown has engaged in a plethora of lobbying activities from creating public service announcements on television to directly lobbying legislators at the federal, state, and local government levels.[45]

In addition to the groups mentioned above, there are a multitude of other single-issue advocacy groups. For example, the Campaign to End the Death Penalty, as the name of the group indicates, seeks to eliminate capital punishment in the United States.[46] Families Against Mandatory Minimums is a group that seeks to reform sentencing laws in the United States, and specifically abolish mandatory prison terms for low-level non-violent drug offenders.[47] Many other groups exist that advocate a number of different positions that are important to criminal justice including the Children's Defense Fund, Reform Sex Offender Laws, Inc., USA Fair, Inc., the National Organization for Victim Assistance, the National Center for Victims of Crime, and countless others.

# General Interest Groups

## *American Civil Liberties Union (ACLU)*

While human rights may seem like a singular issue, inevitably, the campaign for many groups who seek to protect and promote human rights becomes multifaceted. Perhaps the most well-known advocacy group of this type is the **American Civil Liberties Union** (ACLU). According to the ACLU, the group was founded as a reaction to the "Palmer Raids," where the U.S. Department of Justice undertook a nationwide initiative to capture and deport "radical leftists"—especially anarchists—in November of 1919 to January 1920. At that time and in the following years, the United States was fearful that communism might take hold in the country and ultimately overthrow all vestiges of democracy. One of the many reactionaries was former Attorney General Mitchell Palmer, who advocated the searching, detaining, and incarceration of people he believed were potential enemies of democratic order. According to the ACLU, these raids were "egregious civil liberties abuses" and a small group of people formed the organization to combat them. At present, the ACLU claims membership of over 500,000 people, with almost 200 staff attorneys and thousands of volunteers. The current stated mission of the ACLU is "to fight government abuse and to vigorously defend individual freedoms including speech and religion, a woman's right to choose, the right to due process, citizens' rights to privacy, and much more." The group identifies itself as "civil libertarians" and claims the title of the largest public interest law firm in the United States. Indeed, the ACLU has appeared before the Supreme Court more often than any other organization except the United States Department of Justice. The ACLU is willing to represent nearly anyone or any group whose civil liberties have been violated including the American Nazis, the Ku Klux Klan, and the Nation of Islam.[48]

## Southern Poverty Law Center (SPLC)

Similar to the ACLU is the **Southern Poverty Law Center (SPLC)**, which was founded in 1971 by two civil-rights lawyers, **Morris Dees** and **Joseph Levin Jr.** Rather than advocating for civil liberties in their entirety, the SPLC considers itself "dedicated to fighting hate and bigotry and to seeking justice for the most vulnerable members of our society." The organization utilizes litigation, education, and other forms of advocacy with the goal of "equal justice and equal opportunity." In particular, the SPLC tracks and exposes organizations it identifies as "hate groups." SPLC also identifies five areas of advocacy in which it is involved: defending children at risk, combating hate and extremism, defending the rights of immigrants, defending the rights of the Lesbian, Gay, Bisexual & Transgender (LGBT) community, and teaching tolerance to the public at large.[49] The SPLC is best known for representing indigent defendants and suing "the nation's most dangerous hate groups" on behalf of those victimized by these groups. Specifically, the SPLC seeks multimillion-dollar court judgments designed to bankrupt these groups and shut down their activities.[50]

## Amnesty International

More global in scope than the aforementioned groups is **Amnesty International**. In 1961, British attorney **Peter Benenson** published an article in the *Observer* titled "The Forgotten Prisoners." The article discussed the plight of two Portuguese students who had been imprisoned in the United Kingdom for engaging in what Benenson believed was an extremely benign action — raising a toast to freedom. Benenson began the group known as "Appeal for Amnesty" in 1961 and the group's first international meeting was held in July of 1961 and included delegates from Belgium, the United Kingdom, France, Germany, Ireland, Switzerland, and the United States. Beginning with a small office and library staffed entirely by volunteers, Amnesty International now claims over three million members in more than 150 countries.[51] The primary goal of the organization is to "campaign for a world where human rights are enjoyed by all."[52]

Unlike the ACLU and the SPLC, Amnesty International is not a law firm; rather, it is primarily an advocacy group. According to the organization, the group engages in letter writing, online and offline campaigning, demonstrations, vigils, and direct lobbying of "those with power and influence." The organization primarily began by supporting the rights of prisoners in various countries, especially those whom Amnesty International believed were incarcerated only for expressing political beliefs—people the group defined as "prisoners of conscience." In 1968, Amnesty International began to campaign for an end to the death penalty, and a year later the organization advocated an end to racial discrimination. Later, the group began to campaign against political regimes in different countries that Amnesty International believed violated human rights. This included advocacy to end the practice of torturing prisoners and political dissidents. In 1994, Amnesty International began a campaign to advocate for the equal rights of all women.[53]

While the ACLU, the SPLC, and Amnesty International certainly produce and disseminate useful research for their respective agendas, there are other organizations whose primary purpose is to produce and disseminate research. These organizations are often referred to as *think tanks* and are usually composed of researchers with advanced university degrees who specialize in public policy research. Think tanks occupy a myriad of roles in the criminal justice policy process, from trying to inform the policy process to directly affecting the political process. Furthermore, some think tanks self-identify as "non-partisan," while others actively engage in partisan-based research to support a particular policy position.

## RAND Corporation

One of the best-known think tanks in the United States is the **RAND Corporation**. In 1948, Project RAND was developed to use research and development decisions to better inform United States' military planning. Originally part of the Douglas Aircraft Company, RAND was incorporated as a nonprofit corporation in 1948. In its incorporation papers, the purpose of the new organization was "To further and promote scientific, educational, and charitable purposes, all for the public welfare and security of the United States of America." The name RAND was used as a contraction of the two goals of the project: research and development. Several individuals within the United States War Department (now Department of Defense) believed a non-partisan private organization was needed that was entirely separate from government to evaluate the long-term goals of the United States military utilizing scientific research. Specifically, RAND describes its methodology as "a unique style, blending scrupulous nonpartisanship with rigorous, fact-based analysis to tackle society's most pressing problems." Although focusing on the military is still a cornerstone of the research interests of RAND, during the 1960s, RAND began to expand its research portfolio to include "many urgent domestic social and economic problems."[54]

In 2015, RAND employed 1,700 staff in five different offices in the United States, one office in the United Kingdom, one in Belgium, and one in Australia. Of the research staff at RAND, 57% has one or more doctorates and 29% hold one or more master's degrees. The field of studies of RAND researchers is diverse and includes social scientists, political scientists, policy analysts, physical scientists, mathematicians, statisticians, life scientists, engineers, economists, computer scientists, and attorneys to name a few. In 2014, RAND had 350 clients and grantors, completed 590 new projects, and produced more than 350 technical reports and 625 journal articles. In addition to carrying out policy research, RAND is also involved in education. In 1970, it founded a graduate school, which has granted more than 300 doctorates in policy analysis. Thus, not only does RAND produce research that greatly informs and affects the creation of public policy, RAND also directly trains future policy researchers and/or university professors.[55] The different areas of research affecting criminal justice in which RAND has engaged is long and varied, but some of the more important projects have included: evaluations of community justice centers and the National Crime Victim Law Institute's Victim's Rights Clinics; the changing role of criminal law in controlling criminal behavior; and various assessments of the consequences of the legalization of marijuana in the state of Washington.[56]

## The Heritage Foundation

In 1973, the **Heritage Foundation** was established as a research and educational institution. According to the organization, its "mission is to formulate and promote conservative public policies based on the principles of free enterprise, limited government, individual freedom, traditional American values, and a strong national defense." The Heritage Foundation produces "timely, accurate research on key policy issues and effectively market[s] these findings to our primary audiences: member of Congress, key congressional staff members, policymakers in the executive branch, the nation's news media, and the academic and policy communities." The research agenda of the Heritage Foundation is divided into three institutes: The Institute for Economic Freedom and Opportunity, The Institute for Family, Community, and Opportunity, and The Kathryn and Shelby Cullom Davis Institute for National Security and Foreign Policy.[57] On its website, the Heritage Foundation lists twenty-three members on its Board of Trustees,[58] twenty members of senior management,[59] and 281 "team" members.[60] Additionally, in 1977, Ed Feulner, who was president of the Heritage Foundation at that time, created the "Resource Bank to take on the liberal establishment and forge a national network of conservative policy groups and experts." Currently, the Resource Bank includes 2,200 policy experts and 465 policy groups in the United States and other countries.[61] Among the criminal justice issues that the Heritage Foundation has engaged in and disseminated research on are: cyber-terrorism, national security, proposed revisions to criminal codes, sex offender registration, and police brutality.

# Conclusion

Within Chapter 6, we examined the role of politics in criminal justice. Little research has been conducted on the effect of interest groups on criminal justice policymaking, but from the research conducted, some general observations can be made. The authors identified three primary classifications of interest groups, including single-issue, general-issue, and criminal justice employee union interest groups. Examples of both single-issue and general-issue interest groups were reviewed.

# Key Terms

- Interest groups
- Mothers Against Drunk Driving (MADD)
- Amethyst Initiative
- Clery Center for Security on Campus
- National Rifle Association (NRA)
- Taxpayers against Fraud
- Brady Campaign to Prevent Violence
- Everytown for Gun Safety
- American Civil Liberties Union (ACLU)
- Southern Poverty Law Center (SPLC)
- Amnesty International
- RAND Corporation
- Heritage Foundation

# Key People

- Erika Fairchild
- Barbara Ann Stolz
- Robert Borkenstein

- Candy Lightner
- Frank Weed
- Colonel William C. Church
- General George Wingate
- Jim Brady
- Morris Dees
- Joseph Levin Jr.
- Peter Benenson

# Discussion Questions

1) Considering the limited research on the effect of interest groups on criminal justice policymaking, propose a research study that would examine this relationship.
2) Why do you think there has been such little research conducted on the role of interest groups in criminal justice?
3) Of the single-issue interest groups mentioned, which one do you think has had the most influence on criminal justice policies? Make sure to defend your answer.
4) Explain the difference between general-issue and single-issue interest groups. Do the two ever overlap? If so, how?
5) What is the role of the RAND Corporation? How do you think RAND affects criminal justice research?
6) What do you believe will be the role of criminal justice interest groups in the next ten years? What type of issues will be prevalent? Why?

# Notes

1. Fairchild, Erika S. 1981. "Interest Groups in the Criminal Justice Process." *Journal of Criminal Justice*, 9: 181–194.

2. Stolz, Barbara Ann. 2002. "The Roles of Interest Groups in US Criminal Justice Policy Making: Who, When, and How." *Criminology and Criminal Justice*, 2(1): 51–69. Quote on page 58.

3. Stolz, Barbara Ann. 2005. "Educating Policymakers and Setting the Criminal Justice Policymaking Agenda: Interest Groups and the 'Victims of Trafficking and Violence Act of 2000.'" *Criminal Justice*, 5(4): 407–430.

4. Shelden, Randall G. 2011. "Interest Groups and Criminal Justice Policy (Research Brief)." Center on Juvenile and Criminal Justice. Retrieved on January 30, 2015 at: http://www.cjcj.org/uploads/cjcj/documents/interest_groups_and_criminal_justice_policy.pdf. Quote on Page 3.

5. *Ibid.*

6. Stolz, Barbara Ann. 2002. "The Roles of Interest Groups in US Criminal Justice Policy Making: Who, When, and How." *Criminology and Criminal Justice*, 2(1): 51–69.

7. Fell, James C. and Robert B. Voas. 2006. "Mothers Against Drunk Driving (MADD): The First 25 Years." *Traffic Injury Prevention*, 7: 195–212; Stolz, Barbara Ann. 2002. "The Roles of Interest Groups in US Criminal Justice Policy Making: Who, When, and How." *Criminology and Criminal Justice*, 2(1):51–69; Wooster, Martin Morse. February, 2000. "Mothers Against Drunk Driving: Has Its Vision Become Blurred?" *Alternatives in Philanthropy*, 1–6.

8. Stolz, Barbara Ann. 2002. "The Roles of Interest Groups in US Criminal Justice Policy Making: Who, When, and How." *Criminology and Criminal Justice*, 2(1): 51–69.

9. Fell, James C. and Robert B. Voas. 2006. "Mothers Against Drunk Driving (MADD): The First 25 Years." *Traffic Injury Prevention*, 7: 195–212.

10. Fell, James C. and Robert B. Voas. 2006. "Mothers Against Drunk Driving (MADD): The First 25 Years." *Traffic Injury Prevention*, 7: 195–212; Stolz, Barbara Ann. 2002. "The Roles of Interest Groups in US Criminal Justice Policy Making: Who, When, and How." *Criminology and Criminal Justice*, 2(1):51–69; Wooster, Martin Morse. February, 2000. "Mothers Against Drunk Driving: Has Its Vision Become Blurred?" *Alternatives in Philanthropy*: 1–6.

11. Fell, James C. and Robert B. Voas. 2006. "Mothers Against Drunk Driving (MADD): The First 25 Years." *Traffic Injury Prevention*, 7:195–212; Stolz, Barbara Ann. 2002. "The Roles of Interest Groups in US Criminal Justice Policy Making: Who, When, and How." *Criminology and Criminal Justice*, 2(1): 51–69.

12. Weed, Frank J. 1993. "The MADD Queen: Charisma and the Founder of Mothers Against Drunk Driving." *Leadership Quarterly*, 4(3/4): 329–346.

13. *Ibid.*

14. *Ibid.*

15. Weed, Frank J. 1991. "Organizational Mortality in the Anti-Drunk Driving Movement: Failure among Local MADD Chapters." *Social Forces*, 69(3): 851–868.

16. Weed, Frank J. 1993. "The MADD Queen: Charisma and the Founder of Mothers Against Drunk Driving." *Leadership Quarterly*, 4(3/4): 329–346.

17. Fell, James C. and Robert B. Voas. 2006. "Mothers Against Drunk Driving (MADD): The First 25 Years". *Traffic Injury Prevention*, 7:195–212.

18. Wooster, Martin Morse. February, 2000. "Mothers Against Drunk Driving: Has its Vison Become Blurred?" *Alternatives in Philanthropy*: 1–5.

19. Lanza-Kaduce, Lonn and Donna M. Bishop. 1986. "Legal Fictions and Criminology: The Jurisprudence of Drunk Driving." *The Journal of Criminal Law and Criminology*, 77(2): 358–378. Quote on page 361.

20. Lanza-Kaduce, Lonn and Donna M. Bishop. 1986. "Legal Fictions and Criminology: The Jurisprudence of Drunk Driving." *The Journal of Criminal Law and Criminology*, 77(2): 358–378.

21. Wooster, Martin Morse. February, 2000. "Mothers Against Drunk Driving: Has its Vision Become Blurred?" *Alternatives in Philanthropy*, 1–5.

22. Lanza-Kaduce, Lonn and Pamela Richards. 1989. "Raising the Minimum Drinking Age: Some Unintended Consequences of Good Intentions." *Justice Quarterly*, 6(2): 701–716.

23. Amethyst Initiative. Retrieved on December 11, 2014 at: http://www.theamethystinitiative.org/.

24. Clery Center. Retrieved on May 23, 2015 at: http://www.clerycenter.org.

25. Josoph Henry was tried and convicted of raping, torturing, and murdering Ms.

Clery and sentenced to life in prison without possibility of parole.

26. Clery Center: Our Mission. Retrieved on May 23, 2015 at: http://clerycenter.org/our-mission.

27. Sloan, III, John J. and Bonnie S. Fisher 2011. *The Dark Side of the Ivory Tower: Campus Crime as a Social Problem.* New York: Cambridge University Press, pp. 52–80.

28. Burke, Jennifer and John J. Sloan III. 2013. "State-Level Clery Act Initiatives: Symbolic Politics or Substantive Policy?" Pp. 119–133 in Bonnie S. Fisher and John J. Sloan III (Eds.), *Campus Crime: Legal, Social and Policy Perspectives* (3ed). Springfield, IL: Charles C. Thomas Publisher.

29. *Ibid*, p. 79.

30. Originally titled the *Student Right-to-Know and Campus Security Act of 1990* (20 USC 1092(f)), the legislation was renamed in 1998 to honor the memory of Jeanne Clery.

31. Kiss, Allison 2013. "The Jeanne Clery Act: A Summary of the Law and Its Evolution in Higher Education." Pp. 33–45 in Bonnie S. Fisher and John J. Sloan III (Eds.), *Campus Crime: Legal, Social and Policy Perspectives* (3ed). Springfield, IL: Charles C. Thomas Publisher.

32. Jeanne Clery Act Information: Clery Act Complaints. Retrieved on February 13, 2015 at: http://www.cleryact.info/clery-act-complaints.html.

33. Gregory, Dennis E. and Steven M. Janosik 2013. "Research on the Clery Act and Crime Reporting: Its Impact on the Literature and Higher Education Administrative Practice in Higher Education." Pp. 46–62 in Bonnie S. Fisher and John J. Sloan III (Eds.), *Campus Crime: Legal, Social and Policy Perspectives* (3ed). Springfield, IL: Charles C. Thomas Publisher.

34. *Ibid*, pp. 56–57.

35. See, for example, Sloan, III, John J. and Bonnie S. Fisher (2011). *The Dark Side of the Ivory Tower: Campus Crime as a Social Problem.* New York: Cambridge University Press; Fisher, Bonnie, Jennifer L. Hartman, Francis T. Cullen and Michael G. Turner (2002). "Making Campuses Safer for Students: The Clery Act as Symbolic Legal Reform." *Stetson Law Review*, 31: 61–91.

36. District of Columbia v. Heller, (2008). 554 U.S. 570.

37. Freedman, Adam. 2007. "Clause and Effect". *The New York Times.* Retrieved on December 13, 2014 at: http://www.nytimes.com/2007/12/16/opinion/16freedman.html?_r=0.

38. Guberman, Ross. "Million-Dollar Commas." Retrieved on December 13, 2014 at: http://www.legalwritingpro.com/articles/D10-million-dollar-commas.php.

39. NRA History. Retrieved on December 13, 2014 at: http://home.nra.org/history/document/about.

40. NRA-ILA: Institute for Legislative Action. Retrieved on December 13, 2014 at: http://www.nraila.org/legislation.aspx.

41. Brady Campaign to Prevent Gun Violence: Our History. Retrieved on December 13, 2014 at: http://www.bradycampaign.org/our-history.

42. Brady Campaign to Prevent Gun Violence: Jim and Sarah Brady. Retrieved on December 13, 2014 at: http://www.bradycampaign.org/jim-and-sarah-brady.

43. Brady Campaign to Prevent Gun Violence: Our History. Retrieved on December 13, 2014 at: http://www.bradycampaign.org/our-history.

44. Everytown for Gun Safety. Retrieved on December 15, 2014 at: http://www.bradycampaign.org/our-historhttp://everytown.org/who-we-are/.

45. Alman, Ashley. 2014. "New Bloomberg-Backed Gun Safety Group Releases Chilling

PSA Aimed at Parents." *The Huffington Post*. Retrieved on December 15, 2014 at: http://www.huffingtonpost.com/2014/04/16/everytown-for-gun-safety-psa_n_5162887.html.

46. Campaign to End the Death Penalty. Retrieved on December 15, 2014 at: http://www.nodeathpenalty.org/about-us.

47. Families Against Mandatory Minimums. Retrieved on December 15, 2014 at: http://famm.org/about/.

48. ACLU History. Retrieved on January 3, 2015 at: https://www.aclu.org/aclu-history.

49. Southern Poverty Law Center: Who We Are. Retrieved on January 3, 2015 at: http://www.splcenter.org/who-we-are.

50. SPLC History. Retrieved on January 3, 2015 at: http://www.splcenter.org/who-we-are/splc-history.

51. The History of Amnesty International. Retrieved on January 3, 2015 at: https://www.amfnesty.org/en/who-we-are/.

52. Amnesty International: Who We Are. Retrieved on January 3, 2015 at: https://www.amnesty.org/en/who-we-are/.

53. The History of Amnesty International. Retrieved on January 3, 2015 at: http://www.amnesty.org/en/who-we-are/history.

54. A Brief History of RAND. Retrieved on January 4, 2015 at: http://www.rand.org/about/history/a-brief-history-of-rand.html.

55. RAND at a Glance. Retrieved on January 4, 2015 at: http://www.rand.org/about/glance.html.

56. RAND Topics: Law and Business. Retrieved on January 4, 2015 at: http://www.rand.org/topics/law-and-business.html; RAND Topics: Criminal Law. Retrieved on January 4, 2015 at: http://www.rand.org/topics/criminal-law.html.

57. About Heritage. Retrieved on January 4, 2015 at: http://www.heritage.org/about.

58. The Heritage Foundation: Board of Trustees. Retrieved on January 4, 2015 at: http://www.heritage.org/about/board-of-trustees.

59. The Heritage Foundation: Senior Management. Retrieved on January 4, 2015 at: http://www.heritage.org/about/staff?positions=%22Senior+Management%22.

60. The Heritage Foundation: Team. Retrieved on January 4, 2015 at: http://www.heritage.org/about/staff.

61. The Heritage foundation's 35th Anniversary: A History of Achievements. Retrieved on January 4, 2015 at: http://www.heritage.org/about/our-history/35th-anniversary.

# Chapter 7

# The Political Economy
# of Policing

## Chapter Outline

# Learning Objectives

- Identify the types of law enforcement agencies within the United States
- Evaluate the role of money and politics on agencies' behavior
- Examine the role of privatization within security in the United States
- Assess the role of civilianization in police departments
- Evaluate the role of federal discretionary grants in police departments
- Evaluate the role of ticket revenue on police officer discretion

# Introduction

In Chapter 3, we briefly discussed the evolution of modern police in the United States. As presented there, police in the United States evolved out of the watch system used in the colonies, later augmented by the constable system, and in the South, out of slave patrols. The first modern police department in the United States was created in Boston in 1838, and by the end of the 19th century most major American cities had a centralized municipal police department. For over a century, the process of moving the police from an unprofessional, relatively untrained, reactively oriented, highly politicized group to a professional, better trained, proactively focused group that was far less influenced by local politics is still ongoing. In this chapter, we discuss in more detail how money and politics has affected the development and operation of police agencies in the United States across the last two centuries.

# Law Enforcement Agencies

There are many different types of law enforcement agencies. Some law enforcement agencies, such as the New York Police Department (NYPD), are what we may call general law enforcement agencies. In the case of the NYPD, sworn employees of the department are responsible for maintaining order, enforcing state laws and local ordinances, and providing service—the three main functions of police agencies—within the five boroughs of New York. Other law enforcement agencies might have specialized agendas and focus on one area of law enforcement. For instance, a fish and game or fish and wildlife department ensures people are not hunting out of season or without a license, or if a person is fishing, verify that the individual possesses a valid fishing license. In most instances, a fish and game officer would not investigate a robbery or homicide.

In 2008, the most recent year for which data were available, there were over 18,000 U.S. law enforcement agencies functioning at the state and local level of government, employing about 1.3 million people.[1] Additionally, federal law enforcement agencies employed about 120,000 people in 2008, with the four largest agencies employing about two-thirds of all federal law enforcement personnel.[2] There are also specialized police agencies, such as fish and game police, transit police, campus police, and tribal police, operating at the state and local level. Furthermore, there are also specialized police agencies operating at the federal level, including the Supreme Court Police, U.S. Postal Inspection Service, Amtrack Police, and United States Park Police.[3] Finally, there is a large and growing multibillion-dollar private security industry that engages in quasi-law enforcement activities involving the protection of people and property.

## Federal Law Enforcement

Federal law enforcement agencies have jurisdiction over federal crimes, if a crime occurs on federal land, or in a particular field or area, such as illegal drugs. For instance, on March 1, 1932, **Charles Augustus Lindbergh, Jr.,** the twenty-month-old son of the world-famous aviator Charles Lindbergh, who was the first person to fly an airplane non-stop over the Atlantic Ocean, was kidnapped. The kidnappers left a ransom note that demanded $50,000 from the Lindbergh family for return of the baby. The Lindbergh home was near the town of Hopewell, New Jersey, which did not have its own police department. As a result, the New Jersey State Police initially investigated the case. Shortly after, the Director of the Federal Bureau of Investigation (FBI) at the time, J. Edgar Hoover, offered both his assistance as well as that of the FBI in the investigation. At that time, the FBI was only allowed to offer the assistance of the agency, but the agency was not allowed to take over an investigation or a case.[4] While the FBI had more resources at their disposal, there were no federal laws at that time specifically prohibiting kidnapping, so it had no jurisdiction in the case. Indeed, before the automobile and airplane were commonly available, many people did not have the ability to take people across state lines against their will, or at least it was not very common. The problem of kidnapping had become somewhat of a national issue, but many states' rights activists opposed federal legislation. However, in the aftermath of the Lindbergh kidnapping, Congress passed and President Herbert Hoover signed into law the **Federal Kidnapping Act**. The law has been amended several times, but the legislation allows the FBI to take jurisdiction in many, if not most, cases of kidnapping. In addition to kidnapping, there are approximately 3,000 federal crimes.[5]

One interesting fact about the United States is that, unlike many countries, it does not have a national police department. The closest entity that it has to such an agency is the FBI. According to the agency's website, it is responsible for investigating nine different broadly defined areas including terrorism, counterintelligence, cyber-crime, weapons of mass destruction, public corruption, civil rights, organized crime, white-collar crime, and violent crime & major thefts. For the FBI to investigate any of these crimes, a person or group of people must have first violated a federal law.[6]

Most other federal law enforcement agencies have more specialized functions. For example, as the names of two of the organizations clearly imply, the **Drug Enforcement Administration** (DEA) and the **Bureau of Alcohol, Tobacco, Firearms and Explosives** (ATF) investigate federal drug crimes and federal crimes involve alcohol, tobacco, firearms, and explosives. However, some agencies' missions are not as clearly articulated. For example, it is common knowledge that the United States Secret Service (USSS) is responsible for protecting the president of the United States, the vice president of the United States, the families of both, former presidents, and a host of other important dignitaries and foreign leaders who come on official state visits.[7] However, what is less commonly known is that when founded in 1864, the primary purpose of the Secret Service was to investigate the counterfeiting of United States currency. Beginning in 1984, the agency's role was expanded to include the investigation of crimes that involve financial institution fraud, computer and telecommunications fraud, false identification documents, access device fraud, advance fee fraud, electronic funds transfers and money laundering. In general, the Secret Service, in addition to protecting the lives of important political leaders, is also responsible for protecting the well-being of the American economy.[8]

## State Law Enforcement

One of the common themes of this textbook is that there is great variation in how individual states govern their citizens. The organization of state police agencies exemplifies this theme. For this reason, it is difficult to make any generalizations about state police organizations and operations. How these agencies are organized in individual states is entirely dependent upon state law and to what degree the states want to reserve law enforcement duties for state authorities instead of local police departments. Samuel Walker, for example, identified state police, highway patrol, and state investigative agencies as the most common state-level law enforcement agencies. State police are organizations created by law that have general law enforcement duties within a state's geographic boundaries. Highway patrol agencies, as the name would imply, enforce laws on state highways and roads (note that some states actually have separate agencies for state police and highway patrol).[9] The television program ChiPs (which was on the air from 1977–1983 and made the actor Erik Estrada a household name) was a hugely popular depiction of the California Highway Patrol (CHP), which was established in 1929 as a distinct law enforcement agency in California. The agency's mission was to provide uniform traffic law enforcement throughout the state on California's highways.[10] The California State Police (CSP), on the other hand, was in charge of many law enforcement duties, such as guarding the state capital and providing law enforcement assistance to local governments that do not have their own police force. However, critics wondered if the two agencies could not be merged in order to reduce budgetary costs. Ultimately, in 1995, 271 officers within the CSP became employees of the CHP.[11] Presently, the California Department of Justice's Division of Law Enforcement houses the two agencies and five bureaus organized around areas including firearms, forensic services, gambling control, investigation, and Medi-Cal fraud & elder abuse.[12] In addition, the California Department of Alcoholic Beverage Control is responsible for overseeing and administering all provisions of the California Alcoholic Beverage Control Act.[13]

## Local Law Enforcement

While the number and functions of federal and state law enforcement agencies have increased over the past century, the majority of all police agencies are found at the local level of government. As we noted in Chapter 4, the vast majority of the 18,000 law enforcement agencies in the United States are local police departments, and over sixty percent of those employed in law enforcement are employed with local agencies. There are also several different types of local law enforcement agencies, including **municipal/city police departments, sheriff's departments,** and **specialized police,** which include (among other agencies) airport police, transit police, tribal police, and college and university police departments.

## Municipal Police Departments

The most common law enforcement agencies are referred to as municipal/city police departments. These agencies have jurisdiction limited to the geographic boundaries of a particular town/city/municipality or, in some rural locations, may be responsible for an entire county, but are general law enforcement agencies.[14] Some municipal police departments are very large; the NYPD, for example, employs over 30,000 sworn officers.[15] Other city police departments may employ as few as 2–3 officers. In fact, most police agencies in America are relatively small, employing 50 or fewer officers, but most police officers work for large agencies like the NYPD.[16] Needless to say, there is considerable variation in the size and scope of municipal and city police departments in the United States county sheriff's departments.[17] Another component of local law enforcement agencies are county sheriff's departments. A sheriff's office is a local law enforcement agency organized at the county level and directed by a sheriff, nearly all of whom are elected officials. The jurisdiction of sheriffs' offices includes unincorporated areas of a county, excluding areas served by a local police department. In certain counties, municipalities contract with a sheriffs' department for law enforcement services. In the United States, in 2008 (the most recent year for which data were available), there were 3,063 sheriff's departments employing over 353,000 people, including nearly 183,000 sworn employees. States with the most sheriffs' offices in 2008 included Texas (254), Georgia (159), Kentucky (120), Missouri (114), Kansas (104), Illinois (102), and North Carolina (100). Four states—Alaska, Connecticut, Hawaii, and Rhode Island—do not have any local sheriffs' offices. In those states, court-related duties typically performed by local sheriffs' offices are the responsibility of state agencies. The District of Columbia also does not have a sheriff's office; the U.S. Marshals Service performs typical sheriff's department duties for the District.[18]

## *Specialized Law Enforcement Agencies*

The final group of police agencies includes departments whose mission focuses on a narrow aspect of law enforcement, in terms of either the jurisdiction in which the agency operates or the specific activities in which the agency engages. A good example of such specialized agencies is the Los Angeles Airport Police, which was created in 1946 after control of the airport was transferred from the United States War Department to the City of Los Angeles. Originally, six armed "airport guards" were hired to provide security for the facility. Three years later, three additional guards were hired and the nine total airport guards were made "special officers" of the City of Los Angeles. Today, the officers are known as "airport police officers" and the Los Angeles Airport Police employ 1,100 law enforcement and other support personnel.[19]

While some transportation systems are large enough to require a separate police agency, some transportation systems have jurisdictional problems that also require a specialized police agency to serve them. As an example, the Washington Metropolitan Area Transit Authority was created in 1976 to provide police services to the metropolitan transit system in Washington, DC. The agency, now known as the **Metro Transit Police Department** (MTPD), has tristate jurisdiction (District of Columbia, Virginia, and Maryland) with responsibility for a variety of law enforcement and public safety functions in transit facilities throughout the DC metropolitan area. The MTPD has an authorized strength of 490 sworn police officers, 64 security special police, and 91 civilian personnel. Officers provide a variety of law enforcement and public safety services on the Metrorail and Metrobus systems in the Washington metropolitan area. MTPD police officers have arrest powers throughout the 1,500-square-mile transit zone for crimes that occur in or against transit authority facilities. It is the only tri-jurisdictional police agency in the country and serves a population of 3.2 million.[20]

Another example of specialized police agencies are those serving colleges and universities—"campus police." These agencies were generally created during the 1960s and 1970s, partly in response to the unrest that was occurring at many colleges and universities as students protested the Vietnam War or were involved with the civil rights movement.[21] Rather than having local law enforcement patrol their campuses, college and university presidents convinced state legislatures of the need to have a *campus* law enforcement entity to engage in order maintenance, law enforcement, and service on college or university property. College presidents and boards of trustees were then able to convince receptive state legislators to first pass laws to create these agencies and then provide necessary funding to put them into operation. Over the next 40 years, these agencies evolved and became remarkably similar to local police departments in terms of their organizational, administrative, and functional features.[22]

A recent report by Brian Reaves on the results of a national survey of campus law enforcement agencies at public and private four-year secondary institutions enrolling 2,500 or more students during the 2011–2012 academic year revealed that:

- About 75% of the campuses were using armed officers, compared to 68% during the 2004–05 school year;
- About 90% of public campuses used sworn police officers (92%), compared to about 4 in 10 private campuses (38%);
- Most sworn campus police officers were authorized to use a sidearm (94%), chemical or pepper spray (94%), and a baton (93%);
- Most sworn campus police officers had arrest (86%) and patrol (81%) jurisdictions that extended beyond campus boundaries;
- About 7 in 10 campus law enforcement agencies had a memorandum of understanding or other formal written agreement with outside law enforcement agencies;

- Most campus law enforcement agencies serving 5,000 or more students had personnel designated to address general crime prevention (91%), rape prevention (86%), drug education (79%), alcohol education (78%), stalking (75%), victim assistance (72%), and intimate partner violence (69%);
- Compared to private campuses, a higher percentage of campus law enforcement agencies on public campuses met regularly with special interest groups, such as advocacy groups (64% public compared to 43% private) and groups seeking to prevent domestic violence (69% compared to 48%) or sexual violence (76% compared to 58%);
- Nearly all campuses had a mass notification system that used email, text messages, and other methods to alert and instruct students, faculty, and staff in emergency situations.[23]

The final specialized police agency of note is agencies that have responsibility for law enforcement, order maintenance, and service on tribal lands. "Tribal police" agencies were established on Indian reservations throughout the United States because tribal lands were not generally subject to the laws of the individual states. In 1953, Congress passed a law that addressed state jurisdiction over offenses committed by or against indigenous Americans in Indian country. The law required the states of Alaska, California, Minnesota, Nebraska, Oregon, and Wisconsin to take over the criminal justice systems of tribal lands within state borders. The rationale behind the law was that tribal governments were not effective in governing their territories and the states needed to intervene. The law was amended in 1968 to require that a tribe consent to the state taking on criminal justice responsibilities on its land and allowed tribes to opt out of state control. The end result of the law and its amendment is confusion as to who has authority to police these areas.[24] Regardless, a 2003 report by Matthew Hickman found that as of June 2000, American Indian tribes operated 171 law enforcement agencies that employed the equivalent of at least one full-time sworn officer with general arrest powers. In addition, the Bureau of Indian Affairs (BIA) operated 37 agencies providing law enforcement services in Indian country. Tribally operated agencies employed 3,462 full-time personnel, including 2,303 sworn (67%) and 1,159 non-sworn (33%) employees.[25]

## Private Policing Organizations

Both historically and today, many Americans have relied on non-governmental, for-profit, private agencies to protect them from crime. The *types* of services provided by these agencies vary, ranging from providing consumers with security systems for their homes or businesses, to personnel trained to guard individuals and property, to providing technologies designed to protect people and property from crime. As Mark Button has noted, as police forces across the world have grown considerably, so too has the private security sector.[26] As he stated, it is difficult to find exact figures on the complete size and scope of the private security industry, but private security expenditures total more than those spent on government-based policing.[27] Furthermore, as technological advances in security and the global economy continue to grow, there will be an increased need for people to look beyond governments for police services.[28]

As Kevin Strom and his colleagues noted, one of the primary difficulties in defining the scope of the private security industry is developing a universal definition of what exactly constitutes the "security industry." Some studies have defined private security as any organization that charges a fee to protect any person or organization. Yet many organizations will employ personnel for this purpose.[29] For instance, ever walk into a shopping mall or a department store? Although you might see a police officer in the facility on rare occasion, you will more often see privately hired security personnel. While one may argue that this does not completely cover all aspects of private security, Strom and colleagues found that the American Society for Industrial Security (ASIS) identified eighteen distinct aspects of private security: physical security, personnel security, information systems security, investigations, loss prevention, risk management, legal aspects, emergency and contingency planning, fire protection, crisis management, disaster management, counterterrorism, competitive intelligence, executive protection, violence in the workplace, crime prevention, crime prevention through environmental design, and security architecture and engineering.[30]

To give some perspective on the scope of the private security industry, we found one posting on the website Security Degree Hub that lists what is described as the thirty most powerful private security companies in the world. Table 7.1 illustrates the enormity of the top five companies. The premiere company in the group, G4S, is a British company headquartered in London that provides security personnel, monitoring equipment, response units, and secure prisoner transportation to business, government, and industry. The second largest company in the list is Securitas AB, with headquarters in Stockholm, Sweden, that provides guards and patrols, investigations, home alarm systems, loss prevention, security consulting, and guard dogs. Third largest is ADT Corporation, headquartered in Boca Raton, Florida. The company provides alarms and monitoring equipment to 6.4 million clients. Fourth is Allied Barton, which is based in Pennsylvania and provides security to higher education campuses, commercial property, aerospace and defense sites, housing, malls,

Table 7.1. SecurityDegreeHub.com's Five Most
Powerful Security Companies in the World

| Company | Location | Employees | Annual Revenue |
|---------|----------|-----------|----------------|
| G4S | London, England | 620,000 | 12 billion |
| Securitas AB | Stockholm, Sweden | 300,000 | 10 billion |
| ADT Corporation | Boca Raton, FL | 16,000[31] | 3.1 billion |
| Allied Barton | Pittsburgh, PA | 60,000[32] | 1.9 billion |
| Dyncorp | Annandale, VA | 25,000[33] | 3 billion |

Source: Adapted from http://www.securitydegreehub.com.

health-care facilities, and chemical industries. The fifth, DynCorp, is based in
Annandale, Virginia, and is a private military contractor.

## Police Unions

While trade unions emerged in Europe and America generally during the Industrial Revolution, police unions were slow to follow suit, not becoming common until the 1960s. According to Jan Berry and colleagues, the development
of police unions involved seemingly contradictory forces.[34] They argued that
modern police agencies represented centrally led efforts by governments to
control various groups, which frequently resulted in police officers used in actions taken *against* organized labor as it sought to recruit members. Police officers have also typically been recruited from the working class, yet it was
precisely from this class that union members were also recruited. Finally, police officers were effectively blocked from unionizing by many local and state
governments until the 1960s.[35] One of the reasons that police officers were
slow to organize is that many state and local governments argued that police
unionization could threaten the internal security of states and localities. Roy
Adams has argued, however, there is little empirical evidence to support such
claims and instead makes the case that police officers who are allowed to unionize actually act in a more democratic manner while on the job.[36] Further, there
were many reasons that police officers needed to unionize. In particular, one
of the continual complaints about police work is that officers receive low wages.
It does not take a gigantic leap in logic to conclude that police officers receiv-

ing substandard wages will also be those most susceptible to corruption. **Samuel Walker** has credited the formation of police unions as not only improving the salaries and benefits of police officers, but also creating protections for rank-and-file officers from arbitrary discipline by superiors.[37] However, while police unions can be valuable for protecting the rights of rank-and-file officers, unions often stand in the way of changes to the police profession. Those joining the profession not only receive training in the law and tactics necessary for law enforcement, but also learn the cultural values of the profession, one of which is distrust of change—especially when being imposed from police administration. As a result, police unions have a history of opposing new strategies and duties for rank-and-file officers.[38]

One example of a law enforcement union is the **International Union of Police Associations** (IUPA), which is affiliated with the American Federation of Labor and Congress of Industrial Organizations (AFL-CIO). The IUPA officially joined the AFL-CIO in 1976. The union noted that among the most important rights for law enforcement officers is to be able to collectively bargain. In 1986, Congress made the Fair Labor Standards Act applicable to law enforcement agencies, which meant officers could no longer be required to work more than eight hours a day or forty hours a week without overtime compensation, and local police unions would not have to collectively bargain to obtain overtime pay for officers.[39]

# Employees of Law Enforcement Agencies

As police organizations modernized, the structure and operation of these organizations has been primarily compared to both the military and bureaucracies.[40] Comparisons of modern-day police forces with the military stem from the relatively rigid, rank-based hierarchy found in both organizations. According to **O.W. Wilson,** one of the principals responsible for efforts to professionalize American police, rank-and-file officers needed to be subservient to the command structure to ensure orders would be followed and allow for easy deployment of personnel, just like in the military. Wilson also believed a quasi-military command structure made police officers and police departments less susceptible to the undue influence of politicians. Furthermore, organizing police departments as quasi-military institutions helps create bonds among rank-and-file employees while reinforcing their role as crime fighters and the primary agents of social control within communities.[41]

Yet describing police departments as quasi-military organizations is often inappropriate. Police departments are not supposed to be forces invading communities; they are supposed to be part of those communities, serving and protecting members of the community. Playing upon comparison to the military may only lead to further strains in the relationship with communities, especially minority communities who may very well view police departments as marauding hordes.[42]

## The Importance of Rank in Law Enforcement

An alternative way to describe the organization of police departments is to compare them to any other government bureaucracy. David Bordua and Albert Reiss have argued that bureaucratization is a common technique used by organizations to insulate themselves from civic pressures.[43] While officers do have to respect the chain of command, they are also civil servants. Modern police organizations are supposed to be a source of stability between the elites and the masses. Bordua and Reiss argued that the police often draw hostility from the masses that should instead be directed at social elites. Thus, in some ways, elites and the police within a society mutually support one another. According to Bordua and Reiss, describing police forces as quasi-military ignores the broader context of organizations generally and notes that many companies or bureaucratic agencies (most of which are not engaged in policing) also have a rigid command structure. Furthermore, despite the orders of police administrators, once rank-and-file police officers are on a beat or patrol, they are largely left on their own and are not heavily supervised in the field.[44] Michael Lipsky made the same observation in his acclaimed book, *Street-Level Bureaucracy*. He argued that while police officers have numerous policies that govern their behavior, they not only largely supervise themselves but also are responsible for implementing these very policies.[45]

Many people are familiar with the rank structure found in police departments, beginning with patrol officers and moving up through sergeants, lieutenants, captains, deputy chiefs, and chiefs. If you happen to be a fan of *Law & Order: Special Victims Unit*, you are probably familiar with Detectives Elliot Stabler and Olivia Benson investigating cases under the watchful eye of Captain Donald Cragen. Captain Cragen spends most of his time trying to get Stabler and Benson to follow the rules and warns about "the brass" coming down on him when a case is politically sensitive or policy is not followed.

While those who carry some form of badge or have some rank are the most common employees in police organizations, police departments are increasingly employing civilians who are not sworn law enforcement officers, have no arrest powers, and do not carry firearms as part of their jobs.

## Civilian Employees in Law Enforcement Agencies

In Chapter 3, we noted the importance of the two-way radio in changing how police engaged in routine patrol activities. With this invention, it allowed a citizen to call a central office and request assistance. Whoever was manning that telephone line was then able to use a two-way radio to contact any officers on duty and request they proceed to the location where help was needed. Police officers can certainly be the ones to take the phone calls; however, if you watch any police shows on television, one of the duties that officers always hate is "riding a desk." Many police officers join the force so that they can be out in the world—solving problems and helping people. As a result, many police departments hire civilians to do these desk jobs. As Brian Forst has noted, civilians are often cheaper to hire and require fewer benefits than sworn officers. In 1965, there were 8.3 sworn officers for every civilian in police departments across the nation. By 1995, there were only 2.6 sworn officers for every civilian employed in police departments nationwide. This trend of hiring ever more civilians in police departments has been referred to as **civilianization.**[46]

While hiring civilians within police departments may have originally been for the purpose of filling jobs that police officers wanted to avoid, many civilians are now recruited for their special skills. For example, as technology has become more common in policing, civilians have been hired to perform more and more tasks that police officers lack the training to perform. Many policing jobs (for example, communication specialists, crime scene technicians, forensic laboratory scientists, spatial analysts, computer specialists, and others) require people who not only have specialized training, but also often have advanced degrees. Furthermore, since most police training does not include budgeting, strategic planning, or human relations, these tasks are often performed by specialized staff.[47]

While this complaint certainly applies to police organizations as well, many citizens have complained that governments are not responsive to their needs. Police brutality has long been a problem, especially during the American civil rights movement; one of the common complaints was that police disproportionately abused the civil rights of minorities. As a result, many cities established *civilian review boards* dedicated to reviewing the actions and behavior of the police. Many supporters of these boards believed they were necessary because court relief for victims of police brutality was not only inconsistent, but took time and money—something the poor and minorities did not have. Police organizations often fought the creation of civilian review boards, arguing that outsiders did not properly appreciate the dangers of police work. Yet, proponents noted that before the creation of review boards, police organizations rarely disciplined officers unless they had engaged in some form of insubordination.[48]

# Budgets, Costs, and Profits

A common point made by citizens to public officials is "Hey, I pay your salary!" Indeed, most government agencies depend upon tax dollars collected from citizens to fund their operations. And pay we do. According to Stephen Salisbury, in total the federal government (by itself) has appropriated about $635 billion, accounting for inflation, for homeland security-related activities and equipment since the 9/11 attacks.[49] That does not include the amount of money spent by state and local governments for law enforcement and similar homeland security operations, which is also likely in the hundreds of billions of dollars. Policing, in short, is a costly operation.

## The Costs of Policing: Vehicles and Equipment

Police departments have to purchase a wide range of equipment including weapons, vehicles, body armor, handcuffs, and other accessories—all of which costs money. In response to this need, many companies exist that sell equipment to police departments for a profit. For example, the *New Jersey Journal* reported that in 2014, the Lawmen Supply Company won a $500,000 contract to supply firearms and ammunition to the Jersey City police department.[50] When the Ford Motor Company discontinued production of the **Crown Victoria**, a full-size sedan produced from 1992 to 2012, the car was considered the "gold standard" of police vehicles (Ford later introduced the Ford Fusion Police Interceptor, available as both a sedan and as a sport utility vehicle). In wake of the decision to discontinue what many police officers referred to simply as the "Crown Vic," some agencies decided to switch to sport utility vehicles (SUVs). However, critics of this decision noted that SUVs have much poorer gas mileage than do standard automobiles. Police vehicles also spend a lot of time idling, further eroding vehicle fuel efficiency. Thus, two standards were now needed to evaluate police vehicles: miles per gallon while driving and miles per gallon while idling.[51] While some states and localities may purchase vehicles directly from manufacturers, other states such as North Carolina contracted with four different dealerships from which police vehicles were purchased.[52]

In addition to vehicles used by police departments, police officers require myriad pieces of equipment ranging from their personal firearm to their uniform to other devices, such as handcuffs. Galls, which markets itself as "the authority in public safety equipment and apparel" lists twenty different types of first responder gear on its main webpage ranging from uniforms to surveillance equipment.[53] Indeed, there are dozens of companies in the business of providing equipment to both police departments and individual officers.[54]

While one might think these "tools of the trade" are simply provided to all officers by their departments, that is not always the case. Some local police departments provide officers an allowance to cover some or most of the costs of uniforms, personal firearms, ammunition, and flashlights while other departments require officers to cover those costs themselves. For example, Tim Dees, a retired police officer, noted in an online forum that a big expense police departments often do not cover is uniform upkeep. Dees noted that he spent between $800 and $1,200 annually on dry-cleaning charges for his uniforms.[55] Similarly, Meg Handley, writing in 2009, found that a basic full dress uniform for a police officer cost $2,487, a winter field uniform cost $766, and a summer field uniform cost $552.[56]

Thus, when you think about it, there are many companies in the business of supplying goods to police departments. Some of these goods are provided to officers by their departments, while others expect their officers to purchase their own equipment. This can be extremely difficult because local police officers are not especially well paid, but they also do a job where they often put their life on the line. That is difficult or stressful enough. Either not having the most up-to-date equipment or not being able to afford certain necessities for a job will undoubtedly cause even more stress.

## Funding the Police

An obvious source of funding police departments at the state and local levels of government are taxes paid by citizens. Yet, taxes are not the only source by which government organizations like police departments receive funding. Furthermore, in response to recessions and general budgetary shortfalls, many local governments have to either cut budgets or look for alternative avenues to fund their agencies. Some people might think that police departments are a basic necessity—after all, society needs protection from criminals, especially in difficult times. Nonetheless, police departments—like all criminal justice agencies—occasionally suffer budget cuts just like other government agencies. As a result, unless police departments want to simply cut their resources or personnel, they need to identify alternative revenue sources.

## Federal Grants to Fund Local Police

While states and localities can take advantage of taxes to help fund their governmental endeavors, another source of revenue received from the federal government are **federal grants**. According to the Congressional Budget Office (CBO), in fiscal year 2011, the federal government provided $607 billion in federal grants to state and local governments, accounting for 17 percent of total federal outlays, 4 percent of gross domestic product (GDP), and 25 percent of spending by state and local governments that year.[57] Some of these grants are called **block grants**, while others are known as **categorical formula grants**. Block grants are a specified amount of aid the federal government provides to state and local governments to assist them in addressing broad purposes such as community development, social services, public health, or law enforcement. Categorical formula grants, on the other hand, come with strict limitations on how the money can be spent and are given only if the state or local government complies with certain regulations.[58] Categorical grants take two forms. **Project grants** are competitive grants awarded by the federal government to fund research projects, such as projects geared toward reducing gang activity in a major city, and are typically three years in duration. In project grants, Congress or the executive branch establishes a set of criteria that form the basis for evaluating applications received from state or local governments for such projects. Certain grants to implement education reforms, to construct transportation projects, or for law enforcement purposes have recently been awarded through project grant competitions. Robert Lowry and Matthew Potoski have argued that project grants are inherently politicized, representing specific types of federal projects that lawmakers would like to see funded.[59] **Formula grants**, on the other hand, are noncompetitive awards given by the federal government using a predetermined formula based on Census or other similar data. These grants are sometimes also known as *state-administered programs*. Medicare and Medicaid are perhaps the best-known examples of formula grants. In June 2009, the Census Bureau reported that during fiscal year 2007 the federal government obligated over $446 billion to state and local governments through formula grants.[60]

An excellent example of a federal project grant involving the police occurred in 1994 when Congress passed and President **Bill Clinton** signed into law the **Violent Crime Control and Law Enforcement Act of 1994**, popularly known at the time as simply "The Crime Bill."[61] The largest piece of legislation of its type in the history of the United States, the legislation consisted of 356 pages and provided for the hiring of 100,000 new police officers, $9.7 billion in funding for prisons, and $6.1 billion in funding for prevention programs designed with significant input from experienced police officers.[62] Furthermore, a new federal agency was created, the **Office of Community Oriented Policing Services** (COPS), to oversee the awarding of the funds and provide resources on local policing for both practitioners and academics.[63]

While campaigning for the presidency, then Governor Bill Clinton wanted to be seen as a "law-and-order" candidate, a moniker frequently associated with the Republican Party. His idea of adding 100,000 police on the streets was viewed by political pundits as a grand gesture to show that he was seriously committed to a "law-and-order" agenda. Clinton also wanted to ensure this was done in an acceptable way. While Clinton wanted to court Republicans and Independents to vote for him, he also did not want to alienate voters in the Democratic Party. Thus, Clinton made it a condition of receiving Crime Bill funding that departments were pursuing or had already embraced *community-oriented policing* (COP), a developing organizational model for local police departments that shifted emphasis from reactive to proactive policing and stressed improving relationships between local police departments and the people the departments were serving, particularly minority communities.[64]

Federal grants are often tied to such buzz or splashy issues. Edward Maguire noted that the implications of hiring more officers under the Crime Bill were clear: if any police agency wanted to use the program to hire new officers, they would have to embrace community policing. In a study of 236 large metropolitan American police departments, Maguire found that only nine percent of these departments had no plans to implement any aspect of community policing. While some departments had begun community-policing programs prior to passage of the Crime Bill, Maguire believed the bill's funding stipulations clearly affected implementation of these programs in local departments.[65]

## Federal Grants and Moral Panics

In addition to federal grants influencing state and local policy, these grants can also lead to the creation of specific programs or units within police departments. Marjorie Zatz, for example, has argued that the creation of specialized gang units in many local police departments has been dictated by the availability of federal grants. Zatz believed that in the rush to procure gang funding, many police chiefs used stereotypes about race to convince people that gang problems were rampant in their cities when no such problem actually existed. She also argued that *moral panics* were often created to obtain these federal funds.[66] Moral panics surrounding crime are especially important as knee-jerk policy responses to them often occur and, in some cases, billions of dollars are earmarked to address the "problem." While not specifically calling the proliferation of specialized gang units a result of a moral panic, Charles Katz noted in 2001 that 85% of *all* specialized gang units in local law enforcement agencies had been created in the previous ten years. In a study of a Midwestern police department Katz referred to as "Junction City," he argued that creation of the department's specialized gang unit was due more to political pressure than to the reality of a true gang problem in Junction City.[67] In a subsequent study with two additional colleagues, Katz argued that the establishment of gang units illustrated resource dependence theory, which argues that how organizations (like police departments) procure their resources—personnel, funding, etc.—affects their behavior.[68] Some police departments will seek federal grants to obtain new personnel or equipment with the intended purpose of the grant being of secondary concern.[69]

## Federal Grants and the Militarization of the Police

Finally, a more recent federal grant program involving local police departments has created more than a little controversy. Prior to September 11, 2001, local police departments began to arm themselves more heavily. Enhanced firepower was not just occurring in very large police departments, such as New York or Los Angeles, but even in very small departments. In a phenomenon they called "Militarizing Mayberry," **Peter Kraska** and **Louis Cubellis** found that over sixty-five percent of the 311 police departments that served populations between 20,000 and 50,000 people had **Paramilitary Police Units** (PPU), what are more commonly known as **Special Weapons And Tactics (SWAT) teams**. Kraska and Cubellis argued that many of these specialized units were not needed and represented a growing militarization of many rural police departments. Furthermore, to justify the proliferation of these units across small-town America, they began engaging in activities not traditionally associated with SWAT teams, such as serving search warrants and, in some instances, conducting patrols in "high crime areas." Although Kraska and Cubellis do not specifically use the word "cool" to describe the perceptions of local officers about enhanced firepower and increased use of SWAT teams in non-traditional ways, Kraska and Cubellis found many officers essentially thought that it was "cool" to either be a member of these units or have one in their department.[70]

Enhanced firepower for local officers and the proliferation of SWAT units in local departments have been directly tied to federal grants that support such initiatives. According to the American Civil Liberties Union's (ACLU) recent report *War Comes Home*, the Department of Defense (DOD) operates the **1033 Program** through the Defense Logistics Agency's (DLA) Law Enforcement Support Office (LESO), whose motto is "from warfighter to crime fighter." According to the ACLU report, more than 17,000 state and local police agencies are eligible to participate in the 1033 Program, which has transferred $4.3 billion worth of military-style equipment to the departments. Not coincidentally, the use of military equipment by local and state police agencies has increased dramatically, as evidenced by these numbers: in 1990, the value of transferred property was about $1 million; by 2013, the value of military-style property controlled by local and state police departments had skyrocketed to nearly $450 million. The 1033 Program authorizes the Department of Defense to transfer property that is "excess to the needs of the department," which can include *new* equipment. The ACLU report indicates that thirty-six percent of the property transferred pursuant to the program is *brand new*. It seems the DLA can purchase new property from an equipment or weapons manufacturer and then transfer it to a local law enforcement agency *free of charge*. The ACLU also uncovered numerous examples of transfers that might appear curious. For example, during the years covered by their investigation, the ACLU found that North Little Rock, Arkansas, police obtained at least 34 automatic and semi-automatic rifles, two MARCbots (robots designed for use in Afghanistan that are capable of being armed), several ground troop helmets, and a Mamba tactical vehicle. The Arkansas state coordinator found that the LESO application for participation and the required memorandum of agreement between the State of Arkansas and DLA were outdated; many weapons were also unaccounted for in the inventory. In spite of this, the coordinator signed off on a form that said all the inventory forms were accurate. Bay County, Florida, received military-style rifles, a forklift, and several utility trucks. The same county also has numerous M-16s, M-14s, sniper rifles, submachine guns, and ballistic shields, though it is not clear from the records whether Bay County obtained those items through the 1033 Program, from another federal source, or otherwise. Gwinnett County, Georgia, received nearly 60 military-style rifles, as well as numerous combat vests and Kevlar helmets.[71]

Police agencies are also permitted to transfer equipment obtained through the 1033 Program between each other, and the ACLU uncovered numerous examples of such exchanges. There also does not appear to be any limitations on or oversight of this practice. If police departments cannot obtain military-style equipment through federal grant programs, they may be able to do so through such groups as the **National Association for the Exchange of Industrial Resources** (NAEIR), which collects property from the Department of Defense through a federal property dispersal program. For a fee of $595, an agency can purchase five, 200-page catalogs from which it may select free goods. The only catch is that the agencies must either pick up the goods from a main distribution center in Galesburg, Illinois, or pay shipping and handling.[72]

## *Funding Law Enforcement Agencies: Traffic Citations*

While some citizens see taxes as deductions from their paychecks that fund government operations, there is another way that governments and their agencies, including police departments, are able to tax Americans: traffic tickets. Granted, for one to receive a ticket—whether a moving violation or a parking infraction—he or she must (hopefully) have done something wrong. Yet, for some observers, local police departments go beyond simply enforcing the "rules of the road" intended to make driving safer. As Jeffrey Ward and colleagues have noted, some locations become known as "speed traps" out of overzealous police enforcement of traffic laws. In their study, Ward and colleagues analyzed the traffic enforcement actions of members of a small-town police department in Waldo, Florida. To identify and catch more speeders and, therefore, raise revenue, the town changed the speed limit repeatedly over stretches of road within the town's geographic boundaries. By establishing speed limits that required drivers to repeatedly speed up and slow down on various stretches of road, the town actually encouraged drivers to violate posted speed limits. This policy became so well known that the American Automobile Association (AAA) actually posted a large billboard 2½ miles before the town warning that a speed trap was ahead. Waldo, Florida, was only one of two towns in the entire United States to which AAA gave this distinction.[73] Three years after Ward's study was published, the Waldo City Council voted to disband the Police Department after a Florida Department of Law Enforcement (FDLE) investigation determined the police chief had ordered each officer to write at least twelve traffic citations per twelve-hour shift or face some form of discipline. During 2013, the seven officers employed by the department filed 11,603 traffic citations. Roughly half of the town's revenue came from traffic ticket fines.[74]

Yet, while the town of Waldo may be an example of one of the more egregious types of behavior of a town attempting to raise revenue through traffic tickets, there are many other cases that exemplify the importance of traffic ticket revenue to local government budgets. In Missouri, state auditors found that the town of Randolph, with a population of only 47 people, raised more than 75% of the town's $270,000 budget from the collection of traffic tickets.[75] As a result of such abuses, the state legislature passed a law that limited a city or town's revenues from tickets to 35% of total revenues; any funds collected over the 35% cap must then be allocated to the county schools. In the city of Burlington, Vermont, so many citizens were behind on payment of traffic tickets that the city offered a "Driver Restoration Day" that allowed citizens to pay all outstanding traffic tickets for $20 each. More than one thousand people participated, and extra police officers were needed to help keep order during the event.[76]

## Funding Police Departments Using Asset Forfeiture: Policing for Profit?

Have you ever seen a police car or other government vehicle carrying a specific message such as "seized from drug dealers" or "paid for with drug dealer assets"? These messages advertise an important byproduct of the "war on drugs" that is commonly used by local governments and law enforcement agencies to supplement their budgets—**asset forfeiture.** Asset forfeiture can take two forms: criminal asset forfeiture and civil asset forfeiture.

Each time a drug dealer is arrested, charged with a crime or crimes, and convicted, the government may choose to seize their property—including homes, cars, boats, RVs, and other types of property. The government can then either keep the property to be used by the police or sell the property at government-sponsored auctions and keep the proceeds. This situation illustrates criminal asset forfeiture: once an individual is charged with a crime and convicted on those charges, the government can seize any assets that were created by the criminal conduct.

There is another form of asset forfeiture that has many practitioners, attorneys, and academics concerned: civil asset forfeiture. Civil asset forfeiture refers to the government's power to take property *suspected* of being involved in a crime or crimes *without having to charge, let alone convict, the owner of any wrongdoing.* Since civil forfeiture proceedings are against the *property,* the government can take it despite the innocence of its owner. For example, say that Smith and his wife own a motel with 15 rooms. Should any guests use their rooms for criminal activities, such as distributing drugs or for prostitution— either without the Smiths' knowledge or consent, or even if the Smiths work with law enforcement to stop the activities—the government can seize their motel under civil asset forfeiture rules.[77]

According to John Kramer, for most of American history, proceeds from asset forfeitures went not to the law enforcement agencies responsible for the seizures, but to the government's general fund. That began to change in the 1980s when Congress, in 1984, amended portions of the Comprehensive Drug Abuse and Prevention Act of 1970 and created the Assets Forfeiture Fund. It was into this fund that the attorney general was to deposit all net forfeiture proceeds for use by the Department of Justice and other federal law enforcement agencies. Subsequent amendments expanded what law enforcement could do with these funds, including allowing their use for such expenses as purchasing vehicles and overtime pay. After these amendments, federal agencies were able to retain and spend forfeiture proceeds—subject only to very loose restrictions—giving them a direct financial stake in generating forfeiture funds.

Additionally, the United States Department of Justice created a program called Equitable Sharing (ES) under which a state or local law enforcement agency that directly participated in an investigation or prosecution resulting in a federal forfeiture can request an "equitable share" of the net proceeds of the forfeiture, which could deliver up to 80 percent of any seized asset's worth back to local police departments as supplemental revenue.[78] As law enforcement agencies became incentivized to pursue criminal asset forfeiture against drug offenders, it was only a matter of time before these agencies realized that they had another weapon in their arsenal which was much easier to use because it did not require them to charge, let alone convict, a defendant before seizing his or her property. Thus, the police began turning toward civil asset forfeiture as a revenue-generating stream to supplement existing budgets.

With these changes, critics have argued, began the modern era of "policing for profit." Many states followed the federal government's profit-making example by amending their civil forfeiture laws to give law enforcement agencies a direct share of forfeited proceeds. One change of note occurred in 2000 when Congress passed the Civil Asset Forfeiture Reform Act (CAFRA), amending various provisions of federal forfeiture law. Although CAFRA created modest reforms, it failed to fundamentally alter how forfeiture proceeds could be distributed. Perhaps more importantly, it did not eliminate the profit motive that law enforcement agencies have for using civil asset forfeiture. No longer is forfeiture tied to the practical difficulties of obtaining jurisdiction over an individual to seize his or her property. Rather, it is far easier to obtain jurisdiction over the property.

Particularly problematic with civil asset forfeiture is the burden it creates on those seeking to block the government from seizing their property. As described by John Kramer, in criminal proceedings, the government must prove the defendant's guilt "beyond a reasonable doubt" before it can sanction the defendant by seizing his or her property. The standard also helps protect the rights of innocent people wrongfully charged with a crime. However, innocent property owners enjoy no such protections. In only two states (Nebraska and Wisconsin) does the civil forfeiture standard match the criminal standard of "beyond reasonable doubt." Under federal law and in many states, police agencies can seize property using civil asset forfeiture by asserting "probable cause" that the property is involved with illegal activities, and keep the property by showing proof "beyond a preponderance of evidence" that crimes involving the property occurred. Furthermore, the property owner is faced with proving his or her innocence in forfeiture cases. In other words, with civil forfeiture, property owners are effectively guilty until proven innocent. The increased burden (including substantial legal costs) of proving one's innocence can result in owners abandoning rightful claims to seized property. If owners do not fight civil forfeiture and the government wins by default, law enforcement agencies are more likely to engage in it.[79]

The end result of the rise in police use of asset forfeiture is telling. In a survey John Worrall conducted of 1,400 municipal and county law enforcement executives, he found that civil asset forfeiture was deemed a "necessary budgetary supplement" for many of these departments. As a result, Worrall argued, use of civil asset forfeiture has made law enforcement "addicted" to the "war on drugs" and created an inherent conflict of interest for the police. What is more important—enforcing the law or generating revenue?[80] One interesting development occurred in 2015 when United States Attorney General **Eric Holder** announced an end to the Equitable Sharing program.[81] This could signal a shift is occurring in the practice of asset forfeiture, but only time will tell.

# Politics & Current Issues

Much of the modern era of police seems to be devoted to depoliticizing the police. There were many who seemed fed up with the notion that the police were merely political tools or the shock troopers of whatever political machine/regime was in power at that time. Given the fragmented authority that exists in the federalist system of the United States, how much separation exists between the police and local/state governments varies. Depending upon where you live, you may have a rather unique view of law enforcement. Nonetheless, no matter how much people want to take the supposed politics out of law enforcement practices, at a fundamental level this is impossible. Law enforcement, as the name implies, is charged with enforcing the law. Since law is created by a political process, law enforcement is not only engaging in politics, law enforcement is also the primary agent of social control in any society. Completely separating politics from the enforcement of laws is simply not practical.

One example of how law enforcement can engage in the political process is how vigorously law enforcement officers enforce the law. Before marijuana was legalized in the state of Colorado, the city of Denver passed a ballot initiative in 2007 that resulted in an interesting ordinance stating, "The Denver Police Department shall make the investigation, arrest and prosecution of marijuana offenses, where the marijuana was intended for adult personal use, the City's lowest law enforcement priority." Obviously, this law is a little vague. Is law enforcement only supposed to enforce marijuana prohibition when they are bored and have nothing else to do (such as the enforcement of more "important" crimes) or was this law essentially marijuana decriminalization where marijuana is not officially legal? Needless to say, some within law enforcement were not happy. One sergeant within the Denver Police Department argued that he found it rather outlandish to believe that officers would simply not enforce the law.[82] Thus, prior to marijuana legalization in the state of Colorado, officers in Denver were presented with a choice. If they see an adult smoking marijuana, do they arrest them or not? While an officer might respond that they are merely enforcing the law, how they enforce the law is inherently a political action.

In 1968, the Supreme Court delivered a momentous decision that affected the job of police officers. In *Terry v. Ohio*,[83] the Court created the new standard of reasonable suspicion, which allowed law enforcement officers to pat down a suspect if the officer believed that the suspect might be armed with a weapon or pose some danger to the officer. Some people refer to such encounters as "Terry Stops" or "**stop and frisks**." Regardless of what one chooses to call it, the Supreme Court legitimized a tactic that has become inherently controversial. Very few people would question the need for officers to feel safe when they conduct their jobs and in many instances, a lone officer might have to deal with multiple suspects at a time before backup can arrive. A suspect producing a weapon while an officer has his/her back turned is a legitimate fear of police officers. Yet the best of policies can be abused, even if intentions are good.

For a time, New York City, a place some people refer to as the best city in the world, was a cesspool. The city was crime-ridden. It was perceived that decent folks could not go out without fearing for their lives or becoming the victim of a crime. Beginning in the 1990s, the **New York City Police Department** (NYPD) began aggressive new policies where officers were given broad latitude to perform stops and frisks of many people in the city for a variety of crimes—some major and some very minor. Crime in the city went down, much as it did in many other places in the United States during that time. Many credited the new police tactics as a contributing factor to the large drops in crime in New York City.[84] Yet not all was rosy in New York City. As multiple studies have found, the targets of these stop and frisk searches were disproportionately minorities— especially people who were of African-American and Latino heritage. While some people simply saw racism, others saw a less nefarious reason. Crime is more often discovered by law enforcement in poorer and structurally disadvantaged neighborhoods. More often, racial minorities make up a disproportionate amount of the citizens in these neighborhoods. However, in a study conducted by Andrew Gelman and colleagues, they found that stop and frisks seem to disproportionately target minorities—even when controlling for the higher likelihood that they will be charged with committing a crime.[85]

# Conclusion

While we could give you more examples, the political issues surrounding police really boil down to two questions: how do law enforcement officers enforce the law, and are these policies equally enforced? Overall, is it unfeasible that the enforcement of laws will be equal across agencies, or even officers, as it is a system run by human beings, most of whom are fallible. Furthermore, in order for law enforcement to be effective, officers must be able to make split-second decisions in uncertain situations. Thus, officers have a great deal of autonomy and discretion. This can further the inequality of what laws are enforced, and how they are enforced.

While the professionalization of law enforcement has improved tremendously, the United States is still left with a system that is problematic. This is primarily attributable to money—specifically, the monetary contingencies for funding of police agencies, as well as the underpaid officers. In all likelihood, additional funding as a reward, instead of the withholding of funding as a punishment, would eventually aid in determining effective methods of policing.

# Key Terms

- The Federal Kidnapping Act
- The Drug Enforcement Administration
- Bureau of Alcohol, Tobacco, Firearms and Explosives
- Municipal/city police departments
- Sheriff's departments
- Specialized police
- Metro Transit Police Department
- International Union of Police Associations
- Civilianization
- Federal grants
- Block grants
- Categorical formula grants
- Project grants
- Formula grants
- Violent Crime Control and Law Enforcement Act of 1994
- Office of Community Oriented Policing Service
- Paramilitary Police Units
- Special Weapons And Tactics
- 1033 Program

- National Association for the Exchange of Industrial Resources
- Asset forfeiture
- Crown Victoria
- New York City Police Department
- *Terry v. Ohio*
- Stop and frisk

# Key People

- Charles Augustus Lindbergh
- O. W. Wilson
- Eric Holder
- Bill Clinton
- Peter Kraska and Louis Cubellis
- Samuel Walker

# Discussion Questions

1) As we referenced in the text, the NYPD is a general law enforcement agency with over 30,000 officers. Identify the pros and cons of an agency this large. Think in context of enforcement, control, officer discretion, and autonomy.
2) Do you believe tribal lands should have their own police agencies? Why or why not?
3) In addition to being underpaid, police officers are often responsible for a number of expenses (such as uniform maintenance, bullet-proof vests, etc.). What effect do you believe this would have on a police officer's behavior? What effect do you believe this has on the hiring and retention of police officers?
4) Police agencies' budgets are contingent upon federal grants. Do you believe federal stipulations aid or hinder the efficacy of police agencies ability to enforce and prevent crime? Why? Provide examples.
5) In the text, we discussed the use of Terry stops in New York City. Do you believe these stops were attributable to a decrease in crime? Why or why not?

# Notes

1. Reaves, Brian A. 2011. *Census of State and Local Law Enforcement Agencies, 2008*. Washington, DC: Bureau of Justice Statistics.

2. Reaves, Brian A. 2011. *Federal Law Enforcement Officers, 2008*. Washington, DC: Bureau of Justice Statistics.

3. Trex, Ethan. 2010. "12 Specialized Government-Run Police Forces." Retrieved May 24, 2015 from http://mentalfloss.com/article/24463/12-specialized-government-run-police-forces.

4. Famous Cases & Criminals: The Lindbergh Kidnapping. The FBI: Federal Bureau of Investigation. Retrieved on April 6, 2015 at: http://www.fbi.gov/about-us/history/famous-cases/the-lindbergh-kidnapping.

5. Fields, Gary and John R. Emshwiller. 2011. "Many Failed Efforts to Count Nation's Federal Criminal Laws." *Wall Street Journal*, July 23, 2011. Retrieved on May 22, 2015 at: http://www.wsj.com/articles/SB10001424052702304319804576389601079728920.

6. What We Investigate. The FBI: Federal Bureau of Investigation. Retrieved on April 6, 2015 at: http://www.fbi.gov/about-us/investigate/what_we_investigate.

7. Protective Mission. United States Secret Service. Retrieved on April 6, 2015 at: http://www.secretservice.gov/protection.shtml.

8. Investigative Mission. United States Secret Service. Retrieved on April 6, 2015 at: http://www.secretservice.gov/investigations.shtml.

9. Walker, Samuel. 1999. *The Police in America*. 3rd Edition. New York: McGraw-Hill.

10. The Purpose of the California Highway Patrol. California Highway Patrol. Retrieved on April 6, 2015 at: http://www.chp.ca.gov/html/history/purpose.html.

11. CHP & California State Police Merger. California State Police Merger. Retrieved on April 6, 2015 at: http://www.chp.ca.gov/html/history/merger.html.

12. Law Enforcement. State of California Department of Justice: Office of the Attorney General. Retrieved on April 6, 2015 at: https://oag.ca.gov/law.

13. Mission Statement. California Department of Alcoholic Beverage Control. Retrieved on April 6, 2015 at: http://www.abc.ca.gov/mission.html.

14. Walker, Samuel. 1999. *The Police in America*. 3rd Edition. New York: McGraw-Hill.

15. Frequently Asked Questions: Police Administration. NYPD. Retrieved on April 6, 2015 at: http://www.nyc.gov/html/nypd/html/faq/faq_police.shtml#1.

16. Reaves, Brian A. 2011. *Census of State and Local Law Enforcement Agencies, 2008*. Washington, DC: Bureau of Justice Statistics.

17. *Ibid*.

18. *Ibid*.

19. APD History. Los Angeles World Airports. Retrieved on April 6, 2015 at: http://www.lawa.org/airportpolice/.

20. Metro Transit Police. Metro. Retrieved on April 6, 2015 at: http://www.wmata.com/about_metro/transit_police/.

21. Sloan, John J. 1992. "The Modern Campus Police: An Analysis of Their Evolution, Structure, and Function." *American Journal of Police*, 11(2):85–106.

22. Paoline, Eugene A. III and John J. Sloan III. 2003. "Variability in the organizational structure of contemporary campus law enforcement agencies: A national-level analysis." *Policing*, 26(4): 612–639.

23.  Reaves, Brian A. 2012. *Campus Law Enforcement, 2011–2012*. Washington, DC: Bureau of Justice Statistics.

24.  Hart, Rebecca A. and M. Alexander Lowther. 2008. "Honoring Sovereignty: Aiding Tribal Efforts to Protect Native American Women from Domestic Violence." *California Law Review*, 96(1): 185–233.

25.  Hickman, Matthew J. 2003. *Tribal Law Enforcement, 2000*. Washington, DC: Bureau of Justice Statistics.

26.  Button, Mark. 2002. *Private Policing*. Portland, OR: Willan.

27.  *Ibid*.

28.  De Waard, Jaap. 1999. "The Private Security Industry in International Perspective." *European Journal on Criminal Policy and Research*, 7(2): 143–174.

29.  Strom, Kevin et al. 2010. *The Private Security Industry: A Review of the Definitions, Available Data Sources, and Paths Moving Forward*. Retrieved on April 12, 2015 at: https://www.ncjrs.gov/pdffiles1/bjs/grants/232781.pdf.

30.  *Ibid*.

31.  Berry, Jan, Greg O'Connor, Maurice Punch, and Paul Wilson. 2008. "Strange Union: Changing Patterns of Reform, Representation, and Unionization in Policing". *Police Practice and Research*, 9(2): 113–130.

32.  Walker, Samuel. 1999. *The Police in America*. 3rd Edition. New York: McGraw-Hill.

33.  Adams, Roy J. 2008. "The Human Right of Police to Organize and Bargain Collectively". *Police Practice and Research*, 9(2): 165–172.

34.  Walker, Samuel. 1999. *The Police in America*. 3rd Edition. New York: McGraw-Hill.

35.  Skogan, Wesley G. 2008. "Why Reforms Fail". *Policing & Society*, 18(1): 23–34.

36.  IUPA. 2015. "Our History". Retrieved on April 12, 2015 at: https://iupa.org/our-history/.

37.  Walker, Samuel. 1999. *The Police in America*. 3rd Edition. New York: McGraw-Hill.

38.  Jermier, John M. and Leslie J. Berkes. 1979. "Leader Behavior in a Police Command Bureaucracy: A Closer Look at the Quasi-Military Model". *Administrative Quarterly*, 24(1): 1–23.

39.  Walker, Samuel. 1999. *The Police in America*. 3rd Edition. New York: McGraw-Hill.

40.  Bordua, David J. and Albert J. Reiss, Jr. 1966. "Command, Control, and Charisma: Reflections on Police Bureaucracy. *American Journal of Sociology*, 72(1): 68–76.

41.  *Ibid*.

42.  Lipsky, Michael. 1980. *Street-Level Bureaucracy: Dilemmas of the Individual in Public Services*. New York: Russell Sage Foundation.

43.  Forst, Brian. 2000. "The Privatization and Civilianization of Policing". *Criminal Justice*, 2: 19–79.

44.  *Ibid*.

45.  Hudson, James R. 1971. "Police Review Boards and Police Accountability." *Law and Contemporary Problems*, 36(4): 515–538.

46.  Salisbury, Stephan. 2012. "The Cost of America's Police State." *Salon*, March 5, 2012. Retrieved on June 6, 2015 at: http://www.salon.com/2012/03/05/the_cost_of_americas_police_state/.

47.  McDonald, Terrence T. 2014. "Jersey City to Award Contract for Weapons, Ammo Under Controversial New Policy." *The Jersey Journal*. Retrieved on April 14, 2015 at: http://www.nj.com/hudson/index.ssf/2014/09/jersey_city_awarding_contract_for_weapons_ammo_

under_controversial_new_rules.html.

48. Robinette, Eric. 2013. "More Police Departments Choosing SUVs over Sedans". *Journal-News*. Retrieved on April 14, 2015 at: http://www.journal-news.com/news/news/more-police-departments-choosing-suvs-over-sedans/ncPKS/.

49. State Term Contract: 070B—Law Enforcement Vehicles. Retrieved on April 14, 2015 at: http://www.doa.state.nc.us/pandc/070b.pdf.

50. Galls Company Website. Retrieved on April 14, 2015 at: http://www.galls.com/Pages/LAW.

51. See, for example, http://www.policeone.com/manufacturer-directory/.

52. Dees, Tim. 2013. Do Law Enforcement Officers Choose their Own Weapons and Gear? *Quora.com*. Retrieved on April 14, 2015 at: http://www.quora.com/Do-law-enforcement-officers-choose-their-own-weapons-and-gear.

53. Handley, Meg. 2009. "Uniform Coverage: The Price a Chicago Police Officer Must Pay." *Medill Reports*. Retrieved on June 10, 2015 at: http://news.medill.northwestern.edu/chicago/news.aspx?id=134375.

54. Congressional Budget Office. 2013. *Federal Grants to State and Local Governments*. Retrieved on June 6, 2015 at: https://www.cbo.gov/publication/43967.

55. Benz, Rainer. 2015. Categorical Grants: Definitions and Examples. Retrieved June 6, 2015 from http://study.com/academy/lesson/categorical-grants-definition-examples.html

56. Lowry, Robert C and Matthew Potoski. 2004. "Organized Interests and the Politics of Federal Discretionary Grants." *The Journal of Politics*, 66(2): 513–533.

57. General Accounting Office. 2009. *Formula Grants*. Washington, DC: General Accounting Office.

58. Lewis, Neil A. 1994. "President Foresees Safer U.S." Retrieved on June 6, 2015 at: http://www.nytimes.com/1994/08/27/us/president-foresees-safer-us.html.

59. Johnson, Carrie. 2014. "Twenty Years' Later, Parts of Major Crime Bill Viewed as Terrible Mistake." Retrieved June 6, 2015 from http://www.npr.org/2014/09/12/347736999/20-years-later-major-crime-bill-viewed-as-terrible-mistake.

60. Office of Community Oriented Police Services. nd. About Us. Retrieved on June 6, 2015 at: http://www.cops. usdoj.gov/default.asp?Item=2754.

61. Chapman, Steve. 2001. "Invisible Cops" How Clinton's Plan to Field 100,000 New Police turned into a Pork Barrel as Usual". *Slate.com*. Retrieved on April 14, 2015 at: http://www.slate.com/articles/news_and_politics/politics/2001/11/invisible_cops.html.

62. Maguire, Edward R. 1997. "Structural Change in Large Municipal Police Organizations During the Community Policing Era". *Justice Quarterly*, 14: 547–576.

63. Zatz, Marjorie S. 1987. "Chicano Youth Gangs and Crime: The Creation of a Moral Panic." *Contemporary Crises*, 11: 129–158.

64. Krinsky, Charles. 2013."Introduction: The Moral Panic Concept." Pp. 1–14 in Charles Krinsky (Ed.), *The Ashgate Research Companion to Moral Panics*. Burlington, VT: Ashgate Publishers. See also: John Sloan and Bonnie Fisher. 2010. *The Dark Side of the Ivory Tower: Campus Crime as a Social Problem*. New York: Cambridge University Press.

65. Bryant, Lee. 2014. "The Media and Crime." Retrieved from http://www.historylearningsite.co. uk/ media_crime.htm.

66. Katz, Charles M. 2001. "The Establishment of a Police Gang Unit: An Examination of Organizational and Environmental Factors". *Criminology*, 39(1): 37–73.

67. Kraska, Peter B. and Louis J. Cubellis. 1997. "Militarizing Mayberry and Beyond: Making Sense of American Paramilitary Policing". *Justice Quarterly*, 14: 607–629.

68. Dansky, Kara. 2014. *War Comes Home: The Excessive Militarization of American Policing.* New York: ACLU Foundation.

69. Hamilton, Melanie. 2014. "Resources for Law Enforcement Aren't Limited to Federal Grants." Retrieved on April 14, 2015 at: http://www.policegrantshelp.com/news/100253-The-Money-Crunch-Getting-the-Goods/.

70. Ward, Jeffrey T. Matt R. Nobles, Lonn Lanza-Kaduce, Lora M. Levett, and Rob Tillyer. 2011. "Caught in their own Speed Trap: The Intersection of Speed Enforcement Policy, Police Legitimacy, and Decision Acceptance." *Police Quarterly*, 14(3): 251–276.

71. WFLA.Com. 2014. "Waldo Police Department Disbanded after Ticket Quota Scandal." Retrieved on April 14, 2015 at: http://www.wfla.com/story/26671583/waldo-police-department-disbanded-after-ticket-quota-scandal.

72. Aho, Karen. 2011. "The Town that Lived Off Speeding Tickets". Fox Business. Retrieved on April 14, 2015 at: http://www.foxbusiness.com/personal-finance/2011/10/19/town-that-lived-off-speeding-tickets/.

73. Achen, Paris. 2015. "Hundreds Gather to Pay Off Vermont Tickets". *Burlington Free Press.* Retrieved on April 14, 2015 at: http://www.burlingtonfreepress.com/story/news/local/vermont/<d>2015/03/20/thousands-gather-pay-vermont-tickets/25078153/.

74. Kramer, John H. 2015. *Fighting Civil Forfeiture Abuse.* Arlington, VA: Institute for Justice. Retrieved June 6, 2015 from http://www.ij.org/massachusetts-civil-forfeiture-background.

75. Catalog of Federal Domestic Assistance. nd. "Equitable Sharing Program." Retrieved June 7, 2015 from https://www.cfda.gov/index?s=program&mode=form&tab=core&id=2d77abffc79 ad8ad17d0b5427a2cfa1d.

76. Kramer, John E. 2015. *Fighting Civil Forfeiture Abuse.* Arlington, VA: Institute for Justice. Retrieved June 6, 2015 from http://www.ij.org/massachusetts-civil-forfeiture-background.

77. Worrall, John L. 2001. "Addicted to the Drug War: The Role of Civil Asset Forfeiture as a Budgetary Necessity in Contemporary Law Enforcement." *Journal of Criminal Justice*, 29(3): 171–187.

78. O'Harrow, Jr., Robert, Sari Horwitz and Steven Rich. 2015. "Holder Limits Seized-Asset Sharing Process that Split Billions with Local, State Police. *The Washington Post.* Retrieved on April 14, 2015 at: http://www.washingtonpost.com/investigations/holder-ends-seized-asset-sharing-process-that-split-billions-with-local-state-police/2015/01/16/0e7ca058-99d4-11e4-bcfb-059ec7a93ddc_story.html.

79. Nizza, Mike. 2007. "Denver Voters Set 'Lowest Priority' for Cops: Pot." *The New York Times.* Retrieved on April 15, 2015 at: http://thelede.blogs.nytimes.com/2007/11/07/denver-voters-set-lowest-priority-for-cops-pot/comment-page-2/?_r=0.

80. Terry v. Ohio, 392 U.S. 1 (1968).

81. Zimring, Franklin E. 2006. *The Great American Crime Decline.* New York: Oxford University Press.

82. Gelman, Andrew, Jeffrey Fagan, and Alex Kiss. 2007. "An Analysis of the New York City Police Department's "Stop-and-Frisk" Policy in the Context of Claims of Racial Bias." *Journal of the American Statistical Association*, 102(479): 813–823.

83. ADT. 2015. Retrieved on April 19, 2015 at: http://www.adt.com/about-adt.

84. Allied Barton. 2014. About Us. Retrieved on April 19, 2015 at: http://www.allied-barton. com/About-Us.

85.   DynCorp International. 2015. Washington Technology. Retrieved on April 19, 2015 at: http://washingtontechnology.com/toplists/top-100-lists/2012/dyncorp-international.aspx.

# Chapter 8

# The Political Economy of Courts

## Chapter Outline

- Administrative Office of the United States Courts
- Federal Law Clerks
- Assistant United States Attorneys
- State Court Employees
  - Judges
  - Intermediate Appeals Courts
  - Courts of Last Resort
  - State Court Support Staff
  - State Prosecutors
- Budgets, Costs, and Profits
  - Recovering Court Costs
  - Expert Witnesses
  - Legal Search Engines
- Politics and Current Issues
- Conclusion
- Key Terms
- Key People
- Key Cases
- Discussion Questions

# Learning Objectives

- Compare and contrast civil and criminal courts
- Compare and contrast the state and federal court systems
- Identify types of court employees
- Describe the roles and responsibilities of state and federal court employees
- Describe the development of the United States Supreme Court
- Evaluate the roles and responsibilities of the various court systems in the United States
- Evaluate the differences and similarities for defense attorneys and prosecutors
- Identify and define types and purposes of lobbying groups for attorneys
- Critically evaluate the role of money in the American court system
- Critically evaluate the role of politics in the American court system

# Introduction

In Chapter 3, we discussed how courts evolved in the United States. Specifically, we examined how courts progressed from informal and irregular pro-

ceedings, where a judge was the only pseudo-professional in the process, to a
formal adversarial system complete with a judge, prosecutor, and defense attorney. In this chapter, we discuss the different types of criminal courts in the
United States, as well as the people who work in them. Furthermore, we discuss how criminal courts are funded, how these institutions cost taxpayers
money, and how governments and individuals profit from them. Lastly, we
discuss several issues associated with political activity in criminal courts.

## Criminal Courts

One of the difficulties in describing the court system within the criminal justice system is that the court system is not entirely devoted to the prosecution of
crimes. Indeed, the American court system involves both **criminal** and **civil
courts**. Some people have argued that the distinction between **criminal** and
**civil law** is essentially arbitrary. For instance, **Edwin Sutherland** argued that
much of the criminogenic behavior of elites was punished in civil courts, while
street crimes tended to be prosecuted in criminal courts.[1] Legal scholars have
often debated these distinctions as well. For instance, Paul Robinson stated that
the most common explanation of the difference between criminal and civil systems of courts is that crimes are usually actions that require some moral repudiation of the act—something is inherently wrong about the actions of a person
who has been accused of a crime. If a person is found guilty, they should be
punished for their actions. On the other hand, a civil wrong (usually a tort or
breach of contract) implies that a person failed in some sort of duty and wronged
another person. In these instances, the person who failed in their duty owes
the person they harmed either monetary compensation or, in cases of contract
law, what they originally promised. Yet a person found liable in civil court does
not need to be punished beyond providing that compensation. Many countries
beyond just the capitalistic United States have separate court systems and make
some distinction in legal codes between crimes and civil wrongs. The need for
these two systems has puzzled many people, including legal scholars.[2] However,
one distinction exists that cannot be overlooked within the American court system: cases in American criminal courts must be proven "**beyond a reasonable
doubt**," and cases in American civil courts (in most instances) must be proven
by "**a preponderance of the evidence**"—a lesser standard of proof.[3]

So why do we bring up the distinction between criminal and civil courts?
Since court budgets, judges, and many attorneys who handle criminal defense
do not exclusively focus on the disposal of criminal cases, one could certainly
argue that some of the budgets we cite are slightly overinflated and cannot be
attributed exclusively to the criminal justice system. Furthermore, many civil

cases actually originate from actions of the criminal justice system. How does this occur? Most people who are convicted of a crime and sentenced to prison are not happy to be there and will undertake efforts to be released by appealing their convictions. Some of the appeals they file challenge trial procedures in their cases or the competency of their attorney. Some inmates will challenge the legality of their incarceration by filing *habeas corpus* motions in federal court that literally ask the court to order the "body be brought before it." Furthermore, prisoners will file other lawsuits that argue the conditions under which they are being kept violate the Eighth Amendment's prohibition of cruel and unusual punishment. Some of these lawsuits are legitimate; many are not. Nonetheless, this shows how the criminal justice system does not just involve criminal law, but can involve civil law as well.

## *United States Supreme Court*

While many people automatically think of the United States Supreme Court as one of the most powerful governmental entities in the country, it may not have originally been intended that way. Indeed, the Constitution is somewhat vague about the intended duties of the Court. **Article III of the Constitution** indicates, "The judicial power of the United States, shall be vested in one supreme Court, and in such inferior Courts as the Congress may from time to time ordain and establish."[4] Thus, the Founding Fathers seemed to care so little about the Supreme Court that they could not even devote *a single sentence* to defining the duties of the Court. Yet declaring a government action "unconstitutional" is something that many people say rather imprudently, disregarding any thought as to the term's meaning, never mind its origins. In fact, the Court's deciding the constitutionality of government actions did not first occur until the case of *Marbury v. Madison,*[5] in 1803, when the Court gave itself the power of **judicial review**.

Prior to *Marbury v. Madison*, a partisan power struggle between the Federalist Party and the newly formed Democratic-Republican Party was gripping the United States. President **John Adams**, who represented the Federalist Party, was defeated in his re-election bid for president by **Thomas Jefferson** of the Democratic-Republican Party. Once friends, after the American Revolution and the Constitutional Convention were over, the two men had very different visions for the country. After being defeated in the presidential election, Adams wanted to make Jefferson's life difficult and also ensure the Federalists still had a say in the government. Thus, between the time Adams lost the election and Jefferson was inaugurated as president, Adams sought to appoint as many Federalists to office as he could before leaving office. To create positions for these new potential office-holders, Congress passed and President Adams signed the Judiciary Act of 1801, which amended the original Judiciary Act of 1789 (discussed in Chapter 4). Passage of this new law was not entirely a political game. The legislation expanded the federal circuit courts from three to six, and created new positions so that Supreme Court Justices no longer had to preside over lower court proceedings as they once did. After the passage of the legislation, Adams had only two weeks before Jefferson took office. In an incident now referred to as "**The Midnight Judges**," Adams appointed as many Federalists as he could to the new federal circuit court positions. In addition to this expansion of the federal judiciary, the city of Washington, DC, was officially designated the nation's capital city. The creation of the new capital would require additional federal employees to govern, and allowed for more appointments from Adams.[6]

One of the many appointees was **William Marbury**, whom President Adams nominated for the position of Justice of the Peace for Washington, DC. While today we might think of a Justice of the Peace as someone who oversees shotgun weddings, as we discussed in Chapter 4, for much of the 1800s, a Justice of the Peace oversaw court proceedings in minor cases. While the United States Senate approved all of the appointments that Adams had made, not all of these "commissions" became official before Jefferson took office. When he did so, Jefferson decided not to deliver the rest of the commissions, including one that belonged to Marbury. Marbury really wanted to be Justice of the Peace of Washington, DC, so much so that he actually sued the federal government to have the commission delivered to him. Ultimately, the case ended up before the Supreme Court. In *Marbury v. Madison*, the Court ruled that Marbury was entitled to the position and a particular kind of order, known as a **writ of mandamus**, was necessary to order **James Madison**, the Secretary of State in President Jefferson's administration, to deliver the commission. However, there was a conflict between Section 13 of **the Judiciary Act**, which Marbury had relied upon when he filed the lawsuit and which authorized the Supreme Court to issue writs of mandamus, and the Constitution. According to Justice John Marshall, who authored the opinion of the Court, the Supreme Court was governed by Article III of the Constitution and a law passed by Congress could not alter the duties of the Court. Since the Supreme Court interpreted that the Constitution and the Judiciary Act were in conflict, due to the Supremacy Clause within the Constitution, the Constitution trumped the Judiciary Act and Section 13 of the Judiciary Act was unconstitutional.[7]

This may sound peculiar. Marbury won, yet simultaneously lost. This "new" ability of the Supreme Court to determine the constitutionality of legislation, known as **judicial review**, has continued to be controversial. As we stated previously, the Constitution barely mentions the Supreme Court. Thus, it is odd the Court in *Marbury* would know exactly what its duties should be. Judicial review is controversial for many legal scholars. Some scholars have argued that if the Founding Fathers had intended the Supreme Court to have the power of judicial review, the power would have been articulated by the Constitution. Other scholars have countered that not only did the Founding Fathers desire the Court to have the power of judicial review, but that such a power had previously been used by appellate courts and was intended to buttress the separation of powers and system of checks and balances the Founding Fathers deemed necessary to ensure no one branch of government became too powerful.[8]

Through judicial review, the Supreme Court stands as the ultimate authority in interpreting the Constitution and thus is often referred to as *the court of last resort*. While many think of the Supreme Court as simply an appellate court, there are instances where the Supreme Court has original jurisdiction—meaning, certain cases are actually only heard by the Supreme Court. From Article III, Section II of the Constitution, the Supreme Court is granted original jurisdiction "in all Cases affecting Ambassadors, other public Ministers and consuls, and those in which a State shall be Party."[9] One example of the latter was a case between New Jersey and New York over the ownership of **Ellis Island** (home of the Statue of Liberty). New York and New Jersey had previously signed an agreement that gave New York possession of the islands located in the channel between the states. Both Staten Island and Ellis Island are found in this channel and thus, belonged to New York. However, also within the agreement, New Jersey was granted water rights within the channel. Ownership of the islands did not become an issue until Ellis Island became a hub for new immigrants entering the United States. As the need arose for more space, New York began to fill the waterway with soil, which effectively made the island larger. Eventually, Ellis Island became bigger and actually extended into the portion of the channel that belonged to New Jersey. Ultimately, in *New Jersey v. New York* the Supreme Court ruled that part of Ellis Island belonged to New Jersey.[10]

Originally, there were five justices on the Supreme Court. Despite the efforts of President **Franklin D. Roosevelt,** whom we mentioned in Chapter 1, there are now nine justices on the Supreme Court—one chief justice and eight associate justices. The appellate jurisdiction of the Supreme Court extends to appeals from federal courts involving federal legislation and appeals from state courts involving a federal constitutional question. While approximately 7,000 to 8,000 cases are appealed to the Supreme Court every year, only about 150 cases are heard each year. For the Supreme Court to actually hear a case, a minimum of four justices must agree the case is significant enough for the Court to hear it (known as the rule of four).[11]

In Chapter 3, we discussed the Judiciary Act of 1789 in some detail, including how it established the federal court structure of the United States. The only change since that time, beyond increasing the number of federal judges, was the addition of federal magistrates in 1968 to the federal court system. Nonetheless, we believe it is important to describe again the different branches of the federal court system.

## Federal Magistrate Judges

The position of **federal magistrate judge** was created to provide assistance to federal district judges. Federal magistrate judges are appointed by majority vote of the district judges of the court within which the magistrate judge will serve for a term of eight years.[12] In 2012, 573 federal magistrate judges disposed of 1,351,236 cases. As reported in Table 8.1, the most common type of activity involving magistrate judges are preliminary hearings (27.61%).[13] While most of the cases are criminal, civil cases comprise almost 20% (264,981) of cases they hear. Among criminal case matters, proceedings included 199,686 felony pretrial matters, 376,131 felony preliminary hearings, 102,737 initial appearances, 67,747 arraignments, 49,478 detention hearings, 57,714 applications for search warrants, 51,762 applications for arrest warrants/summonses, 30,509 felony guilty pleas, and 126,714 misdemeanor cases. Regarding lawsuits filed by or on behalf of prisoners, magistrate judges issued 26,346 reports and recommendations and they conducted 431 evidentiary hearings.

## Federal District Courts

As mentioned previously, **federal district courts** are the trial courts of general jurisdiction in the federal system. There are a total of 94 federal district courts with 677 federal judges presiding over judicial matters in these courts.[15] Table 8.2 presents a summary of federal district court activity during 2012.

## Federal Appeals Courts

As we mentioned previously, there are thirteen **federal circuit courts of appeal** with a total of 179 judges assigned to them.[17] The smallest appeals court, the First Circuit, has only six judges while the Ninth Circuit, the largest, has 29 judges.[18] As the name of the courts implies, these courts handle all appeals in the federal court system. Most cases that reach federal appeals courts are

Table 8.1. Cases Heard by Federal Magistrate Judges in 2012[14]

| Cases for Federal Magistrate Judges | | Frequency | Percent |
|---|---|---|---|
| Civil Matters | | 264,981 | 19.61 |
| Criminal Matters | | | |
| | Pretrial Matters | 199,686 | 14.78 |
| | Preliminary Proceedings | 373,131 | 27.61 |
| | Initial Appearances | 102,737 | 7.60 |
| | Arraignments | 67,747 | 5.01 |
| | Detention Hearings | 49,478 | 3.66 |
| | Applications for Search Warrants | 57,714 | 4.27 |
| | Applications for Arrest Warrants/ Summons | 51,762 | 3.83 |
| | Felony Guilty Pleas | 30,509 | 2.26 |
| Lawsuits Filed by or on Behalf of Prisons | | 126,714 | 9.38 |
| | Judge-Issued Reports and Recommendations | 26,346 | 1.95 |
| | Evidentiary Hearings | 431 | 0.03 |
| Total | | 1,351,236 | 100.00 |

civil cases. For instance, in 2013, of the 56,475 cases filed, 11,924 of those cases were criminal cases and in 2014, of the 54,988 cases filed, 11,003 of those cases were criminal cases. However, as we mentioned previously, that does not tell the entire story. Of the 30,251 civil cases filed in 2013 and 30,568 cases filed in 2014, 15,031 and 15,180 of those cases were petitions from prisoners in Amer-

Table 8.2. Cases Heard by the Federal District Courts in 2012[16]

| Federal District Court Cases in 2012 | Frequency | Percent |
|---|---|---|
| Civil Cases | | 824,379 |
| | Filed | 278,442 |
| | Terminated | 271,572 |
| | Pending | 274,365 |
| Criminal Cases (Includes Transfers) | | 299,952 |
| | Filed | 94,121 |
| | Terminated | 97,728 |
| | Pending | 107,703 |

ican correctional systems. Thus, around 50% of civil cases filed are still a result of the criminal justice system.[19] Table 8.3 shows the workloads of the circuits in 2012.

## State Court Systems

A common theme throughout this textbook has been the implications of the federalist system in the United States and how the system actually encourages variation among the states. Despite the growing presence of the federal government within criminal justice, the majority of criminal cases are filed in **state courts**.[21] Keeping track of the activity in state courts is a tremendous undertaking; each year a report is disseminated that provides statistics for state court caseloads. As can be seen in Table 8.4, 103.5 million cases were filed in state courts in 2010.[22] While the distribution of legal filings against people is not evenly distributed, to provide context for this rather large number, according to the United States Census Bureau, in 2010 there were about 309.3 million people in the country. This means that in 2010, one of every three people in the United States could have had a legal case of some kind filed against them.

Table 8.3. Appeals Heard by the Federal Circuit Courts in 2012[20]

| Circuit | States | Total Appeals |
|---|---|---|
| DC Circuit | District of Columbia | 414 |
| First Circuit | Maine, Massachusetts, New Hampshire, Rhode Island and Puerto Rico | 3,059 |
| Second Circuit | Connecticut, New York and Vermont | 4,995 |
| Third Circuit | Delaware, New Jersey, Pennsylvania and Virgin Islands | 3,220 |
| Fourth Circuit | Maryland, North Carolina, South Carolina, Virginia, West Virginia | 9,296 |
| Fifth Circuit | Louisiana, Mississippi and Texas | 20,451 |
| Sixth Circuit | Kentucky, Michigan, Ohio, and Tennessee | 6,033 |
| Seventh Circuit | Illinois, Indiana, and Wisconsin | 3,465 |
| Eighth Circuit | Arkansas, Iowa, Minnesota, Missouri, Nebraska, North Dakota, South Dakota | 5,295 |
| Ninth Circuit | Alaska, Arizona, California, Idaho, Montana, Nevada, Guam, Oregon, Washington, and Hawaii | 22,816 |
| Tenth Circuit | Colorado, Kansas, New Mexico, Oklahoma, Utah, and Wyoming | 7,099 |
| Eleventh Circuit | Alabama, Florida and Georgia | 8,018 |

## State Trial Courts

There is no uniform structure for states to process such a gargantuan number of cases; in fact, they vastly differ from state to state. For instance, the Commonwealth of Massachusetts has a supreme judicial court, an appeals court, superior courts, district courts, probate/family courts, housing courts, municipal courts, and land courts. South Dakota, on the other hand, only has circuit courts (for trials) and a supreme court.[23] Thus, from this example, one could gage that the higher the population of a state, the more complex their court system is. Furthermore, one could surmise that states with higher populations are more likely to have a higher number of specialty courts that have

Table 8.4. Types of Cases Heard by State Court Systems

| Type of Case | Frequency of Cases (in Millions) |
|---|---|
| Traffic | 56.3 |
| Criminal | 20.4 |
| Civil | 19 |
| Domestic Relations | 5.9 |
| Juvenile | 1.9 |
| Total | 103.5 |

Source: LaFountain, Robert C., Richard Y. Schauffler, Shauna M. Strickland & Kathryn A. Holt. 2012. *Examining the Work of State Courts: An Analysis of 2010 State Court Caseloads.* National Center for State Courts.

what is referred to as **limited jurisdiction**—meaning these courts can only hear specific cases (the most common being traffic courts).[24] By far the most common specialty court is traffic court.

While oftentimes there is a positive correlation between a state's population and its court system complexity, there are certainly exceptions. Given the sheer diversity of state court systems, the most basic generality we can give, regarding state trial courts, is that states fall into one of two categories: **single-tiered court systems** or **multi-tiered court systems**. States in single-tiered court systems will have many general district courts that can hear any type of case. Only four states fall into this category: California, Illinois, Iowa, and Minnesota. Washington, DC, and Puerto Rico also fall into this category. While not all multi-tiered states share the complexity of the Massachusetts court system, in states with multi-tiered court systems, 79% of cases are processed in limited jurisdiction courts.

## State Appeals Courts and Courts of Last Resort

In federal court, decisions from federal district courts are appealed to federal circuit courts and ultimately appeals from federal circuit courts are heard by the United States Supreme Court. While some states follow this structure, others do not. One of the main rationales behind states establishing intermediate courts has been the ever-increasing caseloads that courts must manage.

David Neubauer and Henry Fradella have noted that approximately a century ago, many states believed there was no need for intermediate appellate courts and did not have them. One state court of last resort was enough to handle all of the appellate case workload.[25] Even today, some states do not have an intermediate court of appeals, meaning that all appeals from trial courts have to be appealed directly to the state court of last resort. Conversely, some states actually have two intermediate courts of appeals.

Why do we call some courts the "**court of last resort**"? Some states do not call their highest courts "Supreme Courts." Indeed, if you have ever watched an episode of one of the many different iterations of *Law & Order*, you would know that New York calls their trial courts "Supreme Courts" and their court of last resort the "Court of Appeals." Furthermore, Texas and Oklahoma actually have two courts of last resort, one for criminal cases and one for civil cases. The variation between state court systems is undoubtedly confusing. In an attempt to break down this information, Table 8.5 provides each state's appeals courts by number of intermediate courts (none, one, two) and number of courts of last resort (one or two).

Appellate cases typically fall into one of four categories: appeals by right, appeals by permission, death penalty appeals, and original proceedings. In 2010, 272,975 cases were filed with state appellate courts. **Appeals by right**, as the name implies, means that certain state laws include an automatic right to appeal the decision in a case and have an appeals court review the decision. This does not mean, however, the court has to engage in a full review of all aspects of the case. If a court decides that such a review is warranted, it can order one, which would include oral arguments by attorneys from both sides. In 2010, 172,632 (63%) appeals by right cases were filed in state appellate courts. In total, intermediate appellate courts hear 91% of appeals by right.

**Appeals by permission** are cases in which appeals courts have the discretion to hear the case or not. In such cases, the losing party must convince the court either that some procedural error occurred in the case or that the case raises a constitutional issue of some kind, either state or federal. In 2010, for example, 55,189 (20%) appeals by permission cases were filed in appellate courts. In total, state courts of last resort heard 79% of appeals by right.

Death penalty appeals arise from capital cases and are automatic. In fact, for a state's death penalty statute to be constitutional, it must include at least one automatic review of the decision by a state appeals court. In 2010, state appellate courts heard 390 **death penalty appeals**. This represented less than 1% of the state appellate court workload. In total, state courts of last resort hear 94% of death penalty appeals.

## Table 8.5. Appeals Courts by State

| State | None | One | Two | One | Two |
|---|---|---|---|---|---|
| | Intermediate Courts | | | Courts of Last Resort | |
| Alabama | | | X | X | |
| Alaska | | X | | X | |
| Arizona | | X | | X | |
| Arkansas | | X | | X | |
| California | | X | | X | |
| Colorado | | X | | X | |
| Connecticut | | X | | X | |
| Delaware | X | | | X | |
| Florida | | X | | X | |
| Georgia | | X | | X | |
| Hawaii | | X | | X | |
| Idaho | | X | | X | |
| Illinois | | X | | X | |
| Indiana | | | X | X | |
| Iowa | | X | | X | |
| Kansas | | X | | X | |
| Kentucky | | X | | X | |
| Louisiana | | X | | X | |
| Maine | X | | | X | |
| Maryland | | X | | X | |
| Massachusetts | | X | | X | |
| Michigan | | X | | X | |
| Minnesota | | X | | X | |
| Mississippi | | X | | X | |
| Missouri | | X | | X | |
| Montana | X | | | X | |
| Nebraska | | X | | X | |
| Nevada | X | | | X | |
| New Hampshire | X | | | X | |
| New Jersey | | X | | X | |
| New Mexico | | X | | X | |
| New York | | | X | X | |
| North Carolina | | X | | X | |
| North Dakota | | X | | X | |
| Ohio | | X | | X | |
| Oklahoma | | X | | | X |
| Oregon | | X | | | |
| Pennsylvania | | | X | | |
| Rhode Island | X | | | X | |
| South Carolina | | X | | X | |
| South Dakota | X | | | X | |
| Tennessee | | | X | X | |
| Texas | | X | | | X |
| Utah | | X | | X | |

Table 8.5. Appeals Courts by State, *continued*

| State | None | One | Two | One | Two |
|---|---|---|---|---|---|
| | Intermediate Courts | | | Courts of Last Resort | |
| Vermont | X | | | X | |
| Virginia | | X | | X | |
| Washington | | X | | X | |
| West Virginia | X | | | X | |
| Wisconsin | | X | | X | |
| Wyoming | X | | | X | |

In addition to reviewing decisions from state trial courts, state appellate courts have other duties to perform. For example, any time an ethics complaint is filed against an attorney or judge, these complaints will be reviewed by state bar organizations. If the state bar decides to punish the attorney or judge, for example by suspending their license to practice law, state appellate courts review these decisions. In 2010, 44,765 (16%) appeals of this type were made to state appellate courts. In total, state courts of last resort heard 51% of these cases.[26]

## *Juvenile Courts*

Throughout much of human history, children have had few rights and have often been subjected to methods of discipline as their parents or guardians saw fit. Until the end of the 19th century, if a child committed a crime, they were tried in adult court and faced the same punishment as adults convicted of the same crime.[27] As the Industrial Revolution transformed the United States during the 1800s, many social reformers became concerned with the seemingly reduced quality of life within the country. One group of reformers known as the **child-savers** was composed primarily of middle- to upper-class women who believed their motherly duties extended not only to their own children, but to every child in the United States. Many of these women were self-avowed feminists who were severely limited in both employment and political opportunities; however, society generally found it acceptable for women to engage in the public advocacy of children. Of particular importance to the child-savers was reforming how the legal system responded to juvenile offenders. The child-savers believed that a separate court system, one based on reform rather than punishment, was needed. Furthermore, proceedings of the court should be informal so that children could be dealt with primarily on a case-by-case basis.[28]

While some courts dealt with juveniles in such an informal manner on an *ad hoc* basis, the first specialized and fully autonomous juvenile court was founded in 1899, in Cook County, Illinois. Over the next twenty-five years, almost every American state created a separate justice system for juveniles.[29] Formally, the only children protected from the adult court system were children under the age of eight. Then as now, children under the age of eight were presumed to be incapable of formulating the necessary intent to commit a crime. Those over the age of eight were presumed to have the capacity to form criminal intent and could thus be tried in adult court. Along with this belief was the developing concept of *parens patriae*, a Latin phrase that literally means "parent of the country" and which has its roots in English common law.[30] In feudal times, various obligations and powers collectively referred to as the "royal prerogative" were reserved for the monarch, who exercised them as the father (king) or mother (queen) of the country. In America, *parens patriae* had its greatest application in the treatment of children, mentally ill persons, and other individuals who are legally incompetent to manage their affairs. The state is considered the supreme guardian of all children within its jurisdiction, and state courts have the inherent power to intervene to protect the best interests of children whose welfare is jeopardized by controversies between parents. This inherent power is generally supplemented by legislative acts that define the scope of child protection in a state.[31]

The peak of juvenile cases processed by juvenile courts was in 1998 when 1,031,900 cases were formally processed in juvenile courts nationwide and 768,400 cases were informally processed. By 2012, only 619,700 cases were formally processed and 526,100 cases were informally processed in the nation's juvenile courts.[32] While such a decline in the number of cases being heard in juvenile courts is partly due to declining crime rates in the United States, another factor that reduced caseloads is that many states enacted automatic waivers or transfers to adult court when very serious charges are being brought against those under the age of majority in the state. Automatic waivers or transfers allow the state to pursue the case in adult court and seek adult punishments for the juvenile, were he or she to be convicted.[33]

## *Problem-Solving Courts*

While civil and criminal litigation in the U.S. is adversarial, critics argue this model is counterproductive, in that adversarial-based justice is not appropriate for certain kinds of cases, such as those involving drug-addicted offenders, those with mental health issues, those who are veterans, etc., who may need treatment rather than punishment. For this reason, jurisdictions around the nation have created *problem-solving courts* that seek to solve the problem (e.g., drug addiction) that caused the criminal behavior.[34] Instead of simply prosecuting a defendant, these courts (or specialized dockets within particular courts) are based on the principle of **therapeutic jurisprudence;** the goal of problem-solving courts is to bring all parties involved to court and to treat defendants rather than merely punish them.

According to Bruce Winick:

> [Problem-solving courts] grew out of the recognition that traditional judicial approaches have failed, at least in the areas of substance abuse, domestic violence, certain kinds of criminality, child abuse and neg-lect, and mental illness.... The traditional judicial model addressed the symptoms, but not the underlying problem. The result was that the problem reemerged, constantly necessitating repeated judicial in-tervention. All these areas involved specialized problems that judges of courts of general jurisdiction lacked expertise in. Moreover, they in-volved treatment or social service needs that traditional courts lacked the tools to deal with.[35]

Winick argued that problem-solving courts represent "a significant new direc-tion for the judiciary." In this model, judges actively and holistically attempt to remedy not only the case before them, but also the underlying cause that resulted in the case. Judges in these courts seek to help people by connecting them with community resources while also using the court's authority to motivate defen-dants to accept services and treatment. Problem-solving court judges also closely monitor the progress of offenders to increase the likelihood of a successful out-come. These courts are effectively applying a public health approach to social and behavioral problems that cause suffering and deterioration in the quality of life for both individual defendants and the larger community.[36]

Some of the first examples of problem-solving courts were specialized court dockets that dealt exclusively with drug cases during the 1950s in Chicago and New York.[37] Later, in the 1970s, New York established "**narcotic courts**" as a response to rising heroin use in New York City. In 1989, the first "**drug court**" was established in Dade County, Florida.[38] Not only are there many different variations of drug courts, but many other types of problem-solving courts have been established as well. Some examples of these courts are mental health courts, veterans' courts, gambling courts, domestic vio-lence courts, and child support courts.[39] According to the National Associa-tion of Drug Court Professionals, in June of 2012, there were 2,734 drug courts in operation in the U.S. and an additional 1,122 problem-solving courts.[40]

# Prosecutors

## *Federal Prosecutors*

While the Judiciary Act of 1789 is primarily known for creating the federal court system, it also laid the groundwork for the system of federal prosecutors. Within the act, the Office of the attorney general was created. Originally, the position was only part-time and one person, the **attorney general**, was employed in the office. To be eligible for the position, a person only needed to be "learned in the law." The attorney general was tasked with prosecuting and conducting all suits in the Supreme Court in which the United States government was a party. Furthermore, the attorney general provided legal advice to the president and other government officials. Needless to say, the job was a little bigger than one person could handle.

Eventually, the attorney general had to hire private counsel to help with the tremendous workload. By 1870, increases in litigation and the growing expense of employing private counsel led Congress to implement several significant changes. The first change was to establish the Attorney General's Office as an executive agency renamed the Department of Justice, with the attorney general as a full cabinet member that needed to be nominated by the president and confirmed by the Senate. Additionally, the department was not only given control over all criminal prosecutions and civil suits propagated by the federal government, but the department also was given supervisory power over federal law enforcement. Needless to say, with all these duties, the attorney general could not be responsible for representing the federal government appellate court proceedings. This duty was given to the newly created position of **Solicitor General**.[41]

To prosecute federal crimes, 93 United States attorneys are directly appointed by the president to oversee 94 judicial districts (one attorney oversees both Guam and the Northern Mariana Islands). United States attorneys report to the United States attorney general through the deputy attorney general. Each attorney is considered the chief law enforcement officer in his or her district. While United States attorneys have both criminal and civil law responsibilities, 79% of personnel are devoted to criminal prosecutions and 21% of personnel are devoted to civil matters. Additionally, 94% of work hours are allocated to criminal prosecutions and 6% are allocated to civil litigation.[42]

While all United States attorneys are ultimately accountable to both the deputy attorney general and attorney general, most are accorded a great deal of discretion in how they run their office. To some degree, there are good reasons for this. Each district has its own crime problems (for example, some districts have many more drug cases than others, while some districts may have more violence than others), and the United States attorney must be given latitude to address them as he or she sees fit. Furthermore, 93 United States attorneys is a large number of personnel to directly manage, especially when many of them are located in districts that are thousands of miles away from the Department of Justice headquarters in Washington, DC. While the attorney general is ultimately responsible for the budget of the Department of Justice and the creation of agency goals, how the individual United States attorneys comply with these goals is often left up to them.[43] In 2010, federal prosecutors filed 68,591 cases against 91,047 defendants. 81,934 of those defendants were convicted, which represented a 93% conviction rate.[44]

## State Prosecutors

Much like the federal government, each state has an attorney general who is considered the chief legal officer for the state. However, for the most part, that is where the similarity ends. To begin, in 43 states, the attorney general is an elected position and does not serve at the pleasure of a governor. Five states have attorney generals that are appointed by governors; one state (Maine) selects its attorney general by a secret ballot of the legislature; and one state (Tennessee) has its attorney general selected by the state supreme court.[45] The implication of this difference in selection method for attorney general does not alleviate controversy. For instance, some have argued that the federal government should follow the primary state method of attorney general selection so that the position would not be so beholden to whoever is the sitting United States president.[46] Others have argued that since many political candidates view the position of state attorney general as a stepping stone from which to later run for a higher office (e.g., governor), their political ambitions may trump the good of the voters; attorney generals should concentrate on their current job instead of gaining the political capital necessary to run for governor.[47] Regarding enforcement of criminal law and prosecution of suspected criminals, how an attorney general is selected may be a moot point. While in three states (Alaska, Delaware, Rhode Island) local prosecutors are actually members of their respective state attorneys general office, in the rest, attorney generals have little (if any) authority to prosecute crime within the state. In Alabama, for example, the attorney general's duties include: providing legal representation for the state, its officers, departments, and agencies; defending the state in all lawsuits in which the state is a named defendant; representing the state in all cases where the constitutionality of a state statute is at issue; initiating criminal or civil court actions to protect the state's interests or enforce state law;

representing the state in all criminal actions in the appellate courts, both state and federal; and issuing legal advice through formal and informal written opinions to public officials and agencies.[48]

In most states, local district attorneys' offices pursue the vast majority of criminal prosecutions. For this reason, most states' attorneys general concentrate on civil law responsibilities within the state.[49] One example of this was the decision by many state attorneys general to challenge the constitutionality of the Affordable Care Act ("Obamacare").[50]

## Local Prosecutors

Local prosecutors, also known as district attorneys, county prosecutors, states attorneys, and prosecuting attorneys, are responsible for the vast majority of criminal cases coming into American courts each year. Most **district attorneys** (DAs) are elected to the office via partisan election, serve a specific term (e.g., four years), and are considered the chief legal officer of the county they serve. These officials have an organization over which they serve as administrators that consists of one or more assistant district attorneys (ADAs) and support personnel, including investigators, administrative assistants, legal secretaries, and paralegals. To illustrate how large these operations can be, the Los Angeles County District Attorney's (LADA) office has a staff of roughly 1,000 lawyers, nearly 300 investigators and about 800 support staff, making it the largest district attorney's office in the United States. In 2014, the LADA prosecuted more than 71,000 felonies and nearly 112,000 misdemeanors.[51]

In a 2007 national survey, Steven W. Perry and Duren Banks identified 2,330 prosecutors' offices operating in the United States, serving populations ranging from 500 people to 9.9 million residents. The offices reported a total estimated operating budget of $5.8 billion and employed nearly 78,000 attorneys, investigators, paralegals, and support staff. Local prosecutors closed 2.9 million cases charged as felonies in 2007, which translated to approximately 94 cases for each prosecuting attorney on staff. Further, Perry and Banks reported that:

- The average annual salary of a chief prosecutor in 2007 was $98,000, with mean salaries ranging from $165,700 for chief prosecutors in the largest offices to less than $45,000 in part-time offices.
- In 2007, the average tenure of a chief prosecutor was 9 years.
- Sixty-four percent of chief prosecutors had been in office for more than 5 years, and 38% had been in office for more than 10 years. The longest serving prosecutor had been in the position for 42 years.

- The average annual salary for assistant prosecutors ranged from $33,460 for entry-level assistant prosecutors in part-time offices to $108,434 for assistant prosecutors with 6 or more years of experience in offices serving jurisdictions of 1 million or more residents.[52]

According to the American Bar Association, the function of the district attorney (and by extension, ADAs) includes 1) having responsibility for all criminal prosecutions in the jurisdiction; 2) serving as an administrator of justice, an advocate for the people of the jurisdiction being served, and an officer of the court; 3) seeking justice and not merely convictions; 4) reforming/improving the administration of criminal justice, including undertaking remedial action when inadequacies of justice arise from either the substantive or procedural law; and 5) having the duty to know and be guided by the standards of professional conduct as defined by applicable professional traditions, ethical codes, and law in the prosecutor's jurisdiction.[53] Most district attorneys have complete authority and control over the policies and practices relating to the prosecution of criminal defendants, constrained only by statute, case law, and procedural law.

More practically, local prosecutors engage in several activities.[54] First, they *review charges* against people who have been arrested by the police, which includes deciding *whether* to charge arrestees with a crime or crimes and determining *what the charges should be*. Second, local prosecutors offer plea bargains to defendants, which may involve *reducing the number or seriousness of the charges filed* ("charge bargains") or agreeing to *recommend a particular sentence* ("sentence bargains") in exchange for a plea of guilty or other consideration by the defendant. Third, local prosecutors *represent the people* of the jurisdiction in criminal trials and appeals arising from cases handled by the DAs office. Finally, local prosecutors play a role at the investigative stage of a case by providing *advisory assistance to the police* to ensure evidence required for a conviction is identified and obtained and that police investigators have access to certain tools the prosecutor controls, such as the grand jury or requests for search warrants or electronic surveillance. The prosecutor may also *assume responsibility for the lawfulness of investigative activities* undertaken by the police.

Examining the historical emergence of local prosecutors, Joan Jacoby, in her seminal exploration, suggested that when the earliest settlers of America rejected the premise of private prosecutions that was the English tradition, they set in motion a series of events that ultimately produced a uniquely American prosecutor, characterized as a locally elected official.[55] Jacoby then presented evidence indicating that the office of local prosecutor can be traced to English, French, and Dutch influences, but none of these can be directly linked to the development of local prosecutors. Rather, prosecutors' role, power, and authority developed from an amalgam of forces not exclusive to any single historical antecedent.[56] Michael Ellis, who traced the history of how local prosecutors came to be elected officials, observed that local prosecutors began as appointed officials during the Colonial Era, but that between 1832 and 1860— as a result of new state constitutions being drafted, amendments occurring to existing constitutions, or via new legislation—nearly three-quarters of the states decided to give voters the right to elect them.[57] Ellis pointed out that supporters of elected prosecutors believed popular elections would give citizens greater control over government, eliminate patronage appointments, and increase the responsiveness of prosecutors to the communities they served. However, he noted that amid the era's democratic impulses, supporters of elected prosecutors gave little consideration to the substantive effect elections might have on prosecutors, including subjecting them to "untoward political influences" leading them to concentrate their efforts on high-profile investigations to win favorable media coverage, opening them up to possible corruption through campaign contributions received, and causing them to seek higher conviction rates.[58]

As Robert Misner has argued, an important point about local prosecutors that cannot be overemphasized is this: they are *the* preeminent actors in the criminal justice system.[59] Over the past 50 years, the diffusion of responsibility for outputs from the criminal justice system, namely criminal convictions, has abated and resulted in power consolidating in the office of local prosecutors. Such centralization of authority became necessary, at least in part, for a coordinated and responsive criminal justice system to exist; simultaneously, however, the prosecutor became increasingly accountable to the electorate for both the successes and failures of the system. Furthermore, because prosecutors exercise enormous discretion in charging and plea bargaining decisions, they effectively control not only the flow of cases into the system via local court dockets but the number of new inmates that must be housed in state prisons or offenders who are placed on probation.[60] Minser continued his analysis by observing that prosecutorial power is very broad, as evidenced by the key role played by prosecutors at bail hearings, in granting of immunity from prosecution, and in trial strategy. Additionally, despite criticisms of the practice, the prosecutor plays a pivotal role in the areas of charging, plea bargaining, and sentencing. Finally, Minser argued that three trends helped solidify prosecutorial power. First, current criminal codes contain so many overlapping provisions that the choice of *how* to characterize conduct as criminal has passed to the prosecutor. Secondly, until recently, increases in reported crime without a concomitant increase in resources dedicated to the prosecution and de-

fense of criminal conduct has resulted in a criminal process that is highly dependent upon plea bargaining with few restraints placed upon the prosecutor.
Finally, the development of sentencing guidelines and a growth of statutes with
mandatory minimum sentences have increased the importance of the initial
charging decision since the charging decision determines the range of sentences available to the court once a conviction is obtained either through plea
bargain or as a result of trial.[61]

Beyond the prosecutor, there is one more attorney whose role in the criminal justice system is important: defense attorneys. Discussion now turns to
the role and function of defense counsel.

# Defense Attorneys

As we mentioned in Chapter 3, early American criminal trials did not promi-
nently feature attorneys, partly because there were few of them. However, as
the country expanded in both territory and population, the role of attorneys
in American life expanded as well.[62] While the prestige of attorneys and their
presence in the legal system seemed to increase after WWII, many of the best
and most accomplished attorneys did not find their way into practicing criminal law. Instead, most of these attorneys sought employment in law firms representing corporate clients or in corporate counsel offices with major companies.

By its nature, the practice of criminal law does not generate the highest fees.
Furthermore, while many white-collar crimes may end up in civil court, many
criminal offenses that actually get prosecuted are more likely to be committed
by economically disadvantaged people who invariably have a hard time paying for legal services. Additionally, many criminal defense attorneys are either
solo practitioners or members of very small law firms.[63] When these considerations are combined with the perception held by many lawyers that criminal defense work is "low status," this type of law practice generally does not
attract the best and brightest attorneys.[64] Given the low prestige of the work
combined with the fact that invariably most defense attorneys' clients will be
found guilty, it may well be that those who practice criminal law are a "different breed" of lawyer.[65]

Besides the general growth of the legal profession in the United States, perhaps no other factor has expanded the need for attorneys to practice criminal
law than the Supreme Court decision in the 1963 case of *Gideon v. Wainwright*.[66] In that case, Clarence Gideon was accused of committing a burglary
at a local pool hall. The crime was a felony, and Gideon requested an attorney
because he could not afford to hire one. The trial court denied his request, be-

cause at the time, Florida law only required appointed counsel in capital cases. Gideon represented himself, was convicted, and was sentenced to five years in prison. His appeal was ultimately accepted by the United States Supreme Court, which had to determine whether the Sixth Amendment's right to counsel in criminal cases extended to felony defendants in *state* courts. In its decision, the Supreme Court ruled that the Sixth Amendment was made applicable to the states via the Fourteenth Amendment and therefore, felony defendants who could not afford counsel would receive appointed counsel. Additional Supreme Court rulings further expanded this right so that any time a defendant faces possible incarceration upon conviction for the offense charged— even if for only one day—the defendant must have appointed counsel if they cannot afford a lawyer.[67]

## *Public Defender Offices*

Even before the decision in *Gideon*, many jurisdictions had created **public defender offices**. These agencies can be publicly funded, either statewide or at the county or local level, or private non-profit law firms that represent indigent defendants in court proceedings. The first such office was created in Los Angeles County in 1914,[68] and by 2007 (the last year data were available), 49 states had public defender offices. In 27 states and the District of Columbia, counties or local jurisdictions funded and administered public defender offices, while in 22 states a single office oversaw indigent defense operations throughout the state.[69]

While the primary reasons to create a public defender's office are to comply with *Gideon* and provide adequate defense for indigent defendants, many localities simply do not have enough criminal cases filed against indigent defendants to justify the creation of a permanent agency for this purpose.[70] Many studies have found that criminal case outcomes for public defenders are comparable to privately hired attorneys, while a few studies have found that public defenders are not as successful. One reason for this discrepancy may be that some defendants hire a private attorney if they believe they have a chance of winning, while if they believe they are likely to lose, they may settle for a public defender. Regardless, public defenders are often viewed as favorable to assigned or contracted counsel.[71]

In 2007, 49 states and the District of Columbia had public defender offices within the state. The only exception is Maine. Twenty-two states had a state-operated public defender program, with 427 public defender offices within these states. Statewide public defender offices are structured around a central office that both funds and administers to all of rest of the offices in the state.

In 27 states, public defenders offices are funded and administered at the county or local level using some combination of state and county funds. In 2007, public defenders programs spent more than $830 million on representation of indigent defendants. Furthermore, there was a median number of 163 public defender attorneys in each state and these programs employed an average of one investigator per six attorneys. Many of the attorneys in these offices are overworked, and fifteen state programs reported that staff attorneys handled more than the maximum recommended number of cases per attorney.[72]

## The Defender Services Program

Prior to 1964, if you were charged with a federal crime and could not afford an attorney—that was your problem. Some attorneys provided *pro bono* representation, but defendants who could not find such representation had to represent themselves. In 1964, the Criminal Justice Act was made law and allowed for attorneys who represented indigent clients in federal court to be reimbursed for "reasonable" expenses, including payment to expert witnesses and for investigative services. In 1970, the act was amended so that the individual federal judicial districts could create federal public defender offices. Today, these offices exist in 91 of the 94 federal districts. A **Chief Federal Public Defender,** appointed to a four-year term by members of the Court of Appeals for the circuit that includes the federal district, oversees each office. Congress purposefully chose the Court of Appeals for nomination so that district courts would not have any authority over public defenders. Federal public defenders offices employ more than 31,000 personnel including attorneys, investigators, paralegals, and support personnel.[73]

## Assigned or Contracted Counsel

Prior to the adoption of public defender offices and still operating in most jurisdictions are **assigned counsel** systems for indigent clients. In such a system, a judge simply appoints an attorney to defend an indigent defendant. This can be done by either appointing an attorney who happens to be in a courtroom during initial appearances (many attorneys purposely spend time in courtrooms during initial appearances for this very purpose), or a judge will have a list of attorneys who are available to defend indigent clients and will randomly select a name from the list.

Another system that is used to provide indigent services to criminal defendants is known as **contracted counsel,** where either a law firm or a group of attorneys bids on the job of defending all indigent defendants within a jurisdiction. While some consideration is given to the quality of attorneys who are seeking to represent these clients, the main consideration, in many places, is cost. With the exception of capital cases, whenever an attorney is assigned an indigent client, there is usually a predetermined maximum fee, which is usually not very much money. In the case of bidding for contracted counsel, the cost of representation is most likely going to be the deciding factor. Therefore, within assigned or contracted counsel, it is typically a volume business. Thus, attorneys are going to seek as many assigned cases as possible to earn more money. In the case of contracted counsel, attorneys might be likely to spend the minimum amount on each client so they could devote other resources to procuring paying clients. Most research has demonstrated that defendants who are represented by assigned counsel or contracted counsel fair worse than privately obtained counsel or public defenders.[74]

# Professional Associations for Attorneys

There are many different professional associations for attorneys, both defense attorneys and prosecutors. These organizations provide professional training and professional development opportunities, sponsor conferences, and engage in lobbying on behalf of their members. While certainly not an exhaustive list, we discuss several major professional organizations for lawyers, including the American Bar Association (ABA), the National Association of Attorneys General (NAAG), the National District Attorneys Association (NDAA), and the National Association of Criminal Defense Lawyers (NACDL).

## *American Bar Association*

On August 21, 1878, seventy-five lawyers from twenty states and the District of Columbia gathered in Saratoga Springs, New York. In the wake of that meeting, the American Bar Association (ABA) was established.[75] Today, the ABA has nearly 400,000 members and describes itself as one of the world's largest voluntary professional organizations. The organization, among other activities, provides different resources for members, advocates for improvements in the administration of justice, accredits law schools, and establishes and helps enforce model rules of professional conduct for the legal profession. People eligible to join the organization are attorneys, law students, and others interested in either the law or the legal profession.[76]

## National Association of Attorneys General

According to the organization's website, the National Association of Attorneys General (NAAG) was created in 1907 when several state attorneys general gathered to discuss how to develop a common strategy to address antitrust issues created by the Standard Oil Company. Until 1936, the activities of NAAG were administered through individual state attorneys general offices. In that year, the organization became a member of the Council of State Governments (CSG), with that organization serving in the role of NAAG secretariat. In 1980, NAAG became an independent organization and separated from CSG.[77] Today, the attorneys general of all fifty states and Washington, DC, as well as the chief legal officers of Puerto Rico, Northern Mariana Islands, American Samoa, Guam, and the Virgin Islands belong to the organization. NAAG seeks to promote both communication and coordination for various legal and law enforcement issues that affect the different states and territories. Additionally, the organization conducts research and policy analysis, as well as provides training for members through the National Attorneys General Training and Research Institute (NAGTRI).[78]

## National District Attorneys Association

The National District Attorneys Association (NDAA) is located in Alexandria, VA, and was founded in 1950 by a group of local prosecutors to give a focal point to advance their causes and issues at the national level.[79] The organization has a board of directors from the individual states who are appointed by various state prosecuting associations as well as current and former officers of NDAA. Officers are chosen annually who then vote for various leadership positions within the organization. Representatives from NDAA regularly meet with members of the Department of Justice, Congress, and other national associations to influence federal and national policies that affect both law enforcement and the prosecution of crimes.[80]

## National Association of Criminal Defense Lawyers

The National Association of Criminal Defense Lawyers (NACDL) describes its mission as "ensuring justice and due process for persons accused of crime, fostering the integrity, independence and expertise of the criminal defense profession, and promoting the proper and fair administration of criminal justice."[81] Membership in NACDL provides an opportunity for criminal defense attorneys to network, share information, and discuss strategy. It not only provides a way for attorneys to contact other attorneys, but also provides training resources, and information that covers changes and updates relevant to the practice of criminal law. Furthermore, the organization provides prospective clients the opportunity to find attorneys who can represent them.[82] NACDL advertises itself as a champion of freedom, which the organization states was integral to the foundation of the United States. The organization's position is that the "war on drugs" and other crackdowns on criminal behavior have eroded many freedoms within the United States and argues that a "rational and humane crime policy" is needed.[83]

# Employees of the Courts

## Federal Judges

In many ways, being a federal judge is a pretty good job. While you have to be appointed by the president and confirmed by the Senate, once approved, you serve for life. The only way you can be removed from your judgeship is through formal impeachment. In addition to having the job for life, the salary is not bad either. In 2015, District Judges made $201,100, Circuit Judges made $213,300, Associate Justices of the Supreme Court make $246,800 and the Chief Justice made $258,100.[84]

## Administrative Office of the United States Courts

While judges are considered the "face" of courts, they certainly do not operate their courts alone. Indeed, in 1939 the **Administrative Office of the United States Courts** (AOC) was created to provide support for federal judges. Today, there are 32,000 employees working in more than 800 locations who provide support for the federal court system. Among AOC employees are lawyers, public administrators, accountants, systems engineers, analysts, architects, statisticians, and other staff that are needed to insure the federal courts can properly function.[85]

## Federal Law Clerks

Included among the 32,000 employees of the AOC is a prestigious appointment many recent law school graduates rigorously compete for—federal law clerk. To be a law clerk, prospects must either have completed law school or have met the requirements for graduation and are awaiting official confer-ral of the degree. Prospects possess one or more of the following attributes: they are ranked in the upper third of the class of a law school approved by the American Bar Association or Association of American Law Schools; they have been a member of the school's law review; they possess an LLM (Master of Laws degree); and/or they have "demonstrated proficiency in legal studies." Federal law clerks, depending upon experience and other qualifications, can make between $51,298 and $85,544 annually.[86] While some budding lawyers might seek a clerkship for the experience itself, earning a federal clerkship, es-pecially the most prestigious clerkship position of a clerk for a Supreme Court justice, is a career-maker for any attorney. Federal law clerks represent the top law students from the best law schools in the country. Being a federal law clerk will greatly help an attorney when applying for positions at the nation's top law firms, but it is also helpful for attorneys who hope to land a faculty posi-tion at a law school. In addition to being beneficial for the attorney, these po-sitions are also beneficial for the federal judiciary. Federal judges rely greatly on the work of law clerks, and if judges did not have law clerks available to help them, the work of the federal courts would be much less efficient.[87]

### Assistant United States Attorneys

In addition to the 93 United States attorneys, in 2010, these offices em-ployed 6,075 full-time assistant United States attorneys (AUSAs) and 5,799 support employees. Attorneys performed 595,680 work hours for courtroom-related activity.[88]

# State Court Employees

## Judges

Historically, in the United States state court judges were typically directly ap-pointed by the governor or selected by state legislatures.[89] Today, judges are selected by one of the following methods: partisan election (judges belong to a political party), non-partisan election (judges' names are listed, but not their political affiliation), appointment by a governor, selection through a merit plan, or appointed by the legislature.[90] Judges often make comfortable incomes and the prestige of the job makes many attorneys desire the position.[91] The lowest salary for a judge is $117,600 (Montana) and the highest is $199,100 (Washington, DC).[92] Table 8.6 provides a breakdown of the caseloads judges have in different jurisdictions.

## Table 8.6. Judges by Court and State

| State | Cases Per Judge (non-traffic) | Full-time Judges[93] | Intermediate Judges[94] | Supreme Judges[95] |
|---|---|---|---|---|
| Alabama | 1,567 | 144 | 10 | 9 |
| Alaska | 537 | 40 | 3 | 5 |
| Arizona | 1,778 | 174 | 22 | 5 |
| Arkansas | 1,863 | 120 | 12 | 7 |
| California | 2,219 | 1,646 | 105 | 7 |
| Colorado | 1,425 | 164 | 16 | 7 |
| Connecticut | 1,960 | 201 | 9 | 7 |
| Delaware | 1,728 | 19 | 0 | 5 |
| District of Columbia | 1,742 | 62 | 0 | 9 |
| Florida | 3,100 | 599 | 62 | 7 |
| Georgia | 2,157 | 205 | 12 | 7 |
| Hawaii | 1,023 | 48 | 4 | 5 |
| Idaho | 516 | 43 | 3 | 5 |
| Illinois | 1,413 | 906 | 52 | 7 |
| Indiana | 2,638 | 315 | 15 | 5 |
| Iowa | 1,569 | 198 | 9 | 8 |
| Kansas | 1,782 | 167 | 14 | 7 |
| Kentucky | 1,340 | 146 | 14 | 7 |
| Louisiana | 1,623 | 236 | 53 | 7 |
| Maine | 2,555 | 53 | 0 | 7 |
| Maryland | 2,068 | 157 | 13 | 7 |
| Massachusetts | 379 | 82 | 25 | 7 |
| Michigan | 1,386 | 221 | 28 | 7 |
| Minnesota | 1,467 | 289 | 16 | 7 |
| Mississippi | 541 | 51 | 10 | 9 |
| Missouri | 1,898 | 334 | 32 | 7 |
| Montana | 1,042 | 44 | 0 | 7 |
| Nebraska | 1,002 | 55 | 6 | 7 |
| Nevada | 1,826 | 72 | 0 | 7 |
| New Hampshire | 1,001 | 21 | 0 | 5 |
| New Jersey | 3,410 | 412 | 34 | 7 |
| New Mexico | 1,569 | 88 | 10 | 5 |
| New York | 1,231 | 455 | 70 | 7 |
| North Carolina | 2,214 | 111 | 15 | 7 |
| North Dakota | 2,192 | 44 | 0 | 5 |
| Ohio | 1,900 | 394 | 68 | 7 |
| Oklahoma | 1,490 | 241 | 12 | 141 |
| Oregon | 1,982 | 174 | 10 | 7 |
| Pennsylvania | 1,725 | 450 | 24 | 7 |
| Rhode Island | 852 | 338 | 0 | 5 |
| South Carolina | 776 | 22 | 9 | 5 |
| South Dakota | 5,060 | 46 | 0 | 5 |
| Tennessee | 2,741 | 41 | 12 | 5 |
| Texas | 2,017 | 154 | 80 | 182 |
| Utah | 1,976 | 454 | 7 | 5 |
| Vermont | 2,644 | 71 | 0 | 5 |
| Virginia | 2,044 | 30 | 11 | 7 |
| Washington | 1,843 | 157 | 22 | 9 |
| West Virginia | 1,329 | 188 | 0 | 5 |
| Wisconsin | 691 | 70 | 16 | 7 |
| Wyoming | 1,956 | 248 | 0 | 5 |

## Intermediate Appeals Courts

Unlike appointment to the federal courts, no judges on state intermediate appeals courts serve for life. Massachusetts is the only state that appoints their judges for terms that last until they reach the age of 70. For election purposes, five states that have intermediate appeals courts have partisan elections, 12 states have non-partisan elections, 18 states have nominating commissions for these judges, two states have governors select these judges, and one state has the state legislature select these judges.[96] Being a judge on an intermediate appellate court provides a nice salary. The lowest salary is $124,616 (New Mexico) and the highest is $211,260 (California).[97]

## Courts of Last Resort

To select judges for state courts of last resort, states use a variety of procedures. Furthermore, states have different terms that judges serve. Unlike the federal judiciary, the vast majority of states appoint judges to courts of last resort for terms considerably shorter than life. Only Rhode Island appoints judges at this level for life, and two states (Massachusetts and New Hampshire) appoint judges at this level to their respective courts of last resort until the judge reaches 70 years of age. Six states elect judges by partisan election, 15 states elect judges from non-partisan elections, 24 states select judges by a nominating commission, four states select judges by nomination from a governor, and one state selects judges by the state legislature. Different states have different procedures to decide if a judge will be retained on the court of last resort they serve beyond their initial appointment or election.[98] Being a judge on a court of last resort provides monetary compensation that most people would be happy with. The lowest annual salary for a judge on a state court of last resort is $124,949 (Montana), and the highest is $225,342 (California).[99]

## State Court Support Staff

As we mentioned when discussing the federal court system, it takes many people, in addition to judges, to run a court. One might also think it would be easy to find information relating to support positions for state courts. Sadly, this is not the case. Finding such information is often very difficult if not impossible. Luckily, the State of Florida has a "Sunshine Law,"[100] that requires the government to provide openness and disclosure concerning the manner in which the state conducts business. For this reason, we found court-related employment information very accessible and learned that Florida has nine different employment codes or categories of workers associated with the state court system, including: officer/administrator, professional, technical, protective services, para professional, office support, skilled craft, custodial/maintenance, and personal staff. Within these nine categories are 194 different positions, such as office support assistant, custodial worker, electronic transcriber, accountant, purchasing specialist, legal secretary, court translator, deputy clerk, mediator, archivist, court analyst, court statistician, budget analyst, magistrate, general counsel and deputy state courts administrator. The lowest paid position in the system comes with an annual salary of $33,416.58 while the top paid position has an annual salary of $230,000.[101]

## State Prosecutors

In 2007, there were 2,330 prosecutor's offices in operation throughout the United States. Seventy-four percent of those offices served jurisdictions with less than 100,000 residents and 15% of offices were part-time offices without a full-time chief prosecutor. During that year, prosecutors closed 2.9 million felony cases, with 2.2 million of those cases resulting in convictions. These offices employed 78,000 full-time staff members, with almost 25,000 of those staff being assistant prosecutors. Offices that served over jurisdictions with over one million people had an average staff size of 535 employees. Included within this staff was an average of 187 assistant prosecutors, 31 supervisory attorneys, 16 victim advocates, 51 investigators, and 183 support staff. By contrast, offices serving less than 100,000 people on average only employed one chief prosecutor, three assistant prosecutors, one victim advocate, one legal services staff member, one investigator, and three support staff members. The average annual salary for a chief prosecutor was $98,000. Within the most populous areas, the average salary was much higher, at $165,700; however, within part-time offices, it dropped to less than $45,000. The average tenure of a chief prosecutor was nine years. Prosecutors who started directly after law school had an average annual salary between $33,460 and $51,354, while prosecutors with six or more years of experience had an average annual salary between $53,113 and $108,434, depending upon the size of the office, as well as the population of the jurisdiction they served. While these salaries may seem lucrative to some, attorneys often borrow a significant amount of money to attend law school, and many of the higher salaries from larger offices will be offset by an increased cost of living. Prosecutors have a high rate of job turnover and after many attorneys get what they believe is enough trial experience, they will often leave their job for more lucrative opportunities.[102]

# Budgets, Costs, and Profits

As the previous discussion illustrates, state and federal court systems are large-scale operations employing thousands of people and costing taxpayers hundreds of millions of dollars each year. The costs of justice are, indeed, high. For instance, when **O.J. Simpson** was charged with the murders of his ex-wife Nicole Brown Simpson and her friend Ron Goldman, Simpson hired a legal team that was dubbed "The Dream Team." While no one seems to know exactly how much money Simpson spent to defend himself, speculation is he paid between $3 million and $5 million to his attorneys and their support staff.[103] Obviously, most people do not have $3–$5 million to spend on their defense and in many ways, the Simpson case is an outlier. However, at least one website has noted that if one needs to hire an attorney to defend themselves against felony charges, they should expect to pay at least a $5,000 to $10,000 retainer for an attorney. If the charge is a serious felony, say murder, the defendant may well have to pay $25,000 or more as a retainer.[104]

In some instances, the costs of a criminal trial can have severe financial repercussions on an entire court system. While Los Angeles County, because of its size and relative wealth, was able to absorb the costs of the O.J. Simpson trial, in other places, the costs of a full-blown trial can weigh heavily on the criminal justice system. In 1997, along with **Timothy McVeigh**, **Terry Nichols** was convicted of several charges related to the bombing of a federal building in Oklahoma City, Oklahoma. While both Timothy McVeigh and Terry Nichols were ultimately convicted in a federal trial and McVeigh was later executed, Terry Nichols received a sentence of life imprisonment without parole. To some observers, this seemed unjust and they wanted Terry Nichols to be executed as well. As a result of political pressure, seven years later, in 2004, the State of Oklahoma tried Terry Nichols on 161 counts of murder arising out of the same bombing. By the time of Nichols's trial, the state had already spent $4 million on the salaries of eleven attorneys and investigators who had worked on the case, and five prison guards who were assigned to watch Nichols 24 hours a day (except for when he was in court). Estimates of the total cost of trying Nichols were $10 million.[105] Again, some observers argued that the added cost was unjustified since Nichols was already slated to spend the rest of his life in a federal prison. The case went to trial in state court and ultimately, just like in the federal trial, Nichols was convicted and received a sentence of life in prison without possibility of parole.[106]

## Recovering Court Costs

Some 40 years ago, Marc Galanter observed the use of courts is not distributed equally across all people or institutions in society—what we will call "social actors." Some social actors "have many occasions to utilize the courts ... to make or defend claims; others do so only rarely. We might divide our actors into those claimants who have only occasional recourse to the courts (**one-shotters** or OS) and **repeat players** (RP) who are engaged in many similar litigations over [an extended] time."[107] Galanter then described how repeat players organize themselves around the fact they play for (not necessarily by) the rules and as a result, accrue major advantages in litigation when compared to one-shotters.

Returning to our point about the costs of running a court system, should not repeat players, because they constantly return to the courts with disputes in which they are involved, have to pay more for using the courts than one-shotters? Is there no way help recover the costs of excessively using the courts? In effect, cannot the people who routinely use the courts pay for them? The short answer is "yes," and many states have developed mechanisms to not only recoup the costs of running the courts but maybe even eke out a profit.

A number of states have passed what are known as recoupment statutes, which seek small payments from indigent defendants as their trial occurs or that force defendants to pay some amount of money to help with court costs after they are acquitted or have been released from incarceration.[108] As we noted in Chapter 7, the goal of many police departments seems to be raising revenue through the collection of monetary fines from traffic tickets. While the court system surely benefits from the imposition of these fines, the court system also has other ways of collecting money, which involves the imposition of court costs on defendants.

For example, in North Carolina, a state statute designates not only the amount of court costs, but also how these charges are calculated. For instance, to appear in District Court for a criminal case, a person can expect to pay $173 in costs. While this may seem like a random number, it is not. Of that $173, a total of $127.05 is earmarked to the general fund, $2.45 is allocated to the state bar legal aid account, $12 is a facilities fee, $4 is a phone systems fee, $18 is a misdemeanor confinement fund fee, $7.50 is for law enforcement officers' retirement/insurance, and $2 is for a law enforcement officers training and certification fee. Additionally, fees accrue if you committed a chapter offense ($10), or are charged with a criminal offense ($2 DNA Fee), and a $5 service fee for each arrest or service of criminal process (including citations and subpoenas). If your trial is in superior court, the price is a little higher—expect to pay $198 in court costs, which includes a $30 facilities fee (instead of the $12 facilities fee collected by the district court). If you are declared indigent—there is a $60 fee. If you receive community service—there is a $250 fee.[109] Thus, while the state may have to pay money to prosecute someone for committing a crime, it fully expects to receive some of that money back.

## Expert Witnesses

While judges, attorneys, paralegals, investigators, and courtroom staff are the most commonly seen personnel, expert witnesses are seen in court far more frequently than they were as recently as 25 years ago. Yet, expert witnesses can often be met with a degree of skepticism. For instance, Judge John Pitt Taylor, writing in 1848, argued that "skilled witnesses" were the least trustworthy of witnesses and could be expected to say essentially whatever the attorney who called them wanted them to say. While the complexity of trials has increased with the advent of various technologies often used in criminal cases (e.g., fingerprints, ballistics tests, DNA samples, and handwriting analysis) and expert testimony has become more common,[110] the cases of *Frye v. United States*[111] and later *Daubert vs. Merrell Dow Pharmaceuticals*,[112] as well as the **Federal Rules of Evidence**,[113] have given considerable guidance on the standards for expert testimony. Still, many people today note that expert witnesses do seem bound by standard rules of contract or tort law, and will often have immunity from lawsuits while testifying on the witness stand.[114]

We do not want to spend this entire section bashing expert witnesses— there are certainly many who are honest. Yet, the ostensible reason many people are skeptical of them is because serving as an expert witness can be quite lucrative. Take, for example, **SEAK, Inc.** (Skills, Education, Achievement, Knowledge), which was founded in 1980 by Steven Babitsky, himself an attorney. His company advertises itself as the world's leading provider of expert witness training and textbooks.[115] According to SEAK, Inc., the average hourly fee for in-court testimony for an expert witness is $248 an hour. Medical experts, the highest paid experts, command an average of $555 an hour while in court. Testifying in court provides the most lucratively hourly rate for expert witnesses, but even engaging in other activities, such as depositions and file review and preparation, can earn expert witnesses lucrative fees.[116]

## Legal Search Engines

Undoubtedly, you have seen a commercial for a law firm or lawyer on television. While these commercials take many forms, perhaps one of these commercials was filmed in the firm's law library. Perhaps you saw all those fancy printed and bound volumes, which contain various statutes and cases that are vital for a lawyer to use in the practice of law. While some attorneys still rely on bound volumes for their legal research, many more conduct their legal research online using **LexisNexis** search engines.

Originally known as Mead Data Central, the company changed its name to LexisNexis (after the popular legal search engine Mead developed) when it was purchased in 1994 by Reed Elsevier P.L.C. for $1.5 billion.[117] LexisNexis search engines can access thousands of databases and retrieve literally millions of articles, cases, statutes, and other items necessary for legal research. In 2013 alone, revenues for LexisNexis Legal & Professional were $2.37 billion.[118] How do LexisNexis and its main competitor, Westlaw, make so much money? The short answer is that neither of these services is cheap. As Ronald Wheeler has noted, a single search in Westlaw Next can cost $60, and there is approximately a $15 charge for each document that is opened from the results of these searches.[119]

Needless to say, if someone uses either legal search engine and does not have free access to the service, huge fees can be quickly accrued. These costs are a major concern of law firms and law schools alike. As Laura Justiss has argued, it is imperative law students be taught how to conduct legal searches that do not cost much money. If a law firm is representing a large corporation, that corporation might be willing to foot the bill for large legal research services. However, smaller firms or solo practitioners, to which many criminal defense attorneys belong, will usually not be able to afford these costs. Thus, they need to figure out other alternatives to conducting online legal research.[120]

# Politics and Current Issues

Any time a trial occurs or two attorneys argue a case before an appellate court, a political process is taking place. A criminal trial is an exercise in reinforcing the creation of law. Additionally, a trial is a substitute for more primitive rituals, such as trial by combat or trial by ordeal. Furthermore, either a judge or a jury is making a determination on whether a person's actions should be punished. In some rare instances, a process called **jury nullification** occurs, where a jury disregards the evidence of a person's guilt and votes to acquit the defendant. They will thus "nullify" the law and acquit. Sometimes, this may simply occur because a jury feels sorry for, or relates to, a defendant. An example of jury nullification is depicted in John Grisham's novel (and the movie inspired by it) *A Time to Kill,* which chronicles the exploits of a "down-on-his-luck" small town attorney who successfully defends a man for killing the two defendants—in open court and in front of dozens of witnesses—on trial for raping his young daughter. Grisham's point here is that some people relate to the notion that an aggrieved father would need to have his own form of justice. Yet, in some instances, jury nullification goes beyond simply relating to a defendant. For example, members of a jury might believe the law a person is accused of violating is in some way wrong or unjust. Thus, a jury may engage in a political decision—ignoring the law.

Ever want to see a circus sideshow? Watch the confirmation hearings of someone nominated to serve on the United States Supreme Court. A group of senators will pepper the nominee with different questions that are meant to ascertain the candidate's judicial philosophy: does the candidate believe in a "strict" or more liberal interpretation of the Constitution? How would the candidate rule in a particular type of case, say one involving abortion? Would the candidate be more likely to side with a defendant claiming some type of violation of his or her Constitutional rights or with the government? In some instances, the nominee will simply demur and say that since there is not a current case pending, they are not sure how they would rule. Technically, while that is probably true, do you really believe someone who has been nominated for the Supreme Court cannot really tell others what he or she thinks about the permissibility of false confessions in a criminal case or of the death penalty? While some people claim "the law is the law" and it is somehow politically neutral, nothing is further from the truth. Law is both politically constructed and evaluated. For someone to be appointed to the Supreme Court, they must be nominated by the president (who is elected) and confirmed by the Senate (the members of which are elected). If this was truly a value-neutral, apolitical process, someone could develop some type of merit or seniority system whereby only the most learned or qualified candidate would be the replacement. Instead, a president (or more often the president's advisors) will closely vet potential nominees whom they believe are most likely to not only advance the president's agenda, but also interpret the law in ways that agree with the president's views. **Dwight Eisenhower** once lamented that the two greatest mistakes of his presidency were nominating Earl Warren and William Brennan to the Supreme Court. The reason? Eisenhower was a conservative Republican and Earl Warren and William Brennan would turn out to be two of the most liberal members of the Court in history and spearhead what critics called the greatest level of "liberal activism" of the Court during the 1960s and 1970s, particularly concerning civil rights.

One of the most basic complaints about the legal system is structural inequality. There is a wide perception by many that if you have a lot of money and can hire the best attorneys, you can "cheat" the legal system. Earlier, we mentioned the cost of O.J. Simpson's defense team and the ultimate result that he was found not guilty in the face of what seemed to be insurmountable guilt. **Alan Dershowitz**, one of the attorneys who represented O.J. Simpson, had previously represented Claus von Bulow, who had been convicted of the attempted murder of his wife, Sunny. As depicted in the novel *Reversal of Fortune* (and later, the movie), Dershowitz handled von Bulow's appellate case and managed to have the conviction overturned. To many, money, prestige, and access to capable representation seem to be the ticket to avoiding a conviction in criminal court. Yet many people have argued that structural inequalities go beyond whether one simply has access to representation.

As we recounted in Chapter 3, criminal justice used to be a system of amateurs. Prosecutors and defense attorneys were not common in early American criminal justice; a judge and jury decided a person's fate. Today, trials are rare, plea bargains are common, and lawyers completely control the process. **William Chambliss** and **Robert Seidman** have argued that those at the highest levels of wealth and status have the greatest ability to have laws passed that reflect their particular values. Their analysis goes beyond simple differences in the legality of white-collar and street crimes. Chambliss and Seidman argued that the very legal system *itself* is designed to insulate and protect the powerful. Laws are created by legislatures, which typically represent powerful people or are composed of people who come from wealthy and powerful families. Furthermore, appellate judges, who are tasked with interpreting the meaning of legislation during the appellate process, typically come from the best law schools and were educated by the best law professors. The top law schools all use some variation of the case method, which relies on the concept of *stare decisis*. Thus, while Chambliss and Seidman did not specifically use the word "brain-washing," they argued that law students are trained by legal scholars to perpetuate the legal system as it exists. Young lawyers who want to advance in their legal careers desire to work for wealthy clients who are best prepared to advance their careers and groom them for the top judicial positions.[121] To some degree, this is also reflected in the federal judicial clerkship program. While clerks are hired to *help* judges, there is little doubt federal judges will have some, if not a dramatic, effect on the legal views of clerks.

While we could be satisfied with a critique of the legal system that simply points out how the law protects the powerful, some critiques go beyond that. For instance, Peter Goodrich has argued that the study of law in some ways can be compared to the study of a language. As he observed, "Despite the common social experience of legal regulation as a profoundly alien linguistic practice, as control by means of an archaic, obscure, professionalized and impenetrable language, no recognition has been provided of the peculiar and distinctive character of law as a specific, sociolinguistically defined speech community and usage."[122] Thus, by its very nature, for the law to function, it requires someone trained in its practice, procedures, and language. Therefore, if you do not have this training yourself, you will need to hire someone who does. Furthermore, you have to hire someone licensed to practice law, which requires passage of the state bar exam, and in most states, that the person attended a law school that carries some accreditation (in order to sit for the bar exam). On one level, these regulations protect consumers from "shysters." Additionally, in hiring an attorney, you are helping to protect your rights. Yet, by creating the system in this way, American society has essentially mandated that it cannot get by without attorneys.

So why does all this matter? Essentially, whether protecting our rights or not, we have created a gigantic need for attorneys. Additionally, in most instances, no one needs an attorney when all is well; we only seek their advice when we have problems. On one occasion when one of the authors of this text was attending law school, a criminal defense attorney who was guest lecturing in class exclaimed, "If drugs were legal, I would not have a job." While what he said was intended as humorous and there is a distinct possibility he could find other legal work if drugs were legal, he made a very important point. The more often people are arrested for violating drug laws, the more often they will need attorneys—like him—to represent them. Every time a law is repealed or a police officer handles law-breaking informally and does not arrest someone, there is one less client available to represent. Generally, we would argue (with certain exceptions) the legal profession would resist changes that reduced the number of clients available for defense attorneys to represent, the number of defendants that prosecutors prosecute, and the number of cases over which judges preside. The more crime, the better it is for their labor market.

Yet the labor market for attorneys can be very fickle. In the late 1980s and early 1990s, law school applications increased rapidly. The practice of law had always been viewed as a prestigious and lucrative career, yet many people struggled to explain why there had been such a tremendous increase in the number of people wanting to attend law school. A culprit many people pointed to was the popular television show *L.A. Law*.[123] While some of you might find this curious, especially considering the sheer number of legal dramas that have inundated television since the days of *L.A. Law*, the show really was a pioneer of the genre. Shows such as *Perry Mason* and *Matlock* presented two lawyers as "advocates" for their always-innocent clients; *L.A. Law* presented the legal profession in a new, glamorous, and slightly cynical way. Attorneys were rich and powerful—who would *not* want to live that life? Yet, as both the number of law schools and applications to them continued to rise, the party did not last. Beginning around 2010, law school enrollment peaked and since then, applications to law school have been declining, in some cases sharply. Reasons for this are plenty. Some prospective attorneys finally noticed the job market for attorneys is oversaturated and, as a result, there are not enough good jobs available. Furthermore, there is a growing realization among some critics of the traditional model of legal education that what has become a weak job market no longer justifies three years of law school and the tremendous debt many law students accrue over that period.[124] In one study of more than 1,200 attorneys who had passed the bar and graduated in the class of 2010, Deborah Merritt found that 25% of the class worked in jobs *that did not require a law degree.* Fully 10% of the class was working as solo practitioners, more than a few of whom were forced to do so because they could not find a job, even with a small firm. Merritt did find that graduates from many of the top law schools (e.g., Harvard, Yale, Stanford) had not been as deeply affected.[125]

What are the long-term consequences of these somewhat dramatic changes to the legal profession? That is difficult to say. Dorothy Brown, a law professor at Emory University, predicted possible dire consequences for law schools due to a continuing decline in the job market combined with fewer applications by potential students. Many law firms are now downsizing, and the proliferation of programs such as LexisNexis and Westlaw have severely reduced the time it used to take to conduct legal research. Brown suggests that some law schools may have to close because the market will demand it.[126] *Will* this happen? We cannot say for sure. Predicting the trends and futures of the job market for lawyers is beyond our expertise. Yet, by analyzing this set of circumstances, we hope it illustrates that the legal profession is a business like any other.

# Conclusion

The American courts constitute a massive system. Included is a dual-system of courts (federal and state), each of which has several different levels. To run this system, thousands of judges are required, as well as countless attorneys serving as prosecutors and defense attorneys. In addition to the attorneys who try the cases and the judges who preside over them, a considerable support staff is required to perform the plethora of tasks necessary so that these courts can function. Many of these positions are simply due to the Durkheimian notion that as societies become more organic they will inevitably become more complex. However, considering the continually growing number of criminal cases filed as well as ever-expanding legal codes, the complexity will only escalate.

# Key Terms

- Criminal court
- Civil court
- Criminal law
- Civil law
- Beyond a reasonable doubt
- A preponderance of the evidence
- Habeas corpus
- Article III of the Constitution
- The midnight judges
- The Judiciary Act
- Judicial review
- Ellis Island
- Federal magistrate judge
- Federal district courts
- Federal appeals courts
- State courts
- Limited jurisdiction
- Single-tiered court systems
- Multi-tiered court systems
- Court of last resort
- Appeals by right
- Appeals by permission
- Death penalty appeals
- Juvenile courts
- Child-savers
- *Parens patriae*
- Problem-solving courts
- Therapeutic jurisprudence
- Narcotic courts
- Drug court
- Federal prosecutors
- Attorney general
- Solicitor general
- State prosecutors
- Defense attorneys
- Public defender offices
- The Defense Services Program
- Chief federal public defender

- Assigned counsel
- American Bar Association
- National Association of Attorneys General
- National District Attorneys Association
- National Association of Criminal Defense Lawyers
- Federal judges
- Administrative Office of the United State Courts
- One-shotters
- Repeat players
- OSCAR
- Federal prosecutors
- State judges
- Intermediate appeals courts
- State court support staff
- State prosecutors
- SEAK, Inc.
- LexisNexis
- Jury nullification
- *A Time to Kill*
- *Stare decisis*

# Key Cases

- *Marbury v. Madison*
- *New Jersey v. New York*
- *Gideon v. Wainwright*
- *Frye v. United States*
- *Daubert v. Merrell Dow Pharmaceuticals*

# Key People

- Edwin Sutherland
- William Marbury
- James Madison
- John Adams
- Thomas Jefferson
- Franklin D. Roosevelt

- O.J. Simpson
- Alan Dershowitz
- Robert Seidman
- William Chambliss
- Timothy McVeigh
- Terry Nichols
- Dwight Eisenhower

# Discussion Questions

1) What is the significance of *Marbury v. Madison*? Describe the events of the case and explain its importance, as well as its legal quandary.
2) What are courts of last resorts? Do these differ among states? If so, how?
3) In Table 8.4, the types of cases heard by state court systems are listed. Did these frequencies surprise you? If so, which ones? Do you think money affects types of cases heard? Why or why not?
4) What do you think the benefits are of problem-solving courts? Do you support them? Why or why not?
5) What is the role of lobbying groups for attorneys? Evaluate the advantages and disadvantages of these lobbying groups.
6) In the section about court costs, we provided an example of specific types of fees. Do you think these fees are fair? Why or why not?
7) What is the role of politics in law? Provide two examples from the book.

# Notes

1. Sutherland, Edwin. 1940. "White-Collar Criminality." *American Sociological Review*, 5(1): 1–12.

2. Robinson, Paul H. 1996. "The Criminal-Civil Distinction and the Utility of Desert." *Boston University Law Review*, 76: 201–214.

3. Clermont, Kevin M. and Emily Sherwin. 2002. "A Comparative View of Standards of Proof." *The American Journal of Comparative Law*, 50: 243–275.

4. United States Constitution, Article III, Section I.

5. *Marbury v. Madison* (1803). 5 U.S. 137.

6. Turner, Kathryn. 1961. "The Midnight Judges." *University of Pennsylvania Law Review*, 109: 494–523.

7. Marbury v. Madison (1803). 5 U.S. 137.

8. Prakash, Saikrishna B. and John C. Yoo. 2003. "The Origins of Judicial Review." *University of Chicago Law Review*, 70: 887–982.

9. United States Constitution, Article III, Section I.

10. New Jersey v. New York (1998). 523 U.S. 767.

11. Champion, Dean John, Richard D. Hartley and Gary A. Rabe. 2012. *Criminal Courts: Structure, Process, and Issues.* 3rd Edition. New York: Pearson.

12. United States Courts: Frequently Asked Questions. Retrieved on April 22, 2015 at: http://www.uscourts.gov/Common/FAQS.aspx.

13. United States Courts: U.S. Magistrate Judges. Retrieved on April 22, 2015 at: http://www.uscourts.gov/Statistics/JudicialBusiness/2012/us-magistrate-judges.aspx.

14. *Ibid.*

15. United States Courts: Federal Judgeships. Retrieved on April 22, 2015 at: http://www.uscourts.gov/JudgesAndJudgeships/FederalJudgeships.aspx.

16. United States Courts: Judicial Caseload Indicators—Judicial Business, 2012. Retrieved on June 10, 2015 at: http://www.uscourts.gov/Statistics/JudicialBusiness/2012/judicial-caseload-indicators.aspx

17. United States Courts: Federal Judgeships. Retrieved on April 22, 2015 at: http://www.uscourts.gov/JudgesAndJudgeships/FederalJudgeships.aspx.

18. United States Courts: Frequently Asked Questions. Retrieved on April 22, 2015 at: http://www.uscourts.gov/Common/FAQS.aspx.

19. United States Courts: U.S. Courts of Appeals. Retrieved on April 22, 2015 at: http://www.uscourts.gov/Statistics/JudicialBusiness/2014/us-courts-of-appeals.aspx.

20. United States Courts: Statistics & Reports. Retrieved on June 10, 2015 at: http://www.uscourts.gov/statistics/table/d/judicial-business/2012/09/30.

21. Friedman, Lawrence M. 1993. *Crime and Punishment in American History.* New York: Basic Books.

22. LaFountain, Robert C., Richard Y. Schauffler, Shauna M. Strickland & Kathryn A. Holt. 2012. *Examining the Work of State Courts: An Analysis of 2010 State Court Caseloads.* National Center for State Courts.

23. Champion, Dean John, Richard D. Hartley and Gary A. Rabe. 2012. *Criminal Courts: Structure, Process, and Issues.* 3rd Edition. New York: Pearson.

24. Champion, Dean John, Richard D. Hartley and Gary A. Rabe. 2012. *Criminal Courts: Structure, Process, and Issues.* 3rd Edition. New York: Pearson; LaFountain, Robert C., Richard Y. Schauffler, Shauna M. Strickland & Kathryn A. Holt. 2012. *Examining the Work of State Courts: An Analysis of 2010 State Court Caseloads.* National Center for State Courts; Neubauer, David W. and Henry F. Fradella. 2014. *America's Courts and the Criminal Justice System.* Belmont, CA: Cengage.

25. Neubauer, David W. and Henry F. Fradella. 2014. *America's Courts and the Criminal Justice System.* Belmont, CA: Cengage.

26. LaFountain, Robert C., Richard Y. Schauffler, Shauna M. Strickland & Kathryn A. Holt. 2012. *Examining the Work of State Courts: An Analysis of 2010 State Court Caseloads.* National Center for State Courts.

27. Friedrichs, David O. 2006. *Law in Our Lives: An Introduction.* 2nd Edition. Los Angeles: Roxbury Publishing Company.

28. Platt, Anthony. 1969. "The Rise of the Child-Saving Movement: A Study in Social Policy and Correctional Reform." *Annals of the American Academy of Political and Social Science,* 381: 21–38.

29. Friedrichs, David O. 2006. *Law in Our Lives: An Introduction.* 2nd Edition. Los Angeles: Roxbury Publishing Company.

30. Neubauer, David W. and Henry F. Fradella. 2014. *America's Courts and the Criminal Justice System*. Belmont, CA: Cengage.

31. The Legal Dictionary. *Parens Patriae*. Retrieved May 26, 2015 from http://legaldictionary.thefree dictionary.com/Parens+Patriae.

32. Office of Juvenile Justice and Delinquency Prevention: Statistical Briefing Book. Retrieved on May 1, 2015 at: http://www.ojjdp.gov/ojstatbb/court/qa06401.asp?qaDate=2012.

33. Steiner, B. and J. Hamilton, 2014. "Transfer of Juveniles to Adult Court." Pp. 1–8 in Jay Albanese (Ed.), *The Encyclopedia of Criminology and Criminal Justice*. New York: Wiley.

34. Winick, Bruce J. 2002. "Therapeutic Jurisprudence and Problem Solving Courts." *Fordham Urban Law Journal*, 30(3): 1055–1103.

35. Winick, Bruce J. 2002. "Therapeutic Jurisprudence and Problem Solving Courts." *Fordham Urban Law Journal*, 30(3): 1055–1103.

36. *Ibid.*

37. Hora, Peggy Fulton, William G. Schma and John T.A. Rosenthal. 1999. "Therapeutic Jurisprudence and the Drug Treatment Court Movement: Revolutionizing the Criminal Justice System's Response to Drug Abuse and Crime in America." *Notre Dame Law Review*, 74(2): 439–538.

38. Belenko, Steven. 1998. "Research on Drug Courts: A Critical Review." *National Drug Court Institute Review*, 1(1): 1–42.

39. Huddleston, III, C. West, Douglas B. Marlowe and Rachel Casebolt. 2008. *Painting the Current Picture: A National Report Card on Drug Courts and other Problem-Solving Court Programs in the United States*. Washington, DC: U.S. Department of Justice.

40. National Association of Drug Court Professionals: Types of Drug Courts. Retrieved on May 1, 2015 at: http://www.nadcp.org/learn/what-are-drug-courts/types-drug-courts.

41. United States Department of Justice: About DOJ. Retrieved on April 28, 2015 at: http://www.justice.gov/about.

42. United States Department of Justice. United States Attorneys' Annual Statistical Report: Fiscal Year 2010. Retrieved on April 28, 2015 at: http://www.justice.gov/sites/default/files/usao/legacy/2011/09/01/10statrpt.pdf.

43. Neubauer, David W. and Henry F. Fradella. 2014. *America's Courts and the Criminal Justice System*. Belmont, CA: Cengage.

44. United States Department of Justice. United States Attorneys' Annual Statistical Report: Fiscal Year 2010. Retrieved on April 28, 2015 at: http://www.justice.gov/sites/default/files/usao/legacy/2011/09/01/10statrpt.pdf.

45. National Association of Attorneys General: How does one become an attorney general? Retrieved on April 29, 2015 at: http://www.naag.org/naag/about_naag/faq/how_does_one_become_an_attorney_general.php.

46. Robinson, Nick. 2009. "Elect, Don't Appoint, the US Attorney General." *The Christian Science Monitor*. Retrieved on April 29, 2015 at: http://www.csmonitor.com/Commentary/Opinion/2009/0130/p09s01-coop.html.

47. Greene, Norman L. 2013. "Selecting State Attorneys General." *American Bar Association: State & Local News*, 36(3). Retrieved on April 29, 2015 at: http://www.americanbar.org/publications/state_local_law_news/2012_13/spring_2013/selecting_state_attorneys_general.html.

48. State of Alabama, Office of the Attorney General. "About the Attorney General." Retrieved May 26, 2015 from http://www.ago.state.al.us/Page-About.

49. Neubauer, David W. and Henry F. Fradella. 2014. *America's Courts and the Crimi-

*nal Justice System.* Belmont, CA: Cengage.

50. Stewart, Brandon. 2011. "List of 27 States Suing Over ObamaCare." Retrieved on May 26, 2015 at: htt://dailysignal.com/2011/01/17list-of-states-suing-over-obamacare/.

51. Los Angeles County District Attorney's Office. "Meet the DA." Retrieved on May 27, 2015 at: http://da.lacounty.gov/about/meet-the-da.

52. Perry, Steven W. and Duren Perry. 2011. *Prosecutors in State Courts, 2007.* Washington, DC: Bureau of Justice Statistics. Retrieved on May 27, 2015 at: http://www.bjs.gov/content/pub/pdf/ psc07st.pdf.

53. American Bar Association. nd. "Prosecution Function." Retrieved on May 27, 2015 at: http:// www. americanbar.org/publications/criminal_justice_section_archive/crimjust_standards. pfunc_blk.html.

54. Heymann, Philip and Carol Petrie (Eds.). 2001. *What's Changing in Prosecution? Report of a Workshop.* Washington, DC: National Academies Press.

55. Jacoby, Joan. 1980. *The American Prosecutor.* Lexington, MA: Lexington Books.

56. *Ibid.*

57. Ellis, Michael. 2012. "The Origins of the Elected Prosecutor." *Yale Law Journal,* 121(6):1286–1583.

58. *Ibid.*

59. Misner, Robert. 1996. "Recasting Prosecutorial Discretion." *Journal of Criminal Law and Criminology,* 86(3):717–777.

60. *Ibid.*

61. Misner, Robert. 1996. "Recasting Prosecutorial Discretion." *Journal of Criminal Law and Criminology,* 86(3):717–777.

62. Friedrichs, David O. 2006. *Law in our Lives: An Introduction.* 2nd Edition. Los Angeles: Roxbury Publishing Company.

63. Heinz, John P., Edward O. Laumann, Robert L. Nelson and Ethan Michelson. 1998. "The Changing Character of Lawyers' Work: Chicago in 1975 and 1995." *Law & Society Review,* 32(4): 751–776.

64. Neubauer, David W. and Henry F. Fradella. 2014. *America's Courts and the Criminal Justice System.* Belmont, CA: Cengage.

65. Luban, David. 1993. "Are Criminal Defenders Different?" *Michigan Law Review,* 91(7): 1729–1766.

66. Gideon v. Wainwright (1963). 372 U.S. 335.

67. Samaha, Joel. 2014. *Criminal Procedure.* 9th Edition. Belmont, CA: Cengage.

68. Neubauer, David W. and Henry F. Fradella. 2014. *America's Courts and the Criminal Justice System.* Belmont, CA: Cengage.

69. Farole, Donald J. and Lynne Langton. 2010. *County Based and Local Public Defender's Offices, 2007.* Washington, DC: Bureau of Justice Statistics.

70. Houlden, Pauline and Steven Balkin. 1985. "Quality and Cost Comparisons of Private Bar Indigent Defense Systems: Contract vs. Ordered Assigned Counsel." *Journal of Criminal Law and Criminology,* 76(1): 176–200.

71. Hoffman, Morris B., Paul H. Rubin, and Joanna M. Shepherd. 2005. "An Empirical Study of Public Defender Effectiveness: Self-Selection by the 'Marginally Indigent.'" *Ohio State Journal of Criminal Law,* 3: 223–255.

72. Langton, Lynn and Donald Farole, Jr. 2010. *State Public Defender Programs, 2007.* Washington, DC: U.S. Department of Justice.

73. United States Courts: The Defender Services Program. Retrieved on April 28, 2015

at: http://www.uscourts.gov/FederalCourts/AppointmentOfCounsel.aspx.

74. Houlden, Pauline and Steven Balkin. 1985. "Quality and Cost Comparisons of Private Bar Indigent Defense Systems: Contract vs. Ordered Assigned Counsel." *Journal of Criminal Law and Criminology*, 76(1): 176–200.

75. American Bar Association: History of the American Bar Association. Retrieved on April 29, 2015 at: http://www.americanbar.org/about_the_aba/history.html.

76. American Bar Association: About the American Bar Association. Retrieved on April 29, 2015 at: http://www.americanbar.org/about_the_aba.html.

77. National Association of Attorneys General: NAAG History. Retrieved on April 29, 2015 at: http://www.naag.org/naag/about_naag/naag-history.php.

78. *Ibid.*

79. National District Attorneys Association. "History of NDAA." Retrieved on May 27, 2015 at: http://www.ndaa.org/ndaa_history.html.

80. *Ibid.*

81. National Association of Criminal Defense Lawyers. Mission and Values. Retrieved on May 27, 2015 at: http://www.nacdl.org/about/mission-and-values/.

82. National Association of Criminal Defense Lawyers: Member Benefits Overview. Retrieved on April 29, 2015 at: http://www.nacdl.org/benefits/.

83. National Association of Criminal Defense Lawyers: Mission & Values. Retrieved on April 29, 2015 at: http://www.nacdl.org/about/mission-and-values/.

84. United States Courts: Judicial Salaries Since 1968. Retrieved on April 22, 2015 at: http://www.uscourts.gov/JudgesAndJudgeships/JudicialCompensation/judicial-salaries-since-1968.aspx.

85. United States Courts: Administrative Office of the United States Courts. Retrieved on April 22, 2015 at: http://www.uscourts.gov/FederalCourts/UnderstandingtheFederalCourts/AdministrativeOffice.aspx.

86. United States Courts: OSCAR: Qualifications, Salary, and Benefits. Retrieved on April 22, 2015 at: https://oscar.uscourts.gov/qualifications_salary_benefits.

87. Avery, Christopher, Christine Jolls, Richard A. Posner and Alvin E. Roth. 2001. "The Market for Federal Judicial Law Clerks." *University of Chicago Law Review*, 68: 793–902.

88. United States Department of Justice. United States Attorneys' Annual Statistical Report: Fiscal Year 2010. Retrieved on April 28, 2015 at: http://www.justice.gov/sites/default/files/usao/legacy/2011/09/01/10statrpt.pdf.

89. Neubauer, David W. and Henry F. Fradella. 2014. *America's Courts and the Criminal Justice System.* Belmont, CA: Cengage.

90. Champion, Dean John, Richard D. Hartley and Gary A. Rabe. 2012. *Criminal Courts: Structure, Process, and Issues.* 3rd Edition. New York: Pearson.

91. Neubauer, David W. and Henry F. Fradella. 2014. *America's Courts and the Criminal Justice System.* Belmont, CA: Cengage.

92. National Center for State Courts: Judicial Salary Tracker. Retrieved on April 28, 2015 at: http://www.ncsc.org/FlashMicrosites/JudicialSalaryReview/2015/home.html.

93. *Ibid.*

94. Neubauer, David W. and Henry F. Fradella. 2014. *America's Courts and the Criminal Justice System.* Belmont, CA: Cengage.

95. *Ibid.*

96. Champion, Dean John, Richard D. Hartley and Gary A. Rabe. 2012. *Criminal Courts: Structure, Process, and Issues.* 3rd Edition. New York: Pearson.

97. National Center for State Courts: Judicial Salary Tracker. Retrieved on April 28,

2015 at: http://www.ncsc.org/FlashMicrosites/JudicialSalaryReview/2015/home.html.

98. Champion, Dean John, Richard D. Hartley and Gary A. Rabe. 2012. *Criminal Courts: Structure, Process, and Issues.* 3rd Edition. New York: Pearson.

99. National Center for State Courts: Judicial Salary Tracker. Retrieved on April 28, 2015 at: http://www.ncsc.org/FlashMicrosites/JudicialSalaryReview/2015/home.html.

100. Government in the Sunshine Act, Pub. L. 94–409, 90 Stat. 1241.

101. Florida Courts: Salary Schedule. Retrieved on April 28, 2015 at: http://www.flcourts.org/administration-funding/employment/salary-schedule.stml.

102. Perry, Steven W. and Duren Banks. 2011. *Prosecutors in State Courts, 2007 — Statistical Tables.* Washington, DC: U.S. Department of Justice.

103. Haynes, V. Dion. 1997. "The $25 Million Question: What is Simpson Worth? Chicago Tribune. Retrieved on May 1, 2015 at: http://articles.chicagotribune.com/1997-02-07/news/9702070269_1_nicole-brown-simpson-los-angeles-civil-lawyer-legal-fees.

104. ExpertLaw: Hiring a Criminal Defense Lawyer. Retrieved on May 1, 2015 at: http://www.expertlaw.com/library/criminal/criminal_lawyer.html.

105. Gold, Scott. 2004. "Cost of Vengeance Divides Oklahoma."" *Los Angeles Times.* Retrieved on May 1, 2015 at: http://articles.latimes.com/2004/feb/29/nation/na-nichols29.

106. CNN: Terry Nichols Fast Facts. Retrieved on May 1, 2015 at: http://www.cnn.com/2013/03/25/us/terry-nichols-fast-facts/.

107. Galanter, Marc. 1974. "Why the 'Haves' Come Out Ahead: Speculations on the Limits of Legal Change." *Law and Society Review,* 9(1):95–124.

108. Wright, Ronald F. and Wayne A. Logan. 2006. "The Political Economy of Application Fees for Indigent Criminal Defense." *William & Mary Law Review,* 47(6): 2045–2087.

109. The North Carolina Court System: Criminal Court Costs 2014. Retrieved on May 1, 2015 at: http://www.nccourts.org/Courts/Trial/Documents/court_costs_chart-Oct2014-criminal.pdf.

110. Gross, Samuel R. 1991. "Expert Evidence." *Wisconsin Law Review,* 1991: 1113–1232.

111. *Frye v. United States* (1923). 293 F. 1013.

112. *Daubert v. Merrell Dow Pharmaceuticals* (1993). 509 U.S. 579.

113. Federal Rules of Evidence. Article VII. Opinions and Expert Testimony. Rule 702: Testimony by Expert Witnesses. Retrieved June 2, 2015 from https://www.law.cornell.edu/rules/fre/rule_ 702.

114. Harrison, Jeffrey L. 2001. "Reconceptualizing the Expert Witness: Social Costs, Current Controls and Proposed Responses." *Yale Journal on Regulation,* 18: 253–314

115. SEAK: About Us. Retrieved on May 1, 2015 at: www.seak.com/about-us.

116. SEAK: Expert Witness Fee Study. Retrieved on May 1, 2015 at: http://www.seak.com/expert-witness-fee-study/.

117. Company News. 1994. "Company News; A Name Change is Planned for Mead Data Central." *The New York Times.* Retrieved on May 1, 2015 at: http://www.nytimes.com/1994/12/02/business/company-news-a-name-change-is-planned-for-mead-data-central.html.

118. Reed Elsevier. Annual Reports and Financial Statements 2013. Retrieved on May 1, 2015 at: http://www.relxgroup.com/investorcentre/reports%202007/Documents/2013/reed_elsevier_ar_2013.pdf.

119. Wheeler, Jr., Ronald E. 2011. "Does WestlawNext Really Change Everything? The Implications of WestlawNext on Legal Research." *Law Library Journal,* 103(3): 359–377.

120. Justiss, Laura K. 2011. "A Survey of Electronic Research Alternatives to LexisNexis and Westlaw in Law Firms." *Law Library Journal,* 103(1): 71–89.

121. Chambliss, William J. and Robert B. Seidman. 1971. *Law, Order, and Power*. Reading, MA: Addison-Wesley.

122. Goodrich, Peter. 1984. "Law and Language: An Historical and Critical Introduction." *Journal of Law and Society*, 11(2): 173–206. Quote on page 173.

123. Abrahamson, Alan. 1989. "Applications Hit Record Highs for U.S. Law Schools: Increase Attributed to Impact of Television Hit 'L.A. Law'." *Los Angeles Times*. Retrieved on May 2, 2015 at: http://articles.latimes.com/1989-08-20/local/me-1216_1_law-school-applications.

124. Olson, Elizabeth. 2015. Burdened with Debt, Law School Graduates Struggle in Job Market. *The New York Times*. Retrieved on May 2, 2015 at: http://www.nytimes.com/2015/04/27/business/dealbook/burdened-with-debt-law-school-graduates-struggle-in-job-market.html?_r=1.

125. Merritt, Deborah Jones. (In Press.) "What Happened to the Class of 2015? Empirical Evidence of Structural Change in the Legal Profession." *Michigan State Law Review*.

126. Brown, Dorothy A. 2015. "Law Schools are in a Death Spiral. Maybe Now They'll Finally Change." *The Washington Post*. Retrieved on May 2, 2015 at: http://www.washingtonpost.com/posteverything/wp/2015/03/09/law-schools-are-in-a-death-spiral-maybe-now-theyll-finally-change/.

# Chapter 9

# The Political Economy of Corrections

## Chapter Outline

- Introduction
- Corrections in America: An Overview
  - The Reach of Corrections in America
- Federal Corrections
- State Corrections: Prisons and Probation/Parole Services
- Local Corrections: Jails and Lockups
- United States Marshals Service
- Intermediate Sanctions and Community Corrections
- Private Corrections Companies
- Correctional Advocacy Groups
- Budgets, Costs, and Profiles
- Politics and Current Issues
- Conclusion
- Key Terms
- Key People
- Discussion Questions

## Learning Objectives

- Describe the federal system of corrections
- Describe the state and local systems of corrections
- Compare and contrast the federal, state, and local systems of corrections
- Describe the correctional population today
- Describe types of correctional advocacy groups

- Define community corrections
- Define intermediate sanctions
- Define net-widening
- Evaluate the costs and benefits of intermediate sanctions
- Assess the role of privatization in the corrections system
- Evaluate the role of politics in corrections

# Introduction

Once individuals have been convicted of a crime, they face an array of sanctions depending on the seriousness of the charges for which they were convicted and their prior criminal record. Sanctioning offenders for violating the law is typically justified on various grounds including deterring them from committing crimes in the future; incapacitating them in jail or prison and eliminating the possibility of victimizing general society while incarcerated; rehabilitating them by eliminating the "causes" of their criminality; or punishing them for their behavior (sometimes known as "just deserts").[1] Practically speaking, offenders can face sanctions that range from a short term of (un)supervised release back into the community (probation) to capital punishment for especially heinous crimes. Offenders may also face monetary fines or have to pay restitution to victims as part of their sanction. If sentenced to probation, offenders may also pay fees that cover at least some, if not all, of the costs of their supervision. In some states, once an offender has served a portion of their sentence in prison, he or she is eligible for parole based on the recommendation of a committee of practitioners who review the offender's record and judge him or her fit for early release. Finally, regardless of the specific component of corrections being discussed—probation, jail, prisons, or parole—the past 25 years has seen major growth in the presence of the private sector in American corrections, to the point where some observers, such as Randall Shelden, have suggested that probation, jails, prisons, and parole have developed into a "corrections-industrial complex."[2] In this chapter, we explore the many aspects of American corrections, including the politics of corrections—policies that many criminologists have argued caused an exponential increase in the number of citizens under some form of correctional supervision—and the economics of corrections, particularly the burgeoning role played by corporations that have profited from those policies.

# Corrections in America: An Overview

In the United States, the stated purpose of corrections is exactly as it sounds—to correct the behavior of those who have broken the law. For the most part, correctional officials do not intervene in the lives of Americans unless they have been charged with or convicted of a crime.

When the topic of corrections arises, many people automatically think of prisons. While prisons are certainly an integral part of corrections in America, these facilities are not the only component. Corrections also include county and local jails and local lockups, probation and parole services, and community-based correctional operations such as halfway houses. In fact, in 2013 (the most recent year for which data were available), just under one-quarter (23%) of those under correctional supervision in this country were in prison; the rest were on either probation or parole, or incarcerated in local jails.[3]

Recall that Cesare Beccaria (whom we discussed in Chapter 2) is generally regarded as the "father of criminology." His primary concern was with the methods of punishment used against criminal offenders during the late 1700s, now viewed by many as draconian. Thus, one could argue that criminology actually began with the study of corrections. Since Beccaria's time, how offenders are treated and how prisons are managed—sometimes known as **penology**—has been a continuing interest of many criminologists, as well as a source of ongoing debate regarding which is the most effective and efficient method of punishment. While politicians claim the specific correctional policies they sponsor are both rational and work at changing the behavior of offenders, the reality is that most policies place cost-effectiveness and popularity with constituents at the forefront. Lastly, the correctional system not only punishes offenders but in so doing presents many money-making opportunities: by fostering educational programs, like degrees in criminal justice; by creating jobs for probation, parole, and correctional officers as well as jail and prison administrators; and by offering various segments of American industry the opportunity to earn a profit.

## *The Reach of Corrections in America*

As previously mentioned, corrections in America touches the lives of many people. Thousands of people work in the corrections sector and millions more are under its supervision. However, many readers may not fully understand how corrections operate in this country. Let us look at the different places in which people can be locked up, which vary by level of government—federal, state, and local. While one might *think* it would be easy to count the number of prisons, jails, and similar types of facilities operating in this country, such is not the case. According to Pete Wagner and Leah Sakala, "[O]ur systems of federal, state, local, and other types of confinement are fragmented. [D]efinitional issues and incompatibilities make it hard to get the big picture."[4] Wagner and Sakala recently used multiple datasets to create the most complete census of known correctional facilities. Based on their sources, Wagner and Sakala estimated that, as of 2005, in the United States there were 1,719 state prisons, 102 federal prisons, 2,259 juvenile correctional facilities, 3,283 local jails, and 79 Indian country jails (they did not include specific numbers for such facilities as military prisons, immigration detention facilities, civil commitment centers, and prisons in the U.S. territories).[5]

Regardless of whether one is talking about prisons, jails, or other aspects of corrections such as probation, American corrections touches the lives of countless citizens. For example, corrections creates jobs. The **Bureau of Labor Statistics** (BLS) provides employment data on people employed as "correctional officers and jailers," a category created by BLS. In 2014, for example, 229,940 people were employed as "correctional officers and jailers" by state governments, 162,840 people were employed by local governments, 23,300 people were employed as facility support services, and 820 people were employed by psychiatric and substance abuse hospitals. The state of Texas employed the most correctional officers and jailers, with 49,040. By contrast, the state of Rhode Island only employed 1,100 correctional officers and jailers.[6] Additionally, the Bureau of Labor Statistics also included first-line supervisors of correctional officers in its employment data. In 2014, 26,300 people were employed as first-line supervisors of correctional officers by state governments, 14,750 people were employed by local governments, 1,430 people were employed by facility support services, and 160 people were employed by psychiatric and substance abuse hospitals. Again, the state of Texas employed the most first-line supervisors, with 5,430. By contrast, the state of Alaska employed only 80 first-line supervisors.[7] In addition to the reports of the Bureau of Labor Statistics, the **Bureau of Justice Statistics** conducted a survey of prisons in 2005 to perform a census of employees that included both state and private facilities. Those data are shown in Table 9.1.

BLS also reported employment data for probation and parole officers in a category referred to as "Probation Officers and Correctional Treatment Specialists." BLS does not differentiate between parole and probation officers, likely because some departments cover both probation and parole, while some departments specialize in one or the other. According to the BLS data for 2014, there were 46,390 individuals who were employed by state governments and 37,770 employed by local governments as "probation officers and correctional treatment specialists." While we cannot say with certainty, it is plausible that the states using the centralized method of probation (which we previously described) employed state employees, while local government employees were employed in locations using the decentralized model. In addition, BLS indicated that 1,020 people were employed in facility support services, 880 people were employed in individual and family service positions, and 440 were employed in other residential care facilities around the nation. California was by far the biggest employer of probation and parole officers, with 12,260 officers working for the state in 2014.[8]

Corrections also touches the lives of people who are in the system. In 2013, the most recent year for which data were available, 6,899,000 people in the United States were under some form of correctional supervision—either in jail, on probation, in prison, or on parole.[9] To put this figure into context, it translates to about 3% of the adult population; the rate of correctional supervision was about 284 per every 100,000 adults. The almost 7 million adults under correctional supervision in 2013 included 3.9 million probationers (56.7%), 853,200 parolees (12.4%), 731,200 jail inmates (10.6%), and 1.5 million prison inmates (22.8%).[10] Figure 9.1 provides a graphical depiction of the distribution of the correctional population in the U.S. during the period 1980 through 2013.[11]

Zeroing in on incarceration, the United States incarcerates its citizens at a rate unprecedented in the world. As of December 31, 2013, the imprisonment rate for U.S. residents of all ages was 478 sentenced prisoners per 100,000 individuals, and for U.S. residents age 18 or older the rate was 623 incarcerated per 100,000 people.

More interesting—and perhaps troubling—is the fact that many American states, were they *countries*, would be among the world leaders in incarcerating their citizens. We return to the work of Pete Wagner and Leah Sakala, along with their colleague Josh Bagley, who in a recent report for the non-profit and non-partisan Prison Policy Initiative analyzed rates of incarceration in the 50 states and the District of Columbia in 2014 and compared them with rates found in other countries.[12] Wagner and his colleagues found that 36 states and the District of Columbia have incarceration rates higher than that of Cuba, the nation with the second highest incarceration rate in the world in 2014. New Jersey and New York follow. Next is Washington State, which claims the same incarceration rate as the Russian Federation. Utah, Nebraska and Iowa lock up a greater portion of their populations than does El Salvador, a coun-

Table 9.1. State Correctional Employees

| Authority | Total | Facilities | All | Administrators | Correction | Service | Education | Prof./technical | Other/N/A |
|---|---|---|---|---|---|---|---|---|---|
| U.S. Total (estimated) | | | 44,505 | 10,769 | 295,261 | 51,993 | 11,526 | 46,016 | 29,489 |
| U.S. Total (reported) | 1,821 | 1,717 | 419,635 | 10,154 | 278,398 | 49,024 | 10,868 | 43,388 | 27,805 |
| Public | 1,406 | 1,317 | 393,699 | 8,290 | 262,718 | 46,481 | 9,827 | 39,618 | 26,765 |
| Private | 415 | 400 | 25,938 | 1,864 | 15,680 | 2,543 | 1,041 | 3,770 | 1,040 |
| State | 1,719 | 1,620 | 389,882 | 9,254 | 264,233 | 42,808 | 9,946 | 38,533 | 25,108 |
| Region (excluding federal) | | | | | | | | | |
| Northeast | 268 | 262 | 70,215 | 1,381 | 47,544 | 9,621 | 2,754 | 7,715 | 1,200 |
| Connecticut | 49 | 49 | 6,402 | 118 | 4,516 | 708 | 239 | 652 | 169 |
| Maine | 7 | 7 | 834 | 41 | 572 | 96 | 42 | 83 | 0 |
| Massachusetts | 17 | 17 | 4,057 | 131 | 3,309 | 297 | 32 | 246 | 42 |
| New Hampshire | 8 | 8 | 876 | 54 | 545 | 60 | 32 | 145 | 40 |
| New Jersey | 42 | 36 | 9,277 | 232 | 6,650 | 686 | 550 | 942 | 217 |
| New York | 77 | 77 | 31,573 | 565 | 21,331 | 4,820 | 1,140 | 3,272 | 445 |
| Pennsylvania | 52 | 52 | 15,195 | 175 | 9,083 | 2,845 | 664 | 2,169 | 259 |
| Rhode Island | 7 | 7 | 1,161 | 17 | 947 | 70 | 14 | 109 | 4 |
| Vermont | 9 | 9 | 840 | 48 | 591 | 39 | 41 | 97 | 24 |
| Midwest | 342 | 338 | 85,256 | 2,702 | 55,322 | 12,567 | 2,580 | 10,496 | 1,589 |
| Illinois | 44 | 40 | 14,167 | 582 | 8,771 | 2,169 | 658 | 1,606 | 381 |
| Indiana | 23 | 23 | 6,310 | 227 | 4,264 | 912 | 177 | 678 | 52 |
| Iowa | 31 | 31 | 3,399 | 131 | 2,107 | 547 | 37 | 551 | 26 |
| Kansas | 13 | 13 | 2,984 | 108 | 1,944 | 438 | 32 | 427 | 35 |
| Michigan | 62 | 62 | 21,202 | 191 | 15,235 | 2,839 | 423 | 2,503 | 11 |
| Minnesota | 18 | 18 | 3,611 | 110 | 2,131 | 545 | 130 | 648 | 47 |
| Missouri | 28 | 28 | 9,439 | 156 | 5,625 | 1,791 | 300 | 987 | 580 |
| Nebraska | 9 | 9 | 1,812 | 89 | 1,261 | 229 | 25 | 155 | 53 |
| North Dakota | 8 | 8 | 625 | 40 | 394 | 86 | 15 | 88 | 2 |
| Ohio | 59 | 59 | 13,318 | 702 | 8,167 | 1,934 | 447 | 1,749 | 319 |
| South Dakota | 6 | 6 | 804 | 19 | 473 | 82 | 31 | 195 | 4 |
| Wisconsin | 41 | 41 | 7,585 | 347 | 4,950 | 995 | 305 | 909 | 79 |

Table 9.1. State Correctional Employees, *continued*

| Authority | Total | Facilities | All | Administrators | Correction | Service | Education | Prof./technical | Other/N/A |
|---|---|---|---|---|---|---|---|---|---|
| **South** | 779 | 775 | 148,923 | 3,753 | 108,036 | 15,893 | 3,703 | 15,385 | 2,153 |
| Alabama | 33 | 33 | 3,250 | 184 | 2,489 | 386 | 0 | 179 | 12 |
| Arkansas | 26 | 26 | 3,559 | 66 | 2,713 | 677 | 3 | 94 | 6 |
| Delaware | 12 | 12 | 1,639 | 33 | 1,363 | 120 | 22 | 89 | 12 |
| District of Columbia | 5 | 5 | 123 | 14 | 51 | 23 | . | 24 | 11 |
| Florida | 109 | 107 | 23,038 | 294 | 17,827 | 692 | 408 | 3,589 | 228 |
| Georgia | 87 | 87 | 14,301 | 553 | 9,670 | 1,993 | 293 | 1,331 | 461 |
| Kentucky | 25 | 25 | 3,946 | 237 | 2,474 | 424 | 129 | 586 | 96 |
| Louisiana | 23 | 23 | 5,921 | 142 | 4,710 | 324 | 59 | 480 | 206 |
| Maryland | 29 | 29 | 7,160 | 85 | 5,384 | 809 | 133 | 522 | 227 |
| Mississippi | 31 | 31 | 3,934 | 167 | 2,932 | 262 | 97 | 339 | 137 |
| North Carolina | 88 | 88 | 15,106 | 412 | 11,388 | 1,056 | 215 | 1,742 | 293 |
| Oklahoma | 53 | 53 | 5,075 | 273 | 2,871 | 804 | 154 | 895 | 78 |
| South Carolina | 33 | 33 | 5,051 | 236 | 3,698 | 607 | 98 | 412 | 0 |
| Tennessee | 19 | 19 | 6,279 | 232 | 4,205 | 674 | 241 | 723 | 204 |
| Texas | 132 | 132 | 38,097 | 627 | 27,737 | 5,065 | 1,333 | 3,250 | 85 |
| Virginia | 59 | 57 | 10,697 | 118 | 7,599 | 1,691 | 374 | 876 | 39 |
| West Virginia | 15 | 15 | 1,747 | 80 | 925 | 286 | 144 | 254 | 58 |
| **West** | 330 | 245 | 85,488 | 1,418 | 53,331 | 4,727 | 909 | 4,937 | 20,166 |
| Alaska | 21 | 21 | 1,339 | 68 | 896 | 152 | 30 | 174 | 19 |
| Arizona | 21 | 21 | 8,235 | 161 | 6,519 | 524 | 167 | 859 | 5 |
| California | 100 | 100 | 47,881 | 47 | 27,803 | 128 | 40 | 230 | 19,633 |
| Colorado | 58 | 58 | 6,902 | 362 | 4,394 | 885 | 242 | 776 | 243 |
| Hawaii | 10 | 10 | 1,724 | 18 | 1,251 | 245 | 25 | 164 | 21 |
| Idaho | 15 | 15 | 1,473 | 58 | 971 | 146 | 51 | 209 | 38 |
| Montana | 11 | 11 | 1,211 | 96 | 700 | 192 | 33 | 183 | 7 |
| Nevada | 22 | 22 | 2,313 | 47 | 1,589 | 221 | 35 | 398 | 23 |
| New Mexico | 11 | 11 | 2,632 | 147 | 1,848 | 269 | 123 | 211 | 34 |
| Oregon | 15 | 15 | 3,739 | 144 | 2,318 | 630 | 103 | 478 | 66 |
| Utah | 7 | 7 | 1,380 | 28 | 1,073 | 141 | 23 | 83 | 32 |
| Washington | 32 | 32 | 6,064 | 201 | 3,599 | 1,094 | 16 | 1,114 | 40 |
| Wyoming | 7 | 7 | 595 | 41 | 370 | 100 | 21 | 58 | 5 |

try with a recent civil war and one of the highest homicide rates in the world. Even when examining the rates of the five states with the lowest incarceration rates (Minnesota, Massachusetts, North Dakota, New Hampshire, and Rhode Island), they all still have higher incarceration rates than countries that have experienced major 20th century social traumas, including several former Soviet republics and South Africa. The two American states that incarcerate the least are Maine and Vermont, but even *those* states incarcerate far more than do the closest allies of the United States, the member countries of the North Atlantic Treaty Organization (NATO). Those nations incarcerate their own citizens at a rate five to ten times *lower* than does the United States.

Just like the rest of the American criminal justice system, corrections operates at the federal, state, and local levels of government and, like police and the courts, is complex and spans multiple agencies. For example, probation agencies (which often include services for parolees) exist at the federal, state, and local levels of government, with most probation officers working for state probation agencies. Prisons, ranging from so-called "supermax" facilities, where inmates are kept in solitary confinement except for a one-hour-per-day allowance for outside exercise, to minimum security facilities for relatively low-level offenders, exist at the federal and state levels, with most prisons in the United States operated by the states. Jails and lockup facilities, on the other hand, are most often found at the local level of government (counties and cities). They serve three primary functions: to house individuals who have been arrested and are awaiting further case processing; to punish those who have been convicted of crimes and sentenced to serve a term of incarceration of less than one year; and to house those who are awaiting transfer to prison after being convicted of a felony.

The point here is that most activities involving corrections occur at the state and local levels of government and those entities bear the financial costs of running probation services, prisons, jails, etc. Because of various budget cuts occurring, many states and localities have chosen to privatize certain aspects of their correctional systems—primarily those involving prisons—by contracting with for-profit companies (e.g., Corrections Corporation of America, or CCA) to build and operate prisons or provide operational support for state-owned facilities and programs. The rise of private correctional organizations, what some refer to as the "prison-industrial complex,"[13] which is discussed below in detail, is the direct result of criminal justice policies associated with various "wars" the country has fought against crime (generally), drugs, gangs, illegal aliens, etc., in the past 30 years. Let us now look at corrections at the federal, state, and local levels of government.

# Federal Corrections

At the federal level of government, there are prisons and related institutions and probation services. Federal prisons are under the administration of the **Federal Bureau of Prisons** (BOP), which is responsible for housing some 200,000 inmates in 121 institutions spread across America with security levels ranging from "low" to "maximum security." BOP also employs some 40,000 professional staff, including attorneys, correctional officers (guards), acquisition specialists, treatment specialists and counselors, information technology practitioners, dieticians, maintenance specialists, and administrative support personnel, among others.

In 1891, Congress passed the "Three Prisons Act," which established the Federal Prison System (FPS) and designated prisons in Leavenworth, Kansas, Atlanta, Georgia, and McNeil Island, Washington, as federal prisons. Theses prisons were operated with limited oversight by the United States Department of Justice. Some three decades later, in 1930, the Bureau of Prisons was established, pursuant to Pub. L. No. 71-218, 46 Stat. 325, and housed within the Department of Justice. The agency was charged with the "management and regulation of all Federal penal and correctional institutions," which at that time included eleven prisons and about 13,000 inmates.[14] The BOP's budget for fiscal year (FY) 2014 was $6.859 billion, which included funding for about 43,000 positions, including 21,000 correctional officers. Table 9.2 presents a breakdown of the BOP's 2014 FY budget. Readers will note the largest budget category is for "institutional security and administration"—which includes correctional officers and equipment for them, as well as security equipment for the institutions –accounting for about 43% of the total budget.

Table 9.2. Federal Bureau of Prisons FY 2014 Operating Budget[15]

| Activity and program | # Permanent Positions | Cost |
|---|---|---|
| Inmate Care and Programs | 15,674 | $2,525,039,000 |
| Institution Security and Administration | 25,738 | $2,966,364,000 |
| Contract Confinement | 413 | $1,074,808,000 |
| Management and Administration—BOP | 1,233 | $202,789,000 |
| **Grand Total** | **43,058** | **$6,769,000,000** |

Probation services are another component of the federal corrections system. According to its website, the United States **Probation and Pretrial Services System** (PPSS) is responsible for probation and pretrial services in the United States district courts. Despite the fact that probation has existed in this country as a sentencing option since 1878, when Massachusetts passed a law allowing judges to impose probation, the sanction did not become a sentencing option in the federal system until some 50 years later.[16]

The first bills for a federal probation law had been introduced in Congress in 1909, but it was not until **The Probation Act** of 1925 became law that a probation system was created in the federal courts (except in the District of Columbia). The act gave the courts the power to suspend the imposition or execution of sentences and place defendants on probation for such period and on such terms and conditions as they deemed best. The act also authorized courts to appoint one salaried probation officer and one or more persons to serve as probation officers without compensation (i.e., volunteers). In 1940, administration of federal probation was transferred from the Bureau of Prisons to the Administrative Office of the United States Courts.[17]

In 1974 Congress enacted the Speedy Trial Act which, among other things, authorized the director of the Administrative Office of the United States Courts to establish "demonstration" pretrial services agencies in 10 judicial districts in order to reduce crime by persons released to the community pending trial and reduce unnecessary pretrial detention. They were to supervise persons released into their custody pending trial and help defendants on bail locate and use community services. The Administrative Office administered five of the agencies, and five were administered by boards of trustees whose members were appointed by the chief judges of the district courts. Finally, in 1982, President Ronald Reagan signed the Pretrial Services Act, which authorized expansion of pretrial services from the ten demonstration districts to every federal judicial district (except the District of Columbia). Most importantly, it allowed each court to choose the form of pretrial services organization that best provided for its needs, considering such factors as criminal caseload and court location. Expanding pretrial services to all districts marked a significant milestone for what was now the "federal probation and pretrial services system." Officers are now involved in the criminal justice process from arrest on a federal charge until the defendant completes community supervision.[18]

United States probation and pretrial services officers, who are considered the "eyes and ears" of the federal courts, investigate and supervise persons charged with or convicted of federal crimes. Among other activities, officers gather and verify information about persons who come before the courts; prepare reports that the courts rely on to make release and sentencing decisions; supervise persons released to the community by the courts and paroling authorities; and direct persons under supervision to services to help them stay on the right side of the law, including substance abuse treatment, mental health treatment, medical care, training, and employment assistance.[19]

In addition to supervising probationer and pretrial services, Federal Probation and Pretrial Services also supervises federal parolees. However, the number of parolees within the federal system is rapidly decreasing. The primary reason for this is that the federal government eliminated parole in 1987; in 2011 there were only 1,992 inmates on parole for federal crimes. While there may be a reduced caseload from federal crimes, the department did inherit parolees who committed crimes in Washington, DC. This occurred in 1997 due to the **National Capital Revitalization and Self-Government Improvement Act**, which eliminated the District of Columbia Board of Parole, thus transferring all parole decisions and supervision responsibilities to Federal Probation and Pretrial Services. In 2011, Federal Parole supervised 500 parolees from Washington, DC. Additionally, Federal Probation and Pretrial Services oversees all military members who have been convicted of crimes and paroled. In 2011, there were 350 people who were on parole from the Military Justice System.[20]

# State Corrections: Prisons and Probation/Parole Services

Across the 50 states and the District of Columbia, in 2005 there were some 1,800 prisons operating. In 2013, nearly 6.6 million adults were under some form of state-level correctional supervision. This included about 4.5 million people on probation or parole and another 2 million individuals incarcerated in state prisons.[21] State-level corrections comprise agencies and services that include community supervision, confinement, and rehabilitation of adults and juveniles; operation and management of prisons, probation and parole offices; and pardon proceedings, to name a few. State agencies and services also cost a significant amount of money to run. For example, Elizabeth Brown observed in 2012 that "corrections spending makes up the fourth largest state expenditure,"[22] while according to Tracey Kyckelhahn, in a recent report compiled for the Bureau of Justice Statistics, total state expenditures on corrections were $48.5 billion in fiscal year 2010. She also reported that between fiscal years 1982 and 2010, state spending on corrections represented between 1.9% and

3.3% of total state expenditures. To place those percentages into a larger context, between 1982 and 2010, states allocated between 29% and 33% of their spending to education, between 22% and 25% to public welfare, between 6% and 9% to highways, and between 6% and 7.5% to health care and hospitals.[23]

State-level corrections is divided into two components: oversight of institutional corrections (prisons) and oversight of probation/parole services. At the state level, prisons are usually administered under a single agency housed in the executive branch. For probation and parole, the picture is more complex. According to Frank Hellum, probation services can be organized along four different organizational models: single agency with primary authority statewide; single state agency with primary authority but local agencies with secondary authority; local agencies with primary authority and a secondary state agency; local agencies with primary authority.[24]

Todd Clear and colleagues suggest that the reality of the organizational models identified by Hellum is whether probation services are *centralized* or *decentralized*.[25] What commentators have suggested is that recent trends have moved probation away from being administered by the state's circuit courts (and, to a lesser degree, the district courts) and toward probation being housed in a centralized authority, typically part of the executive branch.[26] According to Clear and his colleagues, under a centralized model, probation services across the state are housed in a single entity (as was the case in the federal system) under the control of either the executive or the judicial branch of government. Proponents of this model point to issues with the courts administering probation in a decentralized manner, resulting in outmoded practices and a lack of professionalism that negatively affect service delivery and the success of probation. In contrast, a large, statewide agency is able to better train staff, design and implement broader-based programs, and have higher quality supervision and services, resulting in higher levels of success for probationers. Proponents of a decentralized model, where the courts administer probation services around the state, argue that having the courts (in conjunction with a city or county agency) administer probation results in a smaller, more flexible operation that is better able to respond to the unique problems of the community. Since decentralized probation draws its support from the community and the local government, it can offer better supervision for its clients and make better use of existing community resources.[27]

To illustrate how corrections operate at the state level, let us look at how Alabama administers prison and probation services. The Alabama Department of Corrections (ALDOC) oversees the state's 16 prisons and a community corrections operation that includes 12 facilities (both residential and non-residential facilities designed for low-level offenders and/or those returning to the community after a term of incarceration). In fiscal year 2014, ALDOC had expenditures of over $447 million (and a state appropriation of just over $388 million). ALDOC employed over 3,800 staff, including over 2,900 correctional officers. ALDOC was responsible for over 31,000 inmates housed in its facilities, including over 3,700 individuals housed at the agency's community corrections facilities.[28]

Turning to probation, in Alabama there is a primary agency, the Alabama Board of Pardons and Parole (ALBPP), which is responsible for felony probation services around the state. The agency operates sixty-one probation and parole field offices in counties located throughout the state. According to the agency's annual report, in FY 2014 the agency supervised 53,839 probationers, 10,374 parolees, and 321 offenders serving both probation and parole. In FY 2014, ALBPP employed 250 supervising probation and parole officers, each of whom is a state law enforcement officer with arrest powers. Duties of a supervising probation and parole officer in Alabama include monitoring conditions of parolees/probationers on assigned caseloads; seeing offenders during reporting periods; conducting home visits, employment verifications, and drug screenings; collecting DNA samples as statutorily required; collecting supervision fees as statutorily required ($40.00 per month); monitoring payment of court ordered monies/restitution; managing caseloads; making referrals to treatment/programs and completing violation/delinquency reports; using arrest authority when necessary; and preparing for revocation proceedings for parolees/probationers. These officers also complete electronic pre-sentence or post-sentence investigation reports for every offender convicted of a felony in the state. They also complete preliminary investigations and personal/social history investigations, youthful offender investigations, and sentencing standards worksheets.[29] In Alabama, misdemeanor probation is administered by district courts. Thus, Alabama has a primary agency (ALBPP) and secondary agencies (district courts) responsible for probation services.

The final level at which American corrections operates is the local level of government, where the primary components of corrections are county and city jails and local lockups. Discussion now turns to understanding how these entities operate.

## Local Corrections: Jails and Lockups

Jails have a long history traceable back to the very dawn of Western civilization and, more specifically, to feudal practices in 12th century England

where the shire-reeve (the ancestor of today's county sheriff) would, among other duties, hold in *gaol* (jail) people accused of breaking the law. Today, however, to put it succinctly, jails are frequently little more than dumping grounds for people, both those entering and leaving the American system of corrections. As criminologist Rick Ruddell observed:

> Jails remain today as the stepchild of the criminal justice system despite nearly 40 years of litigation and lawsuits. Too many in local government and ... local communities still consider jails with populations of criminals and social misfits as beyond the pale of redemption despite ... commendable efforts [by] some to educate public opinion. When people embrace the 'not in my backyard' factor, one understands the enormity of the challenge [facing jails].[30]

According to a recent report for the Vera Institute of Justice, Ram Subramanian and his coauthors observed, "Although in common parlance jails are often confused with prisons ... jails are locally run facilities, primarily holding people arrested but not yet convicted. Jails are the gateway to the formal criminal justice system."[31] Subramanian and colleagues observed that the more than 3,000 jails operating in the United States hold nearly 750,000 people (approximately the population of Detroit) on any given day; but over the course of a typical year, more than *12 million* jail admissions occur, which is nearly *19 times* the number of annual admissions to state and federal prisons and equivalent to the population of Los Angeles and New York City combined.[32] In 2007, the American Jail Association (AJA) published *Who's Who in Jail Management, Fifth Edition*,[33] which reported that there were 3,096 counties in the United States being served by 3,163 jail facilities. At that time, the total rated capacity of these facilities — the number of inmates or beds determined by an official body and often based on architectural design and construction — stood at 810,966 people.

The AJA distinguishes jails from local lockups as follows. A lockup is a temporary holding facility operated by a local police department or county sheriff's department designed to hold arrestees pending their initial appearance before a judge and subsequent transport to jail for further processing. Lockups are also designed to hold those arrested for public intoxication until they are sober and ready for further processing. Lockups also hold juvenile arrestees pending release to a parent or guardian or transport to a juvenile detention center at the order of a juvenile court.[34] Due to great variability in the locations of lockups, no exact count of them is currently available, but one estimate is there are over 13,000 of these facilities.[35] A jail, on the other hand, is a correctional facility administered by a local law enforcement agency such as a sheriff's office or local corrections department that confines adult offenders (and juveniles under certain circumstances) who are awaiting trial or who have been sentenced to serve up to a one-year term of incarceration.[36]

Jails are typically categorized by their rated capacity and include: small jails (1–49 person capacity); medium jails (50–249 person capacity); large jails (250-999 person capacity) and mega jails (capacity of greater than 1,000 persons). Small jails comprise the bulk of jails operating in the United States.[37] We do note there are 11 federally operated jails in the United States housing some 11,000 people[38] and that six states do not have jails per se, but rather have a unified corrections system that includes both jails and prisons run by a centralized state agency. A recent trend in jails is the creation of **regional jails**, formed by combining several municipal or county jails into a single operation. While fiscally sound, because local politicians and correctional officials are loath to give up their autonomy or control over patronage-based jobs, this new type of jail has been slow to gain much traction. Resistance to regionalization of jails has also arisen from reformers objecting to moving inmates away from their communities and from citizens who oppose having regional jails "in their backyard." Along with the development of these regional jails has been a trend for them to be privately run by for-profit companies.[39]

# United States Marshals Service

Founded in 1789, the **United States Marshals Service** is the oldest law enforcement agency in the country. The original mission of the Marshals Service was to be the enforcement arm of the federal court system. The agency carries on that mission to the present day and is responsible for the security of federal court facilities. Currently, not only does the agency protect the federal judiciary but it is also responsible for capturing any person under some form of federal custody who becomes a fugitive. The agency manages and sells assets that the federal government receives through asset forfeiture, is responsible for housing federal court defendants and transporting federal prisoners, and maintains and operates the federal **Witness Security Program**.[40] Today, the agency has a total budget of $1.195 billion and a total of 5,410 employees. Just like the federal court system, the Marshals Service has one United States marshal for each judicial district. The agency employees 3,843 deputy marshals and criminal investigators, as well as 1,473 administrative employees and detention enforcement officers. Within the 94 judicial districts, there are 218 sub-offices. There are also three foreign field offices to help track federal fugitives who have absconded from United States borders.[41] Furthermore, the Marshals Services supervises more than 5,000 federal court security officers whose wages and activities are funded through the budget of the federal court system.[42]

After a person is arrested by federal law enforcement officers or indicted by a federal court, the Marshals Service becomes responsible for ensuring that that person attend all required court proceedings. For federal defendants who cannot afford or are denied bail, there is one slight problem for the Marshals Service—the federal system operates very few jails. Thus, the Marshals Service has to contract with the state or localities to store federal defendants. Additionally, since so many jails are overcrowded, the Marshals Service also has contracts with fifteen private facilities to store federal defendants. On any given day, the marshals are responsibly for an average of 55,330 prisoners. In 2014, the Marshals Service had to transport 275,468 inmates: 96,985 through the air and 178,483 by ground transportation.[43]

# Intermediate Sanctions and Community Corrections

Many people have argued that the whole notion of prison as punishment is counterproductive. Granted, in what we like to deem a civilized society, it does seem necessary to incapacitate individuals who are considered dangerous and show no potential for rehabilitation. Yet as we have discussed, the United States incarcerates far more of its citizens than any other country and still has one of the highest crime rates in the world. Furthermore, although some people view prison as a natural punishment that will prevent people from offending in the future, many others argue this is foolish. The prison experience for many is brutal, as inmates must not only constantly fear for their safety, but also abide by a unique set of informal rules that govern interactions with one another, with institutional staff, and with outsiders, what researchers have called "the inmate code," which has very little to no resemblance to civil society.[44] Thus, the prison experience seems to inevitably make people worse, not better. On the other hand, of the traditional punishments in the United States, the only alternative less stringent punishment to incarceration is probation. For many crimes, this is not only an inadequate punishment, but also an insult to our notions of justice—even if they are socially constructed.

In their seminal work *Between Prison and Probation*, **Norval Morris** and **Michael Tonry** made the case that the United States needed to embrace sanctions for criminal offenders that are less punitive than incarceration, but stricter than probation—a greater variety of punishments for people who commit crimes. To accomplish this, Morris and Tonry argued that a wide range of **intermediate sanctions** should be implemented as part of criminal sentencing. These types of punishment would be designed so that offenders could remain in the community and avoid the brutal experiences associated with incarceration, but would send a clear message to offenders that they are being punished. As Morris and Tonry noted, probation staffs are universally and chronically overworked. As a result, simply requiring an offender to appear for a once-a-month meeting with a probation officer is neither punitive nor productive. Thus, Morris and Tonry argued that intermediate punishments must have rigorous enforcements and be provided more than adequate enforcement resources.[45]

Since intermediate sanctions allow offenders to remain outside prison walls, many people refer to this range of punishments as **community corrections**. Todd Clear and colleagues have categorized intermediate sanctions into two groups: **low control** and **high control**. Examples of low control community corrections would include requiring offenders to either pay fines to the state or provide restitution to the victim(s) of their crime, participate in community service and in drug and/or alcohol treatment, and be sentenced to home confinement and required to pay some or all of the costs associated with monitoring equipment. Forms of high control community corrections include intensive probation supervision and boot camps or shock incarceration, where low-level offenders spend a short (30–90 day) period in a quasi-military style program that focuses on physical training, drills, manual labor, and strict discipline.[46]

Supporters of intermediate sanctions and community-based corrections argue one of the most important goals of these programs is not only to ensure offenders understand they are being punished, but provide them opportunities for rehabilitation as well. Paul Gendreau and colleagues found that programs emphasizing both punishment and rehabilitation were the most likely to be effective in changing offenders' behavior.[47] Community-based corrections can thus be effective because such programs are cost-effective but simultaneously help ensure offenders feel that they are being punished while also giving back to the community.

In the rush to embrace intermediate sanctions and community-based correctional programs, the system needs to ensure that intermediate sanctions do not completely replace probation. For some people, whether they have committed only minor crimes or are first-time offenders, probation is an adequate punishment. Either giving people harsher punishment than they deserve or punishing offenders who otherwise would not have been punished without the existence of these programs can be indicative of what some refer to as **net-widening,** or the expansion of the corrections system into the lives of those who previously would not have come into contact with the system.[48]

Beyond net-widening, some forms of intermediate sanctions can either be excessively costly or actually do more harm than good. One of the seeming quintessential examples of the latter is "boot camps." Everyone is probably familiar with the fact that new recruits into the armed services begin their service by attending and completing **boot camp,** which trains young men and women—through physical training and psychological shaping that includes developing a healthy respect for authority—to run *toward* gunfire instead of *away* from it. Instilling discipline and respect for authority through physical challenges and hard work are the main reasons military-style boot camps came to be identified as a possible new type of correctional program, particularly for younger offenders facing relatively low-level charges. Yet, think of where many offenders were raised—in broken and economically disadvantaged communities. Boot camps make sense for the armed services because recruits are headed to an environment where discipline and respect are needed. In correctional boot camps, once attendees have completed the program, they return to the same community where they first became involved with the criminal justice system. This leaves open the question of what exactly the point of the punishment was in the first place. Evaluations of boot camp programs further call into question whether they are effective, and there is some evidence they may actually make offenders worse. Furthermore, boot camps are usually more expensive to operate than other forms of community-based programs.[49]

Determining how many people receive intermediate sanctions can be difficult. For instance, many states will not distinguish traditional from intensive supervision probation when releasing correctional statistics. Once again, the Bureau of Justice Statistics (BJS) provides a sense of how often intermediate sanctions are utilized in American corrections. In 2013, according to BJS data, 59,441 people received some form of intermediate sanction, including serving weekends in jail (10,950 people) or being electronically monitored (12,023 people).[50]

One of the main issues with institutional corrections (i.e., prisons/jails) is the cost involved in locking people up, but costs can also be problematic for intermediate sanctions. The annual cost of incarcerating an offender in prison or jail is approximately $27,040 or $18,985, respectively. This can add up quickly! Furthermore, every person in prison or jail is a person neither working in the economy nor supporting his or her family. Thus, since probation costs approximately $1,269 per offender per year and intensive supervision costs only $3,481 per offender per year, savings can be quickly realized if an offender can be safely monitored in this fashion and the crime they committed allows for a lesser sanction than prison. Yet, some programs associated with intermediate sanctions and community-based corrections are not quite as cost effective. Take boot camps, for example. We previously mentioned their high costs and here we can provide details. According to Todd Clear and his colleagues, the annual cost for one person to attend a boot camp is $36,027—dramatically more than either prison or jail. Furthermore, although confining a person to a halfway house, either as a lesser punishment than prison or jail or as a way to better transition them back into the community after their release from prison, has an average per year, per offender cost of $18,985.[51] Thus, when discussing intermediate sanctions, sometimes these measures are cost effective and sometimes that does not seem to be the case. Yet, if someone who receives a lesser sanction than prison or jail does not recidivate in the future, then that lack of a future cost of supervision is not factored in to the immediate cost. This is the greatest difficult in truly measuring the costs of corrections.

# Private Corrections Companies

As previously mentioned, scholars and social commentators have become concerned about a recent trend in corrections relating to the involvement of private, for-profit companies in corrections—whether institutional or community-based. When we speak of **privatization** in corrections, we are not referring to the use of private companies to provide services like food and facility maintenance to prisons, jails, or other correctional programs. Those arrangements have been in place almost from the beginning of American corrections. Rather, we are referring either to the actual transfer of ownership of public services or public property to for-profit firms or outsourcing of government services or functions to private, for-profit firms. Examples of the former situation would include ownership/operation of facilities or programs or construction/lease-purchasing of facilities. One example of the latter situation would be contracting out prison labor.[52]

The privatization movement in corrections appears to have begun during the 1980s when burgeoning prison populations—traceable directly to the "war on drugs" and "get tough" sentencing policies at both the federal and state levels that increasingly mandated imprisonment for even first-time offenders—led to prison overcrowding and rising costs. In response, the private sector saw opportunities for expanding their involvement from contracting for services to contracting to manage and operate entire prisons. The result has been an unprecedented "insertion" of the private sector into corrections.

One reason for corporate involvement in corrections is a belief by some policymakers and scholars that correctional programs run by government agencies are wasteful, poorly managed, inefficient, and ineffective. To some degree, we have probably reinforced such a belief. Many people have argued that the reason that governments suffer from these problems is that they are fueled by tax dollars and essentially have no incentive to work efficiently. Carrying on this line of reason, these people believe that the solution to transforming government is to run government entities as if they were businesses or privatize what have traditionally been government-operated public services. Furthermore, criminal justice has a history of governmental non-intervention in many endeavors that we traditionally associate with state-run activities. For instance, as we have recounted, it was not until the 1900s that the government began to actively engage in many law enforcement activities, such as the investigation of crimes. Law enforcement tended to be, for the most part, a reactionary force that only intervened when a crime was actually witnessed. If a person believed they had been the victim of a crime, they needed to play an active role in pressing charges against the person they believed aggrieved them. Additionally, to this day, people who can afford to pay a criminal defense attorney must do so. Perhaps the only criminal justice function that was not privatized, until recently, was corrections. Government authorities performed executions and administered corporal punishment. Governments have always collected fines, although some places have experimented with paying tax collectors for these purposes. Furthermore, Southern and Western states often leased their prisoners to corporations. Yet, beginning in the early 1980s, what was inconceivable to many happened. Corporations began to form that contracted directly with the government to perform correctional operations.

Perhaps the best-known private provider of correctional operational and management services is the **Corrections Corporation of America** (CCA). Founded in January of 1983 by **T. Don Hutto, Tom Beasley,** and **Dr. Robert Crants,** CCA obtained its first government contract from the United States Department of Justice in November of 1983 to operate and manage an Immigration and Naturalization Services (INS) facility in Texas.[53] The following year, CCA began to manage a 63-bed juvenile facility in Tennessee. Later that same year, CCA opened a detention facility in Houston, Texas, that it had both designed and constructed (and which cost $12,000 per bed less than what the government had estimated the as the per-bed cost). By 1986, CCA became a publicly traded stock on the NASDAQ (National Association of Securities Dealers Automated Quotations) stock exchange. In 2007, the company operated 66 facilities in 19 states and Washington, DC. These facilities were designed to hold more than 75,000 inmates and CCA employed more than 16,000 people. The company operates four types of services: prisons, detention centers, jails, and reentry programs.[54]

## Correctional Advocacy Groups

Advocacy groups in corrections generally fall into two categories: groups that advocate about correctional practices/policies and labor unions that advocate on behalf of correctional workers. In Chapter 6, we mentioned Amnesty International. Although the organization now seeks to protect human rights in many forms, Amnesty International originally was formed to protest the incarceration of people whom they referred to as "prisoners of conscience." Perhaps the best-known advocacy group that disseminates information about correctional policy is the **American Correctional Association** (ACA). Originally founded in 1870 as the National Prison Association, the group changed its name in 1954 to the American Correctional Association as a statement that their interests went beyond simply the "pedagogy of prisons" to correctional practices in general. Today, the ACA claims "thousands of members from all over the world."[55] The ACA's "vision statement" is to "shape the future of corrections through strong, progressive leadership that brings together various voices and forges coalitions and partnerships to promote the concepts embodied in its Declaration of Principles." The mission of the ACA is to provide "a professional organization for all individuals and groups, both public and private that share a common goal of improving the justice system."[56] Essentially, the ACA engages in training and pedagogy of people who are employed within the field of corrections. The ACA provides professional development opportunities, sponsors conferences, publishes research, and creates standards for and accredits correctional agencies, including jails.[57]

There are many labor unions that represent correctional workers. The **American Federation of State, County and Municipal Employees** (AFSCME) is one of the largest trade unions in the United States. Among the many employees the organization advocates for are 62,000 corrections officers and 23,000 other corrections employees. The mission of AFSCME is to lobby for better working conditions, wages, and benefits for workers.[58] The American Correctional Officer (ACO) combines the missions of the ACA and AFSCME. The ACO advocates for better working conditions for officers, disseminates best practices, and educates the media and the public about the conditions correctional officers face on the job.[59]

Finally, one of the best-known correctional workers unions is the **California Correctional Peace Officers Association** (CCPOA). According to the CCPOA's website, the suicide of a corrections officer "during the 1950s" over working conditions in the prisons prompted another officer, **Al Mello**, and eight colleagues to try to form a correctional officers union by rallying officers working at Folsom, San Quentin, and Soledad to unionize. In 1957, the California Correctional Officers Association was officially formed (the name change to CCPOA occurred in 1982). CCPOA has lobbied for better pay, medical plans, uniform allowances, vacation time, pensions, and a legal defense fund for officers, and for the construction of new prison facilities to alleviate overcrowding.[60]

# Budgets, Costs, and Profits

Just like policing and courts, corrections is largely funded by taxpayer dollars. Yet, corrections has a disadvantage that policing and courts do not: corrections agencies, unlike the police or the courts, cannot *not* take in offenders. Consider: if the police lack resources, they can conduct fewer patrols or arrest (or ticket) fewer people—especially for what some would consider lesser or minor crimes. This is not ideal and spreading officers thin can put them at higher risk in some situations. However, ultimately, these circumstances can be managed. While it would not be especially popular, if the courts were flooded with cases, they could make people wait longer to have their cases heard, although they could run afoul of the Sixth Amendment's speedy trial clause (defendants typically have to file a motion to press this issue, however). The plea bargaining process is actually an easy way to dispose of a lot of cases quickly; scholars such as **Herbert Packer** have pointed to the plea bargaining process as a means of making the criminal justice system more efficient.[61] In corrections, however, there are no "quick fixes." The implications of mass plea bargaining can be troubling, but again, this can be done if courts need to clear court dockets quickly.

Correctional agencies usually lack these luxuries. When people are convicted of crimes and sentenced, correctional officials cannot simply turn them away. Offenders have to be kept somewhere, whether they are sentenced to probation, jail, or prison. In some instances, judges might make greater use of probation for offenders deemed a low danger to society. Or, parole boards could speed up processing of parole petitions and grant more of them for offenders deemed low risks for reoffending. The problem is increasing the number of offenders on probation without hiring a requisite increase in probation officers only contributes to increased turnover among officers and staff.[62] Additionally, since 16 states and the federal government have eliminated parole, and other states curtailed its use, paroling more offenders to reduce backlogs in jails is not a viable option. Furthermore, many states have passed sentencing reforms that mandate minimum terms of incarceration for many crimes. Thus, even if judges *wanted* to "give offenders a break" and sentence them to probation, sentencing guidelines preclude them from doing so. Indeed, implementation of mandatory minimum sentencing and "truth in sentencing," where offenders must serve at least 85% of the term of incarceration received, have greatly contributed to prison overcrowding in many jurisdictions.[63] During the 1990s, as ever more offenders were sent to serve time in prison, many states engaged in what some scholars have referred to as a "**prison boom**," where they built more prisons themselves or contracted with private corporations to build a host of new correctional facilities. Paradoxically, most of *those* facilities became full and many remain overcrowded.[64] Now that the prison construction boom has effectively ended and many states are reluctant or unable to construct new facilities, building their way out of the consequences of "get tough" sentencing policies is no longer an option. The best ways to reduce correctional populations are entirely out of the hands of correctional administrators. Instead, that burden lies with legislatures, since only they can change sentencing laws and policies; judges, since only they can make greater use of sanctions not involving incarceration; and police officers, since only they can exercise discretion and *not* arrest low level offenders who likely do not deserve to be prosecuted, convicted, and sentenced to prison in the first place.

In a recent report by the National Association of State Budget Officers (NASBO), total state-level corrections expenditures represented about 4.5% of total state budgets in FY 2014 and grew by about 4% over FY 2013 expenditures.[65] As previously mentioned, the annual costs to incarcerate offenders in prisons/jails runs into the tens of thousands of dollars and new jails/prisons cost in the tens of millions of dollars to build. To illustrate, one estimate (per square foot, which is not the usual way such estimates are presented) on the costs of building a basic, no-frills, three-story, 40,000-square-foot jail in 2013 ranged between $278 and $298 per square foot, or between $11.1 million and $11.9 million.[66] There are also operating costs associated with running prisons/jails and community-based programs, many of which are not directly covered by corrections budgets, such as pensions and medical coverage for retirees, which are quickly growing. Unless steps are taken to rein in the costs of corrections, budgets at all levels of government that allocate funds for those purposes will continue to be strained. One reason for the high costs of corrections relates directly to how prisons are operated. Prior to the 1960s, many states had free rein to treat their inmates essentially however correctional administrators and officers wanted. However, beginning in the 1960s, federal courts became interested in hearing prisoner lawsuits from state courts alleging that conditions in state prisons violated constitutional protections against "cruel and unusual punishment." Prisoners began challenging a variety of conditions, such as overcrowding, and practices, such as corporal punishment, as violating their Eighth Amendment protection against cruel and unusual punishment.[67] While inmate conditions have certainly improved, the *degree* of improvement is questionable. Most courts have generally followed the "**deliberate indifference**" **standard** when evaluating a lack of health care in correctional facilities.[68] One growing fear among many is that as the age of the prison population increases (which is aggravated by longer sentences for many inmates), the costs to provide health care to inmates will skyrocket and further burden correctional budgets.[69] At different times, as many as 40 state correctional systems have either come under the direct control of federal courts or have been ordered to reduce prison populations. Different states have developed different strategies to cope with these court decisions.[70] Thus, many correctional administrators have sought ways to reduce costs, while still maintaining prisoners' rights. Seeking that balance was one of the main drivers behind privatizing prisons — the idea that these facilities, which operate as businesses, could reduce costs while still protecting inmates. Yet, there is scant evidence to demonstrate that private prisons actually reduce costs anywhere near what proponents had projected.[71]

To truly determine how much it costs to house inmates, states must walk a narrow line. Correctional officials must provide basic services to inmates. If they try to cut these services too deeply, prisoners will file lawsuits. While some journalists, social commentators, and scholars have pointed to prisoner lawsuits as necessary to improve correctional care, many others have viewed inmate litigation as frivolous and clogging up the courts' dockets. Concern over "frivolous" lawsuits coming from prisoners challenging their incarceration as

unconstitutionally "cruel and unusual" punishment was the major impetus behind Congressional passage of the **Prison Litigation Reform Act** (PLRA), which
dramatically curtailed inmates' ability to either file lawsuits in, or have their cases
heard by, federal courts.[72] Beyond blocking inmate lawsuits, another frequent
method of cost cutting is either eliminating or reducing the number of rehabilitation programs available in prison. While we have previously discussed
research findings regarding the efficacy of these programs, with the revolving
door of recidivism existing in the correctional system, cutting prison programs
is only a short-term fix to balance correctional budgets. Considering the majority of inmates recidivate, the correctional system will simply be repeating the
cycle with them.

Throughout history, one of the most ubiquitous ways in which people have
been punished is through forced labor. Who knows exactly how many of the
great public works projects have been built by convict labor or by slaves? Thus,
it does not seem hyperbolic to say that since the dawn of time, humankind
has profited from the criminalization of different classes of people. Yet, whether
it was mere lip service to justify exploitive behavior, the congregate system and
lease system models of prisons sought to teach prisoners a work ethic which
correctional officials hoped prisoners would utilize after their release. Writing
in 1913, **Oswald West**, the former governor of Oregon, noted that "the prison
labor problem" seemed a perpetual problem American society would always
have to manage. As he noted, how does one teach another a work ethic without possibly exploiting that person's labor? To some degree, when an offender
is paying his or her debt to society, it seems reasonable that they should also
in some way subsidize the costly correctional facility in which they are housed
because they violated society's laws.[73]

Due to the belief that prison labor was being exploited in the United States,
during the 1920s and 1930s, the federal government and 30 states placed restrictions on how goods manufactured by American prisoners could be sold.
As a result, interest in using prison labor diminished. However, opposition to
prison labor did not originate solely from humanitarian concerns. Many corporations and labor unions opposed the use of prison labor because it allowed
industries that utilized prison labor to unfairly compete or because the use of
what amounted to slave labor negatively affected 1) opportunities for non-
inmates to find jobs or 2) wages in the larger industry where inmates were
working.[74] Yet, ostensibly, something should be done to solve this problem.
The worst thing that prison administrators can do to prisoners is give them
too much free time. As the saying goes, "Idle hands are the devil's workshop."
If inmates are not given productive ways to spend their time, bad things happen not just to them, but to prison staff as well.

If prisoners cannot pay for themselves through inmate labor, there are other methods in which offenders can help pay for correctional services. In both Chapters 7 and 8, we discussed how police agencies raise funds through traffic tickets and how courts charge fees to criminal defendants. Correctional agencies are no different; prisons and jails collect various fees from offenders to offset the costs of housing and supervising inmates. As early as 1846, the State of Michigan passed a law that allowed counties to bill inmates for health care costs they incurred during their incarceration. By 1988, 48 states had laws that required inmates under correctional supervision to pay fees to help cover the costs associated with incarcerating them.

While the notion that inmates should pay for themselves is popular, it can actually cause problems. As Kathryn Morgan found, many probation and parole officers believe their primary mission of supervising probationers or parolees is jeopardized by devoting so much of their time to collecting fees. They have to devote too much of their time to collecting fees from the people they are supervising, which can often take away from their primary mission — the supervision or parolees and probationers so that they will be reintegrated into society.[75] Additionally, as Katherine Beckett and Alexes Harris argued, it is counterproductive to extract fees from people under correctional supervision. One of the many reasons that people resort to crime is because they lack the ability to earn money through legitimate means. Furthermore, after these people are labeled "criminals" as a result of a criminal conviction, their ability to legitimately earn income is often diminished. Thus, the correctional system is taking away money from people who already have trouble earning money. It is little wonder these people will resort to crime to earn money.[76]

Thus far in this chapter we have discussed the number of people who are employed by the correctional industry and discussed how private companies are now providing correctional services. Furthermore, prison labor has been used throughout history. However, the number of people who profit from our correctional system goes beyond these entities. Tara Herivel and Paul Wright have referred to the large number of people who profit from the prison industry as "prison profiteers."[77] Alex Henderson, for example, identified nine different industries profiting from the prison industry: food supply companies, telecommunications, health-care companies, telemarketing and call centers, clothing manufacturers, the technology sector, the bail industry, food processing and packaging, and agriculture. Some of these companies make money by employing prison inmates at below minimum wage. In one case, 80 prisoners in the Snake River Prison in Oregon were making $120–$185 a month working full time in a call center. Other industries make money by providing services to prisons. For example, **Global Tel\* Link** (GTL) makes $500 million a year by providing collect call services to inmates. For this service, people who accept collect calls from inmates pay up to $1.13 per minute—a rate that the average American consumer has not paid in years. One company, **Corizon**, makes approximately $1.4 billion annually providing health care to inmates.[78]

Overall, it seems the business of corrections is extremely profitable. Perhaps one of the best examples of this occurred in 2013, when the **GEO Group**, the "world's leading provider of correctional and detention management and community reentry services to federal, state and local government agencies," offered $6 million ($500,000 annually over twelve years) for the naming rights to the football stadium at Florida Atlantic University. The university initially accepted the deal, but ultimately GEO Group decided to withdraw the offer after considerable backlash, particularly from students, who repeatedly protested the deal and referred to the football stadium as "Owlcatraz," an amalgamation of the school's mascot (the Owls) and the famous prison, Alcatraz, located on an island near San Francisco.[79]

# Politics and Current Issues

While policing and the courts are certainly mired in politics, perhaps even more so is the correctional system. As we mentioned in the Preface, deciding which crimes are the most heinous and deserve the strictest punishments is inherently a political exercise. At times in American history, the killing of certain groups of people could result in a mere fine while the killing of others could result in death. A consistent finding by death penalty research is that killing a person who is white is much more likely to result in a death sentence than is killing a person of color. Such circumstances were one of the reasons that the United States placed a moratorium on the death penalty during the early 1970s.[80] Beyond the imposition of the death penalty, some crimes are prosecuted against minorities more often than whites, especially drug crimes, a large part of which has led to the imposition of mass incarceration.[81] Furthermore, offender race also seems to affect the decision by parole boards on whether to parole inmates.[82]

While racism, sexism, and classism seem to play a role in making the law and punishing those who break the law, an even more basic question exists: How do we settle on the punishment for crimes? Why will the commission of some crimes earn you up to twenty years in prison while other crimes may be punished by probation? To some degree, how much violence was involved in the commission of a crime seems to be an important factor. Yet many white-collar crime scholars have routinely taken issue with such an argument, positing that corporations can kill people in slow ways over time, or they can chalk up deaths as merely industrial "accidents" rather than callous and reckless behavior. Anytime an individual engages in this type of behavior and it results in a person's death, the offender can be convicted of either second-degree or felony murder — depending upon the circumstances — as described by state (or federal) law. Much like the French sociologist **Emile Durkheim** argued, law is a reflection of society's values — the law dictates what is considered acceptable and what is not. While people might argue that notions of deterrence dictate how harshly crimes should be punished, at a more basic level, by setting punishment for crimes, society is making some choice as to which values (and by implication laws) are more important than others. Kill a person during the commission of a felony — you might very well get the death penalty. Get caught driving ten miles over the speed limit — you might get a speeding ticket or, better yet, a police officer may give you a mere warning, a lecture, and tell you to drive more carefully. While this might seem completely natural, at some point in time, the penalties for these offenses were decided and that was done through a political process.

So how do politics affect one's views of corrections? To a degree, the dichotomy of "law and order conservatives" and "due process liberals" seems relevant. **Barry Goldwater**, an Arizona senator and 1964 Republican candidate for president, has often been regarded as the first presidential candidate to make crime a legislative priority and reinforce the view that conservatives support "tough on crime" policies. While Goldwater was ultimately defeated in the presidential election by President Lyndon B. Johnson, later presidents **Richard Nixon** and **Ronald Reagan** would become known as "law and order" presidents who supported measures perceived as "tough on crime," such increasing the use of mandatory minimum sentences and declaring "war on drugs." Especially under the Reagan presidency, the incarcerated population of the United States rose meteorically. President **George H.W. Bush** continued conservative dominance as a supporter of crime control and, by extension, tough corrections policies. Even President **Bill Clinton**, a Democrat, seemingly became as tough on crime as were his Republican predecessors. As Nancy Marion and Willard Oliver noted, by the time of the 1996 presidential election, which pitted Bill Clinton against Robert Dole, himself a proud law and order conservative, there was seemingly no difference in their crime policies.[83]

In addition to stricter laws that incarcerate more people, law and order policies can also lead to fewer services for people who have been convicted of crimes. One problem with many of these policies is that they often promote the belief that while they are incarcerated, criminals receive benefits not available to non-criminals. Take, for example, access to educational programs. One almost universal characteristic of prison (and jail) inmates is that they have very low levels of educational achievement, which has a dramatic effect on re-habilitation efforts. In 1994, President Clinton signed the Violent Crime Control and Law Enforcement Act into law after passage by Congress, which at the time was controlled by the Democratic Party. Among the many provisions in this omnibus crime bill was making state and federal prison inmates ineligible for Pell grants—money given to those below certain income levels to pay for college. The rationale behind the passage the legislation was that prisoners should not receive benefits when many law-abiding citizens could not afford a college education. Omitted from the debate was that of the 3,327,683 college students who received Pell grants in 1994, only 25,168 of them were prisoners.[84]

Another issue is limitations imposed on inmates' ability to exercise while incarcerated. Movies depicting prison life will typically depict the prison yard as a place where inmates go to lift weights and develop their bodies (i.e., "get ripped"). This stereotype became so ingrained in the minds of voters that it actually led to changes in prison policy. Due to fears of muscle-bound inmates committing crimes once they were released from prison (not to mention those same inmates assaulting correctional officers and staff working in prisons), in 1996, the Federal Bureau of Prisons was forced by legislation to no longer purchase any training equipment for boxing, wrestling, martial arts, bodybuilding, or weightlifting. Many states enacted similar policies.[85]

These are examples of a persistent critique of providing services to inmates that can be reduced to a simple question: What do the undeserving deserve?[86] Critics of rehabilitation efforts—including educational programs—often argue that prisoners should not have greater opportunities than do law-abiding folk to better themselves. The problem is that such a critique assumes that offenders purposely break the law and pursue incarceration so they can receive these "extra benefits." This assumption strikes us as ridiculous. Also, given that the vast majority of inmates will be released back into the community, is it not good policy to try to ensure inmates are both educated and healthy? If critics of providing "extra benefits" to inmates are worried these educated and healthy inmates will be preferred over non-offenders when competing for jobs, remember they will check that box on every job application that asks if the ap-

plicant has ever been convicted of a felony. Hardly an advantage for the offender, educated or not. Furthermore, providing inmates with productive activities makes sense, as Matthew Wagner and colleagues found in their study,
where inmates who were allowed to engage in weight training seemed to have
less aggression than other inmates.[87]

While "tough on crime" policies may be popular, even if some of these policies fly in the face of common sense, something else might actually lead to
change, and it is a common theme of this textbook—money. A common cry
of the American Revolution was "no taxation without representation." The cry
is still important today. Generally, it seems that Americans hate to pay taxes.
As we have mentioned repeatedly throughout this textbook, it costs money to
punish people, and in times of budget shortfalls arising from less taxes being
collected during tough economic times, priorities have to be set and, unless people agree to raise taxes or find other sources of revenue, something has to give.
Todd Clear and colleagues noted that in recent years, Texas has been among
the biggest criminal justice reformers across the states, seeking new ways to
reduce its incarcerated population. Similarly, politically conservative South
Carolina and less conservative Michigan have also implemented policies that
stress more treatment programs and less incarceration.[88] A comparable occurrence happened at the federal level with Senators Rand Paul (a Republican) and Cory Booker (a Democrat) recently advocating reforms to federal
sentencing guidelines to give judges more discretion, including sending fewer
people to prison.[89]

Yet it seems implausible leaders in this country would declare that, in the
name of fiscal sanity, state and the federal governments will revamp correctional policy. Among many, mantras of "lock them up, but do it more cheaply"
will win out over other potential reforms less focused on incarceration. Furthermore, as we have hopefully established, politics is not just about ideology,
but also about interests. In addition to discussing all of the money spent on corrections, we have also mentioned how many people are employed by correctional agencies and how many companies earn profits from the American
correctional system. An empty prison is just an empty building and, for the most
part, you do not need to pay people to watch an empty building. While supporters of the status quo may honestly believe that crime control policies stressing incarceration are necessary, thoughtful consideration should also be given
to supporters' level of interest in keeping the correctional machine operating
in its current form. Where there is money to be made, there is money to be lost
as well. Just as criminal defense attorneys and prosecutors need people to be
arrested to keep their jobs, correctional workers need people to supervise. Clos-
ing prisons will inevitably lead to people losing their jobs. Just like other Amer-

icans, correctional workers both pay taxes and vote. Even those who do not firmly believe that they are doing good work still want their jobs protected. Furthermore, as we mentioned earlier, powerful groups—including labor unions—exist that protect the interests of correctional workers. Reforms to correctional policies can help balance budgets, but politicians also have to respect the other monetary benefits of these policies—jobs.

# Conclusion

In this chapter, we discussed the many different agencies that supervise people who have been convicted of crimes. While people may associate the correctional system solely with prisons, most people under correctional supervision are not imprisoned. Arguably, criminology was founded to answer the question of how to effectively punish lawbreakers, and debate over the answer continues in modern America. Research has demonstrated that sanctions other than imprisonment, including probation and intermediate sanctions, may be more effective at reducing recidivism and less harmful than traditional imprisonment. Yet, policy is not routinely established by people who engage in criminological research, and punishment seems to invariably revolve around concerns of what is politically popular and how much these sanctions cost.

# Key Terms

- Penology
- Bureau of Labor Statistics
- Bureau of Justice Statistics
- Probation and Pretrial Services System
- The Probation Act
- National Capital Revitalization and Self-Government Improvement Act
- Federal Bureau of Prisons
- Regional jails
- United States Marshals Service
- Witness security program
- Intermediate sanctions
- Community corrections
- Low-control community corrections
- High-control community corrections
- Net-widening

- Boot camp
- Privatization
- Corrections Corporation of America
- American Correctional Association
- American Federation of State, County and Municipal Employees
- California Correctional Peace Officers Association
- Prison boom
- Deliberate indifference standard
- Prison Litigation Reform Act
- Global Tel* Link
- Corizon
- GEO Group
- Violent Crime Control and Law Enforcement Act

# Key People

- John Augustus
- President Calvin Coolidge
- Norval Morris and Michael Tonry
- Don Hutto, Tom Beasley, and Dr. Robert Crants
- Al Mello
- Herbert Packer
- Oswald West
- Emile Durkheim
- Barry Goldwater
- Richard Nixon
- Ronald Reagan
- George H.W. Bush
- Bill Clinton

# Discussion Questions

1) How did the National Capital Revitalization and Self-Government Improvement Act change responsibilities for Federal Probation and Pretrial Services?
2) What did Norval Morris and Michael Tonry propose as an alternative to prison? What was their rationale?

3) Do you believe boot camps are beneficial? Why or why not? If not, what alternative would you believe to be more effective? Why? Provide examples from the reading.

4) How does the criminal justice system conduct a cost-benefit analysis when examining alternatives to imprisonment? What can be problematic about these assessments? (Immediate cost, recidivism, long-term effects)

5) How does the corrections system differ from policing and courts in regards to its ability to manage its circumstances and population? How does this affect the correctional system?

6) What types of services profit from the prison industry? Using examples from the book, do you believe this kind of profit is fair?

7) What are the pros and cons of privatization of prisons? Do you support privatization? Why or why not?

8) How do politicians use corrections as a campaign platform? How can this be harmful to the system? Provide examples from the reading.

# Notes

1. Carlsmith, Kevin M., John M. Darley, and Paul H. Robinson. 2002. "Why Do We Punish? Deterrence and Just Desserts as Motives for Punishment." *Journal of Personality and Social Psychology*, 83(2):284–299.

2. Shelden, Randall. 2001. "The American Gulag: The Correctional Industrial Complex in America." Retrieved on June 8, 2015 at: http://www.cjcj.org/uploads/cjcj/documents/the _american_gulag.pdf.

3. Glaze, Lauren E. and Danielle Kaeble. 2014. *Correctional Populations in the United States, 2013*. Washington, DC: U.S. Department of Justice.

4. Wagner, Pete and Leah Sakala. 2014. *Mass Incarceration: The Whole Pie*. Northampton, MA: Prison Policy Initiative.

5. *Ibid.*

6. Bureau of Labor Statistics: Correctional Officers and Jailers. Retrieved on May 9, 2015 at: http://www.bls.gov/oes/current/oes333012.htm.

7. Bureau of Labor Statistics: First-Line Supervisors of Correctional Officers. Retrieved on May 9, 2015 at: http://www.bls.gov/oes/current/oes331011.htm.

8. Bureau of Labor Statistics: Probation Officers and Correctional Treatment Specialists. Retrieved on May 8, 2015 at: http://www.bls.gov/oes/current/oes211092.htm.

9. Glaze, Lauren E. and Danielle Kaeble. 2014. *Correctional Populations in the United States, 2013*. Washington, DC: U.S. Department of Justice.

10. *Ibid.*

11. Bureau of Justice Statistics. 2014. *Correctional Population in the United States, 2013*. Washington, DC: Bureau of Justice Statistics.

12. Wagner, Peter, Leah Sakala, and Josh Begley. 2014. *States of Incarceration: The Global*

*Context*. Northampton, MA: Prison Policy Initiative.

13. Origins of this term are credited either to the journalist Eric Schlosser, who used the term in a 1998 article for *Atlantic* magazine or the 1960s activist and scholar Angela Davis, who recorded a speech (later released on CD) in 1997 with the title "The Prison Industrial Complex" that became the basis for a book of the same name.

14. Federal Bureau of Prisons: Historical Information. Retrieved on June 8, 2015 at: http://www.bop.gov/ about/history/.

15. Federal Bureau of Prisons: Federal Prison System. Retrieved on June 8, 2015 at: http://www.justice.gov/sites/ default/files/jmd/legacy/2013/12/21/bop.pdf.

16. United States Courts: Probation and Pretrial Services History. Retrieved on June 8, 2015 at: http://www.uscourts.gov/services-forms/probation-and-pretrial-services/probation-and-pretrial-services-history.

17. *Ibid.*

18. *Ibid.*

19. United States Courts: Probation and Pretrial Services Mission. Retrieved on June 8, 2015 at: http://www. uscourts.gov/services-forms/probation-and-pretrial-services/probation-and-pretrial-services-mission.

20. United States Courts: Parole in the Federal Probation System. Retrieved on May 8, 2015 at: http://www.uscourts.gov/News/TheThirdBranch/11-05-01/Parole_in_the_Federal_Probation_System.aspx.

21. Glaze, Lauren and Danielle Kable. 2014. *Correctional Populations in the United States, 2013*. Washington, DC: Bureau of Justice Statistics.

22. Brown, Elizabeth A. 2012. "Foreclosing on Incarceration? State Correctional Policy Enactments and the Great Recession." *Criminal Justice Policy Review*, 24(3):317–337.

23. Kyckelhahn, Tracey. 2012. *State Corrections Expenditures, FY 1982–2010*. Washington, DC: Bureau of Justice Statistics.

24. Hellum, Frank. 1983. *Adult Probation Systems in the United States*. Washington, DC: National Institute of Corrections.

25. Clear, Todd R. Michael D. Reisig and George F. Cole. 2015. *American Corrections*. Boston: Cengage Learning. Kindle Edition, p. 199.

26. See, for example, Joan Petersilia. 1998. "Probation in the United States: Part I." Retrieved June 10, 2015 from http://www.appa-net.org/eweb/Resources/ PPPSW2013/docs/sp98pers30.pdf.

27. Clear, Todd R. Michael D. Reisig and George F. Cole. 2015. *American Corrections*. Boston: Cengage Learning. Kindle Edition, p. 199.

28. Alabama Department of Corrections. 2015. *Annual Report FY 2014*. Montgomery, AL: Alabama Department of Corrections.

29. *Ibid.*

30. Ruddell, Rick. 2010. "Introduction." Pp. 5–14 in Rick Ruddell (Ed.). *American Jails: A Retrospective Examination*. Richmond, KY: Newgate Press.

31. Subramanian, Ram, Ruth Delaney, Stephan Roberts, Nancy Fishman, and Peggy McGarry. 2015. *Incarceration's Front Door: The Misuse of Jails in America*.

32. *Ibid.*

33. American Jail Association. 2007. *Who's Who in Jail Management* (5ed). Haggerstown, MD: American Jail Association.

34. American Correctional Association. 2002. *National Jail and Adult Detention Direc-*

*tory*. Lanham, MD: American Correctional Association.

35. Clear, Todd R. Michael D. Reisig and George F. Cole. 2015. *American Corrections*. Boston: Cengage Learning. Kindle Edition.

36. Cornelius, Gary F. 2008. *The American Jail; Cornerstone of Modern Corrections*. Upper Saddle River, NJ: Pearson Prentice Hall.

37. American Jail Association. 2015. "Statistics of Note." Retrieved June 9, 2015 from https://members.aja.org/About/StatisticsOfNote.aspx.

38. Clear, Todd R., Michael D. Reisig and George F. Cole. 2016. *American Corrections*. 11th Edition. Boston, MA: Cengage.

39. Clear, Todd R., Michael D. Reisig and George F. Cole (2015). *American Corrections*. Cengage Learning. Kindle Edition, p. 169.

40. United States Marshals Service; Fact Sheet. Retrieved on May 7, 2015 at: http://www.usmarshals.gov/duties/factsheets/overview.pdf.

41. United States Marshals Service: Facts and Figures. Retrieved on May 7, 2015 at: http://www.usmarshals.gov/duties/factsheets/facts.pdf.

42. United States Marshals Service; Fact Sheet. Retrieved on May 7, 2015 at: http://www.usmarshals.gov/duties/factsheets/overview.pdf.

43. United States Marshals Service: Facts and Figures. Retrieved on May 7, 2015 at: http://www.usmarshals.gov/duties/factsheets/facts.pdf.

44. Trammell, Rebecca. 2009. "Values, Rules, and Keeping the Peace: How Men Describe Order and the Inmate Code in California Prisons." *Deviant Behavior*, 30(8):746–777.

45. Morris, Norval and Michael Tonry. 1990. *Between Prison and Probation: Intermediate Punishments in a Rational Sentencing System*. New York: Oxford University Press.

46. Clear, Todd R., Michael D. Reisig and George F. Cole. 2016. *American Corrections*. 11th Edition. Boston, MA: Cengage.

47. Gendreau, Paul, Francis T. Cullen, and James Bonta. 1994. "Intensive Rehabilitation Supervision: The Next Generation in Community Corrections?" *Federal Probation*, 58(1): 72–78.

48. Clear, Todd R., Michael D. Reisig and George F. Cole. 2016. *American Corrections*. 11th Edition. Boston, MA: Cengage.

49. Lundman, Richard J. 2001. *Prevention and Control of Juvenile Delinquency*. 3rd Edition. New York: Oxford University Press.

50. Minton, Todd D. and Daniela Golinelli. 2014. *Jail Inmates at Midyear 2013 — Statistical Tables*. Washington, DC: U.S. Department of Justice.

51. Clear, Todd R., Michael D. Reisig and George F. Cole. 2016. *American Corrections*. 11th Edition. Boston, MA: Cengage.

52. Joel, Dana. 1988. *A Guide to Prison Privatization*. Washington, DC: The Heritage Foundation. Retrieved on June 10, 2015 at: http://thf_media.s3.amazonaws.com/1988/pdf/bg650.pdf.

53. Corrections Corporation of America: Our History. Retrieved June 10, 2015 from http://www.cca.com/our-history.

54. CCA: The CCA Story: Our Company History. Retrieved on May 9, 2015 at: http://www.cca.com/our-history.

55. American Correctional Association: The History of the American Correctional Association. Retrieved on May 9, 2015 at: http://www.aca.org/ACA_Prod_IMIS/ACA_Member/About_Us/Our_History/ACA_Member/AboutUs/.AboutUs_Home.aspx?hkey=0c9cb058-e3d5-4bb0-ba7c-be29f9b34380.

56. American Correctional Association: Our Mission. Retrieved on May 9, 2015 at: http://www.aca.org/ACA_Prod_IMIS/ACA_Member/About_Us/Our_Mission/ACA_Member/AboutUs/MissionStatement_home.aspx?hkey=7a39e689-8de2-47d4-a7d4-93cce9442142.

57. American Correctional Association: Home. Retrieved on May 9, 2015 at: http://www.aca.org/ACA_Prod_IMIS/ACA_Member/Home/ACA_Member/Home.aspx?hkey=08837e63-47fc-4a7a-b9c1-b803481ec936.

58. AFSCME: Our Union: Jobs We Do: Corrections. Retrieved on May 9, 2015 at: http://www.afscme.org/union/jobs-we-do/corrections.

59. American Correctional Officer: About the American Correctional Officer. Retrieved on May 9, 2015 at: http://www.americanco.info/faq.html.

60. California Correctional Peace Officers Association: Our History. Retrieved on May 9, 2015 at: http://www.ccpoa.org/about-us/our-history/.

61. Packer, Herbert L. 1968. *The Limits of the Criminal Sanction*. Stanford, CA: Stanford University Press.

62. Simmons, Calvin, John K. Cochran and William R. Blount. 1997. "The Effects of Job-Related Stress and Job Satisfaction on Probation Officers' Inclinations to Quit." *American Journal of Criminal Justice*, 21(2): 213–229.

63. Bogan, Kathleen M. 1990. "Constructing Felony Sentencing Guidelines in an Already Crowded State: Oregon Breaks New Ground." *Crime & Delinquency*, 36(4): 467–487; Petersilia, Joan. 2008. "California's Correctional Paradox of Excess and Deprivation." *Crime and Justice*, 37(1): 207–278.

64. Spelman, William. 2009. "Crime, Cash, and Limited Options: Explaining the Prison Boom." *Criminology & Public Policy*, 8(1): 29–77.

65. National Association of State Budget Officers. 2014. *State Expenditure Report (2012–2014)*. Washington, DC: NASBO. Retrieved on June 11, 2015 at: https://www.nasbo.org/publications-data/state-expenditure-report/state-expenditure-report-fiscal-2012-2014-data.

66. The Gordian Group, nd. "Construction Cost Estimates for Jail in National, U.S." Retrieved June 11, 2015 from http://www.rsmeans.com/models/jail/.

67. Angelos, Claudia and James B. Jacobs. 1985. "Prison Overcrowding and the Law." *Annals of the American Academy of Political and Social Science*, 478: 100–112.

68. Butler, H. Daniel, O. Hayden Griffin, III and Grayson F. Knight. "Supermax Prisons: Another Chapter in the Constitutionality of the Incarceration Conundrum." *Rutgers Journal of Law & Public Policy*, 9: 1–36.

69. Mitka, Mike. 2004. "Aging Prisoners Stressing Health Care System." *JAMA*, 292(4): 423–424.

70. Pitts, James M.A., O. Hayden Griffin, III, and W. Wesley Johnson. 2014. "Contemporary Prison Overcrowding: Short-Term Fixes to a Perpetual Problem." *Contemporary Justice Review*, 17(1): 124–139.

71. Perrone, Dina and Travis C. Pratt. 2003. "Comparing the Quality of Confinement and Cost-Effectiveness of Public Versus Private Prisons: What We Know, Why We Do Not Know More, and Where to Go From Here." *The Prison Journal*, 83(3): 301–322.

72. Schlanger, Margo. 2003. "Inmate Litigation." *Harvard Law Review*, 116(6): 1555–1706.

73. West, Oswald. 1913. "The Problem of Prison Labor." *Annals of the American Academy of Political and Social Science*, 46: 45–53.

74. Hawkins, Gordon. 1983. "Prison Labor and Prison Industries." *Crime and Justice*, 5: 85–127.

75. Morgan, Kathryn. 1995. "A Study of Probation and Parole Supervision Fee Collection in Alabama." *Criminal Justice Review*, 20(1): 44–54.

76. Beckett, Katherine and Alexes Harris. 2011. "Monetary Sanctions as Misguided Policy." *Criminology & Public Policy*, 10(3): 509–537.

77. Herivel, Tara and Paul Wright. 2007. *Prison Profiteers: Who Makes Money from Mass Incarceration*. New York: The New Press.

78. Henderson, Alex. 2015. "9 Surprising Industries Getting Filthy Rich from Mass Incarceration." *Salon*. Retrieved on May 17, 2015 at: http://www.salon.com/2015/02/22/9_surprising_industries_getting_filthy_rich_from_mass_incarceration_partner/.

79. Myerberg, Paul. 2013. "Prison Operator Withdraws Naming Rights Offer for FAU Stadium." *USA Today*. Retrieved on May 17, 2015 at: http://www.usatoday.com/story/gameon/2013/04/02/florida-atlantic-fau-geo-group-stadium-withdraws-offer/2045581/.

80. Jacoby, Joseph E. and Raymond Paternoster. 1982. "Sentencing Disparity and Jury Packing: Further Challenges to the Death Penalty." *The Journal of Criminal Law and Criminology*, 73(1): 379–387; Radelet, Michael L. 1981. "Racial Characteristics and the Imposition of the Death Penalty." *American Sociological Review*, 46(6): 918–927.

81. Beckett, Katherine, Kris Nyrop and Lori Pfingst. 2006. "Race, Drugs, and Policing: Understanding Disparities in Drug Delivery Arrests." *Criminology*, 44(1): 105–137.

82. Morgan, Kathryn D. and Brent Smith. 2008. "The Impact of Race on Parole Decision-Making." *Justice Quarterly*, 25(2): 411–435.

83. Marion, Nancy E. and Willard M. Oliver. 2006. *The Public Policy of Crime and Criminal Justice*. Upper Saddle River, NJ: Pearson.

84. Anderson, Nick. 2013. "Advocates Push to Renew Pell Grants for Prisoners, Citing Benefits of Higher Education." *The Washington Post*. Retrieved on May 17, 2015 at: http://www.washingtonpost.com/local/education/when-congress-cut-pell-grants-for-prisoners/2013/12/03/fedcabb2-5b94-11e3-a49b-90a0e156254b_story.html.

85. Palmer, Brian. 2011. "Do Prisoners Really Spend All their Time Lifting Weights?" *Slate*. Retrieved on May 18, 2015 at: http://www.slate.com/articles/news_and_politics/explainer/2011/05/do_prisoners_really_spend_all_their_time_lifting_weights.html.

86. Johnson, Robert and Hans Toch. 1982. "What Do the Undeserving Deserve?" Pp. 313–330 in Robert Johnson and Hans Toch (Eds.), *The Pains of Imprisonment*. Thousand Oaks, CA: Sage Publications.

87. Wagner, Matthew, Ron E. McBride and Stephen F. Crouse. 1999. "The Effects of Weight-Training Exercise on Aggression Variables in Adult Male Inmates." *The Prison Journal*, 79(1): 72–89.

88. Clear, Todd R., Michael D. Reisig and George F. Cole. 2016. *American Corrections*. 11th Edition. Boston, MA: Cengage.

89. O'Keefe Ed. 2014. "Cory Booker, Rand Paul Team Up on Sentencing Reform Bill." *The Washington Post*. Retrieved on May 18, 2015 at: http://www.washingtonpost.com/blogs/post-politics/wp/2014/07/08/cory-booker-rand-paul-team-up-on-sentencing-reform-bill/.

# Chapter 10

# Conclusion

A conclusion can be defined as the finish to something or as a decision made based on careful reasoning.[1] Taking that into consideration, we decided that the conclusion of a book should accomplish two goals. First, the author(s) are supposed to provide the reader with highlights of what was said in the book. The second goal of a conclusion is to try to play the role of soothsayer and make some predictions about the future. Sadly, we have no crystal ball and if we did, we would put it to much better or, at least in our case, more lucrative, use (we hear a lot of money can be made wagering on sports). Alternatively, perhaps we could utilize our training as criminologists to make predictions. That is problematic as well. No matter how much we read, no matter how much we research, and no matter how astute are our observations at pointing to future events, seemingly trivial matter, or at least events that should not have been as momentous as they turned out, have dramatically affected criminal justice policy. As Frank Cullen has noted, Robert Martinson was not the first person (or the last) to criticize institutionally based rehabilitation programs, but at the time he published his famous article, American society seemed primed to listen.[2] Thus, instead of giving predictions, we believe it more prudent to imagine how money and politics will shape the debate of criminal justice policy in the coming years.

## Law and Policy are a Function of a Political Process

While many people view the United States Constitution and our republican model of government as sacred, neither are. While the former was certainly a well-thought-out design for a government and the latter has its merits, both the document itself and the form our government took were created by a political process. One must remember that many of our "Founding Fathers" were heavily influenced by the many great works of political philosophy exist-

ing at the time. Furthermore, our republican form of government was undoubtedly shaped in response to the experience of being a colony of Great
Britain, as well as the perceived failure to finalize a government under the Articles of Confederation. While some readers view American government as the
quintessential example of a just and free system, others may disagree with that
assessment. Moreover, there is nothing *inherently* natural or just about the
American system of government—despite President Reagan's characterization
of America as the "shining city on the hill." There are many other ways to govern a collection of people. Believing that the American system of government
is ultimately the "best" system is subject to interpretation.

In fact, we are fence sitters on this subject. Ostensibly, there is evidence to
both support and reject the assertion that the American system of government
is "best." Regardless of your view of this subject, we believe the most important aspect to consider is that American government was both implemented and
evolved though a collection of decisions by human beings, none of whom were
infallible.

Like the basic tenets of American government, the law is also created through
a political process. Granted, in the early years of American history, common
law crimes were codified into legal codes, but that only reiterates our argument. At some point, people pick and choose what behaviors should be allowed and which should not. After something is prohibited for some period,
many people begin to believe the law becomes sacred; it becomes deemed a
value that should not be contradicted. Yet that is simply not the case. Certainly, some values and laws are held more sacred than others. One would be
hard pressed to argue that all forms of homicide should be legally permissible.
However, American society *does* allow people to kill one another without societal condemnation or criminal prosecution under certain circumstances,
such as cases of self-defense or defense of others. If a man sexually assaulted
a woman in early America, he might either pay a fine to the woman's father or
simply agree to marry her. The crime, if it could even be called that, was considered an affront to the woman's father, not the woman herself. Prior to the
1900s, if you wanted to purchase heroin, you could order it out of the Sears
catalog. Identity theft, computer hacking, drunk driving—these were all behaviors that *became* crimes after due consideration, rather than simply the
codification of some inherently evil behavior. Undoubtedly, certain values
seem more important to some people than to others, and we can look to different beliefs that inspire these values, such as religion, morals, and family-
upbringing. Ultimately, law is created. Therefore, while some laws may never
change, that does not mean that others should not.

## Freedom Ebbs and Evolves

In this land that many people affectionately refer to as "Murica," we have many different catch phrases and values concerning how much freedom people should have. To some degree, we can rate these freedoms in terms of the social contract—how much freedom are we willing to give up to be secure? To many, the United States has always prided itself on the amount of freedom it provides its citizens—especially when compared to many other countries—including freedom from unreasonable searches and seizures, freedom of speech and peaceable assembly, freedom from cruel and unusual punishment, the right to remain silent, and many more that are not universal values. These freedoms became constitutional amendments because the Founding Fathers deemed that our British colonial masters did not respect these inherent freedoms. Yet, at the same time, these values were enumerated in the Constitution, individual states were free to ignore them, and certain groups of people (e.g., women and minorities) were not covered by these protections. The amount of freedom a person can expect to enjoy has evolved considerably throughout the course of American history.

Without question, technology has dramatically changed not only America but also its criminal justice system. Technological devices allowed us to first communicate through the telegraph, then the telephone, and finally through the Internet. Advances in technology affected our ability to travel to the point where journeys that in past eras took weeks or months to complete can now be completed in hours or days. All of these changes not only dramatically changed our daily lives, but each one has added layer upon layer to existing legal codes. Contemporary America seems firmly planted in the organic solidarity that Durkheim predicted.

To illustrate, it was not too long ago (before the whole "Internet" thing had really taken off) that a college student could only find out their final grades by waiting patiently for the registrar to mail them to a physical address via the United States Postal Service. If a student was really lucky, their professors would post grades on their office doors or on the doors of the room where the class met. A student only knew what grade was theirs by their assigned student number—which invariably was a student's social security number. Not only was a person's social security number their college number, but it could also be their driver's license number and bank account number. No one had heard of identity theft and until it started to happen, most people were perfectly fine to use their social security number as a universal identifier. Thus, when individuals began stealing identities using social security numbers, there was inevitably a need to create more legislation, which only partially assuaged people's growing fear.

## Punishments Evolve

Until well past the Middle Ages, there were really only four variations of punishments one could receive: death, corporal punishment, banishment, or monetary fines. In some instances, which punishment one received was dependent upon the crime they committed. In other instances, the punishment one received might be determined upon some combination of their social standing in society versus the social standing of the victim of the crime they committed. Sound familiar? Contemporary punishments still to some degree reflect these two considerations. The only variation to punishment came about through creative means of administering execution or corporal punishment. Throughout history, people have been burned alive, crucified, stoned, fed to animals, drowned, decapitated, and subjected to countless other punishments. Incarceration as a punishment was supposed to be a humane way to punish people, and it is likely that compared to some of these methods of punishment, it seemed like a better alternative. However, when examining it independently, there is nothing particularly humane about confining a person to an enclosed space in which they may suffer additional punishments from others who have also been confined to these enclosed spaces. To combat this, probation, parole, and a host of other alternative sanctions have been created to help alleviate the inhumanity associated with incarceration. While there are certainly observable trends of punishment within history, it is challenging to forecast where our system of punishment is headed. As we discussed in Chapter 9, criminology was essentially founded on the question of how to effectively punish, and yet, approximately 250 years later, criminologists are still unsure of how to answer such a question. There is certainly something natural about punishing someone who does wrong—some view it simply as a natural reflex.[3] What is the most important value of punishment? Different people have different answers, and as much as we like to pretend that we have all the answers and can scientifically test and conclude the most effect means of punishment for a particular crime, there is that pesky human factor that leads to individual variability. Not all humans act the same. Not all humans hold the same values. Not all humans share the same life experiences. Lastly, not all humans react the same way to different life circumstances. To some, prison might be a humbling life experience from which a person should make the appropriate life changes so that they will never return. To other people, prison is just like home—a chaotic, socially disorganized place. Other people might view prison as a brutal and shameful experience and view the only way to cope with such an experience is to brutalize and shame others.

## Crime Control as Industry

To be fair, we did not invent this phrase—that honor goes to the Norwegian criminologist Nils Christie. Christie viewed crime control as a solution to two problems: unemployment and the unequal distribution of wealth. To him, people who are willing to be correctional officers are allowed that opportunity, and those who are not become prisoners. Thus, crime control is not an end to itself—it is a business.[4] As we have documented, the criminal justice industry is one of the most heavily funded areas of government. Literally millions of people are employed by the public criminal justice sector, work for private companies that provide some criminal justice service, or work for companies who sell goods that are used by criminal justice agencies. Certain aspects of criminal justice certainly work like any other company. Herbert Packer referred to the criminal justice process as an assembly line that processes cases.[5] In order for this "factory" to be effective, a myriad of players are involved including police officers, attorneys, judges, and correctional officers. In many cases, the criminal justice process has been changed to make the system more efficient. In other cases, the process has attempted to give greater protections to people from the criminal justice system. Yet, because of these protections, many additional people need to be hired to protect these rights. Seemingly, every change that occurs to the system results in the need to hire more people. The machine seems to feed itself.

Perhaps the main lesson of the criminal justice industry is that although it involves billions of dollars and the employment of millions of people, the system is dependent on people to be arrested, convicted, and controlled. While certainly many people belong in the system, there are many whose needed presence in the system is questionable. As the United States has evolved, the number of government employees has grown along with the legal code. In a day and age when many people are questioning if the United States needs to incarcerate or otherwise control so many of its citizens, we always need to remember that many people benefit from the status quo of the system.

# Notes

1. According to www.meriam-webster.com.

2. Cullen, Francis T. 2013. "Rehabilitation: Beyond Nothing Works." *Crime and Justice in America 1976–2025*, 42(1): 299–376.

3. Travis, III, Lawrence. 2012. "Criminal Sentencing: Goals, Practices, and Ethics." In Michael Braswell, Belinda R. McCarthy, and Bernard J. McCarthy. *Justice, Crime, and Ethics*, (pp.165–180 ). New York: Routledge.

4. Christie, Nils. 1999. *Crime Control as Industry: Towards Gulags, Western Style.* 3rd Edition. New York: Routledge.

5. Packer, Herbert. 1968. *The Limits of the Criminal Sanction.* Stanford, CA: Stanford University Press.

# Index

Vollmer, August, 76, 77, 79, 92, 93, 97

Wagner, Pete, 252, 253, 281

Wal-Mart, 109–110, 112

Waldos, 41, 54

Walker, Samuel, 74–78, 92, 94, 96, 97, 172, 194–196

Walnut Street Jail, 83

Walsh, Joe, 118

Walsh, John, 136

war on drugs, 24, 49, 55, 71, 79, 90, 189, 191, 227, 268, 276

Ward, Jeffrey, 188, 198

Warren, Earl, 236

Washington, D.C., 94

Washington, George, 11, 26, 29, 59

Weed, Frank, 151, 165, 166

West Coast Hotel Co. v. Parrish, 17, 26, 30

Westlaw, 235, 239, 247

Whiskey Rebellion, 11, 25, 27, 29

white slavery, 14, 15

white-collar crime, 71, 114–116, 132, 172, 222, 276

Wickersham Commission, 78, 91

Wilson, O.W., 179, 194

Witness Security Program, 263, 279

Worrall, John, 191, 198

writ of mandamus, 205

Zatz, Marjorie, 185, 197